THE PEARSON CUSTOM LIBRARY FOR
CHEMISTRY

PEARSON

ISBN 10: 1-269-70465-6
ISBN 13: 978-1-269-70465-6

Table of Contents

An Overview of Analytical Chemistry

Chapter Outline

1 INTRODUCTION: THE CASE OF THE MYSTERIOUS CHEMIST

We turned down a narrow lane and passed through a small side door, which opened into a wing of the great hospital. It was familiar ground to me, and I needed no guiding as we ascended the bleak stone staircase and made our way down the long corridor, with its vista of white-washed wall and dun-colored doors. Near the further end a low, arched passage branched away from it and led to the chemical laboratory. This was a lofty chamber, lined and littered with countless bottles. Broad, low tables were scattered about, which bristled with retorts, test-tubes, and little Bunsen lamps, with their blue, flickering flames.

There was only one student in the room, who was bending over a distant table absorbed in his work. At the sound of our steps he glanced around and sprang to his feet with a cry of pleasure. "I've found it! I've found it!" he shouted to my companion, running toward us with a test-tube in his hand. "I have found a reagent which is precipitated by hemoglobin and nothing else." Had he discovered a gold mine, greater delight could not have shown upon his features.

"Dr. Watson—Mr. Sherlock Holmes," said Stamford, introducing us.[1]

In this passage from the 1887 story "A Study in Scarlet," Sir Arthur Conan Doyle describes the first meeting between Dr. John H. Watson and the great, fictional detective Sherlock Holmes. Holmes is best known for his use of careful observation and deduction as tools for solving crimes. But he also relied heavily on chemical analysis for providing important clues in some of his cases. In the preceding excerpt, Holmes is working on a new method for confirming blood stains (see Figure 1). This was a problem often encountered by law officials at the time of this story because there was no reliable means for proving whether a spot on a suspect's clothing was blood or a stain from another source, like mud, rust, or food. The method developed by Holmes overcame this problem by specifically looking for hemoglobin, the protein in red blood cells that produces their color.[2] In modern laboratories, chemical tests not only can confirm whether a stain is blood but can determine if the blood is from a human or an animal and if it came from a particular victim or suspect.[3–5]

Blood stain analysis is just one of many examples of how chemical tests are used to solve everyday problems. Other examples include techniques for monitoring pollutants in air or water and methods for detecting bacteria or contaminants in our food. Chemical measurements are also important in various industries for determining the quality or purity of their products. This includes companies that produce food, textiles, drugs, plastics, and metals. In addition, chemical analysis plays an important role in forensic science and clinical

FIGURE 1 Sherlock Holmes at work in his laboratory. Although Holmes was a fictional character, he was one of the earliest advocates in the use of analytical chemistry for crime scene investigations. (Original artwork by Sidney Paget, who drew illustrations for many of the early stories about Holmes.)

testing, and is a vital component of research in biology, biochemistry, medicine, and materials science. In fact, almost every day your life is probably affected in some way by chemical analysis.

The field of chemistry that deals with the use and development of tools and processes for examining and studying chemical substances is known as **analytical chemistry**. A fairly simple, but comprehensive, definition of analytical chemistry is "the science of chemical measurements."[6–8] The purpose of this text is to introduce you to common techniques for identifying, measuring, and characterizing chemicals or mixtures of chemicals. As you go through this text, you will learn how each of these methods works and how each is used to address various real-world problems. The underlying principles behind each technique will also be presented and you will see how knowledge of these principles can guide you in the correct choice and use of such methods.

2 THE HISTORY OF CHEMICAL ANALYSIS

2A Origins of Chemical Analysis

The earliest use of chemical testing dates back to ancient times. This can be illustrated in the analysis of precious metals like gold and silver. We have known since the

beginning of recorded history how to refine these metals, creating a need for methods that can determine the purity of the final product. This analysis was accomplished by using a small-scale version of the process for obtaining silver from lead ore—the use of fire to remove silver from lead and other metals. To perform this *fire assay*, a portion of the gold or silver was weighed, combined with lead, and melted in a furnace. A blast of air was then used to convert the lead and metal impurities to solid metal oxides, which could easily be removed from the surface of the melted silver or gold. The difference in mass before and after this treatment was then used to determine the original silver or gold's purity (see Figure 2). There are several references to this method in the Bible.[9–13] This assay is also mentioned in tablets sent between 1350 and 1375 B.C.E. from King Burraburiash of Babylon to Pharaoh Amenophis IV of Egypt, in which the Babylonian king complains about the quality of some gold that was sent to him by the Pharaoh.[9,12]

Another early example of chemical analysis is a method supposedly developed by the Greek mathematician Archimedes. Archimedes (287–212 B.C.E.) had been asked by King Hiero II of Syracuse to determine whether goldsmiths had cheated the king by mixing silver with the gold he had given them to make a crown for use as a ceremonial wreath (see Figure 3). After thinking about how to answer this question without damaging the crown, Archimedes developed an approach in which he compared the amount of water displaced by the crown and an equal mass of pure gold.[9,10] According to legend, Archimedes came up with this scheme as he lowered himself into a bath and watched water spill over the sides. Once he realized this effect could be used to examine the gold content of the crown, he is said to have jumped from the bath and exclaimed "Eureka!" (which means "I have found it!"), giving us an expression that has now become associated with scientific discovery.

In the years spanning from the time of the Roman empire through the Middle Ages, other chemical measurements were developed for looking at the quality of water, metals, medicines, and dyes.[9] It wasn't until the Renaissance, however, that these techniques became important in the systematic study of nature. During this era the phrase "chemical analysis" was first coined for describing such measurements. This term was suggested by Robert Boyle in his 1661 book *The Skeptical Chymist*.[9–11] Boyle was a nobleman who helped popularize the careful use of experiments for studying the physical properties and composition of matter, thus setting the stage for modern chemistry. In fact, it was by using this approach that he was able to develop what is now known as "Boyle's law," which describes the relationship between the pressure and volume of a fixed number of moles of a gas at a constant temperature.

For many years thereafter, chemical analysis was regarded as simply a tool and not as a field of study in its own right. This situation changed in the late 1700s, when a Swedish scientist named Torbern Bergman began to

FIGURE 2 The *fire assay*, a technique that has been used since ancient times for determining the purity of gold and silver. This technique is also called *cupellation*, a name derived from this method's use of a special container known as a *cupel*. (This image is from a book written in 1540 by Vannoccio Biringuccio entitled *De la Pirotechnia*, the earliest book published in Europe on the subject of metallurgy.)

systematically organize existing methods of chemical analysis according to the substances they were used to examine. His work was published between 1779 and 1790 as a collection of five volumes entitled *Opuscula physica et chemica*. It is this event that some think represents the beginning of chemical analysis as a distinct branch of chemistry. As Bergman's work became better known, other books on this topic also began to appear. One of

FIGURE 3 A golden wreath (or "crown") from the late second to early first century B.C.E. This wreath is probably similar to the crown that was examined by Archimedes. (Reproduced with permission, courtesy of the Benaki Museum Athens, © 2010.)

these was a textbook written by C. H. Pfaff in 1821 (*Handbuch der analytischen Chemie*) in which the name "analytical chemistry" was used for this new field of science.[9]

2B Chemical Analysis in the Modern World

During our industrial age, the use of chemical analysis has continued to grow and is now an important part of almost every aspect of our lives. A few of these applications are shown in Figure 4. They range from forensic science to biotechnology, agriculture, and materials science. Chemical analysis is also widely used in commercial applications, including the testing of foods, metals and other manufactured products. You will see many examples of such applications in this text, as we discuss the various approaches used for chemical measurements.

Much of the analytical chemistry that is performed daily has a very practical and applied aspect to it. Many of the chemical measurements made in industrial laboratories are concerned with determining the composition or properties of a product or raw material to ensure this item is satisfactory for sale or further use (an application known as *quality control*). Other examples involve the use of chemical analysis in hospitals for patient testing or in environmental laboratories that monitor the quality of our air, food, and water.

Another important application of analytical chemistry is its use in studying the world around us. This application includes cancer research, the discovery of new drugs, and the development of new synthetic materials, to name a few. The use of analytical methods for such work is often a two-way process, because the need

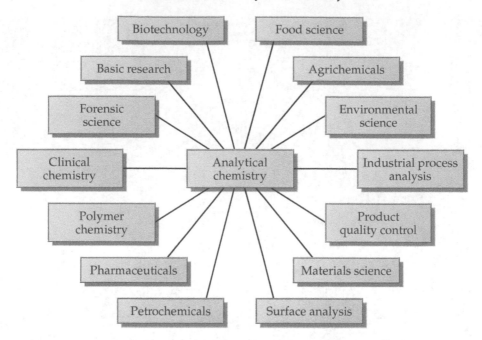

FIGURE 4 Common applications of analytical chemistry in today's world.[7]

for more detailed chemical information promotes the development of new techniques, which leads to further research made possible by the ability to obtain more data about a sample. As an example, the techniques of infrared spectroscopy (IR) and mass spectrometry (MS) both appeared in the early 1900s as research tools for characterizing specific properties of atoms and molecules. During World War II, however, there was a large growth in the synthesis and use of polymers. This growth led to a need for techniques that could analyze polymers and other compounds, such as the use of IR for examining functional groups and MS for determining the masses and structures of molecules. These developments, in turn, made it easier to synthesize and study other types of chemicals.

Because analytical chemistry impacts so many areas, it is not surprising that contributions to this field have been made by individuals from a variety of backgrounds. Table 1 lists the Nobel Prizes that have been awarded for research resulting in new or improved analytical methods. This list includes people from fields such as chemistry, physics, and medicine, and reflects the importance of chemical analysis in all these areas of science.

3 GENERAL TERMS USED IN CHEMICAL ANALYSIS

3A Sample-Related Terms

Now that we have seen the role analytical chemistry plays in our world, we need to define a few terms we will use throughout this text to discuss this topic. The first terms we will consider are those used to describe the material we wish to characterize. In most situations, it is not desirable or practical to look at all of the material of interest, so we instead take a smaller, representative portion for study. An example would be when a nurse or doctor takes a sample of blood to determine the amount of a particular drug that is present in your body. The portion of material taken for analysis is referred to as the **sample**.[14] Ideally, we would like this sample to be as representative as possible of the rest of the material to be examined. Ways for meeting this goal will be described when we discuss approaches for acquiring a chemical sample.

Within most samples there is a large variety of substances present. The entire group of substances that makes up a sample is called the sample **matrix**. The particular substance we are interested in measuring or studying in the sample is known as the **analyte**.[14] In some cases, the analyte might be an atom, molecule, or ion, while in others it might be a larger substance such as a polymer, virus particle, or cell. The technique used to examine the analyte should produce a signal that is related to the presence of this analyte in the sample. Although we are not always interested in looking at other components in the sample, we still have to consider these components as we choose and use an analysis method. This is the case because not all analysis methods are compatible with all types of samples. In addition, some sample components in the matrix may cause an error in the final result if they have not been properly dealt with before or during the analysis.

Another way we can classify an analyte is in terms of its relative contribution to the overall sample. At one extreme we have analytes that make up a significant portion of the sample. The term **major component** (or *major constituent*) is used to refer to such substances, especially if they make up more than 1% of the sample.

TABLE 1   Nobel Prizes Awarded for Developments in Chemical Analysis

Year and Area of Award	Awardees	Area of Study
1915–Physics	Sir William L. Bragg and Sir William H. Bragg	X-ray crystallography
1922–Chemistry	F. W. Aston	Mass spectrometry
1923–Chemistry	Fritz Pregl	Microanalysis of organic compounds
1930–Medicine	Karl Landsteiner	Blood typing
1930–Physics	Sir Chandrasekhara Venkata Raman	Raman spectroscopy
1943–Chemistry	George De Hevesy	Radioactive tracers
1948–Chemistry	Arne Wilhelm Kaurin Tiselius	Electrophoresis
1952–Chemistry	A. J. P. Martin and Richard L. M. Synge	Partition liquid chromatography
1952–Physics	Felix Bloch and Edward M. Purcell	Nuclear magnetic resonance spectroscopy
1953–Chemistry	Frits Zernike	Phase-contrast microscopy
1959–Chemistry	Jaroslav Heyrovsky	Polarography
1960–Chemistry	Willard Frank Libby	Carbon-14 dating
1977–Medicine	Rosalyn Yalow	Radioimmunoassays
1978–Medicine	Daniel Nathans, Werner Arber, and Hamilton O. Smith	Genetic studies with restriction enzymes
1980–Chemistry	Walter Gilbert and Frederick Sanger	DNA sequencing
1981–Physics	Nicolaas Bloembergen and Arthur L. Schawlow	Laser spectroscopy
1982–Chemistry	Sir Aaron Klug	Crystallographic electron microscopy
1985–Chemistry	Herbert A. Hauptman and Jerome Karle	Direct methods for determining crystal structures
1986–Physics	Gerd Binning and Heinrich Rohrer	Scanning tunneling microscopy
1986–Physics	Ernst Ruska	Electron microscopy
1991–Chemistry	Richard R. Ernst	High-resolution nuclear magnetic resonance spectroscopy
1993–Chemistry	Kary B. Mullis	Polymerase chain reaction
1999–Chemistry	Ahmed Zewail	Femtosecond spectroscopy
2002–Chemistry	John B. Fenn and Koichi Tanaka	Soft desorption ionization for mass spectrometry
2002–Chemistry	Kurt Wüthrich	Nuclear magnetic resonance spectroscopy for 3-dimensional studies of biological macromolecules
2003–Medicine	Paul C. Lauterbur and Sir Peter Mansfield	Magnetic resonance imaging
2005–Physics	John L. Hall and Theodor W. Hänsch	Laser-based precision spectroscopy
2008–Chemistry	Osama Shimomura, Martin Chalfie, and Roger Y. Tsien	Discovery of green fluorescent protein

Source: This information was obtained from *The Nobel Prize Internet Archive* (www.almaz.com/nobel).

For instance, a gold bar that is 99% pure would have gold as its major component. A substance present at lower levels, such as 0.01–1% of the total sample, is called a **minor component**. Likewise, a substance present at a level below 0.01% (100 parts-per-million) is known as a **trace component**. Table 2 illustrates these concepts using the composition of dry air as an example.[15] Such a classification scheme is important because the relative amount of an analyte in a sample is often a key factor in determining what techniques can be used for examining this analyte. This type of classification has lead to a division of methods according to whether they are used for **major component analysis**, **minor component analysis**, or **trace analysis**.[16]

3B Method-Related Terms

The Analytical Process.   A second group of terms we need to define concern the method being used to characterize our sample. Some words we have already used to describe this include *assay, analysis,* and *determination.* To illustrate this, we could say in our opening example that Sherlock Holmes was developing an *assay* for the *determination* of hemoglobin in

TABLE 2 Types of Sample Components Based on Relative Amount in the Sample*

Type of Sample Component	Relative Amount in Sample	Example: Composition of Dry Air (Without Water Vapor)
Major Component	1–100%	Nitrogen (78.1%), Oxygen (20.9%)
Minor Component	0.01–1%	Argon (0.9%), Carbon Dioxide (0.03%)
Trace Component	< 0.01% (100 ppm)	Neon (18.2 ppm), Helium (5.2 ppm), Methane (2 ppm), Krypton (1.1 ppm), Hydrogen (0.5 ppm), Nitrogen Dioxide (0.5 ppm), Xenon (0.09 ppm)

* All values are expressed in terms of the volume of gas per unit volume of air (v/v). The abbreviation *ppm* in this table stands for "parts-per-million," where 1 ppm = 0.0001% (see Chapter 3). The ranges given in the table for major, minor, and trace component analysis are only approximate and vary slightly depending on the technique and type of sample that is being examined.

Source: This information was obtained from the *CRC Handbook of Chemistry and Physics, 81st Ed.*, CRC Press, Boca Raton, FL, 2000.

blood or that he was conducting a hemoglobin *analysis*. Each of these terms concerns the general act of examining the sample and its analyte. The approach used to perform this assay is the **analytical method** or "analytical technique." Again going back to the opening example, we can say Holmes was using the *analytical method* of selective precipitation to determine whether hemoglobin was present in his sample. The entire group of operations used for the analysis is known as the *procedure* or *protocol*.

As shown in Figure 5, there are many steps in the overall procedure for a chemical analysis. You first need to determine what question is being asked about the sample and to identify the information that will be needed to answer this question. In the work by Holmes, the general question was "Is the sample a

blood stain?", which he sought to answer by looking for hemoglobin. The second step is to select an appropriate sample. To select a sample you must consider the nature of the material being examined, the types of analytes to be measured, and the distribution and suspected levels of these analytes within the material. For a blood stain, this process would involve locating a sample at the scene of a crime and obtaining a representative portion for analysis.

The third step in an analysis is sample preparation. The degree of preparation needed will depend on the sample's complexity, the types of analytes being examined, and the measurement method. For the technique used by Holmes, sample preparation probably involved placing a small part of the stained material into a container to which reagents could be added. The fourth and fifth steps in an analysis are the actual examination of the sample and use of these results for chemical measurement or characterization. In the technique developed by Holmes, these steps were represented by the addition of a reagent to the stained material and the observation of whether a precipitate was formed by the presence of hemoglobin.

Types of Analytical Methods. The large number of chemicals and samples that occur in our world means we also need many different methods for their measurement or characterization. Some common types of analytical techniques are listed in Figure 6. These techniques can be placed into three categories: classical methods, instrumental methods, and separation methods. **Classical methods** were the first analytical techniques developed and produce a result by using experimentally determined quantities such as a mass or volume, along with the use of atomic or molecular masses and well-defined chemical reactions.[17,18] An example of a classical method is gravimetric analysis, which is

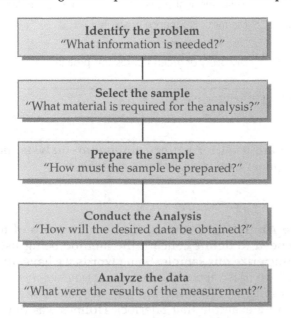

FIGURE 5 The general steps in a procedure for chemical analysis.

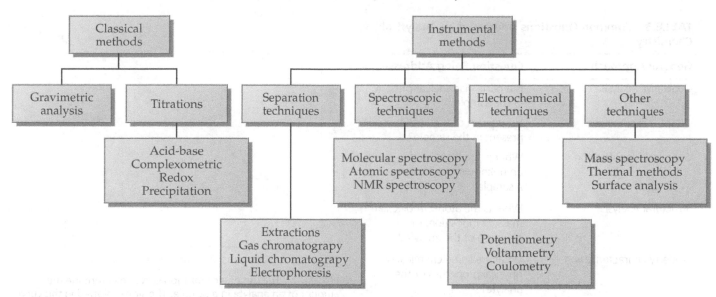

FIGURE 6 General categories of analytical techniques.

based on measuring the mass of a chemical product that either contains or is related to the analyte. The fire assay for gold is an example of a gravimetric method. Another such method is a titration, in which a chemical substance is measured by determining the volume or amount of a well-defined reagent that is needed to react with this analyte. Most classical methods are performed as manual techniques; however, some are conducted in modern laboratories with the aid of automated systems.

An **instrumental method** uses an instrument-generated signal for detecting the presence of an analyte or determining the amount of an analyte in a sample. There are many instrumental methods, ranging from electrochemical methods (which make use of the production or consumption of electrons by chemicals) to spectroscopic methods (which use electromagnetic radiation to characterize or measure analytes). Other techniques in this category are mass spectrometry, thermal methods, and approaches for surface analysis. Instrumental techniques were developed long after classical methods of analysis but are used in most of today's chemical measurements.[19,20]

A **separation method** is an approach used to remove one type of chemical from another. A separation method is often needed when the goal is to examine a chemical or group of chemicals in a complex sample. Chemical separations can be used as part of either a classical method or an instrumental method to isolate an analyte from a sample, remove interfering chemicals, or place the analyte in an appropriate matrix for further study. Some separation methods are carried out manually (for instance, an extraction), while others require special equipment and are considered "instrumental methods" (as occurs for gas chromatography and high-performance liquid chromatography). Separation techniques are quite common and make up an important part of modern methods for chemical analysis.[19,20]

4 INFORMATION PROVIDED BY CHEMICAL ANALYSIS

Each chemical assay has its own unique set of requirements, but we can sort these methods into general categories based on the type of information they provide about a sample (see Table 3). Most chemical assays involve a comparison between the sample and a material known to contain the analyte of interest (known as the **standard**). This comparison provides a means for the positive identification or measurement of the analyte in a sample.

The first type of chemical measurement that might be carried out is a **qualitative analysis**. The goal here is to simply determine whether a particular analyte is present in a sample. An example would be the fictitious assay for hemoglobin that was developed by Sherlock Holmes for the detection of blood. In methods for qualitative analysis we are not necessarily interested in how much of the analyte is present, although there must be a certain minimum amount present for its detection. Instead, we only care if the compound of interest is present above this minimum level. This approach is also sometimes called a **screening assay** and is often used to help decide whether further tests should be conducted on a sample.

Another question that can be asked is "How much of the analyte is present in the sample?" This question is answered by using **quantitative analysis**. The goal here is to measure, **quantitate**, or **quantify** (to provide a numerical value for) the actual amount of analyte in a sample. Such an approach is utilized when it is necessary to determine the concentration of an analyte or its contribution to the overall composition of a sample. For instance, quantitative analysis would be used by a food company to measure the protein, carbohydrate, and fat content in a product. This type of analysis would also be used by a hospital laboratory to determine whether a drug given to a patient is within the proper range for treatment of a disease.

TABLE 3 Common Questions Addressed by Analytical Chemistry

General Approach	Question Being Addressed
Qualitative analysis	Is a particular analyte present in the sample?
Quantitative analysis	How much of the analyte is present in the sample?
Chemical identification	What is the identity of an unknown chemical in a sample?
Structural analysis	What is the atomic/molecular mass, composition, or structure of the analyte?
Property characterization	What are some chemical or physical properties of the analyte?
Spatial analysis	How is the analyte distributed throughout a sample?
Time-dependent analysis	How does the amount of an analyte or a property of the analyte change over time?

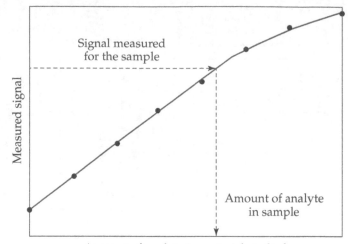

FIGURE 7 The use of a calibration curve to determine the amount of an analyte in a sample. The signal plotted in this curve is determined by using standards containing known amounts of the analyte. The experimental results obtained for the standards are represented by the solid dots, and the solid line is the best-fit curve that passes through these results.

Quantitative analysis is probably the most common type of analytical chemistry that is conducted on a routine basis. A quantitative analysis can be used directly on a sample or may follow an earlier screening assay. Although the response of some methods (such as a gravimetric analysis or titration) can be used directly to determine the amount of an analyte in a sample, most quantitative methods require the use of standards for this purpose. This task is accomplished by making a plot of the signals given by a method for standards that contain known amounts of the analyte. This process is referred to as **calibration** and gives a graph known as a **calibration curve** (see Figure 7). When a sample is later examined by the same method, the signal it produces is compared to the calibration curve and used to determine the amount of analyte that must have been present in the sample to give such a response.

Besides using analytical chemistry to measure a substance, it is also often necessary to identify a substance in a sample. This application, known as **chemical identification**, might be used by a chemist to identify a potential drug candidate that has been isolated from a plant, or it might be used by an environmental scientist to determine the nature of a new pollutant found in a water or soil sample. One way chemical identification can be carried out is by comparing the unknown compound's behavior in an analytical method to that observed for standard samples of known chemicals. Another way chemical identification might be accomplished is by using techniques that provide direct clues regarding the compound's composition and structure.

Two types of testing that are closely related to chemical identification are **structural analysis** and **property characterization**. In structural analysis, the goal is to determine features such as the mass, composition, functional groups, or structure of the analyte. Structural analysis might provide a detailed description of a chemical or help identify an unknown substance. In property characterization, measurement of some specific chemical or physical property of the analyte is desired. Property characterization of a material might involve examining how the material interacts with light or electrons, its ability to react with other chemicals, or its color, crystal shape, and mechanical strength. Like structural analysis, property characterization can be conducted with either standard samples of known chemicals or with unknown compounds that are to be identified through their measured properties.

Many materials have compositions that are different from one section of their matrix to the next. In these cases, the method of *spatial analysis* can be used to provide more detailed information about the material's composition. Spatial analysis deals with determining how a particular analyte is distributed throughout a matrix by examining small sections of the material, thus allowing chemical information to be obtained from different regions. This type of analysis is valuable when you are examining a *heterogeneous material* (that is, a material with a composition that varies from one point to the next within its structure). One example is *surface analysis,* which is used in areas such as the semiconductor industry during the production of storage media and computer chips.

Numerous samples that are studied by chemical analysis are taken from systems that change over time. For instance, if a doctor measures the amount of glucose in your blood, a sample taken shortly after you have eaten will give a much higher result than one that is taken just after you awake in the morning. This change in concentration can be studied by using *time-dependent (temporal) analysis*, which examines how the amount of one or more analytes varies as a function of time. Changes in an analyte over long periods of time can often be examined by using the same methods that are employed for quantitative analysis. However, for shorter periods of time more specialized techniques may be required.

EXERCISE 1	What Information Is Required from a Chemical Analysis?

What general type of chemical test (for instance, qualitative analysis, quantitative analysis, etc.) is needed in each of the following situations?

a. An assay of drinking water to determine if the concentration of a particular pollutant is within legal limits
b. Studies to determine the nature of an unknown toxin in a food sample
c. The location of a specific type of protein within a cell

SOLUTION

(a) This is an example of a quantitative analysis, because the amount of a specific chemical is to be measured. (b) These studies will involve some form of chemical identification. This may be done by comparing an isolated sample of the unknown compound to known samples of standard chemicals, or by performing structural analysis or property characterization on the toxin to provide clues as to its identity. (c) Spatial analysis is required for this application because it is necessary to look at the protein's distribution and location in the cell. This analysis might be carried out in a microbiology or biochemistry laboratory to identify a cell or to provide clues as to a protein's function within the cell.

5 OVERVIEW

In this chapter, we have had our first glimpse at the field of analytical chemistry. We have discussed the origins of this field and considered some of its applications in today's world. We have also considered some general terms used within analytical chemistry and discussed the types of information that can be obtained by chemical analysis.

Key Words

Analyte	Instrumental method	Property characterization	Separation method
Analytical chemistry	Major component	Qualitative analysis	Standard
Analytical method	Major component analysis	Quantitate (quantify)	Structural analysis
Calibration	Matrix	Quantitative analysis	Trace analysis
Calibration curve	Minor component	Sample	Trace component
Chemical identification	Minor component analysis	Screening assay	
Classical method			

Other Terms

Analysis (assay, determination)	Heterogeneous material	Spatial analysis	Time-dependent (temporal) analysis
Fire assay (cupellation)	Procedure (protocol)	Surface analysis	
	Quality control		

Questions

INTRODUCTION AND HISTORY OF CHEMICAL ANALYSIS

1. Define the terms "analytical chemistry" and "chemical analysis."

2. What was the first use of chemical analysis? How have the uses of analytical chemistry changed from ancient to modern times?

3. Describe some general applications of analytical chemistry in the modern world.
4. What is the relationship between research in analytical chemistry and research in other fields, such as medicine, environmental science, or biology?

GENERAL TERMS USED IN CHEMICAL ANALYSIS

5. What is meant in analytical chemistry by the term "sample" (when used as a noun)? How is this related to or different from the terms "analyte" and "matrix"?
6. Identify the sample, analyte, and matrix in each of the following situations.
   (a) Estimation of the amount of sulfur in coal
   (b) Analysis of the drug content in a tablet by a pharmaceutical company
   (c) Measurement of carbon monoxide in fumes emitted by an industrial plant
7. Explain the difference between major, minor, and trace components within a sample.
8. Determine whether each of the following substances in common household items is an example of a major, minor, or trace sample component.
   (a) The amount of protein and fat in a portion of 95% lean beef (5% fat)
   (b) The amount of aspirin (acetylsalicylic acid) in a 250 mg nonprescription tablet that contains 80 mg of this drug
   (c) The vitamin C in an orange, which typically contains 50–60 mg vitamin C per 100 g total mass
9. What are the five general steps in any type of chemical analysis?
10. Explain what is meant in analytical chemistry by a "classical method." What is meant by an "instrumental method"? How do these two types of methods differ?
11. Discuss why a separation method might be used as part of a chemical analysis. What are some examples of separation methods?

INFORMATION PROVIDED BY CHEMICAL ANALYSIS

12. What is a standard? What is a calibration curve? How is each of these used in chemical analysis?
13. Compare and contrast the information that is provided by each of following types of general analytical methods.
    (a) Qualitative analysis vs. quantitative analysis
    (b) Structural analysis vs. property characterization
    (c) Spatial analysis vs. temporal analysis
14. What general approach (for instance, qualitative analysis, quantitative analysis, etc.) is needed in the following situations?
    (a) An analysis of samples from athletes to determine whether they are using performance-enhancing drugs
    (b) Identification of an unknown compound from a plant that is believed to have antitumor properties
    (c) Measurement by a pharmaceutical company of the actual amount of a drug that is present in one of their products
    (d) Location of the point where a pollutant is entering a river

CHALLENGE PROBLEMS

15. Trace analysis can be divided into many subcategories, depending on how small of an amount of analyte must be detected and on the size of the sample that is being used.[14,16]
    (a) Look up the definitions for each of the following terms and explain how they differ from each other: microtrace analysis, nanotrace analysis, and picotrace analysis.
    (b) Differentiate between what is meant by "microtrace analysis" and "ultratrace analysis" in chemical testing.
    (c) Identify several examples of analytes and samples that would fit into the various categories listed in (a) and (b).
16. Look up a research paper that discusses the development or use of an analytical method. Identify each of the following factors within the paper.
    (a) The sample, analyte, and matrix being examined
    (b) The type of assay, analytical method, and procedure being used
    (c) The general type of analytical method (classical or instrumental method)
    (d) The type of question that is being asked
    (e) The general analysis format (qualitative analysis, quantitative analysis, etc.)
17. A general indication of the role analytical chemistry plays in our world can be seen by references that are made to such testing in literature and popular media. An example is the opening excerpt in this chapter from "A Study in Scarlet." Locate another example from a book, movie, or television show (for example, see Reference 21). Identify the types of analytes that are being measured and the approach that is used in your example. Determine whether the analytical method is a real technique or a fictional one.
18. The development of improved electronics led to a huge growth in the development of new instrumental methods in the 1940s and 1950s. Similar growth occurred with the introduction of personal computers during the 1970s and 1980s.[19,20] What current trends and recent advances do you think will be important in the future development of chemical analysis?

TOPICS FOR DISCUSSION AND REPORTS

19. The modern analysis of precious metals such as gold and silver often combines classical methods of chemical analysis with more modern instrumental methods.[9] Report on how such assays are currently performed.
20. Obtain more information on one of the individuals listed in Table 1 and write a report on the contribution that person made to chemical analysis. Discuss how this development impacted the person's field of research or other areas of science.
21. The availability of reliable, commercial equipment for performing instrumental or classical methods has often been a key step in determining how quickly a new analysis technique sees widespread use. Several people and companies who have played important roles in the past development of such equipment are discussed in References 19 and 20. Obtain information on one of these individuals or companies and discuss how that person's work contributed to the field of analytical chemistry.
22. The journal *Analytical Chemistry* is an important source of reviews and research articles on methods for chemical measurements. Reference 22 describes how this journal has changed over the past century. Examine this article and discuss how this journal has reflected the changes in chemical analysis over the past 100 years.
23. Select an article from a current newspaper or magazine that discusses a topic in which chemical analysis was used to provide key information. Describe the type of chemical analysis that was conducted and the type of information it provided. Also, discuss how this information was used in the article.

References

1. A. C. Doyle, "A Study in Scarlet," *Beeton's Christmas Annual*, 1887.
2. S. M. Gerber, "A Study in Scarlet: Blood Identification in 1875," *Chemistry and Crime: From Sherlock Holmes to Today's Courtroom*, S. M. Gerber, Ed., American Chemical Society, Washington, DC, 1983, Chapter 3.
3. F. M. Gdowski, "Bloodstain Analysis-Case Histories," *Chemistry and Crime: From Sherlock Holmes to Today's Courtroom*, S. M. Gerber, Ed., American Chemical Society, Washington, DC, 1983, Chapter 7.
4. L. Kobilinsky, "Bloodstain Analysis-Serological and Electrophoretic Techniques," *Chemistry and Crime: From Sherlock Holmes to Today's Courtroom*, S. M. Gerber, Ed., American Chemical Society, Washington, DC, 1983, Chapter 8.
5. C. S. Tumosa, "The Detection and Species Identification of Blood—A Bibliography of Relevant Papers from 1980 to 1995," *Forensic Science Review*, 8 (1996) 74–90.
6. R. W. Murray, "Analytical Chemistry: The Science of Chemical Measurements," *Analytical Chemistry*, 68 (1991) 271A.
7. J. Tyson, *Analysis: What Analytical Chemists Do*, Royal Society of Chemistry, London, 1988.
8. M. Valcarcel, "A Modern Definition of Analytical Chemistry," *Trends in Analytical Chemistry*, 16 (1997) 124–131.
9. S. Kallmann, "Analytical Chemistry of the Precious Metals: Interdependence of Classical and Instrumental Methods," *Analytical Chemistry*, 56 (1984) 1020A–1027A.
10. F. Szabadvary, *History of Analytical Chemistry*, Pergamon Press, New York, 1966.
11. G. D. Christian, "Evolution and Revolution in Quantitative Analysis," *Analytical Chemistry*, 66 (1995) 532A–538A.
12. J. O. Nriagu, "Cupellation: The Oldest Quantitative Chemical Process," *Journal of Chemical Education*, 62 (1985) 668–674.
13. Examples of citations for the fire assay in the Bible include Numbers 31:22, 1st Peter 1:7, and Revelation 3:18.
14. H. M. N. H. Irving, H. Freiser, and T. S. West, *Compendium of Analytical Nomenclature: Definitive Rules—1977*, Pergamon Press, New York, 1977.
15. *CRC Handbook of Chemistry and Physics, 81st ed.*, CRC Press, Boca Raton, FL, 2000.
16. H. A. Laitinen, "History of Trace Analysis," *Journal of Research of the National Bureau of Standards*, 93 (1988) 175–185.
17. C. M. Beck II, "Classical Analysis: A Look at the Past, Present and Future," *Analytical Chemistry*, 63 (1991) 993A–1003A.
18. C. M. Beck II, "Classical Analysis: A Look at the Past, Present and Future," *Analytical Chemistry*, 66 (1994) 224A–239A.
19. J. Poudrier and J. Moynihan, "Instrumentation Hall of Fame," *Made to Measure: A History of Analytical Instrumentation*, J. F. Ryan, Ed., American Chemical Society, Washington, DC, 1999, pp. 10–38.
20. J. T. Stock, "A Backward Look at Scientific Instrumentation," *Analytical Chemistry*, 65 (1993) 344A–351A.
21. C. A. Lucy, "Analytical Chemistry: A Literary Approach," *Journal of Chemical Education*, 4 (2000) 459–470.
22. D. Noble, "From Wet Chemistry to Instrumental Analysis: A Perspective on Analytical Science," *Analytical Chemistry*, 4 (1994) 251A–263A.

Selected Answers

6

a. Sample = coal, analyte = sulfur, matrix = group of all substances in the coal

b. Sample = drug tablet, analyte = drug, matrix = group of all substances in the tablet

c. Sample = fumes emitted by industrial plant, analyte = carbon monoxide, matrix = group of all substances in the fumes

8

a. Major components

b. Major component

c. Minor component

14

a. Qualitative analysis would be used initially to determine if these drugs are present in the samples above an accepted cut off limit. If any samples are found to give positive results for the drugs, they would probably be reanalyzed using quantitative analysis to determine the amount of drug that is present.

b. A structural analysis could be used to provide information on the structure of the compound, which could then be used to identify this chemical. Property characterization might also be used for this purpose.

c. Quantitative analysis would be utilized in determining the amount of drug that is present in the product.

d. This is an example of spatial analysis because it seeks to obtain information on how a particular analyte is distributed in space along a river bed. This work would also involve quantitative analysis as the amount of pollutant is measured at different locations in the river.

Systems of Measurement

Systems of Measurement

Learning Objectives

At the end of this chapter, the student should be able to do the following:

1. Use metric units and their prefixes properly
2. Convert between metric prefixes
3. Convert between U.S. customary units and metric units
4. Use dimensional analysis as a technique for unit conversions
5. Use the ratio method as a technique for unit conversions
6. Calculate formula weight and molar mass
7. Convert between mass and number of moles
8. Interconvert values in the Fahrenheit, Celsius, and Kelvin temperature scales

Key Terms

Avogadro's number

Celsius

dimensional analysis

Fahrenheit

formula weight

International System of Units (SI)

Kelvin

metric system

molar mass

mole

ratio method

United States Customary System of Units

This chapter presents systems of measurement, their units and symbols, and strategies and procedures for converting among them.

UNITED STATES CUSTOMARY SYSTEM OF UNITS

The **United States Customary System of Units** is also called the "English Imperial" or "American" system. The most commonly used units in this system appear below.

Length	inch (in)	
	foot (ft)	= 12 inches
	yard (yd)	= 3 feet
	mile (mi)	= 1760 yards = 5280 feet
Volume	cup (c)	
	pint (pt)	= 2 cups
	quart (qt)	= 2 pints
	gallon (gal)	= 4 quarts
Weight	ounce (oz)	
	pound (lb)	= 16 ounces
	(short) ton	= 2000 pounds

THE METRIC SYSTEM

In contrast to the U.S. system, the **metric system** has only one basic unit for length, one for volume, and one for weight.

Length	meter (m)
Volume	liter (L)*
Weight**	gram (g)

* The symbol for "liter" is usually a capital "L" because in some typefaces the lowercase letter "l" is confusingly similar to the number "1" and to the letter "I."
** Although we use the terms "weight" and "mass" interchangeably, mass is the amount of matter in a substance, whereas weight is the gravitational force on that matter. Under ordinary circumstances in the laboratory, we use the two terms as though they had the same meaning. In some other contexts, however, they are not interchangeable.

Prefixes and How to Interpret Them

The metric system exploits the convenience of the number "10." As Table 1 ★ shows, we attach a prefix to the basic unit of measure to create a decimal multiple or submultiple. The purpose of prefixes is to reduce the number of zeros in the value; it is much easier to write "μg" than it is to write "0.000001 g" or "1×10^{-6} g."

Let us consider some examples, starting with the basic unit of "gram" (g), which is about the weight of a typical paper clip. If we have an object that weighs 1000 g, we can report the weight as such, or we can call it "1 kilogram" (1 kg). As Table 1 shows, 1 kg is the same as 1000 of its basic unit, the gram:

$$1 \text{ kg} = 1000 \text{ g}$$

If we have an object that weighs 0.001 g, we can report the weight as such, or we can call it "1 milligram" (1 mg). As Table 1 shows, 1 mg is the same as $\frac{1}{1000}$, or one-thousandth, of its basic unit, the gram:

$$1 \text{ mg} = 0.001 \text{ g}$$

★ **TABLE 1** Metric Prefixes and the Arithmetic Relationships They Indicate

Prefix	Symbol	Factor (How many, or how much, of the basic unit)		Power of 10 (10^x)	American Term
giga	G	1,000,000,000		9	billion
mega	M	1,000,000		6	million
kilo	k	1000		3	thousand
hecto	h	100		2	hundred
deka (or deca)	da	10		1	ten
No prefix. This is the level of the *basic unit* (meter, liter, gram)		1		0	one
deci	d	1/10	(0.1)	−1	one-tenth
centi	c	1/100	(0.01)	−2	one-hundredth
milli	m	1/1000	(0.001)	−3	one-thousandth
micro	μ*	1/1,000,000	(0.000001)	−6	one-millionth
nano	n	1/1,000,000,000	(0.000000001)	−9	one-billionth
pico	p	1/1,000,000,000,000	(0.000000000001)	−12	one-trillionth
femto	f	1/1,000,000,000,000,000	(0.000000000000001)	−15	one-quadrillionth
atto	a	1/1,000,000,000,000,000,000	(0.000000000000000001)	−18	one-quintillionth

*This is the proper symbol for "micro," although some clinics and hospitals prefer the abbreviation "mc" because the handwritten letter "μ" can be mistaken for "M" or "m".

Likewise, a microliter (μL) is a millionth of a liter:

$$1 \ \mu L = \frac{1}{1,000,000} L = 0.000001 \ L = 10^{-6} \ L$$

A kilometer (km) is 1000 meters:

$$1 \ km = 1000 \ m = 10^3 \ m$$

Converting Between Units

It is often necessary to convert one unit into another, whether within one system or between systems. Always remember that *in moving to a larger unit, we divide;* we do not multiply. Conversely, *in moving to a smaller unit, we multiply;* we do not divide. This is true in all unit conversions, regardless of the system. For example, in moving from "minutes" to "hours," the number goes down, not up:

$$60 \ minutes \rightarrow 1 \ hour$$

In moving to the larger unit ("hours"), we have divided by "60."

However, in moving from "hours" to "minutes," the number goes up, not down; we multiply by "60" in moving to the smaller unit:

$$1 \ hour \rightarrow 60 \ minutes$$

In the metric system, there are several equally effective ways to think through a conversion involving prefixes. We present two approaches now and two more later.

APPROACH 1

This approach comprises two steps.

Step 1 In Table 1, locate the starting prefix and the target prefix and note their corresponding powers of 10. Subtract the target power of 10 from the starting power of 10:

$$starting \ power \ of \ 10 - target \ power \ of \ 10 = \Delta x$$

Step 2 Multiply the starting value by $10^{\Delta x}$, where Δx is the difference between the powers of 10.

Consider, for example, the conversion of "100 g" to "kg."

Step 1

	Prefix	Unit	Power of 10
Starting	None	gram	0
Target	Kilo	kilogram	3

$$\Delta x = \text{Starting power of 10} - \text{Target power of 10} = 0 - 3 = \underline{-3}$$

Step 2

$$(\text{Starting value}) \times 10^{\Delta x} = 100 \times 10^{-3} = 100 \div 1000 = 0.1$$

Therefore, 100 g = 0.1 kg

Notice that, in moving to the larger unit (g → kg), the value went down, not up; the procedure was the same as *division* by 1000. Here is a way to visualize the conversion:

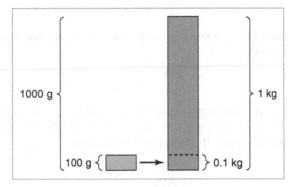

Now let us take an example that converts in the opposite direction, say, from "0.1 mg" to "μg."

Step 1

	Prefix	Unit	Power of 10
Starting	Milli	milligram	−3
Target	Micro	microgram	−6

$$\Delta x = \text{Starting power of 10} - \text{Target power of 10} = (-3) - (-6) = \underline{3}$$

Step 2

$$(\text{Starting value}) \times 10^{\Delta x} = 0.1 \times 10^3 = 0.1 \times 1000 = 100$$

Therefore, 0.1 mg = 100 μg

Notice that, in moving to the smaller unit (mg → μg), the value went up, not down; the procedure was the same as *multiplication* by 1000. Here is a way to visualize the conversion:

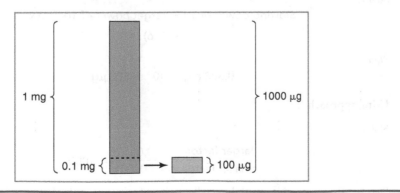

APPROACH 2

This approach also comprises two steps.

Step 1 In Table 1, locate the starting prefix and the target prefix and note their corresponding factors. Calculate the ratio of the larger to the smaller.

$$\frac{\text{larger factor}}{\text{smaller factor}}$$

Step 2 If the conversion is going toward the larger unit, then *divide* the value by the above ratio. If it is going toward the smaller unit, then *multiply*.

Let us turn to the same two examples we saw in the first approach. In the conversion of "100 g" into "kg," the larger factor is 1000 (for "kilo"), and the smaller is 1 (for "gram," a basic unit). Therefore, the ratio of the larger to the smaller is

$$\frac{1000}{1} = 1000$$

Because the conversion is going toward the larger unit, we *divide* the original value by the ratio, which is 1000:

$$\frac{100}{1000} = 0.1 \text{ kg}$$

In the second example, we carry out a conversion toward the smaller unit, that is, from "0.1 mg" to "μg". The larger factor is 0.001 (for "milli"), and the smaller is 0.000001 (for "micro"). Therefore, the ratio of the larger to the smaller is

$$\frac{0.001}{0.000001} = 1000$$

Because the conversion is going toward the smaller unit, we *multiply* the original value by the ratio, which is 1000:

$$0.1 \times 1000 = 100 \text{ μg}$$

APPROACHES 3 AND 4

Dimensional analysis and the *ratio method* are two more approaches to solving problems of this type, but because their usefulness extends far beyond the conversion of metric prefixes, we treat them in their own later sections of this chapter.

Let us consider a final example that has a numeral other than "0" or "1," say, the conversion of 0.382 mg into "μg."

Using approach 1:

Step 1.
$$\text{Starting power of 10} - \text{target power of 10} = \Delta x$$
$$(-3) - (-6) = 3$$

Step 2.
$$0.382 \text{ mg} \times 10^3 = 382 \text{ μg}$$

Using approach 2:

Step 1.
$$\frac{\text{larger factor}}{\text{smaller factor}} = \frac{0.001}{0.000001} = 1000$$

Step 2. Conversion is toward the smaller unit. Therefore, we multiply:

$$0.382 \text{ mg} \times 1000 = 382 \text{ μg}$$

INTERNATIONAL SYSTEM OF UNITS

The **International System of Units**, abbreviated "SI" for the French *Système International d'Unités*, is a modern version of the metric system. Established in 1960, the SI has become the most widely used system of measurement in the world, although the United States still employs customary units alongside it.

There are seven basic units of measurement in the SI.

Length	meter (m)
Weight (Mass)	kilogram (kg)
Amount of Substance	mole (mol)
Time	second (s)
Electric Current	ampere (A)
Temperature	kelvin (K)
Luminous Intensity	candela (cd)

Some non-SI units are acceptable for use within the SI. In the clinical laboratory, the most important of these units is the "liter." Furthermore, it is acceptable to use metric prefixes with SI units, although there is one exception. Because the basic unit "kilogram" already has a multiplying prefix, we may not attach another prefix to it. For example, we may *not* report a "microkilogram" (μkg). Instead, we attach a prefix to the unit "gram" (that prefix would be "milli").

☑ CHECKPOINT 1

Carry out the following conversions.

(a) 1 dL → mL   (b) 100 μL → L   (c) 4 cg → mg

(d) 150 cm → m   (e) 2.0×10^4 ng → kg   (f) 6.7×10^{-3} L → mL

(a) Using approach 1:

$$\Delta x = (-1) - (-3) = 2 \qquad 1 \text{ dL} \times 10^2 = 100 \text{ mL}$$

Using approach 2:

$$\frac{\text{larger factor}}{\text{smaller factor}} = \frac{0.1}{0.001} = 100 \qquad 1 \text{ dL} \times 100 = 100 \text{ mL}$$

(b) 0.0001 L   (c) 40 mg   (d) 1.5 m   (e) 2.0×10^{-8} kg   (f) 6.7 mL

EQUIVALENCIES BETWEEN SYSTEMS

It is possible to interconvert U.S. customary units and metric units. The following table lists the most common equivalencies used in the clinical laboratory.

Length	Volume	Weight
1 in = 2.54 cm	1 c = 236.6 mL	1 oz = 28.35 g
1 yd = 0.914 m	1 gal = 3.785 L	1 lb = 0.454 kg
1 mi = 1.609 km		
1 cm = 0.394 in	1 mL = 0.00423 c	1 g = 0.0353 oz
1 m = 1.094 yd	1 L = 0.264 gal	1 kg = 2.20 lb
1 km = 0.622 mi		

THE MOLE

A **mole**, which we symbolize as "mol," is the amount of a substance that consists of as many entities (molecules, ions, particles, etc.) as there are atoms in exactly 12 grams of the element ^{12}C (carbon-12). Although that definition is just a bit convoluted, the number in question is

$$6.022137 \times 10^{23} \text{ or } 602,213,700,000,000,000,000,000$$

We call this **Avogadro's number**.[1] In other words, 12 grams of ^{12}C consists of 602,213,700,000,000,000,000,000 atoms. The classic illustration of this number's unimaginable enormity is to try to appreciate an Avogadro's number of dollars. If a person started with 6.022137×10^{23} dollars, and spent a billion dollars every second for 75 years, more than 99.99% of the starting balance would still be available.

Like the prefixes on basic units of measurement, the term "mole" simplifies quantities by deleting zeros. After all, it is much easier to talk about frequent-flyer "miles" than it is to talk about frequent-flyer "inches." To erase even more zeros, we can affix those same metric prefixes to "mole" or "mol." For example,

$$0.001 \text{ mol} = 1 \text{ millimole} = 1 \text{ mmol}$$

$$0.000001 \text{ mol} = 1 \text{ micromole} = 1 \text{ } \mu\text{mol}$$

$$0.000000001 \text{ mol} = 1 \text{ nanomole} = 1 \text{ nmol}$$

$$0.000000000001 \text{ mol} = 1 \text{ picomole} = 1 \text{ pmol}$$

If the masses of two atoms differ, then a mole of one substance weighs more than a mole of the other. Consequently, a mole of ^{12}C atoms weighs 12.0 grams, and a mole of Fe (iron) atoms weighs 55.8 grams.

The **formula weight** of a substance is the sum of all the atomic weights in the formula. For example, the formula weight of water (H_2O) is 18.0 g:

$$\underbrace{2 \times 1.0 \text{ g}}_{\text{H atoms}} + \underbrace{1 \times 16.0 \text{ g}}_{\text{O atom}}$$

Therefore, one mole of water molecules weighs 18.0 grams. Likewise, a mole of glucose ($C_6H_{12}O_6$) weighs 180 grams:

$$\underbrace{6 \times 12.0 \text{ g}}_{\text{C atoms}} + \underbrace{12 \times 1.0 \text{ g}}_{\text{H atoms}} + \underbrace{6 \times 16.0 \text{ g}}_{\text{O atoms}}$$

The **molar mass** of a substance is numerically equal to the formula weight and is defined as the mass of one mole of the substance. Table 2 ★ lists several selected elements and their average atomic weights.

★ **TABLE 2** Selected Elements and Their Atomic Weights

Element	Average Atomic Weight (g/mol)
Hydrogen (H)	1.01
Calcium (Ca)	40.08
Carbon (C)	12.01
Chlorine (Cl)	35.45
Cobalt (Co)	58.93
Magnesium (Mg)	24.31
Nitrogen (N)	14.01
Oxygen (O)	16.00
Phosphorus (P)	30.97
Potassium (K)	39.10
Sodium (Na)	22.99
Sulfur (S)	32.07

[1]The value of 6.023 is also used widely as the significand. Because the difference between 6.023 and 6.022 is only 0.02%, this chapter uses both values.

Compute the formula weight of each of the following chemical compounds.

   (a) CO_2 (b) H_2S (c) $MgSO_4$ (d) Na_2O

   (a) $(1 \times 12.01 \text{ g/mol}) + (2 \times 16.00 \text{ g/mol}) = 44.01 \text{ g/mol}$
   (b) 34.09 g/mol   (c) 120.38 g/mol   (d) 61.98 g/mol

DIMENSIONAL ANALYSIS

Mentioned earlier, **dimensional analysis** is a unit-conversion technique based on the fact that any quantity can be multiplied by "1" without its value being changed. We use this technique to convert one unit into another by multiplying by what we call "unit factors." Let us consider four examples.

EXAMPLE 1

To convert "3.0 in" to "cm," we employ the equivalence of

$$1 \text{ in} = 2.54 \text{ cm}$$

From this equivalence, we can create two unit factors:

$$\frac{1 \text{ in}}{2.54 \text{ cm}} \quad \text{and} \quad \frac{2.54 \text{ cm}}{1 \text{ in}}$$

Next, we multiply our original value, "3.0 in," by the unit factor that gives us our target unit, "cm":

$$3.0 \text{ in} \times \frac{2.54 \text{ cm}}{1 \text{ in}} = 7.6 \text{ cm}$$

The units of "in" cancel, leaving the units of "cm", and we conclude that 3.0 inches is the same as 7.6 centimeters.

   To convert in the reverse direction, say, from "9.1 cm" to "in," we follow the same procedure by multiplying our original value by the unit factor that gives us our target unit:

$$9.1 \text{ cm} \times \frac{1 \text{ in}}{2.54 \text{ cm}} = 3.6 \text{ in}$$

The units of "cm" cancel, leaving the units of "in."

EXAMPLE 2

It is sometimes necessary to string several unit factors together. For example, let us calculate the number of ounces in one ton. We start with "1 ton," identify our target as "ounces", and then note any unit factors that link "tons" to "ounces."

Conversion: 1 ton → ? oz

Relevant Unit Factors:

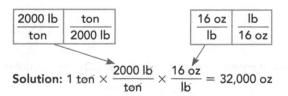

$$\text{Solution: } 1 \text{ ton} \times \frac{2000 \text{ lb}}{\text{ton}} \times \frac{16 \text{ oz}}{\text{lb}} = 32,000 \text{ oz}$$

   We solve the problem by multiplying the original value ("1 ton" in this case) by unit factors in such a way that only the target units emerge at the end of the calculation. The units of "ton" cancel, as do the units of "lb." We conclude that there are 32,000 ounces in one ton.

EXAMPLE 3

Let us now try a slightly longer conversion, one that is more germane to laboratory work. How many micromoles are there in 6.0 milligrams of glucose (molar mass = 180 g/mol)?

Conversion: 6.0 mg → ? μmol

Relevant Unit Factors:

$$\dfrac{1000 \text{ mg}}{g} \quad \dfrac{g}{1000 \text{ mg}} \qquad \dfrac{180 \text{ g}}{mol} \quad \dfrac{mol}{180 \text{ g}} \qquad \dfrac{1 \times 10^6 \text{ μmol}}{mol} \quad \dfrac{mol}{1 \times 10^6 \text{ μmol}}$$

Solution: $6.0 \text{ mg} \times \dfrac{g}{1000 \text{ mg}} \times \dfrac{mol}{180 \text{ g}} \times \dfrac{1 \times 10^6 \text{ μmol}}{mol} = 33 \text{ μmol}$

As in the earlier example, we solve this problem by multiplying the original value (6.0 mg) by unit factors in such a way that only the target units emerge at the end of the calculation. The units of "mg," "g," and "mol" cancel. For glucose, then, we conclude that 6.0 mg is the equivalent of 33 μmol.

EXAMPLE 4

This example of dimensional analysis involves a concentration. Suppose we must convert a test result of 0.739 mmol/L to "nmol/mL." Although the strategy is the same as in the preceding two examples, we now have *two* units to convert.

Conversion: 0.739 mmol/L → ? nmol/mL

Relevant Unit Factors:

$$\dfrac{1000 \text{ mmol}}{mol} \quad \dfrac{mol}{1000 \text{ mmol}} \qquad \dfrac{1 \times 10^9 \text{ nmol}}{mol} \quad \dfrac{mol}{1 \times 10^9 \text{ nmol}} \qquad \dfrac{1000 \text{ mL}}{L} \quad \dfrac{L}{1000 \text{ mL}}$$

Solution: $\dfrac{0.739 \text{ mmol}}{L} \times \dfrac{mol}{1000 \text{ mmol}} \times \dfrac{1 \times 10^9 \text{ nmol}}{mol} \times \dfrac{L}{1000 \text{ mL}} = 739 \text{ nmol/mL}$

☑ CHECKPOINT 3

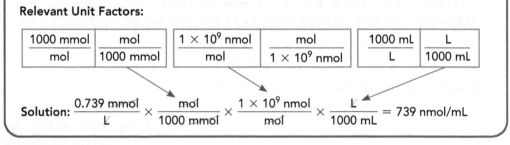

1. Using dimensional analysis, convert "890 nmol/L" to "μmol/dL."

$$\dfrac{890 \text{ nmol}}{L} \times \dfrac{mol}{1 \times 10^9 \text{ nmol}} \times \dfrac{1 \times 10^6 \text{ μmol}}{mol} \times \dfrac{L}{10 \text{ dL}} = 0.089 \text{ μmol/dL}$$

2. Using dimensional analysis, convert "0.864 g of CO_2" to "mmol of CO_2."

$$0.864 \text{ g } CO_2 \times \dfrac{mol \ CO_2}{44.01 \text{ g } CO_2} \times \dfrac{1000 \text{ mmol } CO_2}{mol \ CO_2} = 19.6 \text{ mmol } CO_2$$

THE RATIO METHOD

The **ratio method** is another way to convert between units. For example, if we want to convert "13 yards" to "feet," we can set up an equation of ratios and then cross-multiply:

$$\frac{3 \text{ ft}}{\text{yd}} = \frac{x}{13 \text{ yd}}$$

$$(3 \text{ ft})(13 \text{ yd}) = (1 \text{ yd})x$$

$$\frac{(3 \text{ ft})(13 \text{ yd})}{\text{yd}} = x$$

$$39 \text{ ft} = x$$

For longer conversions, a sequence of ratio calculations can substitute for dimensional analysis. Consider example 3 above, the conversion of "6.0 mg" of glucose to "micromoles." The order in which we convert the units is

$$mg \rightarrow g \rightarrow mol \rightarrow \mu mol$$

This is the same order in which we converted them using dimensional analysis above.

$$\textit{Conversion 1 (mg} \rightarrow \textit{g)} \qquad \frac{1000 \text{ mg}}{g} = \frac{6.0 \text{ mg}}{x}$$

$$x = 0.0060 \text{ g}$$

$$\textit{Conversion 2 (g} \rightarrow \textit{mol)} \qquad \frac{180 \text{ g}}{mol} = \frac{0.0060 \text{ g}}{x}$$

$$x = 3.3 \times 10^{-5} \text{ mol}$$

$$\textit{Conversion 3 (mol} \rightarrow \textit{\mu mol)} \qquad \frac{1 \times 10^6 \ \mu mol}{mol} = \frac{x}{3.3 \times 10^{-5} \text{ mol}}$$

$$x = 33 \ \mu mol$$

☑ CHECKPOINT 4

Using the ratio method, carry out the following conversions.

(a) 6.2 m → yd   (b) 535 μL → mL   (c) 0.5844 g NaCl → μmol NaCl

(a) $\dfrac{1.094 \text{ yd}}{m} = \dfrac{x}{6.2 \text{ m}}$ $x = 6.8$ yd

(b) 0.535 mL   (c) 10,000 μmol = 1.0×10^4 μmol

TEMPERATURE SCALES

There are three temperature scales, each with its own history and utility. On the **Fahrenheit** scale, the freezing point of water (at sea level) is 32 degrees (°F) and the boiling point is 212°F, setting these two temperatures 180F° apart. On the **Celsius** scale, however, water freezes at 0°C and boils at 100°C, the interval being 100C°.

Thus, 180 Fahrenheit degrees covers the same range as 100 Celsius degrees, making each Celsius degree 1.8 times a Fahrenheit degree:

$$\frac{180 \text{ F}°}{100 \text{ C}°} = 1.8 \text{ F°/C°}$$

There are two formulas for converting between Fahrenheit and Celsius temperatures:

$$°F = \left(°C \times \frac{9}{5}\right) + 32°$$

$$°C = \frac{5}{9}(°F - 32°)$$

The third temperature scale bears the name of its developer, Lord Kelvin. On the **Kelvin** scale, the zero-degree point corresponds to the theoretical absence of all thermal energy, "absolute zero." A temperature on the Kelvin scale is represented by "K," *with no degree symbol.*

Each degree, or increment, on the Kelvin scale is a "kelvin" (all lowercase). Each increment on the Kelvin scale is the same as an increment on the Celsius scale. Therefore, the two scales have a simple relationship, and the formula for interconverting them is

$$K = °C + 273.15$$

Summary

1. The *metric system* has only one basic unit for length, one for volume, and one for weight. The *United States Customary System of Units* has several units for each quantity.

2. The metric system is built on the number "10." Prefixes create decimal multiples and submultiples of basic units.

3. The *International System of Units (SI)* has seven basic units but permits the use of some non-SI units.

4. U.S. customary units and metric units are interconvertible.

5. The *mole* ("mol") is the amount of a substance that consists of as many entities (molecules, ions, particles, etc.) as there are atoms in exactly 12 grams of the element ^{12}C (carbon-12). The number is 6.022137×10^{23} or 602,213,700,000,000,000,000,000. It is called *Avogadro's number.* We can affix metric prefixes to "mole" or "mol."

6. The *formula weight* of a substance is the sum of all the atomic weights in the formula. The *molar mass* of a substance is numerically equal to the formula weight and is defined as the mass of one mole of the substance.

7. *Dimensional analysis* is a problem-solving technique based on the fact that any quantity can be multiplied by "1"

without its value being changed. We use this technique to convert one unit into another by multiplying by "unit factors."

8. The *ratio method* is useful in the conversion of units. An equation of ratios is established, and then cross-multiplication gives the value of the unknown quantity. For longer conversions, a sequence of ratio calculations can substitute for dimensional analysis.

9. There are three temperature scales: *Fahrenheit, Celsius,* and *Kelvin.* Their values are interconvertible by these equations:

$$°F = \left(°C \times \frac{9}{5}\right) + 32°$$

$$°C = \frac{5}{9}(°F - 32°)$$

$$K = °C + 273.15$$

Practice Problems

1. (LO 1, 2, 4, 5) Carry out each of the following unit conversions.

(a) 3.1 mL → μL

(b) 420 ng → mg

(c) 0.002 mL → μL

(d) 0.78 μg → ng

(e) 8.5 dL → L

(f) 1445 mg → g

(g) 0.0364 L → mL

(h) 13 pg → ng

(i) 620 nmol → μmol

(j) 9.7×10^{-5} mol → mmol

(k) 4.0 dL → mL

(l) 73 μg → mg

(m) 400 μL → mL

(n) 2.5×10^{-4} μg → pg

(o) 6.09×10^{4} μmol → mol

(p) 0.62 L → dL

(q) 705 μmol → pmol

(r) 2 ng → pg

2. (LO 6) Calculate the molar mass of each of the following substances.

(a) KCl   (b) NH_3 (c) K_3PO_4 (d) Na_2S (e) $MgCl_2$

3. (LO 4, 5, 7) For each of the following substances, suppose you have either the actual mass or the actual number of moles specified. Complete the table by supplying the missing information.

Substance	Molar Mass (g/mol)	Actual Mass (g)	Actual Moles
sodium chloride (NaCl)	58.44	3.50	(a)
sucrose ($C_{12}H_{22}O_{11}$)	342.3	(b)	0.0004
urea (CH_4N_2O)	60.06	0.70	(c)
potassium hydrogen phosphate ($KHPO_4$)	174.18	(d)	0.062
glucose ($C_6H_{12}O_6$)	180.2	5.66	(e)

4. (LO 8) Convert each of the following Celsius temperatures to its Fahrenheit equivalent.

(a) 37°C   (b) 82°C   (c) 140°C   (d) −20°C   (e) 4°C

5. (LO 8) Convert each of the following Fahrenheit temperatures to its Celsius equivalent.

(a) 72°F   (b) 230°F   (c) −7°F   (d) 45°F   (e) 10°F

6. (LO 8) Convert each of the following Celsius temperatures to its Kelvin equivalent.

(a) 0°C   (b) 100°C   (c) −273.15°C

7. (LO 3, 4, 5) Carry out the following conversions.

(a) 53 km → mi   (b) 5.6 in → cm   (c) 128 lb → kg

(d) 2 kg → oz   (e) 31 ft → m   (f) 3500 yd → km

(g) 8.9 L → gal   (h) 0.20 cups → mL   (i) 6.2 qt → L

Contextual Problems

1. (LO 1, 2, 4) If the typical red blood cell has a volume of 90 fL, then how many such cells could theoretically occupy a volume of 1 mL?

2. (LO 1, 2, 4, 5) One of the automated instruments in your laboratory requires the preparation of a special cleaning solution, made by mixing 30 mL of concentrate with enough water to bring the final volume to 250 mL. How much concentrate do you use to make 1 L of the cleaning solution?

3. (LO 2, 4, 5) On a balance that reads in "grams," you must weight out 450 mg of a substance. How many grams does this represent?

4. (LO 2, 4, 5) Using a pipet that reads in "microliters," you must deliver 0.080 mL of a solution. How many microliters does this represent?

5. (LO 2, 4, 5) Some of your laboratory's instruments return test results in units that must be converted into other units before being released into the hospital information system. Convert each of the following results into the units specified.

(a) 628 pg/mL → ng/L

(b) 0.0198 μmol/L → pmol/mL

(c) 1.74 μg/dL → mg/mL

(d) 0.49 mmol/L → μmol/dL

Answer Key

Practice Problems

1. (a) $3.1 \text{ mL} \times \dfrac{\text{L}}{1000 \text{ mL}} \times \dfrac{1 \times 10^6 \text{ μL}}{\text{L}} = 3100 \text{ μL}$

(b) $420 \text{ ng} \times \dfrac{\text{g}}{1 \times 10^9 \text{ ng}} \times \dfrac{1000 \text{ mg}}{\text{g}} = 4.2 \times 10^{-4} \text{ mL}$ (c) 2 μL   (d) 780 ng

(e) 0.85 L   (f) 1.445 g   (g) 36.4 mL   (h) 0.013 ng   (i) 0.620 μmol   (j) 0.097 mmol
(k) 400 mL   (l) 0.073 mg   (m) 0.400 mL   (n) 250 pg   (o) 0.0609 mol   (p) 6.2 dL
(q) 705,000 pmol   (r) 2000 pg

2. (a) 74.55 g/mol   (b) 17.04 g/mol   (c) 212.10 g/mol
(d) $(2 \times 22.99 \text{ g/mol}) + 32.07 \text{ g/mol} = 78.05 \text{ g/mol}$ (e) 95.21 g

3. (a) $3.50 \text{ g} \times \dfrac{\text{mol}}{58.44 \text{ g}} = 0.0599 \text{ mol}$ (b) 0.137   (c) 0.012   (d) 10.8   (e) 0.00314

4. (a) 98.6°F   (b) 179.6°F   (c) 284°F   (d) −4°F   (e) 39.2°F

5. (a) 22.2°C   (b) 110°C   (c) −21.7°C   (d) 7.2°C   (e) −12.2°C

6. (a) 273.15 K   (b) 373.15 K   (c) 0 K

7. (a) $53 \text{ km} \times \dfrac{\text{mi}}{1.61 \text{ km}} = 32.9 \text{ mi}$ (b) 14.2 cm   (c) 58.2 kg   (d) 70.4 oz

(e) $31 \text{ ft} \times \dfrac{\text{mi}}{5280 \text{ ft}} \times \dfrac{1.61 \text{ km}}{\text{mi}} \times \dfrac{1000 \text{ m}}{\text{km}} = 9.5 \text{ m}$ (f) 3.2 km   (g) 2.3 gal

(h) 47.2 mL   (i) 5.8 L

Contextual Problems

1. First, convert one of the units into the other:

$$1 \text{ mL} \times \frac{1 \text{ L}}{1000 \text{ mL}} \times \frac{1 \times 10^{15} \text{ fL}}{1 \text{ L}} = 1 \times 10^{12} \text{ fL}$$

Next, we take the ratio of the 1-mL volume to the 90-fL volume:

$$\frac{1 \times 10^{12} \text{ fL}}{90 \text{ fL}} = 1.1 \times 10^{10}$$

Thus, we conclude that 1.1×10^{10} (11 billion) red blood cells could theoretically occupy a volume of 1 mL.

2. First, convert one of the units into the other:

$$250 \text{ mL} \times \frac{\text{L}}{1000 \text{ mL}} = 0.250 \text{ L}$$

Next, set up an equation of ratios:

$$\frac{30 \text{ mL concentrate}}{0.250 \text{ L solution}} = \frac{x}{1 \text{ L solution}}$$

$$(30 \text{ mL concentrate})(1 \text{ L solution}) = (0.250 \text{ L solution})x$$

$$120 \text{ mL concentrate} = x$$

3. $450 \text{ mg} \times \dfrac{\text{g}}{1000 \text{ mg}} = 0.450 \text{ g}$

4. $0.080 \text{ mL} \times \dfrac{\text{L}}{1000 \text{ mL}} \times \dfrac{1 \times 10^6 \text{ µL}}{\text{L}} = 80 \text{ µL}$

This step can be shorter because 1 µL = 0.001 mL. Therefore, just multiply the number of milliliters by 1000 to give the number of microliters:

$$0.080 \text{ mL} \times 1000 \text{ µL/mL} = 80 \text{ µL}$$

5. (a) Here are four approaches to this problem.

APPROACH 1
Straightforward dimensional analysis.

$$\dfrac{628 \text{ pg}}{\text{mL}} \times \dfrac{\text{g}}{1 \times 10^{12} \text{ pg}} \times \dfrac{1 \times 10^9 \text{ ng}}{\text{g}} \times \dfrac{1000 \text{ mL}}{\text{L}} = \dfrac{628 \text{ ng}}{\text{L}}$$

APPROACH 2
Use the relationship that 1 ng = 1000 pg.

$$\dfrac{628 \text{ pg}}{\text{mL}} \times \dfrac{\text{ng}}{1000 \text{ pg}} \times \dfrac{1000 \text{ mL}}{\text{L}} = \dfrac{628 \text{ ng}}{\text{L}}$$

APPROACH 3
Two-step reasoning.

Step 1.

$$\dfrac{628 \text{ pg}}{\text{mL}} \times \dfrac{\text{ng}}{1000 \text{ pg}} = \dfrac{0.628 \text{ ng}}{\text{mL}}$$

Step 2. Every mL contains 0.628 ng. Thus, 1 L, which is 1000 mL, contains 1000 times as much, or 628 ng. The concentration is 628 ng/L.

APPROACH 4
The ratio method.

$$\dfrac{1 \times 10^{12} \text{ pg}}{\text{g}} = \dfrac{628 \text{ pg}}{x} \qquad x = 6.28 \times 10^{-10} \text{ g}$$

$$\dfrac{\text{g}}{1 \times 10^9 \text{ ng}} = \dfrac{6.28 \times 10^{-10} \text{ g}}{x} \qquad x = 0.628 \text{ ng}$$

Because 1 L = 1000 mL,

$$\dfrac{0.628 \text{ ng}}{\text{mL}} = \dfrac{x}{1000 \text{ mL}} \qquad x = 628 \text{ ng}$$

Therefore, there are 628 ng in every liter.

(b) 19.8 pmol/mL   (c) 17.4 mg/mL   (d) 49 µmol/dL

Glossary

Avogadro's number—the number of elementary particles in one mole of a substance: 6.022×10^{23}) (some resources: 6.023×10^{23}).

Celsius scale—the temperature scale on which the freezing point of water is 0° and the boiling point is 100°.

Dimensional analysis—a unit-conversion technique based on the fact that any quantity can be multiplied by "1" without its value being changed.

Fahrenheit scale—the temperature scale on which the freezing point of water is 32° and the boiling point is 212°.

Formula weight—the sum of all the atomic weights in the formula of a substance.

International System of Units—adopted in 1960, a modern version of the original metric system, based on the number 10 and built on seven base units.

Kelvin scale—the temperature scale on which the 0-degree point corresponds to the theoretical absence of all thermal energy. Each degree on the scale equals one Celsius degree, and a temperature on this scale is greater than the Celsius temperature by 273.15.

Metric system—a system of measurement established in 1791, based on the number 10. The term itself has become synonymous with "International System of Units."

Molar mass—the mass of a substance numerically equal to its formula weight; the mass of one mole of the substance.

Mole—the amount of a substance that consists of as many entities as there are atoms in exactly 12 grams of the element ^{12}C. That value is Avogadro's number.

Ratio method—a unit-conversion technique involving an equation of ratios followed by cross-multiplication.

United States Customary System of Units—a system of measurement in common use in the United States, rooted in the system of pre-1824 English units that had evolved from Anglo-Saxon and Roman units of measurement.

Mass and Volume Measurements

Mass and Volume Measurements

Chapter Outline

1 INTRODUCTION: J. J. BERZELIUS

J. J. Berzelius has been called the greatest experimental chemist of all time. This Swedish scientist was the leading figure in chemistry during much of the first half of the 1800s (see Figure 1A). Working with no more than a few students at a time, he was responsible for discovering several elements, determining the atomic weights of 50 elements, and devising the system of elemental symbols (H for hydrogen, O for oxygen, and so on) that we use to this day. He also determined the chemical composition of approximately 2000 minerals, put together the first comprehensive list of atomic weights, coined the terms "protein" and "catalyst," and invented many pieces of glassware that are still found in modern laboratories.[1-3]

A key feature of Berzelius's work was his insistence on the use of good laboratory techniques and careful measurements (see Figure 1B). The result is that all of the atomic masses he reported (when normalized to the value he used for oxygen) are within 1% of the values listed in the modern periodic table.[1,2] This level of accuracy is particularly impressive because instrumental methods of analysis, as we now know them, did not exist at his time. Instead, Berzelius used classical analysis methods that employed known chemical reactions and mass or volume measurements of the reactants or products.

Mass and volume determinations are still important in today's laboratories, where they form the basis of many

FIGURE 1A Jöns Jakob Berzelius (1779–1848), an early pioneer in analytical chemistry and one of the founders of modern chemistry. A balance that was used by Berzelius is shown in the back of his portrait. The portrait above shows Berzelius in 1843 and is from a painting by O. J. Soedermark. (Reproduced with permission and courtesy of the Royal Swedish Academy of Sciences.)

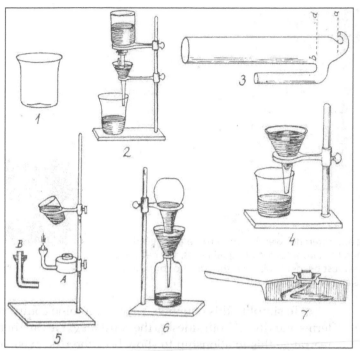

FIGURE 1B The drawings of the equipment shown above are from an 1836 book entitled *Lehrbuch der Chemie* by Berzelius, and include several items of glassware that Berzelius used in his research.

reference methods and are used to prepare samples and reagents for other analytical techniques. In this chapter we discuss mass and volume measurements and the procedures to follow in these measurements. We also consider how mass and volume can be combined to describe the content of samples and reagents.

2 MASS MEASUREMENTS

Mass is one of the most fundamental properties of matter and is defined as the quantity of matter in an object. This quantity is typically determined in a laboratory by using a **balance**, which is a precision weighing instrument used to measure small masses.[4] The balance is the earliest known measurement device. References to balances and weights can be found in cultures that range from ancient Egypt to China.[5] The device in the painting of Berzelius in Figure 1A is typical of what most people imagine when they think of a balance, in which two weighing pans are held by a beam on either side of a central fulcrum. The name "balance" comes from the Latin word *bilanx*, which means "having two pans."[4] The operation of such a device is relatively simple. The object to be measured is placed on one of the two pans while objects of a known mass are added to the other side. When the two sides are level, the mass of the object is determined by adding the masses of the weights on the opposite side.

In analytical chemistry, balances and mass measurements are used for many purposes. Balances are used to measure samples for analysis, to weigh chemicals for the preparation of reagents, and to determine the amount of a product that results from a reaction. The advantages of

mass measurements are that they can be made quickly, accurately, and reproducibly with relatively simple and inexpensive equipment. The only requirements are that you have enough material to examine and that the mass of this material is sufficiently stable to be measured.

2A The Determination of Mass

Weight versus Mass. The process of determining either the mass or weight of a substance is often called **weighing**, but the terms "mass" and "weight" actually refer to quite different things. *Mass* refers to the quantity of matter in an object. The base SI unit for mass is the *kilogram*, but mass can also be expressed in related units like the gram and milligram. **Weight** differs from mass in that it is a measure of the pull of a force on an object.[4] In most cases, gravity is the main force acting on an object as it is weighed, but other forces can also play a role.

The difference between mass and weight can be illustrated if you consider what would happen if you were weighed on both the Earth and the Moon. Your mass would be the same in each location because your body would contain the same amount of matter. However, your weight on the Moon would be about 1/6 of that on Earth because the Moon's gravity is only 16.7% as strong as the Earth's. Even if you move from the equator to the North or South poles on Earth your weight will differ by as much as 0.5% at sea level. This change occurs because the Earth is not a perfect sphere, a feature that causes your weight and distance from the Earth's center (which affects gravitational attraction) to vary at different locations. Similar changes occur as you move up or down in altitude, but none of these factors will alter your mass.[4,6,7]

Converting Weight to Mass. It is important to know the difference between mass and weight because when you place an object on a laboratory balance you are measuring the net force of gravity plus other forces on this object (or the object's *weight*). What we would really like to determine, however, is the object's *mass*. The way a balance makes this conversion is by comparing the object to a reference weight with a known mass. If the object and reference weight are placed on opposite sides of the balance, they will have the same forces acting on them from the surrounding medium and will be experiencing the same local gravitational field. Thus, the difference in force between the two sides should be directly related to their difference in mass.

The forces that act on an object when it is on a balance are illustrated in Figure 2. First, there is the force of gravity that is pulling downward on the object. This force is described by Equation 1.

$$\textbf{Force due to gravity} = m_{obj} \cdot g \qquad (1)$$

where m_{obj} is the mass of the object and g is the *gravitational acceleration constant*, which is a measure of

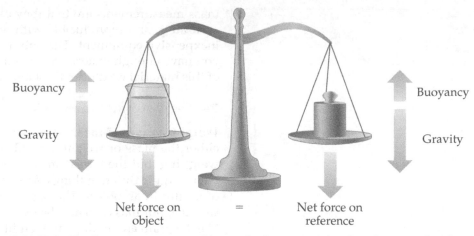

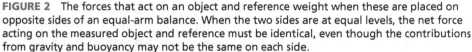

FIGURE 2 The forces that act on an object and reference weight when these are placed on opposite sides of an equal-arm balance. When the two sides are at equal levels, the net force acting on the measured object and reference must be identical, even though the contributions from gravity and buoyancy may not be the same on each side.

the pull of gravity at a particular location. A similar relationship can be written for the reference weight, where the force due to gravity will be equal to $m_{ref} \cdot g$.

Gravity is not the only force that determines an object's weight. Another important factor is **buoyancy**. Buoyancy is a force that works against gravity when you are weighing an object.[4] This force occurs whenever an object is surrounded by air or any medium other than a vacuum. If an object is less dense than its surrounding medium, this medium will displace the object to a region of lower density, causing the object to rise. This effect is why a helium balloon floats into the sky. The size of this force when we are weighing an object is related to the gravitational pull on the medium (usually air) that is displaced when the object and reference weight are placed on the balance. The size of this force is given by Equation 2, where the negative sign indicates that the force due to buoyancy is working against the force of gravity.

$$\text{Force due to buoyancy} = -m_{air} \cdot g \qquad (2)$$

In this relationship, the mass of displaced air can be determined from the air's density (d_{air}) and the volume of the object that displaced this air ($m_{air} = d_{air} \cdot V_{obj}$). Another way of determining the displaced air's mass is to use the density of air and the mass and density of the weighed object, where $m_{air} = m_{obj} \cdot (d_{air}/d_{obj})$.

When the object and reference weight are at the same level on an equal-arm balance, the overall forces acting on the object and reference weight must also be the same. We can describe this situation by combining Equations 1 and 2 to produce the following new relationship.

Weight of Object   **Weight of Reference**

$$m_{obj} \cdot g - m_{obj} \cdot (d_{air}/d_{obj}) \cdot g = m_{ref} \cdot g - m_{ref} \cdot (d_{air}/d_{ref}) \cdot g$$
$$(3)$$

To simplify this equation, we can combine common terms and divide both sides by the constant g. We can then rearrange this relationship to show how the true mass of the object (m_{obj}) is related to its apparent mass, as represented by the mass of reference (m_{ref}).

$$m_{obj} = m_{ref} \cdot \frac{[1 - (d_{air}/d_{ref})]}{[1 - (d_{air}/d_{obj})]} \qquad (4)$$

Equation 4 indicates that the mass of the measured object will indeed be directly related to the value of m_{ref}. It is this principle that allows the mass of this object to be measured on a balance. However, this equation also indicates that m_{ref} and the actual mass of our object are not necessarily the same value. This difference occurs because the ratio $[1 - (d_{air}/d_{ref})]/[1 - (d_{air}/d_{obj})]$ also appears in Equation 4. This ratio represents the different buoyancy effects that are acting on the object and reference weight. Although this ratio is often ignored in routine mass measurements, it must be considered when highly accurate masses are required. We will come back to this topic in Section 2C when we learn how to adjust mass values for buoyancy effects. (See Box 1 and Figure 3 for further discussion of how force measurements can be used in chemical analysis.)

2B Types of Laboratory Balances

Mechanical Balances and Electronic Balances. One type of laboratory balance is a mechanical balance. This device uses a mechanical approach for determining mass. An example is the equal-arm (or two-pan) balance, in which a sample and reference weights are placed on opposite sides of a beam that is held across a central fulcrum. This type of balance has been used for thousands of years and was found in analytical laboratories through the mid twentieth century, but it is not common in modern laboratories.[7] Another type of mechanical balance is the *substitution balance*, or *single-pan mechanical balance*. This device has a

BOX 1
Atomic Force Microscopy

There are other ways besides the use of laboratory balances in which scientists make use of force measurements to obtain information on a chemical sample. One important example is the method of *atomic force microscopy* (or *AFM*). Atomic force microscopy is a high-resolution method that is capable of imaging individual atoms or molecules on the surface of a sample. This technique was first developed in 1986 and has since become one of the most valuable tools for examining and manipulating chemicals at the nanoscale.[8-10]

The instrument that is used to perform AFM is called an *atomic force microscope* (see Figure 3). The basic design of this instrument includes a small cantilever with a sharp tip (called the "probe") that is passed over the surface of the sample. The end of this tip has a width on the order of nanometers, which is comparable to the size of atoms and small molecules. As this tip is passed gently over the sample, forces between the tip and sample will cause a slight deflection in the tip and cantilever. These deflections are typically measured by using a laser beam that is aimed at the cantilever and deflected onto a detector array that monitors any small changes in the position of this laser beam. This information is then used to create an image of the surface of the sample.

Although modern AFM instruments are capable of atomic-scale resolution, they are commonly utilized in examining materials on a slightly larger scale, as shown in Figure 3. A big advantage of AFM is that, unlike some other high-resolution imaging methods, this technique can be used with both conductive and nonconductive samples. AFM can also be employed with samples that are in air or in liquids and that are hard or soft in nature. These properties have made AFM an important tool in fields that range from materials science to biomedical research.[9,10]

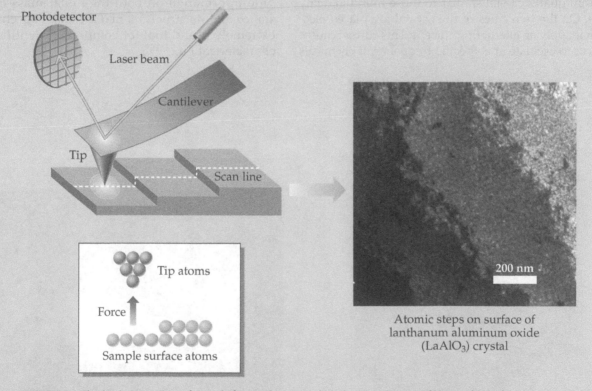

Atomic steps on surface of lanthanum aluminum oxide ($LaAlO_3$) crystal

FIGURE 3 The basic operation of atomic force microscopy (AFM) and an image of the surface of a lanthanum aluminum oxide crystal that was obtained by this technique. (Reproduced with permission and courtesy of C. L. Cheung, University of Nebraska.)

single pan placed on one side of a beam along with a set of removable weights. The other side of the beam is connected to a fixed counterweight. When no sample is present, both sides of the beam are in balance. When a sample is placed onto the pan, the positions of the two sides are disturbed and some weights on the sample side are removed to restore these positions. The mass of these weights is then used to determine the mass of the sample.

The most popular type of balance in modern chemical laboratories is the **electronic balance** (see Figure 4). This balance uses an electronic mechanism to determine the mass of an object, which is accomplished by attaching the sample pan to one or more bars that are held between the two ends of a permanent magnet. When a sample is placed onto the pan, the bars are pushed downward. A position sensor signals the balance to apply a current through the bars, which produces an electromagnetic force that causes the bars to again move upward. The size of the applied current that is needed to move the bar and sample pan to their original positions is then measured, providing a value that is proportional to the mass of the sample.[4,7] The low cost and ease of use of electronic balances have made them popular in analytical laboratories.[4,7,11] With these balances, it is possible to correct electronically for the mass of a sample container and for variations in the instrument's response with changes in temperature. Most electronic balances are also able to perform automatic calibration with built-in reference weights and can interface directly with computers for data collection.

Other Mass-Measuring Devices. There are a variety of other instruments that use mass measurements for chemical analysis. One example is a *quartz crystal microbalance (QCM)*. Rather than being used to measure relatively large amounts of material, a QCM is employed as a sensor for trace amounts of chemicals. This device is constructed from a thin quartz crystal similar to those found in many watches. On the two sides of the crystal are placed electrodes that apply an alternating current. This current causes the quartz to oscillate at a specific frequency. If chemicals adsorb to the surface of the crystal, as might occur when it contains a coating that favors such binding, the mass of the crystal will change. This adsorption process can produce a measurable change in the frequency at which the crystal is vibrating, allowing the mass of deposited material to be measured. The maximum amount of a substance that can be measured by this device is around a few hundred micrograms and it can be used to examine changes in mass as small as a fraction of a nanogram.[12]

Another mass-measuring device that we will encounter throughout this text is a *mass spectrometer*. Unlike laboratory balances, which estimate the total mass of a sample, a mass spectrometer measures the masses of *individual* atoms or molecules. This type of measurement is accomplished by first converting the atoms or molecules into gas-phase ions, which are then separated and analyzed based on their mass and charge. The result is a graph known as a *mass spectrum*, in which the amount of each detected ion is plotted versus its *mass-to-charge ratio (m/z)* (see Figure 5). This plot can provide information on both the molar mass of the substance and its structure, making mass spectrometry an extremely useful tool for compound identification and characterization.[13–15]

Analytical balance

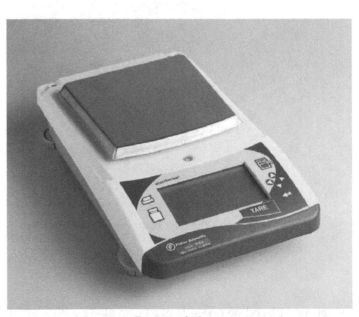

Precision balance

FIGURE 4 Some examples of electronic balances. The balance with the enclosed weighing compartment is known as an **analytical balance,** and the balance that has the open weighing area is called a **precision balance,** or *top-loading balance.* (These images are for the AB-S/FACT Class Analytical Balance and accuSeries II Electronic Toploading balance and are reproduced with permission and courtesy of Mettler Toledo and Fisher Scientific, respectively.)

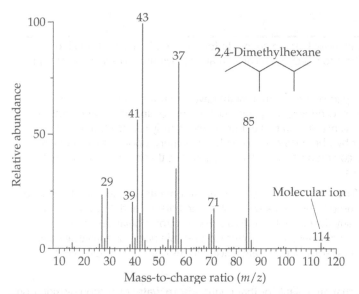

FIGURE 5 An example of a mass spectrum.

2C Recommended Procedures for Mass Measurements

Selection and Use of Balances. Most laboratories have several types of balances, so a question you often need to ask is "What is the best balance for my particular mass measurement?" An important thing to consider is the *maximum load* (or *capacity*) of each balance, which refers to the largest mass a balance can reliably measure. Another feature to consider is the *readability*, which is the smallest division in mass that can be read on the balance's display.[4,7] A third factor used to compare balances is their *resolution*, which is determined by dividing the capacity of a balance by its readability.[7]

$$\text{Resolution} = \frac{\text{Capacity}}{\text{Readability}} \qquad (5)$$

As you can see from this relationship, the resolution is a direct measure of how many distinct masses can be determined by a particular balance (1.0000 g vs. 1.0001 g, and so

on). Most laboratory balances have a resolution of at least 10,000 and some have resolutions as high as 20 million.

Table 1 lists the capacities, readabilities, and resolutions of various laboratory balances. These devices can be placed into one of two general groups based on their readability and design. A balance that has an enclosed weighing compartment (for greater stability and accuracy) and that can provide mass measurements to within at least 0.1 milligram is known as an **analytical balance**. If the balance has an open weighing area, it is called a **precision balance** (or *top-loading balance*).[4,7] Of the various balances that are listed in Table 1, the standard precision balance and macroanalytical balance are the ones most often seen in analytical laboratories, due to their good readabilities and their ability to handle the range of masses needed for most routine assays.

After you have selected a balance, you next must make sure you are familiar with its proper use and care. Using good laboratory practices with the balance will help ensure the balance is operating correctly and is providing the best possible mass measurements. Table 2 summarizes a few guidelines that pertain to the care of any balance, including the handling of samples and chemicals on a balance and the proper recording of mass measurements.

Weighing Methods. Another choice you must make before making a mass measurement is the technique you will employ during the weighing process. There are two common approaches for weighing.[6] The first approach is *direct weighing*, which is carried out by simply placing an object on the balance pan and recording its mass from the display. This approach is commonly used for inert and solid objects, such as reference weights. It is important to remember that chemicals should *never* be placed directly onto a balance. Instead, the chemicals should be weighed while they are in or on a container (for instance, a piece of weighing paper, a plastic weighing boat, or a beaker). This precaution protects the balance from exposure to the chemical, but it also makes it difficult to use direct weighing for chemicals on most mechanical balances.

TABLE 1 Common Types of Balances			
Analytical Balances	**Capacity (g)**	**Readability (g)**	**Resolution**
Macroanalytical balance	50–400	0.0001	$(0.5 - 4) \times 10^6$
Semimicrobalance	30–200	0.00001	$(0.3 - 2) \times 10^7$
Microbalance	3–20	0.000001	$(0.3 - 2) \times 10^7$
Ultramicrobalance	2	0.0000001	2×10^7
Precision Balances	**Capacity**	**Readability**	**Resolution**
Industrial precision scale	30–6,000 kg	0.0001–0.1 kg	$(0.1 - 6) \times 10^5$
Precision balance	100–30,000 g	0.001–1 g	$(0.3 - 2) \times 10^5$

Source: This classification scheme and list of characteristics are from M. Kochsiek, *Glossary of Weighing Terms: A Practical Guide to the Terminology of Weighing*, Mettler-Toledo, Switzerland, 1998; and W. E. Kupper, "Laboratory Balances," In *Analytical Instrumentation Handbook*, 2nd ed., G. W. Ewing, Ed., Marcel Dekker, New York, 1997, Chapter 2.

TABLE 2   Good Laboratory Practices for Using a Balance

Balance Selection	The balance should have a capacity and readability that are adequate for the sample size that is being measured. In any mass determination it is best to select the balance that will give the most significant figures for the measurement at hand.
Balance Location	The balance should be kept away from any part of a room that might have air currents or that is near a source of cold or heat (for example, by doors, windows, hot plates, heating or cooling vents, and areas of heavy traffic through the laboratory). The balance should be kept on a rigid, sturdy surface that is not affected by the presence of the operator or by vibrations due to nearby machinery, doors, or elevators. It should be kept away from and not share a common circuit with any equipment that might cause erratic power fluctuations, such as electrical motors.
Balance Care and Maintenance	The balance should be properly leveled before it is used for any mass measurements. In addition, it should be calibrated at its final site of use before it is used to process any samples. The balance and its surrounding area should always be kept clean and free from any dust or spilt chemicals. For electronic balances, be sure to tare the device back to zero after you have removed a weighed item from the sample pan. For analytical balances, keep the doors to the weighing area closed except when you are placing items onto the sample pan or removing them from it.
Sample Handling	For accurate mass measurements, samples that are volatile or that might adsorb water or carbon dioxide from the air should be weighed in a closed container. The sample should be at the same temperature as the balance and its surroundings, if possible, to avoid the production of local air convection around the sample pan. Normal air humidity should be kept in the laboratory to minimize the presence of static electricity in samples, which can lead to erratic mass measurements. Avoid touching the measured object or its weighing container with your hands, because fingerprints and the moisture they adsorb can add a detectable mass to these items. Always place an object on the middle of the sample pan for the most accurate results. Do not place a liquid sample that contains a magnetic stir bar onto a balance, because the magnet will create additional force acting on the sample that can lead to errors in the weighing procedure.
Recording Mass Measurements	The measured mass values should be recorded *directly* into the laboratory notebook, using the full number of significant figures that are provided by the balance. An indication should be made in the notebook as to whether any buoyancy correction was made. Such a correction is usually required if the final mass needs to be within 0.1% of its true value. If a buoyancy correction is made, the density of the sample and the surrounding air should both be recorded in the notebook. Determining the air density will also require that you determine and record the barometric pressure, temperature, and relative humidity of the air during the time of the mass measurement.

Direct weighing can be conducted on an electronic balance by using a feature known as *taring*. Taring involves placing an empty weighing container onto the balance and resetting the balance's display (by pressing a "tare," "zero," or "rezero" button) so that it reads zero when the container is present.[4] When a chemical is placed into this container, the display can then be used as a direct reading of the amount of added substance. After the object and container have been removed, the "tare" button can be pressed again to provide a reading of zero when nothing is present on the balance. This last step is important when you are working with balances that have automatic calibration, because failure to reset the tare value might affect the calibration process.

The mass of a chemical can also be determined through an approach known as *weight by difference*. In this procedure, a sample's mass is calculated by taking the difference between the mass of the sample plus its container and the mass of the container alone. The best results are obtained when the sample is weighed in the same container that will be used for its final study or preparation. If the sample must be transferred from its weighing container to another vessel, the container should be weighed again after the sample has been removed. The difference in mass for the final container and the container plus the sample is then used to determine the mass of the substance that was transferred. This method is more accurate than using only the initial weight of the container in that some sample may have remained behind after the transfer.

Buoyancy Corrections. Up to this point we have assumed the mass that is displayed by a balance is equal to the mass of the sample being weighed. This assumption is valid if the buoyancy term $[1 - (d_{air}/d_{ref})]/ [1 - (d_{air}/d_{obj})]$ in Equation 4 is approximately equal to one and can be ignored. But when do we need to consider buoyancy effects? We can answer this question by looking more closely at what affects the ratio $[1 - (d_{air}/d_{ref})]/[1 - (d_{air}/d_{obj})]$. First, there is the density of the surrounding medium, which appears in both the top and bottom of this ratio as the term d_{air}. For air, this density will have an average value of $1.2 \times 10^{-3} g/cm^3$. A second factor to consider is the density of the reference weight (d_{ref}). By international convention, such weights usually have a density of 8.0 g/cm^3 and are made of stainless steel.[4,6] The third factor is the density of the object being weighed (d_{obj}). This density can have a wide range of values and will depend on the type of sample we are measuring.

An illustration of how the true and measured masses of an object will differ at various sample densities is shown in Figure 6. Samples with lower densities than the reference weight (8.0 g/cm^3 in this example) will give apparent masses that are lower than their true values, while samples with densities greater than the reference weight will have high apparent masses. The size of this error will depend on how different the sample and reference weights are in their densities. Sample materials with densities of $2-15 \text{ g/cm}^3$, as occur in many solids, have an error of less than 0.01% in the measured mass, as indicated by Figure 6. For samples with densities of $0.8-2.0 \text{ g/cm}^3$, which includes many liquids, this error is around 0.1–0.2%.

A useful guideline to remember is that buoyancy effects should be considered whenever you want to measure a mass with *four* or *more* significant figures (that is, when errors of less than 0.1–0.2% become important). The process of adjusting for these effects is known as making a **buoyancy correction**. This correction can be accomplished by using a modified version of Equation 4, in which the mass of the reference weight is replaced by the equivalent apparent mass that is read from the balance's display ($m_{display}$).

$$m_{obj} = m_{display} \cdot \frac{[1 - (d_{air}/d_{ref})]}{[1 - (d_{air}/d_{obj})]} \qquad (6)$$

Equation 6 shows that you can obtain the correct measured mass of an object if you know (1) the apparent mass given on the balance's display, (2) the density of the sample, (3) the density of the reference weight used to calibrate the balance, and (4) the density of the surrounding medium.

| EXERCISE 1 | Correcting for Buoyancy Effects |

A weighing container is placed onto a balance and the display is tared so that it reads zero. Calcium carbonate is then placed into this container, giving a displayed mass of 10.0150 g. It is desired in this case to know the true mass of the calcium carbonate to five significant figures. The balance has previously been calibrated with 8.0 g/cm^3 stainless steel weights and is operated in a laboratory that has an air density of $1.2 \times 10^{-3} \text{g/cm}^3$. It is known that the density of pure calcium carbonate (calcite) is 2.710 g/cm^3. What is the true mass of the calcium carbonate sample?

SOLUTION

The true mass can be obtained by substituting the measured mass and the densities of the sample, air and reference weights into Equation 6.

$$m_{obj} = m_{display} \cdot \frac{[1 - (d_{air}/d_{ref})]}{[1 - (d_{air}/d_{obj})]}$$

$$= (10.0150 \text{ g})$$

$$\cdot \frac{[1 - (0.0012 \text{ g/cm}^3)/(8.0 \text{ g/cm}^3)]}{[1 - (0.0012 \text{ g/cm}^3)/(2.710 \text{ g/cm}^3)]}$$

$$m_{obj} = 10.0179 \text{ g} = \mathbf{10.018 \text{ g}}$$

In checking our answer by dimensional analysis, we get a final answer with the same units as the measured mass (grams). Also, we see that the measured and actual masses differ by less than 0.03%, which agrees with the type of error we would expect from Figure 6.

You may have noticed in the preceding exercise that we did not consider the effects of buoyancy on the weighing container itself. This simplification was possible because we used the tare feature of the balance to subtract the container's weight from the weight of the container plus calcium carbonate. If the taring and mass measurements are carried out in a reasonably short period of time (so that the density of the air is unchanged), the buoyancy of the container should remain constant, thus allowing the container's weight to be canceled out when we tare the balance. The same assumption would have been true if we had used weight by difference to determine the mass of the calcium carbonate.

To help you make a correction like the one in the last exercise, the densities of many common chemicals can be found in references like the *CRC Handbook of Chemistry and Physics* or *Lange's Handbook of Chemistry*.[16,17] It is also important that you know the exact density of the weights used to calibrate your balance. Although 8.0 g/cm^3 stainless steel is usually employed for this purpose, other types of calibration weights may be used in some cases. Another factor to keep in mind is that $1.2 \times 10^{-3} \text{g/cm}^3$ is only an average value for the density for air. The actual air density for your laboratory will depend on the barometric pressure, temperature, and relative humidity and can vary by as much as 3% from this average value.[7] Using the actual density of air in a buoyancy correction is especially crucial when *five* or *more* significant figures are needed in a mass measurement.

3 VOLUME MEASUREMENTS

Another important property of matter is **volume**. *Volume* can be defined as the amount of space that is occupied by a three-dimensional object. For solid materials, volume

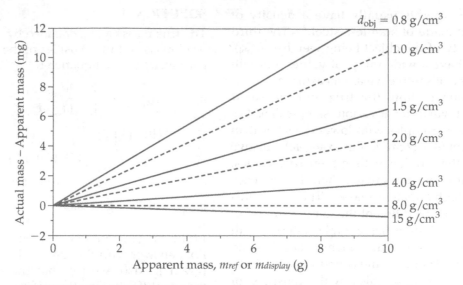

FIGURE 6 Difference in the actual and measured masses for samples or objects of various densities. These samples are being compared to a reference weight with a density of 8.0 g/cm³ and are assumed to be surrounded by air with a density of 1.2 × 10⁻³g/cm³.

can be calculated from the object's height, width, and length, or by measuring the volume of liquid that is displaced by the solid. For a liquid, volume is determined by measuring the amount of space the liquid occupies in a container. Volume measurements have been made since ancient times in areas such as architecture, cooking, and commerce. These measurements also play a key role in the preparation of samples and reagents for chemical analysis, the subject that we will focus on in this chapter. Volume measurements can also be utilized directly for measuring chemical content. We will examine this last topic later in this text when we discuss a technique known as a "titration."

3A The Determination of Volume

Volume versus Mass. Although both volume and mass are related to the size of an object, volume has several advantages when it comes to describing materials. For instance, the volume of a sample is easier to visualize than its mass. Volumes are more convenient to measure for liquids, where all that is required is to place the liquid in a suitably marked container. A disadvantage of using volumes is that a sample's volume, unlike its mass, can vary with temperature and pressure. The mass of an object can also usually be measured with a higher precision than its volume.

The base unit of volume in the SI system is the *cubic meter* (m^3), but this unit is relatively large and not particularly convenient for use in routine chemical testing. Chemists instead often use the *liter* (L), which is now defined in the SI system as being equal to 1 cubic decimeter (or 1000 cm³). The volume and mass of a material are related to each other through that substance's **density**. Density refers to the mass (m) per unit volume (V) of a material and is often represented by the symbols d or ρ, where $d = m/V$. We have already used this relationship in the previous section when we discussed corrections for buoyancy effects. Like volume, the density of an object changes with pressure and temperature. However, the density of a material does have the same value regardless of the material's actual size, which makes density more useful than volume or mass as a means for chemical identification.

Analytical Volume Measurements. Many people are familiar with common pieces of laboratory glassware such as the beaker, Erlenmeyer flask, test tube, and graduated cylinder. These pieces of glassware are designed for the heating, mixing, and handling of solutions, but are not usually designed for the accurate determination of volumes. Even a good-quality graduated cylinder will provide a volume measurement that is accurate to within only 1% of its true value. In modern chemical laboratories more accurate volume measurements must be made on a routine basis. This higher level of accuracy is obtained by using devices that are especially designed for volume measurments, such as volumetric flasks and volumetric pipets (some of which can determine a volume to an accuracy of 0.025%).

One unique feature of these volume-measuring devices is the materials from which they are constructed. Berzelius and other scientists of his time made their own glassware out of conventional *soda-lime glass*, as is obtained by combining sand (SiO_2) with limestone ($CaCO_3$) and sodium carbonate (Na_2CO_3).[18] The most common glass you will find in today's laboratory is *borosilicate glass*, which contains a significant amount of boron oxide (B_2O_3) and a lower percentage of sodium oxide (Na_2O) and other oxides than ordinary glass. Borosilicate glass is more resistant than ordinary glass to strong acids or bases and has a third the change in size and volume with temperature.[1,18] These properties make borosilicate glass better for constructing devices for accurate volume measurements.

One problem with any type of glass is that it will eventually lose some of its mass when exposed to acids or bases over long periods of time. This effect causes the interior of the glass container to be "etched." This process will change the actual volume of the container and makes the container easier to break. Another disadvantage of glass is it may contain trace levels of metal ions that can enter and contaminate solutions. This contamination can be a problem when you are preparing samples and reagents for the analysis of trace-level metals. Because of these limitations, some analytical laboratories use special plastic containers that are made out of Teflon, polymethylpentene, or polypropylene. These materials offer good resistance to most chemical reagents and contain only trace amounts of metals. Their main disadvantage is they melt at much lower temperatures than glass, limiting the range of conditions over which they can be employed.

3B Types of Volumetric Equipment

There are a large number of volume-measuring devices used for analytical measurements. These devices include *volumetric flasks, volumetric pipets, burets, micropipets,* and *syringes.*

Volumetric Flasks. A **volumetric flask** is a device that is used to prepare solutions and to dilute them to a specific volume (generally 1–2000 mL). The general shape of a volumetric flask is shown in Figure 7 and consists of a long upper neck plus a round, flat-bottomed lower region for mixing and holding solutions. The top of the neck contains an opening where a stopper can be placed for mixing the flask's contents. There is also a line etched on the neck, which indicates where the *meniscus* (or curved upper surface) of the solution should be located when the volume of liquid in the flask is equal to its stated volume. Most volumetric flasks have the abbreviation "TC" on their side, indicating that they are designed "To Contain" the stated volume of liquid.

On a volumetric flask you will usually see a letter such as "A" or "B," indicating whether it is *Class A* or *Class B glassware.* The properties needed for a volumetric flask to be designated as Class A glassware are given in Table 3. Both Class A and Class B volumetric flasks provide much better volume measurements than routine glassware, but Class A flasks have only half of the maximum errors than those for Class B flasks. Class B flasks are less expensive than Class A flasks and are often fine for use in teaching or in general purpose work. Class A flasks, however, are the devices of choice whenever high-quality volume measurements are desired during solution preparation.

The procedure for using a volumetric flask is fairly simple. You begin by making sure the flask is clean and clear of any cracks or other defects. You then put into the

flask a small amount of solvent and the solid or liquid you would like to place into solution. Next, you swirl the contents until all of the added material has dissolved. More solvent is then added (not yet totally filling the flask) and the swirling is repeated. While the flask is sitting on a firm flat surface, any solvent needed to fill the flask to its calibrated mark is carefully added. As you near the calibration line, it is recommended that single drops of the solvent be added with a small pipet (*not* a squirt bottle, which is harder to use for this purpose). When the bottom of the solvent's meniscus lies directly on the line, a stopper is firmly placed on the flask and the flask is repeatedly mixed by inverting it for several minutes (for example, inverting 10 times over the course of 4 to 5 minutes). This procedure ensures the flask's contents will have a uniform composition.

Volumetric Pipets. Another important device for measuring liquids is a **volumetric pipet** (also known as a *transfer pipet*). This type of pipet, shown in Figure 8, is designed to measure and deliver a single specific volume of liquid to a separate container, such as a volumetric flask. Volumetric pipets are used to handle volumes that range from 0.5 mL to 100 mL and are employed when volume measurements are needed that are reliable to within a few hundredths of a milliliter.

Like volumetric flasks, a volumetric pipet contains a label that gives the volume and temperature at which the pipet was calibrated. There is also a mark around the pipet's neck that indicates where this calibrated volume occurs, as well as a label indicating whether the pipet is a Class A or Class B device. Class A pipets have the

TABLE 3 Characteristics of Class A Volumetric Flasks[*]	
Type of Flask (mL)	Maximum Allowable Error (mL)
1	± 0.01
2	± 0.015
5	± 0.02
10	± 0.02
25	± 0.03
50	± 0.05
60	± 0.05
100	± 0.08
110	± 0.08
200	± 0.10
250	± 0.12
500	± 0.20
1000	± 0.30
2000	± 0.50

[*]The properties contained in this table are those specified by the American Society for Testing Materials. The term "tolerance" is often used in place of "maximum allowable error" when describing the properties of these devices.

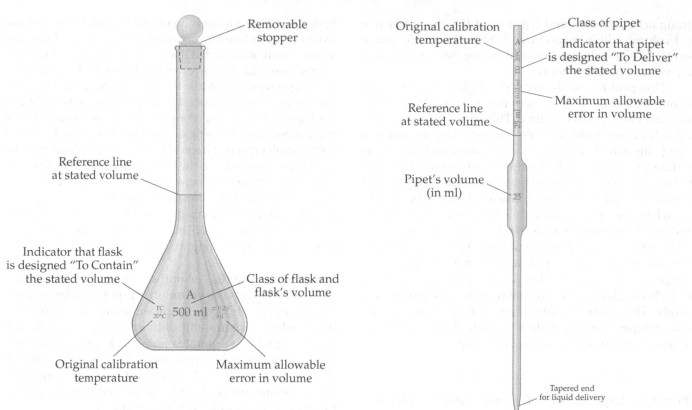

Removable stopper

Reference line at stated volume

Indicator that flask is designed "To Contain" the stated volume

A
TC 20°C 500 ml ± 0.20 ml

Class of flask and flask's volume

Original calibration temperature

Maximum allowable error in volume

Original calibration temperature

Class of pipet

Indicator that pipet is designed "To Deliver" the stated volume

Maximum allowable error in volume

Reference line at stated volume

Pipet's volume (in ml)

25

Tapered end for liquid delivery

FIGURE 7 The general design of a volumetric flask. A line is etched on the neck of this flask to indicate the point at which the meniscus of the solution should be located when the volume of liquid in the flask is equal to the flask's stated volume. The size of this volume and the temperature at which the flask was calibrated are given near the bottom of the flask along with the symbol "TC," which means that the flask is designed "To Contain" the stated amount of liquid.

FIGURE 8 The general design of a volumetric pipet. A line is etched on the neck of the pipet to indicate the point at which the meniscus of a liquid should be located when its volume is equal to the pipet's stated volume. The size of this volume and the temperature at which the pipet was calibrated are given on the side along with the symbol "TD," which means that the pipet is designed "To Deliver" the stated amount of liquid without any added force or pressure.

characteristics listed in Table 4, while Class B pipets have maximum allowable errors that are twice these levels. One important difference from volumetric flasks is that volumetric pipets are designed "To Deliver," as represented by the symbol "TD" on their sides. This symbol means these pipets will provide the indicated volume when their contents are allowed to drain (*without* blowing or any forced delivery) into another container.

When you are using a volumetric pipet, you first need to inspect the pipet to make sure it is clean and free from any cracks or chips, especially at the end where the solvent is delivered. If the pipet is in good shape, you should then rinse its interior by using a rubber or plastic bulb or related device to draw in a small amount of the liquid you would like to measure. After you have carefully swirled this liquid within the pipet (including the region past the calibration mark), discard the rinse liquid. It is wise to carry out this rinsing step at least twice to ensure there is no dust or chemicals in the pipet from previous work. Once the pipet has been rinsed, draw a fresh portion of the desired liquid into the pipet and up past the calibration mark. The bulb or device used to draw up the liquid is then removed from the flat upper end of the pipet and this end is quickly sealed by placing the tip of your

finger onto it. Next, you gently wipe the other end of the pipet with a tissue to remove any excess liquid from the outside. The tip is then touched to the side of a waste container and the pipet is allowed to slowly drain until the bottom of the liquid's meniscus is at the calibrated mark. The pipet is then ready to be moved to the final desired container, into which its liquid contents are allowed to drain freely while the tip of the pipet is kept in contact with the container's wall. At the end of this step, keep the pipet's tip against the container for a few extra seconds to make sure that draining of the liquid is complete.

It is important to *never* blow out the final contents of a volumetric pipet or to use any force other than gravity to cause liquid to flow out of such a device. It is also important to always use a rubber or plastic bulb or related device to draw liquids into the pipet and to *never* draw in a liquid by using your mouth. Finally, after you have finished using a pipet you should rinse it with water or a cleaning solution to avoid any buildup of materials that may clog the pipet or contaminate its interior.

Burets and Other Volumetric Devices. Figure 9 shows some other volume-measuring devices that are often found in analytical laboratories. One of these

TABLE 4 Characteristics of Class A Volumetric Pipets*

Type of Pipet (mL)	Maximum Allowable Error (mL)	Minimum Flow Time (s)
0.5	± 0.006	5
1	± 0.006	10
2	± 0.006	10
3	± 0.01	10
4	± 0.01	10
5	± 0.01	15
6	± 0.02	15
7	± 0.02	15
8	± 0.02	15
9	± 0.02	15
10	± 0.02	15
15	± 0.03	25
20	± 0.03	25
25	± 0.03	25
30	± 0.05	25
40	± 0.05	25
50	± 0.05	25
75	± 0.08	30
100	± 0.08	30

*These properties are those specified by the American Society for Testing Materials. The term "tolerance" is often used in place of "maximum allowable error" when describing the properties of these devices. The "minimum flow time" is the shortest amount of time that is acceptable for all the liquid in a pipet to drain into another container.

devices is the **buret,** which is used to accurately measure and deliver variable amounts of a liquid. A buret consists of a graduated glass tube with an opening at the top for the addition of a liquid and a stopcock at the bottom for the precise delivery of this liquid into another container. A buret is used in the method of titrations, where accurate volume measurements of a reagent solution and a known reaction of this reagent with a sample are used to measure an analyte's concentration. Burets are available as both Class A and Class B devices, with common burets holding from 10 mL to 100 mL of liquid. The scale on the side of the buret varies with the device's size, with the Class A 10 mL burets having 0.05 mL divisions and maximum allowable errors of ± 0.02 mL, and 100 mL burets having ± 0.20 mL divisions and maximum errors of 0.10 mL. There are also special designs for working with smaller or larger volumes of liquids.

Another type of volumetric device is a *Mohr pipet* (or *measuring pipet*). This type of pipet has many marks on its side that allow it to measure and deliver a variety of liquid volumes within its calibrated range. Like a volumetric pipet, a Mohr pipet is designed "To Deliver" liquids through the process of natural draining, without blowing or any forced delivery. Mohr pipets have maximum volumes of 0.1–25 mL and calibrated marks at 0.1, 0.01, or 0.001 mL intervals. Mohr pipets are not as accurate as volumetric pipets, but they are more convenient when measuring a variety of volumes or when using volumes that cannot be delivered by standard volumetric pipets.

Two other types of volumetric devices are the *serological pipet* and the *Ostwald–Folin pipet*. These devices are useful when you are working with small liquid volumes or when you want *all* of a measured liquid to be delivered to a container. These pipets are similar in appearance to the Mohr pipet and volumetric pipet, respectively. An important difference is that serological pipets and Ostwald–Folin pipets are designed *"To Deliver/Blow Out,"* which means they deliver the indicated volume only when the last bit of their contents is blown out with a pipet bulb.

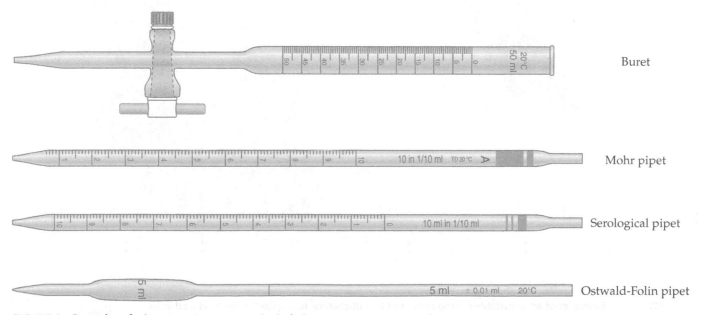

Buret

Mohr pipet

Serological pipet

Ostwald-Folin pipet

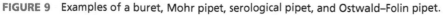

FIGURE 9 Examples of a buret, Mohr pipet, serological pipet, and Ostwald–Folin pipet.

Because of the different ways these pipets are operated, it is essential that you always be familiar with the type of pipet you are using during an experiment.

For handling very small liquid volumes, a *micropipet* (or *pipetter*) can be employed. These devices come with volume capacities often ranging from $0.1~\mu L$ to $5000~\mu L$ and have typical allowable errors of $\pm~0.5$–2.0%. A micropipet uses disposable tips that can easily be replaced between samples or changed to deliver liquids over different volume ranges. Micropipets are convenient when you are dealing with small or precious samples and when errors of a few percent are acceptable. Some micropipets are operated manually, while others are electronically controlled or even equipped with several tips, allowing up to 8–12 samples to be measured and delivered at once (see Figure 10).

A *syringe* is a volumetric device that consists of a graduated glass or plastic barrel that holds the sample of interest. An open needle allows the sample to enter or leave the barrel, while a plunger is used to push out and dispense this sample. Syringes come with volume capacities of 0.5–$500~\mu L$ or larger and, like micropipets, are used to measure and deliver small volume samples. Unlike micropipets, syringes can work with either gases or liquids. One application of syringes is their use for injecting samples into instruments for chemical measurements.

3C Recommended Procedures for Volume Measurements

Selection and Use of Volumetric Devices. Four factors to consider when you are choosing a volumetric device are (1) the general goal of the volume measurement, (2) the volume or range of volumes to be measured, (3) the degree of reliability needed for the measurement, and (4) the number of measurements that are to be made. If you need to deliver a well-defined 5 mL volume of a liquid, a volumetric pipet would be a good choice. However, if you want to measure many different volumes (for instance, in the 3–6 mL range), a Mohr pipet might be better. If volumes less than a milliliter are to be measured, a syringe or micropipet would be preferred. Like mass measurements, volume determinations require appropriate care to provide good results. The procedures to employ when you are using volumetric flasks and volumetric pipets were discussed in Section 3B. Similar procedures for syringes and micropipets can be obtained from the manufacturers of these devices. Table 5 gives several general rules to follow when using a volumetric device.

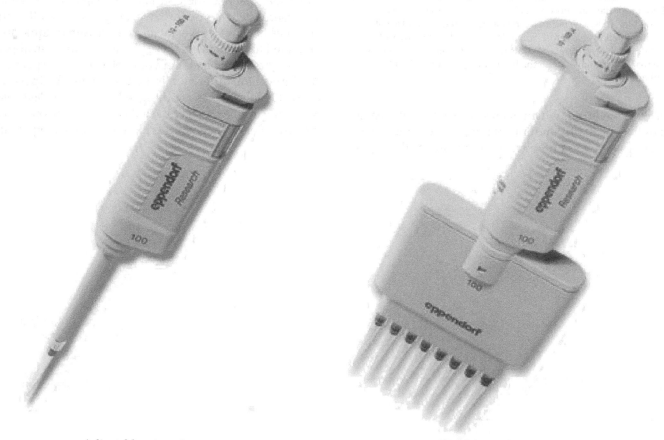

Adjustable micropipet   Multichannel micropipet

FIGURE 10 Examples of an adjustable micropipette and a multichannel micropipette. (Reproduced with permission and courtesy of Eppendorf.)

TABLE 5   Good Laboratory Practices for Using Volumetric Glassware

Selection of Glassware	Be familiar with the properties of your volumetric equipment, such as whether you are working with a Class A or Class B device and whether it is designed "To Deliver," "To Contain," or "To Deliver/With Blowout." Make a note of the temperature at which the glassware was calibrated and whether this will differ from the temperatures you will be using.
Glassware Condition	Always inspect your glassware before you use it. Do not use any glassware that has cracks or chips. Dirt or grease within glassware can block the openings and slow down the drainage of liquids. Dirty glassware can also place undesired substances into the measured liquid and take up part of the container's volume, causing the measured volume to be less than what is stated on the glassware.
Glassware Cleaning	Clean volumetric glassware by using a nonabrasive detergent, an acidic solution of dichromate, or an acidic alcohol solution. Follow this with several rinses of distilled or deionized water. Immediately before use, rinse your glassware with the liquid it will be used to measure or deliver.
Glassware Calibration	All volumetric equipment should be calibrated before its first use or if it is to be employed at a temperature different from that at which it was originally calibrated. Select a device with a volume and level of reliability that matches what is needed in your analytical method.
Equipment Handling	When you place a liquid into volumetric glassware, allow the liquid to settle for a short period of time before you estimate its volume. Make sure there are no air bubbles trapped in the device, which can lead to a low volume measurement. There should also be no undissolved materials remaining in your solution, because these can create inaccurate volume estimates and clog certain types of glassware (such as volumetric pipets).
Recording Results	For equipment that has reference marks for volume measurements, be sure to look at the level of your liquid and the calibrated marks at eye level. Record the measured volumes immediately in your laboratory notebook. Also record the type of device used (for example, a Class A 100.00 mL volumetric flask calibrated at 20°C) and the temperature during this measurement.

One aspect of correctly using volumetric glassware involves knowing how to properly read the level of a liquid in such devices. For volumetric flasks and pipets, the bottom of the meniscus of the liquid should be at the top of the calibration mark when viewed on a horizontal surface at eye level (see Figure 11). You can tell when you are looking at the mensicus properly when the calibration marks on both sides of the flask or pipet overlap one another. If you were to instead look at the liquid above or below this level,

it would give an apparent volume reading that is too high or low (an effect known as *parallax error*).[1] You can make the meniscus easier to see by placing a piece of paper, preferably with a dark color, behind the glassware. Also, when you are using a piece of glassware that has many calibrated marks on it (such as a Mohr pipet or serological pipet), remember to estimate the extent to which the liquid level occurs between the calibrated marks, thus providing one additional significant figure in your measurement.

Calibration of Volumetric Devices. It is a good idea to calibrate your volumetric equipment from time to time. This is especially true when you receive a new volumetric device or are using volumetric glassware at a temperature other than the one used for its original calibration because glassware will expand or contract with a change in temperature. Table 6 indicates that a 1000.00 mL volumetric flask made from borosilicate glass will have a change in volume of approximately 0.01 mL (or 0.001%) for every 1°C change in temperature.[1] This relative change applies to any device made from borosilicate glass. For instance, a Class A 250.00 mL volumetric flask calibrated at 20°C would have an expected volume of 0.99950 · 250.00 mL = 249.88 mL at 15°C.

One way you can determine the true volume of a piece of glassware is to simply use it to measure a sample of distilled water. You then measure the mass of water that is contained by the device and, from the known density of water at various temperatures (see Table 7), you can calculate the volume of water that was present. It is important to correct for buoyancy

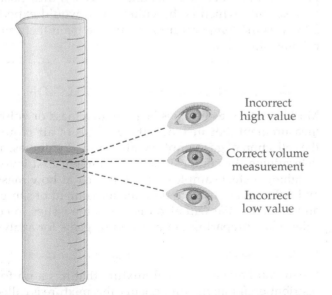

FIGURE 11 Parallax error and the correct approach for reading liquid volumes on a calibrated piece of glassware. The point where each line intersects the outer wall of the glassware is the point at which the meniscus will appear to be located.

Incorrect high value

Correct volume measurement

Incorrect low value

TABLE 6   Change in Volume with Temperature for Borosilicate Glassware*

Temperature (°C)	Change from Volume at 20°C
10	$0.99990 \cdot V_{20°C}$
15	$0.99995 \cdot V_{20°C}$
20	$1.00000 \cdot V_{20°C}$
25	$1.00005 \cdot V_{20°C}$
30	$1.00010 \cdot V_{20°C}$

*These results were calculated based on data provided in H. Diehl, *Quantitative Analysis: Elementary Principles and Practice*, Oakland Street Science Press, Ames, IA, 1970. The term $V_{20°C}$ refers to the volume of the glassware at 20°C.

effects during this process (as described in Section 2C), because you will generally need to use mass measurements with four or more significant figures. An example of this calibration process is given in the next exercise.

TABLE 7   Density of Water at Various Temperatures*

Temperature (°C)	Density (g/cm³)	Buoyancy Correction
10	**0.999 702 6**	$m_{display} \cdot$ **1.001 052**
11	0.999 608 4	$m_{display} \cdot$ 1.001 052
12	0.999 500 4	$m_{display} \cdot$ 1.001 052
13	0.999 380 1	$m_{display} \cdot$ 1.001 052
14	0.999 247 4	$m_{display} \cdot$ 1.001 052
15	**0.999 102 6**	$m_{display} \cdot$ **1.001 052**
16	0.998 946 0	$m_{display} \cdot$ 1.001 052
17	0.998 777 9	$m_{display} \cdot$ 1.001 053
18	0.998 598 6	$m_{display} \cdot$ 1.001 053
19	0.998 408 2	$m_{display} \cdot$ 1.001 053
20	**0.998 207 1**	$m_{display} \cdot$ **1.001 053**
21	0.997 995 5	$m_{display} \cdot$ 1.001 054
22	0.997 773 5	$m_{display} \cdot$ 1.001 054
23	0.997 541 5	$m_{display} \cdot$ 1.001 054
24	0.997 299 5	$m_{display} \cdot$ 1.001 054
25	**0.997 047 9**	$m_{display} \cdot$ **1.001 055**
26	0.996 786 7	$m_{display} \cdot$ 1.001 055
27	0.996 516 2	$m_{display} \cdot$ 1.001 055
28	0.996 236 5	$m_{display} \cdot$ 1.001 056
29	0.995 947 8	$m_{display} \cdot$ 1.001 056
30	**0.995 650 2**	$m_{display} \cdot$ **1.001 056**

* All of the densities shown for pure air-free water are at a pressure of 101.325 kPa (1 atmosphere). The buoyancy corrections assume that the air density is 1.20×10^{-3} g/cm³ and the density of the reference weight is 8.00 g/cm³.

EXERCISE 2   Calibration of a Volumetric Flask

A 200.00 mL volumetric flask is placed on an electronic balance, the display is set to zero, and the flask is filled to the mark with distilled water at 25°C. The displayed mass for the water in this flask is 199.2094 g. The density of the surrounding air is 1.20×10^{-3} g/cm³ and the balance has been calibrated using a 8.00 g/cm³ reference weight. What is the true volume of the flask at 25°C?

SOLUTION

Because we need a final mass for water with at least four significant figures, the displayed mass of the water must first be corrected for buoyancy effects. The density of water and the corresponding buoyancy correction at 25°C can be found in Table 7. (*Note:* The same result is obtained by using Equation 6 and the densities of the water, air, and reference weight.)

$$m = 199.2094 \text{ g} \cdot (1.001055)$$
$$= 199.4196 \text{ g}$$

Now that we know the mass of water in the flask, the flask's volume can be determined by dividing this mass by the density of water, giving the true volume of the flask at 25°C.

$$V = \frac{199.4196 \text{ g}}{0.9970479 \text{ g/cm}^3}$$

$$V = 200.0100 \text{ cm}^3 = \mathbf{200.01 \text{ mL}}$$

In this case we rounded the final answer to be consistent with the expected error in using the flask ($\pm$ 0.10 mL, as listed in Table 3) and we converted the units from cm³ to mL. You could also use this result to estimate the flask's volume at other temperatures. As an example, the calculated volume at 20°C would be 200.01 mL/1.00005 = 200.00 mL, which is the volume you would expect if 20°C was the temperature used by the manufacturer to calibrate this flask.

4 SAMPLES, REAGENTS, AND SOLUTIONS

Most analytical techniques begin with a mass or volume measurement. For instance, the analysis of air requires the collection of gas samples with specified volumes, and determining the composition of steel might first involve weighing a steel sample. Let's now look at how masses and volumes are used to describe the content of samples and reagents. We will also discuss some issues to consider when preparing samples and reagents for analysis.

4A Describing Sample and Reagent Composition

When you have a chemical mixture that has a uniform distribution for all its components, this mixture is called a **solution**. The most abundant component of the solution (or the component that is used to dissolve and contain the other chemicals) is known as the **solvent**. All other substances in the mixture are called **solutes**. As an example, when a small amount of sodium chloride is dissolved in water, this salt dissociates to form sodium ions and chloride ions (the solutes) in water (the solvent).

True solutions have the same composition throughout, so their overall content will be identical for any reasonably sized portion of the solution. As a result, we can describe the content of a solution by using a **concentration**. Concentration can be defined as the amount of a substance that is present within a given volume or mass of solution.[19] We will now examine several ways for reporting the concentration of a solution, as well as how we might describe the composition of non-uniform mixtures of chemicals.

Weight and Volume Ratios. The easiest approach for describing the composition of any chemical mixture is to simply use the masses or volumes of the various components that are present in the mixture. One way this can be done is by using a **weight-per-weight** ratio (w/w). This ratio is calculated by dividing the mass of the analyte or substance of interest by the total mass of the mixture. A major component of a mixture is often described by using a *percent weight-per-weight* (% *w/w*), which is found by multiplying the weight-per-weight ratio by 100.

$$\% \, \text{w/w} = 100 \cdot \frac{\text{Mass of chemical}}{\text{Mass of mixture}} \qquad (7)$$

For example, the body of a 120 pound person contains about 72 pounds of water, so the percent weight-per-weight of water would be $100 \cdot (72 \, \text{lb})/(120 \, \text{lb})$, or 60% w/w. It is important when calculating this value to have the same units for the weights or masses of both the chemical and its mixture so that the answer will be expressed as a true fraction or percent.

The element cerium was discovered by J. J. Berzelius and other scientists in 1803. One source of cerium is the mineral bastnasite-(Ce), which has the formula $Ce(CO_3)F$. If you have one mole of pure bastnasite-(Ce), what would be the % w/w of cerium in this ore?

SOLUTION

From the given chemical formula, the formula weight for bastnasite-(Ce) is 219.12 g/mol. We also know that each mol of bastnasite-(Ce) contains one mol of cerium (atomic weight = 140.12 g/mol), so the amount of cerium in one mole of pure bastnasite-(Ce) would be as follows.

$$\% \, \text{Cerium (w/w)} = 100 \cdot \frac{\text{Mass of cerium}}{\text{Mass of bastnatite-(Ce)}}$$

$$= 100 \cdot \frac{(1 \, \text{mol} \cdot 140.12 \, \text{g/mol})}{(1 \, \text{mol} \cdot 219.12 \, \text{g/mol})}$$

$$\% \, \textbf{Cerium (w/w)} = \textbf{63.947\%}$$

An identical % w/w value for cerium would be obtained if we were working with 0.5 mol or 2.0 mol of this ore because the *relative* content of cerium in this material will still be the same.

When you are working with minor or trace components of a mixture, other multiplying factors besides 100 can be used with weight-per-weight ratios. Using 1000 in place of 100 would give a result in *parts-per-thousand*, which is sometimes represented by the symbol $^0/_{00}$. If even lower amounts of a substance are present, multiplying factors like a million (10^6), billion (10^9), or trillion (10^{12}) might be used. This process would provide results given in units of *parts-per-million* (*ppm*), *parts-per-billion* (*ppb*), or *parts-per-trillion* (*ppt*), respectively. This idea can be illustrated using rare earth metals like lanthanum that can be found in bastnasite. If a 100 g sample of bastnasite-(Ce) contained 2 mg lanthanum, the relative amount of lanthanum would be $10^6 \cdot (2 \times 10^{-3} \, \text{g La})/(100 \, \text{g Bastnasite-(Ce)}) = 20 \, \text{ppm La}$, or 20 parts-per-million. Note that the use of ppm, ppb and ppt is mostly a matter of convenience in that it allows us to describe chemical compositions in a simpler manner, such as saying "20 ppm La" instead of "0.000020 g La/g sample."

A second way of describing chemical composition is to use a **volume-per-volume (v/v)** ratio. This type of ratio is employed when you are working with mixtures of liquids or gases, for which volumes are easier to measure than masses. These ratios are often expressed as % v/v (see Equation 8), but can also be given as parts-per-thousand, ppm, ppb, or ppt.

$$\% \, \text{v/v} = 100 \cdot \frac{\text{Volume of chemical}}{\text{Volume of mixture}} \qquad (8)$$

One common application of volume-per-volume ratios is to describe mixtures of alcohols with water. For instance, a container labeled "25% methanol (v/v)" should contain 25 mL of methanol for every 100 mL of solution. However, this label does *not* mean the solution contains 25 mL of methanol for every 75 mL of solvent, because the volumes of the components in a liquid mixture are not strictly additive. You can get around this problem by simply stating the amount of each component that was placed into the solution. Thus, a "25:75 (or 1:3) solution of methanol in water" would be a better way of describing a solution that is formed by adding 25 mL of methanol to 75 mL of water.

The **weight-per-volume (w/v)** ratio is another means of stating chemical content. This ratio is calculated by determining the mass of a chemical that is present in the total volume of a mixture, and is often used in describing solutions that contain dissolved solids as solutes.

$$\text{w/v} = \frac{\text{Mass of chemical}}{\text{Volume of mixture}} \qquad (9)$$

An illustration would be a 4.0 g/L solution of iron(III) chloride in water, which could be prepared by placing 0.40 grams of solid $FeCl_3$ into water and diluting the entire solution to a final volume of 100.0 mL. The advantage of using weight-per-volume ratios in this situation is it combines the convenience of volume measurements for liquids with the ease of mass measurements for solids.

In addition to being expressed as a ratio of mass and volume units (like g/L or mg/L), weight-per-volume ratios are sometimes given as a percent or in related terms like ppm, ppb, and ppt. These units are typically employed when weight-per-volume ratios are used to describe dilute solutions of chemicals in water. The basis for this approach is that the density of water at room temperature is approximately 1.0 g/mL, meaning that one milliliter of water weighs about 1 gram. Because of this, the mass of water (in grams) can be substituted for its volume (in mL).

EXERCISE 4   **Working with Weight-per-Volume Ratios**

Figure 12 shows a warning sign posted near a well found to have high levels of nitrate. The amount of nitrate–nitrogen found in this water was 27.5 mg/L. What would this value be if it were given in parts-per-million?

SOLUTION

This is a dilute solution of water that is probably at or near room temperature, so we know the density will be about 1.0 g/mL. As a result, we can rewrite 27.5 mg/L as shown below.

Nitrate−nitrogen (w/v) =

$$\frac{(27.5 \text{ mg nitrate−nitrogen}) \cdot (1 \text{ g}/10^3 \text{ mg})}{(1.000 \text{ L solution}) \cdot (1.0 \text{ g/mL solution}) \cdot (10^3 \text{ mL/L})}$$

$$= \frac{(27.5 \text{ g nitrate−nitrogen})}{1.000 \text{ g solution} \cdot 10^6}$$

Nitrate−nitrogen (w/v) = **27.5 ppm**

We can see from the last exercise that a concentration of 1 ppm (w/v) in a dilute aqueous solution is approximately equal to 1 mg/L (or 1 μg/mL). Similarly, a 1 ppb (w/v) aqueous solution is approximately the same as 1 μg/L (or 1 ng/mL), and 1 ppt is roughly equal to 1 ng/L (or 1 pg/mL). It needs to be emphasized that these relationships are valid *only* if the final solution has a density of 1.0 g/mL. If this is not the situation, the weight-per-volume ratio should not be given as a percent or related fraction. Instead, this ratio should be written by using the mass and volume units of the solute and solution, such as g/mL.

Molality and Molarity.   Weight and volume ratios are valuable when dealing with the masses or volumes of chemicals. To understand how chemicals might react with each other, it is even more valuable to know the actual *number* of a given type of molecule, atom, or ion that might be present in solution. Previously, we learned that the SI unit for the number of any substance is the mole, which is equal to 6.02×10^{23}. Although this number may seem rather large, it is convenient for describing the chemical content of many materials, which often contain solutes or compounds that approach or even exceed a mole in quantity.

To relate the number of moles of a particular molecule to its mass, a chemist uses that substance's **molar mass**. The molar mass for any substance is defined as the number of grams that are contained in one mole of that substance. For molecular compounds, the molar mass is commonly referred to as the *molecular weight* (MW), while for ionic compounds and elements the molar mass is also called the *formula weight* or *atomic weight* (or *formula mass* and *atomic mass*), respectively.

One concentration unit that measures the amount of solute in moles is **molality** (represented by the symbol *m*). Molality is equal to the number of moles of a solute per kilogram of solvent.

$$m = \frac{\text{Moles of solute}}{\text{Kilograms of solvent}} \quad (10)$$

As an example, 0.025 mol of iron(II) chloride in 0.500 kg water would give a solution that has a concentration of 0.025 mol/0.500 kg = 0.050 *m* iron(II) chloride, or a 0.050 *molal* solution. It is important to note here that the mass given in the bottom of Equation 10 is for the solvent and not for the total final solution. Because molality is based on a ratio of masses, it is an important unit to use when changes in temperature, and thus changes in volume, are expected during an analysis. Molality is also useful in describing the relative amount of *both* the solute and solvent in a solution.

A disadvantage of using molality is that the total volume of a solution is much easier to measure than the mass of the solvent. This is especially true when you are using a volumetric flask to prepare solutions. Using units of molality also does not directly tell what the total volume of the solution will be. This can be a big problem if volume measurements are to be used during solution preparation or handling. It is more common in routine laboratory work to use a related unit known as **molarity** (*M*). Molarity is defined as the number of moles (or the *number of gram molecular weights*) of a substance that is present in each liter of solution.

$$M = \frac{\text{Moles of solute}}{\text{Liters of solution}} \quad (11)$$

To illustrate this relationship, a solution with a total volume of 500 mL that contains 1.00 g glucose (or 5.56×10^{-3} mol) would have a glucose concentration of 5.56×10^{-3} mol/0.500 L = 0.0111 *M*. This mixture could also be referred to as a 0.0111 *molar* solution.

> **Nebraska Department of Roads**
>
> # NOTICE
>
> In accordance with the Nebraska Department of Health *Regulations Governing Public Water Supply Systems*, the consumers of the
>
> ## Chappell Eastbound Rest Area
>
> public water supply systems are hereby notified that the system is in violation of the established drinking water standard of "10.0" mg/l for nitrate-nitrogen. The nitrate concentration as determined by the Nebraska Department of Health Laboratory from samples collected on:
>
> ## 27.5 mg/l
>
> Nitrate contamination above "10.0" mg/l in drinking water has been associated with the incidence of infant methemoglobinemia or "blue baby syndrome." Symptoms occur when nitrate is reduced to nitrate in the infant internal tract. The nitrate, in turn, reacts with the blood to reduce the capacity of oxygen to reach to body cells. Infants under six months of age are at a greater risk of developing methemoglobinemia. Reports of methemoglobinemia in older children and adults from ingestion of nitrate have not been reported.
>
> Water from the
>
> ## Chappell Eastbound Rest Area
>
> system should not be used in the preparation of infant formula or as a source of drinking water for infants six months of age or less, nursing mothers or pregnant women. Please note that the boiling water *will not* lower the nitrate concentration.
>
> *For additional information regarding this notice, interested persons may contact:*
>
> Nebraska Department of Roads   (308) 254-4712

FIGURE 12 Sign posted in western Nebraska that alerts travelers to the hazards of drinking water from a local well contaminated with nitrate.

EXERCISE 5	**Using Molarity and Molality to Describe a Solution**

A 2.500 g portion of sodium hydroxide (NaOH) is placed into a 250.00 mL volumetric flask and diluted to the mark with water. It is later found that the added mass of water was 497.2 g. What is the final concentration of the NaOH in units of molarity and molality?

SOLUTION

The molarity is found by dividing the moles of added NaOH by the total volume of the final solution. The moles of NaOH present in 2.500 g can be found by using a molar mass of 40.00 g/mol for NaOH, which gives (2.500 g NaOH)/(40.00 g NaOH/mol NaOH) = 0.6250 mol. The molar concentration would be (0.6250 mol NaOH/500.00 mL) · (1000 mL/1 L) = 1.250 M. The molality of the solution is obtained by dividing the moles of NaOH by the kilograms of added solvent. The result is a solution concentration of (0.6250 mol NaOH/497.2 g water) · (1000 g water/1 kg water) = 1.257 m NaOH.

If a solute dissociates into ions or produces several forms when it is placed in solution, the number of moles of this solute that is used in Equation 11 would be based on the *number of gram formula weights* instead of gram molecular weights. This approach is then used to describe the total amount of solute that was placed into solution, giving a concentration in units of moles per liter of solution and referred to as the *formality (F)*. For instance, placing 60.05 g acetic acid (1.000 mol) into 1.000 L of an aqueous solution would give a 1.000 *formal* solution of acetic acid, even though the acetic acid could be present in two forms, acetic acid (HAc) and the acetate ion (Ac^-). We can also describe the concentrations of these individual forms by using molarity, but this can lead to some confusion because formality and molarity have the same net units (mol/L). Because of this, some authorities recommend using molarity to describe the concentrations of both molecular *and* ionic solutes, a practice that will be followed in this text. As part of this process, we will use the term **analytical concentration** (**C**) instead of formality to refer to the total concentration of a substance in solution and brackets to represent the concentration of an individual form for the substance (for example, [HAc] or [Ac^-] to describe the individual concentrations of acetic acid and the acetate ion).

When you are dealing with a relatively dilute aqueous solution at room temperature (for instance, 0.01 *M* NaCl or 0.01 *m* NaCl), the molality and molarity of the solution will have about the same numerical value even though they have different units (mol NaCl/L solution versus mol NaCl/kg solvent). This situation occurs because the density of water and of the solution will both be approximately 1.0 g/mL, which means 1 kg of water will roughly be equivalent to 1 L of solution. This relationship will not be true if you have a different solution density, as would happen when you have a nonaqueous solvent or a solution with a moderate-to-high concentration of solutes. For concentrated solutions, molality is the preferred unit because it provides temperature-independent values. When working with dilute solutions, like those found in many samples for chemical analysis, molarity is the preferred unit because of the greater ease with which a solution's volume can be measured versus a solvent's mass. For this reason, molarity will be the main concentration unit used in this text.

Other Units. There are other measures of chemical content that you will also encounter from time-to-time in books, scientific articles, or chemical catalogs. One such case is when you must describe the amount of a chemical on a surface. For instance, the amount of iron oxide (rust) on the surface of an iron bar could be expressed as a "surface concentration" with units of moles per square meter. Other units for chemical contents depend on the ability of a substance to take part in a particular reaction, like the rate at which an enzyme solution catalyzes the formation of a product. Another example is the use of radioactivity to describe chemical content, such as the measurement of carbon-14 decay for determining the age of an organic sample.

Another measure of chemical reactivity is the unit of *normality* (represented by the symbol *N*). Normality describes the amount of a chemical that is available for a specific type of reaction, as is accomplished by using the *equivalents* of the chemical per liter of solution. The number of equivalents you have of a chemical will depend on that chemical's structure and the type of reaction in which it is going to be employed. In an acid–base reaction, an equivalent is given by the moles of a chemical needed to produce or consume one unit of titratable hydrogen ions. For a reduction–oxidation reaction, an equivalent is related to the moles of a chemical that are needed to produce or consume one unit of electrons. Although chemical equivalents are still employed to describe reactions in analytical chemistry, the use of normality as a unit of concentration is now discouraged.[19] Thus, this unit will not be used in this text except to illustrate how it may be converted to other units of concentration.

4B Solution Preparation

Chemical Purity. When you are preparing a solution for an analytical method, one factor that must be considered is the purity of the chemicals that will be placed into your samples and reagents. Ideally, you do not want to have compounds in the reagents that may interfere with detection of the analyte and cause an inaccurate result to be obtained. You also do not want to accidentally add the same chemicals as those you want to determine, which will create a false "positive" result. For these and other reasons, you should always use high-purity chemicals in any analytical method.

To help in this selection, commercial chemicals are often classified according to their purity, as shown in Table 8. Routine work that requires good but not exceptionally high quality chemicals can be performed with materials that are "Technical Grade" or "Laboratory Grade." For general analytical work, substances with higher purity can be obtained by using chemicals that meet requirements set by the American Chemical Society or by agencies that regulate analytical laboratories. There are also chemicals that have been prepared to meet the needs of particular methods. Examples are "HPLC Grade," "Trace Metal Grade," and "Biotechnology Grade" chemicals.

In some cases, chemicals with special properties may be needed. This situation occurs when a solution is to be used as a reagent in a titration, where the actual concentration of this solution is first determined by reacting it with a compound known as a *primary standard*. A primary standard is a pure substance that is stable during storage, can be weighed accurately, and undergoes a known reaction with the solution it is used to characterize. The reagent solution that is characterized by this process is then referred to as a *secondary standard*.

It is important when selecting chemicals to also consider the purity of your solvents. High-purity water is particularly crucial because many of the samples and reagents in analytical chemistry are aqueous solutions. Table 9 shows some contaminants that can be found in ordinary water. To remove these contaminants, the water should be purified before it is used to prepare samples or

TABLE 8 Common Grades of Commercially Available Chemicals

Type of Chemical	Meaning of Grade	Common Uses
Certified ACS Grade	Reagent chemicals that meet or exceed specifications by the American Chemical Society (ACS)	Various analytical applications
USP, BP, EP, NF, or FCC Grade	Reagent chemicals that meet or exceed specifications made by the U.S. Pharmacopeia (USP), the British Pharmacopeia (BP), the European Pharmacopeia (EP), the National Formulary (NF), or the Food Chemicals Codex (FCC)	Food and drug laboratories, biological testing
Technical or Laboratory Grade	Chemicals of reasonable purity for cases where no official standards exist for quality or impurity levels	Manufacturing and general laboratory use
Biotechnology Grade	Chemicals and solvents that have been purified and prepared for use in biotechnology	Molecular biology, electrophoresis assays, DNA/RNA or peptide sequencing and synthesis
HPLC Grade	Chemicals that have been purified and prepared for use in high-performance liquid chromatography (HPLC)	Preparation of reagents and samples for HPLC
Trace Metal Grade	Chemicals prepared to have low levels of trace metals	Preparation of reagents and samples for trace-metal analysis

reagents. A common approach for water purification is to use *distillation*. This is a relatively inexpensive method in which the water is heated to boiling, with the steam then being condensed and used in a purified form known as *distilled water*. Distillation is one of the oldest methods for water treatment and is good for obtaining water that is free of particulates, dissolved solids, microorganisms, and pyrogens. (*Note:* a "pyrogen" is a substance that produces a fever.) Distillation can also reduce the amount of some dissolved organic compounds, but does not help much in removing dissolved gases.[20]

Some laboratories take distilled water and treat it further by employing a second method, such as *deionization*. The method of deionization uses cartridges that take the cations or anions in water and exchange these for hydrogen ions (H^+) and hydroxide ions (OH^-), which will then react to form more water. The purified water that is obtained by this method is called *deionized water* (or *DI water*). This approach is good at removing ions and dissolved gases like carbon dioxide (which is present in water as carbonic acid), making it a nice complement to distillation as a means for water treatment.[20] Systems for preparing DI water also often contain cartridges with activated carbon to remove organic compounds, as well as submicron filters to remove bacteria and microbes.

Aliquots and Dilutions. Let's next examine some terms that are used to describe the preparation of solutions. One of these is the term **stock solution**, which is a reagent used to make other less concentrated solutions for an assay. The advantage of making a stock solution is that it allows the use of a large mass of solute, which will be easier to handle and measure than smaller quantities. Stock solutions are also easier to store than more dilute solutions because they occupy less space for the same amount of solute.

When part of a stock solution or sample is used to prepare a second less concentrated solution, the portion that is taken from the original solution or sample is known as an **aliquot**. An aliquot is often drawn and measured by using a pipet, micropipette, or syringe. If more solvent is then added to the aliquot, this process is known as a **dilution**. For instance, suppose a 10.00 mL aliquot of a stock solution were placed into a 50.00 mL volumetric flask, and this flask was then filled to the mark with water. The result would be a new solution in which the contents of the original solution had undergone a fivefold dilution. A dilution step is used to adjust

TABLE 9 Types of Contaminants Found in Water

Type of Contaminant	Examples
Dissolved inorganic solids	Calcium ions, magnesium ions, chloride, fluoride, iron(II) and iron(III) ions, silicates, phosphates, and nitrates
Dissolved inorganic gases	Carbon dioxide, oxygen
Dissolved organics	Pesticides and herbicides, decayed plant and animal matter, gasoline, alcohols, chloramines
Particulates (Particulate matter)	Sand, silt, clay, colloidal particles, and debris from pipes
Microorganisms	Bacteria, algae, amoebae, protozoa, diatoms and rotifers
Pyrogens	Cell wall fragments and lipopolysaccharides from bacteria

Source: The information in this table was obtained from *A Guide to Laboratory Water Purification*, Labconco, Kansas City, MO, 1998.

the concentration of samples and reagents to place them in an appropriate range for a chemical analysis.

When you are taking aliquots and conducting a dilution, it is important to keep track of the volumes you are using in each step. This practice is necessary so that you can relate the concentration of your final solution back to the contents of its initial sample or solution. As is shown in Figure 13, the moles of each chemical in the aliquot will be the same as the moles present in the diluted solution (assuming the same chemicals are not in the solvent or other added components). We can use this fact to relate the initial and final concentrations of the analyte as shown below.

$$(\text{mol solute})_{\text{Dilution}} = (\text{mol solute})_{\text{Aliquot}} \quad (12)$$

or

$$M_{\text{Dilution}} \cdot V_{\text{Dilution}} = M_{\text{Aliquot}} \cdot V_{\text{Aliquot}} \quad (13)$$

In these equations, M_{Aliquot} and M_{Dilution} are the molar concentrations of the solute in the aliquot and diluted sample, and V_{Aliquot} and V_{Dilution} are the volumes of the aliquot and dilution in liters. Similar equations can be written for situations in which you are working with concentrations that are in units of molality and weight or volume ratios. In the following exercise you will see how these relationships can be used to calculate what solute concentration will be present in a diluted solution. You can also use these equations to determine the aliquot size and extent of dilution that are needed to prepare a reagent from a particular stock solution or sample.

EXERCISE 6 — Preparing a Diluted Solution

A diluted solution of sodium chloride is to be prepared from a 0.1000 M stock solution. A 10.00 mL aliquot of the stock solution is obtained with a 10.00 mL volumetric pipet and placed into a 50.00 mL volumetric flask. The contents of this flask are then diluted to the mark with water. What is the final concentration of sodium chloride in the diluted solution?

SOLUTION

The aliquot is the only source of sodium chloride in the solution, so the moles of NaCl in the diluted solution will be equal to the moles of NaCl that were in the 10.00 mL aliquot, or (0.1000 mol/L) (0.01000 L) = 1.000×10^{-3} mol. When we place this amount of sodium chloride into a total volume of 50.00 mL water (10.00 mL of which comes from the aliquot), the final concentration of NaCl is (1.000×10^{-3} mol)/(0.05000 L) = 0.02000 M. The same result is obtained by rearranging Equation 13 into the form shown below.

$$M_{\text{Dilution}} = M_{\text{Aliquot}}(V_{\text{Aliquot}}/V_{\text{Dilution}})$$
$$= 0.1000 \ M \ \text{NaCl} \cdot (0.01000 \ \text{L}/0.05000 \ \text{L})$$
$$\mathbf{M_{\text{Dilution}} = 0.02000 \ M \ NaCl}$$

Because this expression uses a ratio of volumes ($V_{\text{Aliquot}}/V_{\text{Dilution}}$), we would have arrived at the same final answer by keeping the original units of milliliters, where 0.01000 L/0.05000 L = 10.00 mL/50.00 mL (or a 1:5 dilution of the original solution).

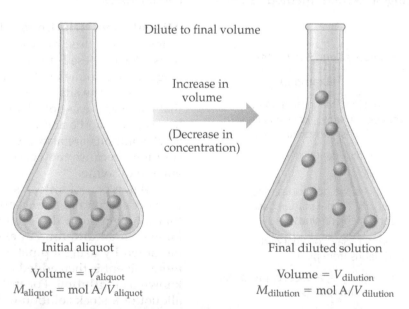

Dilute to final volume

Increase in volume

(Decrease in concentration)

Initial aliquot

Volume = V_{aliquot}
M_{aliquot} = mol A/V_{aliquot}

Final diluted solution

Volume = V_{dilution}
M_{dilution} = mol A/V_{dilution}

FIGURE 13 The relationship between the amount of a chemical that is present in an aliquot and the final concentration of this chemical in a diluted solution. In this example, the total moles of analyte (A) is the same in both the initial aliquot and the final diluted solution. However, the concentration of this analyte is lower in the final diluted solution because this diluted solution has a larger volume than the original aliquot.

Temperature Effects. Another factor to consider when you are preparing solutions is the temperature at which you are making and using your samples and reagents. The volume and concentration of a solution can change as the temperature changes (see Figure 14). This change can result in significant errors if overlooked. When you prepare a solution, the total moles of each added chemical should be constant, provided these chemicals do not degrade or react to form other substances. Thus, if you know the volume (V_1) and molar concentration (M_1) of the solution at its original temperature and you measure the volume (V_2) of the same solution at its final temperature, the new concentration (M_2) at the final temperature can be determined by using Equation 14.

$$M_1 \cdot V_1 = M_2 \cdot V_2 \qquad (14)$$

Imagine that you had a 0.1000 M solution of sodium chloride in water that was prepared at 20°C in a 500.00 mL volumetric flask. If you look at this solution later when the temperature is 25°C, you will find that the volume has increased by 0.58 mL. This change in volume will affect the molar concentration of sodium chloride. This new concentration can be found by using Equation 14, which gives $M_{25°C} = (0.1000\ M) \cdot (0.50000\ L)/(0.50058\ L) = 0.09988\ M$.

If you do not know the volume of your final solution, but do know the densities of the original and final solutions (d_1 and d_2), the new solution volume can be found by using Equation 15.

$$d_1 \cdot V_1 = d_2 \cdot V_2 \qquad (15)$$

You can then use the value obtained for V_2 with Equation 14 to determine the molarity of the final solution. An example of this process is given in Exercise 7. If you look more closely at Equations 14 and 15 you will find that the volume units on each side cancel out to give moles = moles or mass = mass. In other words, both expressions are based on the fact that the total mass or moles of solute will be constant in the solution.

EXERCISE 7   **Effects of Temperature on Concentration**

A $1.0000 \times 10^{-3}\ M$ solution of hydrochloric acid in water is prepared in a 1000.00 mL volumetric flask at 20°C. This solution is set aside for later use. The temperature of this solution is later found to be 25°C. It is known that the density was 0.998232 g/mL at 20°C and that the same solution has a density of 0.997074 g/mL at 25°C. Determine the concentration of hydrochloric acid at 25°C.

SOLUTION

We don't know the exact volume of the final solution but we do know its density, so we first need to use Equation 15 to find the new volume.

$$d_1 \cdot V_1 = d_2 \cdot V_2$$
$$(0.998232\ g/mL) \cdot (1000.00\ mL)$$
$$= (0.997074\ g/mL) \cdot V_2$$
$$V_2 = 1001.16\ mL$$

We can then use this volume with Equation 14 to calculate the molar concentration at 25°C.

$$M_1 \cdot V_1 = M_2 \cdot V_2$$
$$M_2 \cdot (1001.16\ mL) = (1.0000 \times 10^{-3}\ M) \cdot (1000.00\ mL)$$
$$\mathbf{M_2 = 0.9988 \times 10^{-3}\ M}$$

Thus, because the volume of solution has increased from 20°C to 25°C, we see a slight *decrease* in the molar concentration of hydrochloric acid.

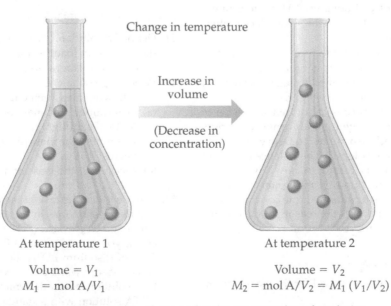

Change in temperature

Increase in volume

(Decrease in concentration)

At temperature 1

Volume = V_1
M_1 = mol A/V_1

At temperature 2

Volume = V_2
M_2 = mol A/V_2 = $M_1\ (V_1/V_2)$

FIGURE 14 Change in the volume and molar concentration of a solution with temperature. The total moles of analyte (A) is the same in the solution at both temperatures. However, the concentration of this analyte is lower in the solution on the right because this solution has a larger volume than the solution on the left.

Key Words

Aliquot	Density	Precision balance	Volumetric pipet
Analytical balance	Dilution	Solute	Weighing
Analytical concentration	Electronic balance	Solution	Weight
Balance	Mass	Solvent	Weight-per-volume
Buoyancy	Mechanical balance	Stock solution	Weight-per-weight
Buoyancy correction	Molality	Volume	
Buret	Molar mass	Volume-per-volume	
Concentration	Molarity	Volumetric flask	

Other Terms

Atomic force microscope	Equivalent	Ostwald–Folin pipet	Readability (of a balance)
Atomic force microscopy	Formality	Parallax error	Resolution (of a balance)
Borosilicate glass	Gravitational acceleration constant	Parts-per-billion	Secondary standard
Capacity (of a balance)	Mass spectrometer	Parts-per-million	Serological pipet
Class A glassware	Maximum load	Parts-per-thousand	Substitution balance
Class B glassware	Meniscus	Parts-per-trillion	Syringe
Deionized water	Micropipet	Primary standard	Taring (to "tare")
Direct weighing	Mohr pipet	Quartz crystal microbalance	Weight by difference
Distilled water	Normality		

Questions

THE DETERMINATION OF MASS

1. Define what is meant by the terms "mass" and "weight." How do these terms differ? Which of these is preferred for use in scientific measurements?
2. Explain what is meant by "weighing" a sample? What is the goal of this process?
3. Describe what is meant by "buoyancy." How does buoyancy affect the measurement of weight? How does it affect the measurement of mass?
4. Write equations that show how the forces of gravity and buoyancy act on an object when it is on a balance. Show how these equations can be combined to relate the mass of the object to the mass of a reference weight.
5. A single-pan electronic balance is calibrated with a set of standard weights in Los Angeles, California (elevation, 340 ft above sea level), and then moved to Denver, Colorado (elevation, 5280 ft above sea level). The balance arrives in good working order but is found to now give a mass reading that is off by a few hundred milligrams for a 1 kg weight. After the balance is recalibrated, the correct result is obtained. What do you think was the reason for the original error after the balance was moved?

TYPES OF LABORATORY BALANCES

6. What is a "balance" and how is it used for the measurement of weight or mass?
7. What is a "mechanical balance"? Explain how this type of balance operates.
8. What is an "electronic balance"? Describe how this type of balance works.

9. What is a "quartz crystal microbalance"? How is this device constructed and how is it used to provide a mass measurement?
10. Describe how the mass of individual chemical species can be examined by using a mass spectrometer. How are the results of this measurement usually displayed?

RECOMMENDED PROCEDURES FOR MASS MEASUREMENTS

11. Define "resolution," "capacity," and "readability." What are the maximum load, readability, and resolution for the balances in your laboratory?
12. Which type of balances in Table 1 would you use for each of the following measurements.
    (a) Determining the mass of a 150 g sample to the nearest tenth of a milligram
    (b) Examining the mass of a 1.00 kg chemical product to the nearest 0.01 g
    (c) Measuring the mass of a 100 mg protein sample to the nearest 0.01 mg
13. You are given the task of measuring the amount of calcium and magnesium ions in a water sample by using ethylenediamine tetraacetic acid (EDTA) as a reagent. To perform this assay, you must prepare 1.00 L of a reagent that contains 7.4 g of disodium EDTA. Because disodium EDTA tends to slowly absorb water as it is weighed, the concentration of its final solution is later determined by reacting a portion of the EDTA solution with a standard solution of calcium carbonate, which is prepared to contain 0.35 g calcium carbonate in 250 mL water. Your laboratory has two electronic balances that you could use in this method. The first is a precision balance with a capacity of 200 g and a readability of 0.001 g. The

other is an analytical balance with a capacity of 80 g and readability of 0.0001 g. Which balance would you use to weigh the disodium EDTA and which would you use for the calcium carbonate?

14. Describe how "direct weighing" and "weight by difference" are performed. What are the advantages and disadvantages of these methods?

15. What is "taring"? How is taring used on laboratory balances?

16. What does it mean when you make a "buoyancy correction" in a mass measurement? When is such a correction important, and how is this type of correction performed?

17. Potassium hydrogen o-phthalate ($KHC_8H_4O_4$, or KHP) is a chemical used as a primary standard for determining the exact concentration of a base in a reagent. A sample of KHP is placed into a weighing container and gives a mass reading of 10.4194 g. The KHP is then transferred to a volumetric flask and the weighing container is measured again, now giving a mass of 5.3052 g. It is known that the density of KHP is 1.636 g/cm^3. If the density of the surrounding air was $1.2 \times 10^{-3} g/cm^3$ and that the balance was calibrated with a 8.0 g/cm^3 reference weight, what actual mass of KHP was placed into the volumetric flask?

18. The amount of iron in an ore sample can be determined by dissolving the ore sample and precipitating the resulting iron ions as hydrated ferric oxide, $Fe_2O_3 \cdot x\ H_2O$. The water in this precipitate is driven off by heating this material with a flame, creating solid Fe_2O_3.

$$Fe_2O_3 \cdot x\ H_2O \xrightarrow{\Delta} Fe_2O_3 + x\ H_2O \qquad (16)$$

The mass of Fe_2O_3 is then measured and used to calculate the amount of iron in the original sample. An ore sample with a known mass of 9.85 g is examined by this method and produces an amount of Fe_2O_3 that has an apparent mass of 0.3369 g. The density of pure Fe_2O_3 is known to be 5.25 g/cm^3, and it is known that only Fe_2O_3 was in the measured product. If air density and types of reference weights were the same as in the previous problem, what was the true mass of Fe_2O_3 that was formed from the sample? What would be the amount of iron in the original sample when given as a percent weight-per-weight?

19. Although reference weights with a density of 8.0 g/cm^3 are now used to calibrate most balances, all of these weights, in turn, are ultimately compared against a platinum–iridium cylinder with a density of 21.5 g/cm^3 that is used as the international definition of the kilogram. Suppose that a 1 kg stainless steel weight is compared to a copy of this 1 kg platinum–iridium cylinder. If the density of the surrounding air is $1.2 \times 10^{-3} g/cm^3$, what is the size of the buoyancy correction that must be used to adjust the apparent mass of the stainless steel weight to its true value?

THE DETERMINATION OF VOLUME

20. How is the volume of an object related to the object's mass? What are the advantages and disadvantages of using volume in place of mass to describe a material?

21. How do the requirements for volumetric glassware, such as for volumetric flasks and pipets, differ from those for more routine glassware, like Erlenmeyer flasks and graduated cylinders?

22. What is "borosilicate glass"? How does borosilicate glass differ from ordinary soda-lime glass? What properties of borosilicate glass make it valuable for use in glassware for analytical volume measurements?

23. What are some materials besides glass that are used to make volumetric devices? What are the advantages and disadvantages of these other materials versus glass?

TYPES OF VOLUMETRIC EQUIPMENT

24. State the function for each of the following devices and describe how the design of each device helps it to perform this function.
    (a) Volumetric flask
    (b) Volumetric pipet
    (c) Buret
    (d) Micropipet
    (e) Syringe
    (f) Serological pipet
    (g) Ostwald–Folin pipet
    (h) Mohr pipet

25. What is meant by "Class A glassware" and "Class B glassware"? Which type of glassware is preferred for analytical volume measurements?

26. What is the meaning of the terms "To Deliver," "To Contain," and "To Deliver/Blow Out"? What devices are associated with each of these labels?

RECOMMENDED PROCEDURES FOR VOLUME MEASUREMENTS

27. List four factors that should be considered when you are selecting a volumetric device.

28. What types of volumetric devices could be used for each of the following applications?
    (a) Transferring 10.00 mL of a solution from a volumetric flask to a separate container
    (b) Measuring a 250 μL solution that contains a DNA sample
    (c) Repeated dispensing of 2.0 mL portions of a reagent to a series of test tubes
    (d) Measuring a 0.2 mL blood sample from a newborn baby
    (e) Measuring a 2.0 mL gas sample
    (f) Delivery of various volumes of a 0.100 M NaOH solution for the titration of an acid

29. What are some general procedures that you should follow when examining, handling, and cleaning a volumetric device?

30. What is parallax error? What steps can be taken to minimize this type of error when you are using a volumetric device?

31. Explain why it is important to calibrate volumetric devices. How does temperature affect this calibration?

32. A 50.00 mL volumetric flask is filled at 30°C with deionized water. The mass of water found to be in the flask at this temperature (as read directly from the balance) is 49.7380 g.
    (a) What is the true internal volume of the flask at 30°C? (Note: You may assume a density for the surrounding air of 0.0012 g/cm^3 and that the balance has been calibrated with a 8.0 g/cm^3 reference weight.)
    (b) What is the true volume of the volumetric flask at 20°C?

33. A pipette is set to a volume of 250 μL and used at 25°C to deliver a sample of deionized water to a small beaker on a tared balance. The mass of water that is delivered to the beaker (uncorrected for buoyancy effects) is 0.2509 g.
    (a) What is the true volume of water that was delivered by the pipette under these conditions?
    (b) If the volume that is delivered by the pipette remains the same, what mass of water would be delivered by this pipet at 20°C?

DESCRIBING SAMPLE AND REAGENT COMPOSITION

34. Define the terms "solution," "solute," "solvent," and "concentration." Use a reagent that contains 0.10 M NaOH in water to illustrate each of these terms.

35. Antifreeze is a solution that is prepared by combining the liquid ethylene glycol ($C_2H_6O_2$) with water. The freezing point of the antifreeze will depend on the relative amount of each chemical in the solution. If 10.0 kg of ethylene glycol liquid is combined with 5.0 L of water (density = 1.00 g/mL), which chemical in this mixture is the solvent and which is the solute?

36. Define each of the following measures of chemical content. State how these units differ and describe the general types of situations in which each is employed.
    (a) Weight-per-weight
    (b) Volume-per-volume
    (c) Weight-per-volume

37. Calculate the content or concentration for each substance in the following mixtures.
    (a) A solution that contains 250 mL of acetonitrile and 500 mL of methanol diluted with water to a total volume of 2.00 L
    (b) A 15.2 g steel sample that contains 10.69 g iron, 2.67 g chromium, 1.22 g nickel, 0.306 g manganese, 0.153 g silicon, and 0.122 g carbon
    (c) A 5.00 L river-water sample that contains 25 g of dissolved solids

38. Determine the content or concentration of the analyte in the following samples.
    (a) A gaseous mixture for the measurement of oxygen that contains 20 mL oxygen in a total volume of 3.5 L
    (b) A 2.00 mL sample of blood that contains 12.5 μg of a drug
    (c) A 5.00 g sample of coal that contains 4.15 g carbon

39. Define each of the following terms and state how they are used to describe the content of chemical solutions and mixtures.
    (a) Parts-per-thousand
    (b) Parts-per-million
    (c) Parts-per-billion
    (d) Parts-per-trillion
    (e) Percent

40. Calculate the content for each stated chemical in the following mixtures. Give the results in percent, parts-per-thousand, ppm, ppb, or ppt.
    (a) 0.010 g Cu^{2+} in a 2.0 L aqueous solution
    (b) 6.2×10^{-3} g Be^{+2} in a 750 mL aqueous solution
    (c) 255 mg $NaIO_3$ in a 1.5 L aqueous solution

41. According to the U.S. EPA, the herbicide atrazine cannot appear in drinking water at levels above 3 μg/L. At this concentration, what is the maximum allowable mass of atrazine that can be present in a glass of water (volume, roughly 240 mL)?

42. What is meant by the "molar mass" of a chemical? Explain how molar mass is related to the terms "molecular weight," "formula weight," or "atomic mass."

43. Define what is meant by the terms "molarity" and "molality." What are the advantages and disadvantages to using each of these units?

44. Calculate the molarity of the following solutions.
    (a) 49.73 g H_2SO_4 dissolved in 500.0 mL of solution
    (b) 4.739 g $RuCl_3$ dissolved in 1.000 L of solution
    (c) 5.035 g $FeCl_3$ dissolved in 250.00 mL of solution
    (d) 27.74 g $C_{12}H_{22}O_{11}$ dissolved in 750.0 mL of solution

45. A solution is prepared by adding 5.84 g of formaldehyde (CH_2O) to 100.0 g water. The final volume of this solution is 104.0 mL. Calculate the molarity and molality of the formaldehyde in this solution.

46. The density of a 10.0% (w/w) solution of NaOH is 1.109 g/cm^3. Calculate both the molar and molal concentration of NaOH in this solution.

47. What is meant when the unit of "formality" is used to describe the concentration of a chemical? How is this related to the "analytical concentration" of that chemical?

48. A 500.00 mL aqueous solution of acetic acid is found to contain 0.00538 mol of acetic acid and 0.00321 mol of its conjugate base, acetate. What are the concentrations for the acetic acid and acetate in units of formality or molarity? What is the analytical concentration of acetic acid plus acetate in this solution?

49. A 25.00 mL portion of the solution in Problem 48 is diluted with water to a total volume of 100.00 mL, and the pH is adjusted to a predetermined value. The new solution is found to contain 0.000322 mol acetic acid and 0.000108 mol acetate. What are the individual concentrations of acetate and acetic acid in this diluted solution? What is the analytical concentration of acetic acid plus acetate in this solution?

50. Explain why the molarity and molality of a dilute aqueous solution are approximately the same at room temperature. Why do differences occur in these values when you work at higher concentrations at other temperatures and when using solvents other than water?

51. Describe each of the following measures of chemical content. In what types of situations might you find each of these measures of content employed?
    (a) Surface concentration (mol/m^2)
    (b) Normality (eq/L)

SOLUTION PREPARATION

52. State the meaning for each of the following terms as related to chemical purity. Which of these grades would be found in most routine analytical laboratories?
    (a) Certified ACS Grade
    (b) Technical Grade
    (c) USP Grade
    (d) Trace Metal Grade
    (e) HPLC Grade
    (f) Biotechnology Grade

53. In titrations, what is meant by a "primary standard" and a "secondary standard"?

54. What types of impurities are often found in water? Give a specific example for each type of impurity.

55. Explain how distillation and deionization are used to purify water. What are the advantages and disadvantages of each approach? Which method is used in your laboratory?

56. Define the terms "stock solution," "aliquot," and "dilution" and state the role played by each during the preparation of a solution.

57. Describe how you would prepare the following solutions.
    (a) 100.00 mL of 1.00 M NaCl in water, beginning with solid sodium chloride
    (b) 250 mL of 1.0 M Na_2SO_4 in water, beginning with a 2.5 M sodium sulfate solution
    (c) 250 mL of 0.500 M HCl in water, beginning with 12 M HCl

58. Nitric acid (HNO_3) is commercially available as a 72% (w/w) solution (density, 1.42 g/cm^3). How many milliliters of this reagent are needed to prepare 2.00 L of a 1.00 M HNO_3 solution?

59. A 1.00 mL urine sample is removed from a collection container and placed into a test tube with 19.0 mL water, giving a final volume of 20.0 mL. If the chemical creatinine has a concentration of 8.5 mM in the original sample, what will be its concentration in the final diluted solution?

60. A 25.00 g portion of 1.435 M NaOH is placed into a 250.00 mL volumetric flask and diluted to the mark with deionized water. A 25.00 mL aliquot of this stock solution is removed and placed into a 500.00 mL volumetric flask. This solution is then mixed and diluted to the mark with more deionized water. What is the molar concentration of NaOH in the final solution?

61. Explain how a change in temperature can affect the concentration of a sample.

62. A pharmaceutical chemist wishes to examine the binding of a drug to its target molecules. To do this, he carefully prepares a 50.0 μM solution of the drug in an aqueous buffer. This solution is made at room temperature (25°C) but is to be used at temperatures that range from 4°C to 45°C. Assuming that the drug's solution has essentially the same density as water (1.00000 g/cm^3 at 4°C and 0.99025 g/cm^3 at 45°C), how much will the drug's concentration change in going from 25°C to the other temperatures that will be used in this study?

63. A biochemist prepares a standard solution that contains 25.0 mg/mL of the protein bovine serum albumin (BSA) in water. This solution is prepared at 30°C and placed into a −20°C freezer for storage. When it is time to use this standard, it is removed from the freezer, thawed, remixed, and allowed to warm before being used in the assay. If this solution is only at 10°C when it is used, what will be the actual concentration of the protein?

CHALLENGE PROBLEMS

64. The method that was allegedly used by Archimedes for the examining the crown of King Hiero involved placing both the crown and an equal mass of pure gold into water and examining the amount of water that each displaced. If you have a crown of pure gold (density, 19.3 g/cm^3) that has a mass of 1000 g, what volume of water would be displaced at 25°C by this crown? If the density of pure silver is 10.5 g/cm^3, what volume of water will be displaced by a 1000 g crown that contains 80% (w/w) gold and 20% silver?

65. The value of g, the local gravitational acceleration constant, changes on Earth as you move to different altitudes or change your distance north or south of the equator. The way in which g varies with the position on the Earth is described by Equation 17,

$$g = 9.80632 - 0.02586 \cdot \cos(2\ v) + 0.00003 \cdot \cos(4\ v) - 0.00000293 \cdot h \tag{17}$$

where v is the location above or below the equator (in degrees) and h is the height above or below sea level (in meters).[4]

(a) Obtain the approximate altitude and latitude of the city in which your laboratory is located. What is the value of g for your location? Ignoring buoyancy effects, how much would the weight of a 1.000 kg object change in going from the equator at sea level to your laboratory?

(b) Imagine that you are given the task of moving a balance from the ground floor of a building to one that is five stories higher, an increase in height of approximately 20 m.

How much would this move affect the value of g around the balance? If this change were to go uncorrected, what effect would the move have on measurements that are performed on the balance?

66. The plots given in Figure 6 were obtained by using the relationship shown in Equation 18 between the density of a sample and the measured versus actual mass,

$$(m_{obj} - m_{display})$$
$$= m_{display} \cdot \frac{[(0.0012\ \text{g/cm}^3)/d_{obj}] - 0.00015}{1 - [(0.0012\ \text{g/cm}^3)/d_{obj}]} \tag{18}$$

where m_{obj} is the actual mass of the object being measured, $m_{display}$ is its apparent mass, and d_{obj} is the density of the object.

(a) Demonstrate how this equation can be derived from Equation 6. What assumptions were made in obtaining this relationship?

(b) Based on Equation 18, create a spreadsheet that can be used to generate graphs like the ones shown in Figure 6 for each of the following substances: cork (density, 0.2 g/cm^3), gasoline (0.7 g/cm^3), silicate-based rock (3.0 g/cm^3), and platinum (21.4 g/cm^3). Which of these materials would be expected to have the largest buoyancy effect? Which would have the smallest buoyancy effect?

67. Although a value of 0.0012 g/cm^3 is often used as the density for air in buoyancy calculations, a more exact air density (in units g/cm^3) can be found by using Equation 19,

$$d_{air} = 0.0012929 \cdot \frac{(273.13\ \text{K})}{T} \cdot \frac{(P - 0.3787 \cdot h)}{760} \tag{19}$$

where T is the absolute temperature (in K), and P is the barometric pressure (in mm Hg). The factor h is the vapor pressure of water (in mm Hg), which is a measure of the air's relative humidity. This last term can be determined through measurement or by using the dew point of the air.[16]

(a) Using Equation 19, estimate the density of air at a temperature of 28°C, a barometric pressure of 745 mm Hg, and a vapor pressure of 11.99 mm Hg (corresponding to a dew point of 14°C).

(b) Under the same conditions as in Part (a), determine what the actual mass would be for a 10.000 g sample that has a density of 0.89 g/cm^3 and is being compared to a reference with a density of 8.00 g/cm^3. How do your results compare to what is obtained when 0.0012 g/cm^3 is used as the density of air?

68. Mercury is sometimes used in place of water to calibrate volumetric equipment, especially when small volumes of liquids are being measured. Look up the physical and chemical properties of mercury in its material safety data sheet (MSDS) and the *CRC Handbook of Chemistry and Physics*.[16] Based on this information, what advantages do you think there might be to using mercury for calibrating volumetric devices? What disadvantages might there be to such a procedure?

69. Equation 14 was used earlier to show how an adjustment can be made for temperature effects when you are dealing with molar concentrations. What type of relationship would you use to make a similar correction for solutions that have

their contents expressed as weight-per-volume ratios (w/v)? Would this same type of correction be needed when working with units of molality, % w/w or % v/v? Explain your answer.

70. It is sometimes necessary during an analysis to convert from one unit of concentration to another. Show how you would convert between each of the following pairs of concentration units. (*Note:* Some of these conversions can be found in sources such as the *CRC Handbook of Chemistry & Physics*.)[16] State what additional information would be needed for each of these conversions. Confirm your approach by using dimensional analysis.
  (a) Converting a concentration in g/L to molarity
  (b) Converting a concentration in molarity to molality
  (c) Converting a concentration in mg/L to ppm (w/w)
  (d) Converting a concentration in % (w/w) to g/L

71. A unique feature of mass spectrometry is that it cannot only provide the mass of molecules but can give information on the isotopic composition of these molecules. One result of mass spectrometry's ability to discriminate between isotopes is that it can give multiple "molecular ion" peaks for a single chemical. Examples of these isotope peaks are shown in Figure 15.

(a) The presence of isotope peaks makes it necessary to distinguish between several ways of describing the molecular weight of a compound in mass spectrometry. Using Reference 19 as a guide, define the terms "average mass," "nominal mass," and "monoisotopic mass" as used in Figure 15.

(b) Chlorpheneramine ($C_{16}H_{19}ClN_2$) is a drug found in many over-the-counter cold medicines. Based on the isotopic masses and abundances given in Reference 16, calculate the nominal mass and monoisotopic mass for this drug, with the latter value being based on the most abundant isotopes for each element in this compound. How do these values compare with the molecular mass that is found when you use the atomic masses listed in the periodic table? Explain the reason for any differences in these values.

TOPICS FOR DISCUSSION AND REPORTS

72. Visit a local analytical laboratory and discuss how mass and volume measurements are used at that facility. Obtain information on the types of mass- and volume-measuring devices that are employed in that laboratory and on the procedures that are followed in the use of this equipment. Also, learn about the types of samples or reagents that are being measured with these devices and any special precautions that are followed during these determinations.

73. Using Reference 12 and other resources, obtain further information on the quartz crystal microbalance. Discuss how a quartz crystal microbalance works. Give examples of some analytical applications for this device.

74. There are several other methods that can be used to purify laboratory water besides distillation and deionization. A list of some of these alternative techniques is provided below.[18] Obtain information of one or more of these methods and describe how they work. How do these methods compare to deionization and distillation in the removal of unwanted substances from water?
  (a) Reverse osmosis
  (b) Activated carbon filtration
  (c) Ultrafiltration
  (d) Microporous filtration
  (e) Ultraviolet oxidation
  (f) Electrodialysis

75. Locate a recent research article that used the method of atomic force microscopy (AFM). Discuss how AFM was used in this article and describe the types of information that it provided.

76. Atomic force microscopy is part of a larger family of techniques known collectively as *scanning probe microscopy* (*SPM*). SPM is a type of microscopy that uses a physical probe to scan a surface and form an image of a sample. Below is a list of several types of scanning probe microscopy.[9,10,20,21,22] Obtain information on one of these methods from the Internet, a book, or a review article. Write a report that describes how this method works. Include in your report some examples of applications for this method in the area of chemical analysis
  (a) Scanning tunneling microscopy
  (b) Scanning electrochemical microscopy
  (c) Force modulation microscopy
  (d) Magnetic force microscopy

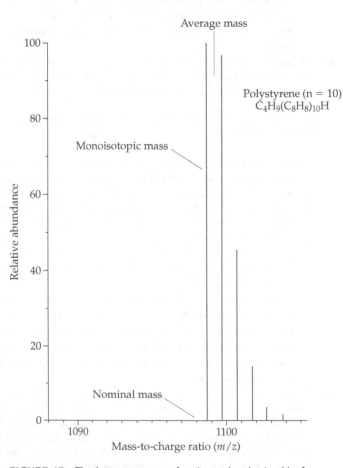

FIGURE 15 The isotope pattern for the molecular ion(s) of polystyrene, illustrating the differences between the nominal mass, monoisotopic mass and average mass for this chemical. (Adapted with permission from J. Yergey, D. Heller, G. Hansen, R. J. Cotter, and C. Fenselau, "Isotopic Distributions in Mass Spectra of Large Molecules," *Analytical Chemistry*, 55 (1983) 353–356.)

References

1. H. Diehl, *Quantitative Analysis: Elementary Principles and Practice*, Oakland Street Science Press, Ames, IA, 1970.
2. F. Szabadvary, *History of Analytical Chemistry*, Pergamon Press, New York, 1966.
3. "Baron Jöns Jakob Berzelius," *Columbia Electronic Encyclopedia*, Columbia University Press, New York, 2000.
4. M. Kochsiek, *Glossary of Weighing Terms: A Practical Guide to the Terminology of Weighing*, Mettler-Toledo, Switzerland, 1998.
5. B. Kisch, *Scales and Weights: A Historical Outline*, Yale University Press, New Haven, CT, 1966.
6. M. W. Hinds and G. Chapman, "Mass Traceability for Analytical Measurements," *Analytical Chemistry*, 68 (1996) 35A–39A.
7. W. E. Kupper, "Laboratory Balances," In: *Analytical Instrumentation Handbook*, 2nd ed., G. W. Ewing, Ed., Marcel Dekker, New York, 1997, Chapter. 2.
8. G. Binnig, C.F. Quate, and C. Gerber, "Atomic Force Microscope," *Physical Review Letters*, 56 (1986) 930–933.
9. E. Meyer, H. J. Hug, and R. Bennewitz, *Scanning Probe Microscopy: The Lab on a Tip*, Springer, New York, 2003.
10. P. Carlo Braga and D. Ricci, Eds., *Atomic Force Microscopy: Biomedical Methods and Applications*, Humana Press, Totowa, NJ, 2003.
11. N. Singer, "The Quiet Revolution in Analytical Balance Technology," *Chemistry*, Springer, New York, (2000) 14–16.
12. C. Henry, "Measuring the Masses: Quartz Crystal Microbalances," *Analytical Chemistry*, 68 (1996) 625A–628A.
13. M. L Gross, "Mass Spectrometry," In *Instrumental Analysis*, 2nd ed., G. D. Christian and J. E. O'Reilly, Eds., Allyn & Bacon, Boston, MA, 1986, Chapter 16.
14. D. A. Skoog, F. J. Holler, and T. A. Nieman, *Principles of Instrumental Analysis*, 5th ed., Saunders, Philadelphia, PA, 1998, Chapter 20.
15. D. O. Sparkman, *Mass Spectrometry Desk Reference*, Global View, Pittsburgh, PA, 2000.
16. D. R. Lide, Ed. *CRC Handbook of Chemistry and Physics*, 83rd Ed., CRC Press, Boca Raton, FL, 2002.
17. J. A. Dean, *Lange's Handbook of Chemistry*, 15th ed., McGraw-Hill, New York, 1999.
18. "Glass," *Encyclopedia Britannica*, Encyclopedia Britannica, Inc., Chicago, IL, 1999.
19. J. Inczedy, T. Lengyel, and A. M. Ure, *Compendium of Analytical Nomenclature*, 3rd ed., Blackwell Science, Malden, MA, 1997.
18. *A Guide to Laboratory Water Purification*, Labconco, Kansas City, MO, 1998.
19. J. Yergey, D. Heller, G. Hansen, R. J. Cotter, and C. Fenselau, "Isotopic Distributions in Mass Spectra of Large Molecules," *Analytical Chemistry*, 55 (1983) 353–356.
20. A. I. Kingon, P. M. Vilarinho, and Y. Rosenwaks, *Scanning Probe Microscopy: Characterization, Nanofabrication and Device Application of Functional Materials*, Kluwer Academic, Norwell, MA, 2005.
21. R. Wiesendanger, Ed., *Scanning Probe Microscopy: Analytical Methods*, Springer, New York, 1998.
22. D. Bonnell, Ed., *Scanning Probe Microscopy and Spectroscopy: Theory, Techniques and Applications*, 2nd ed., Wiley, New York, 2001.

Selected Answers

5 The change in the gravitational pull from that which occurs at 340 ft above sea level to that which occurs at 5,280 ft above sea level would account for the error.

12

a. Macroanalytical balance or semimicrobalance

b. Precision balance

c. Microbalance or ultramicrobalance

13 The precision balance has a resolution of 200,000; this balance would be used to weigh the calcium carbonate. The resolution of the analytical balance is 800,000 and this balance would be used to weigh the EDTA.

17 5.3083 g

28

a. Volumetric pipet

b. Micropipet

c. Several devices might be used here, such as a 2.00 mL volumetric pipet, a micropipette, or a Mohr pipet

d. Several devices might be used here, such as a micropipette, a Mohr pipet or a serological pipet

e. Syringe

f. Buret

32

a. 50.008 mL

b. 50.003 mL

35 This solution contains 161 mol ethylene glycol and 278 mol water, so water is the solvent and ethylene glycol is the solute.

37

a. 12.5% (v/v) acetonitrile, 25.0% (v/v) methanol

b. 70.3% (w/w) iron, 17.6% (w/w) chromium, 8.03% (w/w) nickel, 2.01% (w/w) manganese, 1.01% (w/w) silicon, 0.803% (w/w) carbon, 0.257% (w/w) other elements

c. 5.0 g/L dissolved solids

39

a. 5.0×10^{-6} g/L or 5.0 ppm Cu^{2+}

b. 8.3×10^{-6} g/L or 8.3 ppm Be^{+2}

c. 1.7×10^{-4} g/L or 0.17 parts-per-thousand $NaIO_3$

44

a. 1.014 M b. 0.02285 M

c. 0.1242 M d. 0.1081 M

45 1.87 M or 1.94 m formaldehyde

48 Individual concentrations, 0.0108 M acetic acid and 0.00642 M acetate; analytical concentration of acetic acid plus acetate, 0.0172 M

58 120 mL

59 0.425 mM creatinine

62 50.1 μM at 4°C, 49.7 μM at 45°C

Solutions and Concentrations

Solutions and Concentrations

Learning Objectives

At the end of this chapter, the student should be able to do the following:

1. Explain the nature of solutions and distinguish between the solute and solvent
2. Explain the various expressions of concentration
3. Calculate and interpret concentrations expressed in any of these four systems: percentage, molarity, molality, and normality
4. Use specific gravity in diluting concentrated solutions
5. Describe the relative convenience of the pH scale
6. Calculate pH values and interconvert them with molarity
7. Interconvert expressions of concentration

Key Terms

aqueous
concentration
dissolve
equivalent
equivalent weight
immiscible
insoluble
miscible
molality
molarity
normality
pH

ppb
ppm
ppt
soluble
solute
solution
solvent
sparingly soluble
specific gravity
(v/v)
(w/v)
(w/w)

A **solution** is a homogeneous mixture of two or more substances that do not chemically react with each other. Because the distribution of substances is uniform throughout a homogeneous mixture, a solution's composition, appearance, and properties are the same in any one portion as they are in any other portion. The substance present in the largest amount is called the **solvent**, whereas every other component of the solution is referred to as a **solute**. As a mixture forms, the solute is said to **dissolve** in the solvent. In the clinical laboratory, the most common solvent is water, and a solution of anything in water is referred to as **aqueous**.

A solution may consist of a solid and a liquid, a common example being hot tea sweetened with sugar. An example from the clinical laboratory is normal saline, which is a well-defined solution of sodium chloride in water. The solids in these cases are **soluble**, meaning they dissolve in water. **Insoluble** solids do not dissolve in water, whereas **sparingly soluble** solids dissolve only to a small degree.

A solution may be composed of two liquids, common examples of which are (1) rubbing alcohol, which is a mixture of isopropyl alcohol and water, and (2) vinegar, which is a mixture of acetic acid and water. In such cases, the liquids are **miscible** with each other, meaning that they are capable of being mixed in any ratio without separating. Two **immiscible** liquids, such as gasoline and water, do not form solutions but instead separate on standing, with the less dense liquid rising to the top.

A solution may comprise a gas dissolved in a liquid. Two common examples are (1) sparkling water, which is just an aqueous solution of carbon dioxide gas, and (2) household ammonia, which is an aqueous solution of ammonia gas.

Depending on the test we are conducting, serum and other body fluids can be regarded as any or all of the three kinds of solution outlined above. For example, when we quantify alcohol in blood, the serum is a liquid-in-liquid solution. However, we can view it as a solid-in-liquid solution when glucose is the analyte of interest or as a gas-in-liquid solution when the partial pressure of oxygen is being determined.

This chapter focuses on the calculation and expression of **concentration**, which is a measure of how much solute and solvent are present in a solution. It is difficult to exaggerate the importance of mastering this material because the consequences of reporting an incorrect concentration on a patient sample can be grave, as, for example, when it leads to the misdiagnosis of an illness or the administration of an inappropriate drug. Nearly every liquid in a clinical laboratory—from reagents to control solutions, from serum to spinal fluid, from disinfectants to cleaning agents—has a concentration that we must specify correctly and unambiguously.

Quantifying an analyte in a patient sample requires that the concentration of every reagent used in the assay be accurate to an acceptable degree. Although some reagents do come ready to use from the manufacturer, others must be prepared in the laboratory directly before use. Erroneous concentrations can even have repercussions not directly related to patient results. Consider two examples. First, the concentration of an unconsumed reagent that has expired may determine whether the solution is poured down the drain or consigned to hazardous waste—a decision that affects both the environment and the laboratory's budget. Second, there is the issue of laboratory hygiene. We commonly use bleach as a general disinfectant for surfaces in the laboratory. The required concentration, however, depends on the purpose; it may be as high as 10% for surface disinfection or as low as 0.5% for decontaminating the tubing in an automated instrument. If the concentration is too low, the bleach will fail to disinfect thoroughly; if too high, it might damage expensive parts. When bleach is an unsuitable disinfectant, alcohol serves as an alternative, most effective when its concentration is 70%; it is markedly less bactericidal at higher or lower concentrations. Thus, a solution labeled "70%" that was improperly prepared will lack the expected disinfecting power, possibly creating a risk to laboratory personnel.

EXPRESSING CONCENTRATION

There are many ways to express concentration, some deriving from convenience and others from tradition; it can be based on mass, volume, or number of moles.

Percentage

The following are the three common systems for expressing concentration as a mass or volume percentage.

- **Weight of solute per volume of solution (w/v).** In this system, the value is the number of grams of solute in 100 mL of solution. For example, "10% NaCl (w/v)" describes an aqueous solution of 10 grams of sodium chloride in every 100 mL of solution. Understand that this is *not* the same as 10 grams of NaCl in 100 mL of water (see "Molality"). Preparation of 10% NaCl entails dissolving 10 g NaCl in a small volume of water in a volumetric flask and then adding water until the volume is 100 mL.

- **Weight of solute per weight of solution (w/w).** In this system, the value is the number of grams of solute in 100 grams of solution. Thus, 6% KOH (w/w) is a solution of 6 grams of sodium hydroxide in 100 grams of solution. In simple terms, it is prepared by dissolving 6 g KOH in a small volume of water in a suitable vessel resting on a balance and then adding water until the weight of the solution is 100 g.

- **Volume of solute per volume of solution (v/v).** Used for liquid solutes, this system gives the number of milliliters of solute in 100 mL of solution. Therefore, 70% ethanol (v/v) is a solution of 70 mL of ethanol in 100 mL of solution, prepared by transferring 70 mL of ethanol into a volumetric flask and then adding water until the volume is 100 mL. Because we can weigh liquids, of course, we may also express the concentration of a liquid-in-liquid solution in the other two systems (w/v, w/w).

At this point, it should be clear that expressing concentration just as a percentage (e.g., "10% $C_6H_{12}O_6$") is inadequate because it does not give the basis for the ratio. Therefore, it is necessary to specify the system in a suffix: "10% $C_6H_{12}O_6$ (w/w)."

Parts-Per Notation

For very dilute solutions, when the value of the percentage is inconveniently small, we can express the concentration as "parts per million" (**ppm**), "parts per billion" (**ppb**), or "parts per trillion" (**ppt**). Strictly speaking, "1 ppm" means "one part in one million parts," such as 1 gram of solute in 1,000,000 grams of solution. Because the units in the numerator and denominator are the same, they cancel each other and the value turns out dimensionless. Thus, this system is similar to that of expressing concentrations as weight-per-weight percentages, or "% (w/w)." Consider this example:

$$10 \text{ ppm} = 10 \text{ g solute}/1{,}000{,}000 \text{ g solution}$$

$$= 0.001 \text{ g solute}/100 \text{ g solution}$$

$$= 0.001\% \text{ (w/w)}$$

For aqueous solutions, however, parts-per notation is sometimes used as an alternative to weight-per-volume (w/v) percentages, even though this practice can cause confusion by mixing units. Because the scientific community knows that 1000 grams of water has a volume of 1 liter, and because a very dilute aqueous solution has the same mass as an equal volume of water, exchanging mass for volume in the parts-per expression does not appreciably change the information it gives us. For example,

$$6 \text{ ppm} = 6 \text{ g of solute}/1{,}000{,}000 \text{ g of solution}$$

$$= 0.006 \text{ g of solute}/1000 \text{ g of solution}$$

$$= 0.006 \text{ g of solute}/\text{liter of solution}$$

Therefore, we can use "ppm" to mean 1 mg of solute in 1 L of very dilute solution:

$$1 \text{ ppm} = 1 \text{ g}/1{,}000{,}000 \text{ mL}$$

$$= 0.001 \text{ g}/1000 \text{ mL}$$

$$= 1 \text{ mg/L}$$

Expressing this concentration as "1 ppm" is clearly easier than writing it out as a percentage, "0.0001% (w/v)":

$$1 \text{ ppm} = 0.001 \text{ g}/1000 \text{ mL}$$

$$= 0.0001 \text{ g}/100 \text{ mL}$$

$$= 0.0001\% \text{ (w/v)}$$

☑ CHECKPOINT 1

1. What is the % (w/v) of a solution that comprises 8.2 g of NaOH per 100 mL?
2. How many grams of KCl are present in 200 mL of 10% KCl (w/v)?

   1. 8.2%
   2. Each 100 mL contains 10 g of KCl. Thus, 200 mL contains 20 g.

Molarity

Whereas percentage expresses concentration in terms of a measurable quantity (weight or volume), molarity does not. Rather, **molarity** refers to something that we can neither measure nor count: the molecules, ions, or atoms of a substance.

Molarity is the number of moles of a substance in 1 liter of solution (Equation 1). Thus, if 1 mole of glucose is dissolved in water and the volume is brought to 1 liter, the resulting solution is said to be "1 molar in glucose," and its concentration is written as "1 м." Often, we write the molarity of a substance as the name or chemical symbol in brackets: [glucose] or [Na^+].

$$\text{molarity} = \frac{\text{moles of solute}}{\text{liters of solution}}$$

◀ EQUATION 1

Preparing a solution with its concentration expressed as molarity requires the ability to interconvert grams and moles. Remember that 1 mole equals 6.023×10^{23} particles, in the same way that a dozen is equal to 12 particles and a gross equals 144 particles. Remember also that the formula mass (or formula weight) is the sum of the masses of all the atoms and/or ions in a formula unit, and that the mass of 1 mole of a substance is its molar mass.

A 1.0 м solution of glucose ($C_6H_{12}O_6$), then, comprises 1.0 mole of glucose, or 180 grams, in a volume of 1.0 liter. Of course, the solution should be at room temperature and at atmospheric pressure, or its concentration may not be exactly 1 м.

There are variations on the molarity theme intended to simplify the expression of low concentrations. For example, if the concentration is 0.001 м, there is 1 millimole in every liter of solution. A simpler representation of this solution is "1 mм," or "1 millimolar." Likewise, if the concentration is 0.000001 м, there is 1 micromole per liter of solution; this is more easily expressed as "1μм," or "1 micromolar." Another unit commonly used in the laboratory, especially in research, is "nм," or "nanomolar."

Because molarity is a function of volume, its value changes with temperature. Therefore, a cold solution may have a different molarity than it does when warm.

☑ CHECKPOINT 2

1. What is the molarity of a solution comprising 2 moles of sucrose (table sugar) in 4 liters?
2. How many moles of sucrose are in 0.500 L of the above solution?

1. 0.50 м. The ratio is 2 mol per 4 L:

$$\frac{2 \text{ mol}}{4 \text{ L}} = 0.50 \text{ mol/L} = 0.50 \text{ м}$$

2. 0.25 mol. The quantity 0.500 L is, of course, half a liter, and a liter contains 0.5 moles:

$$0.500 \text{ L} \times \frac{0.50 \text{ mol}}{\text{L}} = 0.25 \text{ mol}$$

Molality

Molality denotes the amount of solute in solution per kilogram of *solvent*—not per kilogram of *solution*. The symbol is "*m*," pronounced "molal." For example, dissolving 1 mole of molecules in 2 kilograms of solvent constitutes a 0.5 *m* solution.

$$\text{molality} = \frac{\text{moles of solute}}{\text{kilograms of solvent}}$$

◀ EQUATION 2

Unlike molarity, molality is not a function of volume, and its value, therefore, does not depend on temperature. Thus, a cold solution has the same molality as it does when warm.

Normality

Normality, symbolized by "*N*," is similar to molarity except that it expresses concentration in terms of **equivalent weight** rather than formula mass. The equivalent weight of a substance is the amount that contains, theoretically combines with, or theoretically replaces 1 mole of hydrogen ions (H^+).

Consider, for example, a 1 N (pronounced "one-normal") HCl solution. By definition, this solution comprises 1 equivalent weight of HCl, or 36.5 g, in a volume of 1 L. The amount of HCl that contains 1 mole of hydrogen ions is, of course, 1 mole; the molar mass of HCl is 36.5 g, which is, therefore, the equivalent weight. Thus, for HCl the normality and molarity are equal.

By contrast, consider a 1 N H_2SO_4 solution. Although this solution, like 1 N HCl, comprises 1 equivalent weight of H_2SO_4 in 1 L, only one-half a mole of H_2SO_4 contains 1 mole of hydrogen ions. Because the molar mass of H_2SO_4 is 98.1 g, the equivalent weight is half that value, or 49.0 g. Thus, for H_2SO_4, a 1 N solution is the same as a 0.5 M solution.

For an acid, then, an **equivalent** is one hydrogen ion in the formula. Thus, 1 mole of HCl is 1 equivalent, whereas 1 mole of H_2SO_4 is 2 equivalents and 1 mole of H_3PO_4 is 3 equivalents.

For a base or a salt, an equivalent is the number of hydrogen ions with which it can theoretically combine; however, we can just as easily regard it as 1 mole of ionic charges. For example, because the bicarbonate ion (HCO_3^-) carries a single charge and can combine with 1 hydrogen ion, then obviously 1 mole of bicarbonate ions carries 1 mole of charges and can combine with 1 mole of hydrogen ions. Therefore, 1 equivalent of HCO_3^- ions is 1 mole.

The magnesium ion (Mg^{2+}), by contrast, carries two charges and can theoretically replace two hydrogen ions. Thus, 1 mole of Mg^{2+} ions is the same as 2 equivalents.

In general, then, the number of equivalents is the product of the number of moles and the number of charges:

EQUATION 3

$$\text{equivalents} = \text{moles} \times \text{charges}$$

In fact, we can express concentration in terms of equivalents ("Eq"), a system widely used in medicine because it directly reports the concentration of positive or negative charges. For example, the concentration of potassium ion in serum typically can be about 5 mEq/L, which is the same as 5 mmol/L (or 5 mM). However, calcium ion (Ca^{2+}) can also typically be present in serum at about 5 mEq/L, which is *not* 5 mmol/L, but half of that, or 2.5 mmol/L. Clearly, a mole of potassium ions gives the same concentration of positive charges as does half a mole of calcium ions, but expressing that concentration in terms of equivalents makes it necessary to convert from moles to charges.

☑ CHECKPOINT 3

1. What is the normality of a solution consisting of 2 mol NaCl in 1 liter?
2. A 2 N H_2SO_4 solution has how many grams of H_2SO_4?

   1. 2 N. One mole of NaCl is 1 equivalent.
   2. An equivalent weight for sulfuric acid is half a mole, 49 g. Therefore, 2 equivalent weights is 98 g, the molar mass.

Preparing for Possible Changes

At this writing, the National Institute of Standards and Technology (NIST) considers obsolete the previously discussed three concentration terms "molarity," "molality," and "normality," along with their symbols, "M," "m," and "N," respectively. Nevertheless, the term "molarity" and its symbol remain very common in chemistry and probably will be so for a long time to come. The terms "molality" and "normality," despite being used less often than "molarity," are still common enough that it is necessary to understand them. Table 1 ★ summarizes the changes proposed by NIST.

SPECIFIC GRAVITY

Specific gravity is the ratio of the density of a solution to the density of water at 4°C (1 g/mL). A substance with a value greater than 1 is denser than water, and a substance with a value smaller than 1 is less dense. And, because specific gravity is a ratio of two densities, the units cancel each other, leaving only a magnitude.

Specific gravity is helpful in diluting concentrated commercial acids in the laboratory. Measuring the weight of a liquid is awkward and, when that liquid is a concentrated acid, dangerous. Measuring its volume, however, is markedly easier, although precautions are still necessary.

★ **TABLE 1** Concentration Terms That NIST Considers Obsolete, and Their Proposed Replacements

Obsolete Quantity and Symbol	Proposed Term	Proposed Symbol	Proposed Units
Molarity (M)	Amount-of-substance concentration of B	c_B	mol/dm³ mol/L kmol/m³
Molality (m)	Molality of solute B	b_B	mol/kg
Normality (N)	Amount-of-substance concentration of H_nA	$c[(1/n)H_nA]^*$	mol/dm³ mol/L kmol/m³

*In this notation, n represents the number of hydrogen ions an acid can release. For example, if the acid is sulfuric (H_2SO_4), then rather than writing "a 0.5 N solution of sulfuric acid," we would write "a solution of sulfuric acid with an amount-of-substance concentration of $c[(1/2) H_2SO_4]$ of 0.5 mol/L."

Suppose, for example, that you have a bottle of concentrated aqueous HCl, the label of which states the specific gravity to be 1.18 and the purity 36%. What these two values mean is that 1 mL of the liquid in the bottle weighs 1.18 g and that 36% of this weight is HCl (the rest is water). If your task is to dilute this acid to a concentration of 1 N in a final volume of 100 mL, then the final solution must have 1 equivalent weight of HCl in every liter.

To do this, you must first determine the equivalent weight of HCl in 100 mL of the dilute acid. Because HCl contains one hydrogen ion, the equivalent weight is the formula mass, or 36.5 g. Therefore,

$$100 \text{ mL} \left(\frac{1 \text{ L}}{1000 \text{ mL}} \right)\left(\frac{36.5 \text{ g}}{1 \text{ L}} \right) = 3.65 \text{ g}$$

What this means is that the diluted acid has 3.65 g of HCl in a final volume of 100 mL. Next, you must calculate the volume of concentrated aqueous HCl that contains 3.65 g—the volume that you will subsequently dilute to that final volume of 100 mL. You know that 36% of the weight of the concentrated aqueous acid is HCl; therefore,

$$0.36 \times \left(\frac{1.18 \text{ g}}{1 \text{ mL}} \right) = 0.425 \text{ g/mL}$$

This means that every mL of the liquid contains 0.425 g of HCl. Now you can calculate the volume needed for dilution to 100 mL:

$$3.65 \text{ g HCl} \times \left(\frac{1 \text{ mL}}{0.425 \text{ g HCl}} \right) = 8.6 \text{ mL}$$

Thus, you pipet 8.6 mL (slowly and under a hood) of the concentrated aqueous HCl into water and then add enough water to bring the final volume to 100 mL. The result is a solution of 1 N HCl.

THE pH SCALE

The concentration of hydrogen ions profoundly affects many chemical reactions in the laboratory and nearly all physiological processes in the human body. Understanding the expression of hydrogen-ion concentrations, therefore, is critical both to the physician, who makes medical decisions, and to the laboratorian, who generates the test results that help guide those decisions.

Serum, urine, other biological fluids, and common laboratory solutions have H^+ concentrations that are ponderous to express in the units discussed previously. For example, the concentration of H^+ in the blood is 0.00000004 M (4×10^{-8} M). To simplify such inconvenient numbers, Danish biochemist Søren Sørenson proposed the quantity "pH" in 1909. He defined the term **pH** as the *puissance d'hydrogène*, which translates as the *power of hydrogen*, expressing [H^+] as a negative logarithm of 10. In other words, [H^+] $= 10^{-pH}$.

Rearranging this equation gives

$$pH = -\log[H^+]$$

EQUATION 4

★ **TABLE 2** The pH Scale

[H$^+$] (mol/L)		pH	
0.1	10^{-1}	1	
0.01	10^{-2}	2	
0.001	10^{-3}	3	
0.0001	10^{-4}	4	
0.00001	10^{-5}	5	
0.000001	10^{-6}	6	Acidic
0.0000001	10^{-7}	7	Neutral
0.00000001	10^{-8}	8	Alkaline
0.000000001	10^{-9}	9	
0.0000000001	10^{-10}	10	
0.00000000001	10^{-11}	11	
0.000000000001	10^{-12}	12	
0.0000000000001	10^{-13}	13	
0.00000000000001	10^{-14}	14	

The pH of blood, then, is

$$pH = -\log(4 \times 10^{-8} \text{ M})$$

$$pH = 7.4$$

Clearly, "7.4" is much simpler than "0.00000004" or "4×10^{-8}." Now, let us look at the pH scale (Table 2 ★) that emerges from Equation 4.

This scale has at least four salient features:

1. As pH increases, the concentration of H$^+$ decreases. Thus, their relationship is inverse.
2. A difference of 1 pH unit—for example, 8 to 9 or 5 to 4—represents a 10-fold change in the H$^+$ concentration. This is so because the scale is logarithmic and its base is 10. Thus, with respect to H$^+$, a solution at pH 6 is 100 times more concentrated than it is at pH 8.
3. The concentration of H$^+$ is in "mol/L." The pH convention is valid *only* for this unit of concentration.
4. By virtue of being a logarithm, the pH is dimensionless; that is, it has no units. Thus, we say "the pH is 7," not "the pH is 7 moles per liter."

A solution at pH 7 is "neutral." At pH < 7, it is acidic, and at pH > 7, it is alkaline, or basic. (Strictly speaking, this is true only at 25°C. At other temperatures, these guidelines vary somewhat.)

Although a whole pH unit corresponds to a factor of 10, every decrement of 0.30 pH units reflects a doubling of the H$^+$ concentration, and every increment reflects a halving of the H$^+$ concentration. This knowledge is helpful in a quick comparison of two pH values. If the H$^+$ concentration doubles, the pH goes down by 0.30, and if the H$^+$ concentration halves, the pH goes up by 0.30. For example, if the pH decreases from 4.50 to 4.20, the H$^+$ concentration has risen by a factor of ~2 from 3.16×10^{-5} M to 6.31×10^{-5} M. Likewise, if the pH increases from 7.10 to 7.40, the H$^+$ concentration has fallen by a factor of ~2 from 7.94×10^{-8} M to 3.98×10^{-8} M.

This relationship comes about because the logarithm of 2 is 0.30. Consider what happens when the H$^+$ concentration doubles:

$$pH = -\log([H^+] \times 2)$$

$$pH = -\log[H^+] - \log 2$$

$$= -\log[H^+] - 0.30$$

What the last equation in this sequence says is that when [H$^+$] doubles, the original pH goes down by 0.30. When the H$^+$ concentration halves, the original pH goes up by 0.30:

$$pH = -\log([H^+] \times {}^1\!/_2)$$

$$pH = -\log[H^+] - \log{}^1\!/_2$$

$$= -\log[H^+] + 0.30$$

☑ CHECKPOINT 4

1. What is the pH of a solution in which $[H^+]$ is 0.062 M?
2. What is $[H^+]$ of a solution whose pH is 8.5?

  1. $pH = -\log(0.062 \text{ M}) = 1.21$
  2. $10^{-pH} = [H^+] = 10^{-8.5} = 3 \times 10^{-9}$ M

CONVERTING BETWEEN UNITS

We can convert between two sets of units in any of several ways. Let us consider three such ways, using the example of converting a result for serum glucose of 80 mg/dL to "mM" ("mmol/L").

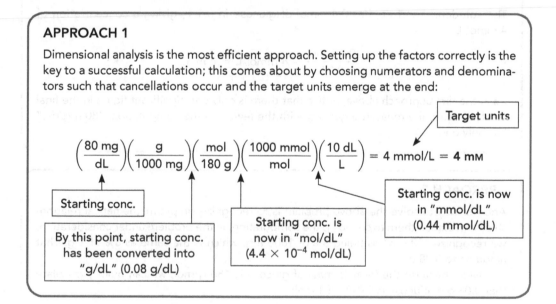

APPROACH 1

Dimensional analysis is the most efficient approach. Setting up the factors correctly is the key to a successful calculation; this comes about by choosing numerators and denominators such that cancellations occur and the target units emerge at the end:

Target units

$$\left(\frac{80 \text{ mg}}{dL}\right)\left(\frac{g}{1000 \text{ mg}}\right)\left(\frac{mol}{180 \text{ g}}\right)\left(\frac{1000 \text{ mmol}}{mol}\right)\left(\frac{10 \text{ dL}}{L}\right) = 4 \text{ mmol/L} = \textbf{4 mM}$$

Starting conc.

By this point, starting conc. has been converted into "g/dL" (0.08 g/dL)

Starting conc. is now in "mol/dL" (4.4×10^{-4} mol/dL)

Starting conc. is now in "mmol/dL" (0.44 mmol/dL)

Notice that there is only one significant figure in the final result because the measured quantity with the fewest in the computation, "80 mg/dL," has only one.

APPROACH 2

An alternate approach to solving the above problem is the ratio method. Using this method, our first objective is to convert "80 mg" into "mmol," which requires taking it to "grams," then to "moles," and finally to "millimoles." In the first step, we set up equivalent ratios:

$$\frac{1000 \text{ mg}}{1 \text{ g}} = \frac{80 \text{ mg}}{x}$$

Cross-multiplication gives

$$(1000 \text{ mg})(x) = (80 \text{ mg})(1 \text{ g})$$

$$x = 0.08 \text{ g}$$

(continued)

In the next step, we convert "0.08 g" into "moles" (the molar mass of glucose is 180 g/mol):

$$\frac{180 \text{ g}}{1 \text{ mol}} = \frac{0.08 \text{ g}}{x}$$

$$x = 0.0004 \text{ mol}$$

Finally, we convert "0.0004 mol" into "millimoles":

$$\frac{1 \text{ mol}}{1000 \text{ mmol}} = \frac{0.0004 \text{ mol}}{x}$$

$$x = 0.4 \text{ mmol}$$

Thus, this solution contains 0.4 mmol of glucose in each dL. To complete the conversion, we change "dL" into "liters":

$$\frac{10 \text{ dL}}{1 \text{ L}} = \frac{1 \text{ dL}}{x}$$

$$x = 0.1 \text{ L}$$

The solution, therefore, has 0.4 mmol of glucose in 0.1 L, giving a concentration of 4 mmol/L:

$$\frac{0.4 \text{ mmol}}{0.1 \text{ L}} = 4 \text{ mmol/L} = \textbf{4 mM}$$

As in the first approach above, notice that there is only one significant figure in the final result because the measured quantity with the fewest in the computation, "80 mg/dL," has only one.

APPROACH 3

Another way to solve the above problem is to recognize simple mathematical relationships and exploit them to speed up the computation. In the problem under consideration, we recognize "80 mg" as being 8% of 1000 mg, which is the same as 8% of 1 g. That amounts to 0.08 g.

Next, because the formula mass of glucose is 180 g/mol, we can quickly calculate that 0.08 g of glucose is 0.04% of 1 mol:

$$\frac{0.08 \text{ g}}{180 \text{ g}} \times 100\% = 0.04\%$$

And 0.04% of 1 mol is 0.0004 mol. Thus, at this point in the computation, we know that 1 dL of our glucose solution contains 0.0004 mol.

We recognize that 1 mol of anything—glucose molecules, golf balls, or votes—is the same as 1000 mmol. In other words, there are 1000 mmol per mol. Therefore, no matter the number of moles, we merely multiply it by 1000 mmol/mol to convert the units to "millimoles"; the number of millimoles is always 1000 times greater than the number of moles. In this case, we have 0.0004 mol:

$$0.0004 \text{ mol} \times 1000 \text{ mmol/mol} = 0.4 \text{ mmol}$$

Now we know that our glucose solution has 0.4 mmol per dL. All that remains at this point is to convert "dL" to "L." We also know that 1 liter of any liquid—glucose solution, gasoline, or tea—occupies the same volume as 10 deciliters. In other words, there are 10 dL per L. Therefore, no matter the number of deciliters, we merely divide it by 10 dL/L to convert the units to "liters"; the number of liters is always 1/10 the number of deciliters. In this case, we have 1 dL:

$$1 \text{ dL} \div 10 \text{ dL/L} = 0.1 \text{ L}$$

At the end of our computation, we see that there are 0.4 mmol of glucose in 0.1 L of our solution. Therefore, the concentration is

$$\frac{0.4 \text{ mmol}}{0.1 \text{ L}} = 4 \text{ mmol/L} = \textbf{4 mM}$$

As in the first and second approaches above, notice that there is only one significant figure in the final result because the measured quantity with the fewest in the computation, "80 mg/dL," has only one.

☑ CHECKPOINT 5

1. For a glucose solution, convert "2.3 mg/mL" to "mol/L" (honor figure significance).

    Approach 1

    $$\left(\frac{2.3 \text{ mg}}{\text{mL}}\right)\left(\frac{\text{g}}{1000 \text{ mg}}\right)\left(\frac{\text{mol}}{180 \text{ g}}\right)\left(\frac{1000 \text{ mL}}{\text{L}}\right) = 0.013 \text{ mol/L}$$

    Approach 2

    $$\frac{1000 \text{ mg}}{1 \text{ g}} = \frac{2.3 \text{ mg}}{x} \qquad x = 0.0023 \text{ g}$$

    $$\frac{180 \text{ g}}{1 \text{ mol}} = \frac{0.0023 \text{ g}}{y} \qquad y = 1.27 \times 10^{-5} \text{ mol}$$

    $$\frac{1000 \text{ mL}}{1 \text{ L}} = \frac{1 \text{ mL}}{z} \qquad z = 0.001 \text{ L}$$

    $$\frac{1.27 \times 10^{-5} \text{ mol}}{0.001 \text{ L}} = 0.013 \text{ mol/L}$$

2. For a KOH solution, convert "5 µmol/mL" to "mg/L" (honor figure significance).

    Approach 1

    $$\left(\frac{5.0 \text{ µmol}}{\text{mL}}\right)\left(\frac{\text{mol}}{10^6 \text{ µmol}}\right)\left(\frac{56.1 \text{ g}}{\text{mol}}\right)\left(\frac{1000 \text{ mg}}{\text{g}}\right)\left(\frac{1000 \text{ ml}}{\text{L}}\right) = 280 \text{ mg/L}$$

    Approach 2

    $$\frac{1 \times 10^6 \text{ µmol}}{1 \text{ mol}} = \frac{5.0 \text{ µmol}}{w} \qquad w = 5.0 \times 10^{-6} \text{ mol}$$

    $$\frac{1 \text{ mol}}{56.1 \text{ g}} = \frac{5.0 \times 10^{-6} \text{ mol}}{x} \qquad x = 0.00028 \text{ g} = 2.8 \times 10^{-4} \text{ g}$$

    $$\frac{1 \text{ g}}{1000 \text{ mg}} = \frac{2.8 \times 10^{-4} \text{ g}}{y} \qquad y = 0.28 \text{ mg}$$

    $$\frac{1000 \text{ mL}}{1 \text{ L}} = \frac{1 \text{ mL}}{z} \qquad z = 0.001 \text{ L}$$

    $$\frac{0.28 \text{ mg}}{0.001 \text{ L}} = 280 \text{ mg/L}$$

Summary

1. A *solution* is a homogeneous mixture of substances. The *solvent* is the substance present in largest amount, whereas every other substance is a *solute*.
2. The *concentration* of a solution is a measure of the amounts of solute and solvent in the mixture.
3. The expression of concentration by percentage has three commonly used systems: (a) weight per volume (*w/v*), which gives the number of grams of solute in 100 mL of the solution; (b) weight per weight (*w/w*), which gives the number of grams of solute in 100 g of the solution; and (c) volume per volume (*v/v*), which gives the number of milliliters of solute in 100 mL of the solution.
4. *Molarity* expresses concentration as the number of moles of solute in 1 liter of solution. Its symbol is "M."
5. *Molality* expresses concentration as the number of moles of solute per kg of solvent. Its symbol is historically "*m*."
6. *Normality* expresses concentration as the number of equivalent weights in 1 liter of the solution. An *equivalent weight* is the amount of a substance that contains, theoretically combines with, or theoretically replaces 1 mole of hydrogen ions (H^+).

7. For an acid, an *equivalent* is one hydrogen ion in the formula. For a base or a salt, an equivalent is the number of hydrogen ions with which it can theoretically combine; however, it can just as easily be regarded as 1 mole of ionic charges.
8. *Specific gravity* is the ratio of the density of a solution to the density of water at 4°C (1 g/mL).
9. The *pH* system for expressing concentration simplifies the numbers involved. The *pH* value is the negative logarithm of the H^+ concentration:

$$pH = -\log[H^+]$$

10. The *pH* scale has four important properties: (a) the relationship between *pH* and $[H^+]$ is inverse, (b) a difference of 1 *pH* unit represents a 10-fold difference in $[H^+]$, (c) the *pH* is valid only for molarity, and (d) the *pH* value is dimensionless.
11. A *pH* difference of 0.30 reflects a two-fold difference in $[H^+]$.

Practice Problems

1. (LO 3) Calculate % (w/v) for each of the following solutions.

    (a) 400 g KOH in 1 L

    (b) 60 g KCl in 500 mL

    (c) 1.8 g NaCl in 200 mL

    (d) 0.5 g glucose in 1 dL

    (e) 250 mg $Pb(NO_3)$ in 300 mL

    (f) 3.08 g NaOCl in 50 mL

2. (LO 3) Calculate % (w/w) for each of the following solutions.

    (a) 9.2 g $CaCl_2$ dissolved in 800 g of water

    (b) 500 mg cholesterol dissolved in 5 g of ethyl acetate

    (c) 200 mg Na_2CO_3 dissolved in 25 g of water

3. (LO 3) If isopropyl alcohol is added to 50 mL of water until the volume of the solution is 150 mL, what is the % (v/v)?

4. (LO 3) Calculate the molarity of each of the following solutions.

    (a) 4 g KOH in 1 L of solution

    (b) 60 g NaCl in 400 mL of solution

    (c) 0.18 mmol Fe^{2+} in 200 mL of solution

    (d) 0.70 μmol HCl in 50 μL of solution

    (e) 164 mg $Ca(NO_3)_2$ in 10 mL of solution

    (f) 0.130 mg $Co(NO_3)_2$ in 300 μL of solution

5. (LO 3) Calculate the normality of each of the following solutions.

    (a) 14.9 g KCl in 200 mL of solution

    (b) 320 g NaOH in 2 L of solution

    (c) 24.53 g H_2SO_4 in 250 mL of solution

6. (LO 3, 7) Complete the following table for $MgCl_2$.

Molarity	% (w/v)
1.0	
	2.6
3.4×10^{-4}	
	29.1
0.0025	

7. (LO 3, 7) Complete the following table for NaCl.

Molarity	% (w/v)
2.0	
	0.90
1.7×10^{-3}	
	16.0
0.082	

8. (LO 3, 7) Complete the following table for glucose ($C_6H_{12}O_6$).

Molarity	% (w/v)
0.80	
	5.0
9.6×10^{-4}	
	0.83
0.066	

Contextual Problems

1. (LO 2, 3, 7) If the reference range for serum Ca^{2+} is 8.5–10.5 mg/dL, would a result of 2.3 mmol/L be within that range? A result of 4.8 mEq/L?

2. (LO 2, 3, 7) If the reference range for serum Mg^{2+} is 1.8–3.0 mg/dL, would a result of 2.6 mEq/L be within that range? A result of 0.8 mmol/L?

3. (LO 6) Complete the following table.

pH	$[H^+]$ (M)
3.90	
	1.9×10^{-6}
7.05	
	2.29×10^{-10}
11.38	
	8.71×10^{-14}

4. (LO 6, 7) Complete the following table. Note the units requested.

pH	$[H^+]$ (mM)
2.61	
	0.0200
7.00	
	7.10×10^{-8}
12.27	
	1.00×10^{-11}

5. (LO 3) Consider a 2.00 m glucose solution. In 2720 g of this solution, what is the total mass of the glucose?

6. (LO 2, 3, 7) Your laboratory analyzes samples that are part of the proficiency testing program being conducted by an oversight agency. For eight of the analytes, the agency requests units that happen to differ from those that your laboratory uses. Convert your results appropriately in the following table.

Analyte	Your Result	Result in Requested Units
creatinine (112.3 g/mol)	6.4 mg/L	μM
folic acid (441.6 g/mol)	14 ng/mL	nmol/L
phenobarbital (230.8 g/mol)	15 μg/mL	μM
lead	4.2 μM	μg/L
phosphorus	1.62 mM	mg/L
iron	22.9 μmol/L	μg/L
glucose	160 mg/dL	mmol/L
uric acid (168.1 g/mol)	77 mg/L	μM

7. (LO 2, 3, 7) Your laboratory's method for quantifying a particular drug in whole blood requires regular decontamination by running through the instrument a solution of bleach (sodium hypochlorite, NaOCl) at a concentration between 0.6% and 1% (w/v). A lower concentration fails to decontaminate the apparatus, and a higher concentration damages it. You have a NaOCl solution at 0.083 M. Does this concentration fall within the range specified?

8. (LO 2, 3, 7) You work in a private laboratory that is about to implement a new method for quantifying ionized calcium in serum. Your supervisor explains that the new method gives results in units of "mg/dL," whereas the physicians in the clinics want results in units of "mmol/L." Therefore, your supervisor instructs you to routinely multiply the first result by 0.2495 to get the second result, which you may then release to the physician. Is your supervisor correct?

9. (LO 2, 3, 7) Ethylene glycol is a toxic substance used in such products as brake fluid, inks, synthetic waxes, and antifreeze. In cases of accidental ingestion, the physicians in your hospital treat the patient with hemodialysis when the ethylene glycol concentration in the serum is greater than 50 mg/dL (molar mass = 62 g/mol).

From the emergency room, you receive a serum sample for a suspected case of ethylene glycol poisoning. Your test for ethylene glycol in the sample returns a result of 9.2 mmol/L. Does this concentration make the patient a candidate for hemodialysis?

10. (LO 4) One of the assays your laboratory routinely carries out requires 1 N H_2SO_4. You have in stock a bottle of concentrated sulfuric acid with a specific gravity of 1.84 and a purity of 97%. To achieve the target concentration of 1 N, how many milliliters of this acid must be diluted to a final volume of 100 mL?

PEARSON
myhealthprofessionskit™

Go to www.myhealthprofessionskit.com <http://www.myhealthprofessionskit.com/> to access the Companion Website created for this textbook. Simply select "Clinical Laboratory Science" from the choice of disciplines. Find this book and log in using your username and password to access additional practice problems, answers to the practice and contextual problems, additional information, and more.

Answer Key

Practice Problems

1. In each case, calculate the number of grams present in 100 mL of solution. Given that 100 mL is the same as 0.1 L, we may solve problem **a** this way:

$$\left(\frac{400 \text{ g}}{1 \text{ L}}\right)\left(\frac{0.1 \text{ L}}{100 \text{ mL}}\right) = 40 \text{ g}/100 \text{ mL} = 40\% \text{ (w/v)}$$

And because 100 mL = 1 dL, we might also solve the problem this way:

$$\left(\frac{400 \text{ g}}{1 \text{ L}}\right)\left(\frac{0.1 \text{ L}}{\text{dL}}\right) = 40 \text{ g/dL} = 40\% \text{ (w/v)}$$

(b) 12% (w/v) (c) 0.9% (w/v) (d) 0.5% (w/v) (e) 0.08% (w/v) (f) 6.16% (w/v)

2. (a) The total solution mass is 800 g + 9.2 g = 809.2 g. Therefore, the concentration is the mass of the solute divided by the total solution mass:

$$\frac{9.2 \text{ g}}{809.2 \text{ g}} \times 100\% = 1.1\% \text{ (w/w)}$$

(b) 9% (w/w) (c) 0.8% (w/w)

3. The concentration is the volume of alcohol divided by the total solution volume:

$$\frac{50 \text{ mL}}{150 \text{ mL}} \times 100\% = 33\% \text{ (v/v)}$$

4. (a) $4.0 \text{ g} \left(\dfrac{\text{mol}}{56.1 \text{ g}} \right) \left(\dfrac{1}{1 \text{ L}} \right) = 0.071 \text{ M}$ (b) $60.0 \text{ g} \left(\dfrac{\text{mol}}{58.5 \text{ g}} \right) \left(\dfrac{1}{0.400 \text{ L}} \right) = 2.56 \text{ M}$

(c) 9.0×10^{-4} M   (d) 0.014 M   (e) 0.10 M   (f) 2.37×10^{-3} M

5. (a) 1 mol KCl = 1 Eq KCl. Therefore,

$$14.9 \text{ g} \left(\dfrac{\text{mol}}{74.6 \text{ g}} \right) \left(\dfrac{1}{0.200 \text{ L}} \right) = 1.0 \, N$$

(b) 4 N (c) 2.0 N

6. Sample calculation, first row in the table. A 1.0 M solution of $MgCl_2$ is the same as 0.10 moles per 100 mL:

$$\dfrac{1.0 \text{ mol}}{\text{L}} = \dfrac{0.10 \text{ mol}}{100 \text{ mL}}$$

Therefore, it is necessary to convert "0.10 moles" into "grams" (formula mass of $MgCl_2$ is 95.21 g/mol):

$$\dfrac{95.21 \text{ g}}{1.0 \text{ mol}} = \dfrac{x}{0.10 \text{ mol}} \qquad x = 9.5 \text{ g (in 100 mL)}$$

Thus,

$$\dfrac{9.5 \text{ g}}{100 \text{ mL}} \times 100\% = 9.5\% \text{ (w/v)}$$

Sample calculation, second row in the table. At 2.6% (w/v), the solution has 2.6 g of $MgCl_2$ in every 100 mL.

$$2.6\% \text{ (w/v)} = \dfrac{2.6 \text{ g}}{100 \text{ mL}}$$

Therefore, it is necessary to convert "2.6 grams" into "moles":

$$\dfrac{95.21 \text{ g}}{1 \text{ mol}} = \dfrac{2.6 \text{ g}}{x} \qquad x = 0.027 \text{ mol (in 100 mL, or 0.1 L)}$$

The number of moles in 1 liter, then, is

$$\dfrac{0.027 \text{ mol}}{0.1 \text{ L}} = 0.27 \text{ mol/L} = 0.27 \text{ M}$$

Molarity	% (w/v)
1.0	9.5
0.27	2.6
3.4×10^{-4}	0.0032
3.06	29.1
0.0025	0.024

7. See problem 6 for sample calculations (formula mass of NaCl is 58.44 g/mol).

Molarity	% (w/v)
2.0	12
0.15	0.90
1.7×10^{-3}	0.0099
2.74	16.0
0.082	0.48

8. See problem 6 for sample calculations (formula mass of glucose is 180.16 g/mol).

Molarity	% (w/v)
0.80	14
0.28	5.0
9.6×10^{-4}	0.017
0.046	0.83
0.066	1.2

Contextual Problems

1. A result of 2.3 mmol/L is within range. Dimensional analysis converts mmol/L to mg/dL:

$$2.3 \text{ mmol} \left(\frac{1 \text{ mol}}{1000 \text{ mmol}} \right) \left(\frac{40.08 \text{ g}}{\text{mol}} \right) \left(\frac{1000 \text{ mg}}{\text{g}} \right) \left(\frac{1}{10 \text{ dL}} \right) = 9.2 \text{ mg/dL}$$

The ratio method gives the same result:

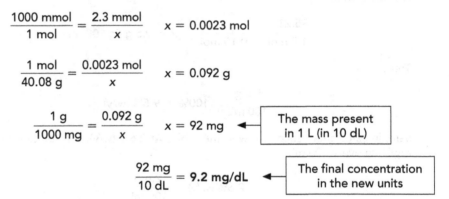

$$\frac{1000 \text{ mmol}}{1 \text{ mol}} = \frac{2.3 \text{ mmol}}{x} \qquad x = 0.0023 \text{ mol}$$

$$\frac{1 \text{ mol}}{40.08 \text{ g}} = \frac{0.0023 \text{ mol}}{x} \qquad x = 0.092 \text{ g}$$

$$\frac{1 \text{ g}}{1000 \text{ mg}} = \frac{0.092 \text{ g}}{x} \qquad x = 92 \text{ mg} \quad \longleftarrow \boxed{\begin{array}{c} \text{The mass present} \\ \text{in 1 L (in 10 dL)} \end{array}}$$

$$\frac{92 \text{ mg}}{10 \text{ dL}} = 9.2 \text{ mg/dL} \quad \longleftarrow \boxed{\begin{array}{c} \text{The final concentration} \\ \text{in the new units} \end{array}}$$

A result of 4.8 mEq/L is also within range. Remember that because 1 mole of Ca^{2+} can theoretically replace 2 hydrogen ions, it is the same as 2 equivalents:

$$1 \text{ mol } Ca^{2+} = 2 \text{ Eq } Ca^{2+}$$

Likewise, 1 millimole is the same as 2 milliequivalents:

$$1 \text{ mmol } Ca^{2+} = 2 \text{ mEq } Ca^{2+}$$

Therefore, 4.8 mEq/L equals 2.4 mmol/L, which falls in the reference range:

$$4.8 \text{ mEq } Ca^{2+} \left(\frac{1 \text{ mmol } Ca^{2+}}{2 \text{ mEq } Ca^{2+}} \right) = 2.4 \text{ mmol} \quad \text{(the amount in every liter)}$$

By the ratio method:

$$\frac{2 \text{ mEq } Ca^{2+}}{1 \text{ mmol } Ca^{2+}} = \frac{4.8 \text{ mEq } Ca^{2+}}{x} \qquad x = 2.4 \text{ mmol } Ca^{2+} \quad \text{(the amount in every liter)}$$

2. A result of 2.6 mEq/L is not within range. Dimensional analysis converts mEq/L to mg/dL:

$$2.6 \text{ mEq} \left(\frac{0.5 \text{ mmol}}{1 \text{ mEq}} \right) \left(\frac{\text{mol}}{1000 \text{ mmol}} \right) \left(\frac{24.305 \text{ g}}{\text{mol}} \right) \left(\frac{1000 \text{ mg}}{\text{g}} \right) \left(\frac{1}{10 \text{ dL}} \right) = 3.2 \text{ mg/dL}$$

A result of 0.8 mmol/L is within range:

$$0.8 \text{ mmol} \left(\frac{\text{mol}}{1000 \text{ mmol}} \right) \left(\frac{24.305 \text{ g}}{\text{mol}} \right) \left(\frac{1000 \text{ mg}}{\text{g}} \right) \left(\frac{1}{10 \text{ dL}} \right) = 1.9 \text{ mg/dL}$$

3. To go from pH to [H$^+$], rearrange Equation 4 to give

$$10^{-pH} = [H^+]$$

Thus, we can solve the first row of the table using this equation:

$$10^{-3.90} = [H^+]$$

$$1.26 \times 10^{-4} = [H^+]$$

Going from [H$^+$] to pH requires direct substitution into Equation 4. The second row of the table gives

$$pH = -\log(1.91 \times 10^{-6})$$

$$pH = 5.72$$

pH	[H$^+$] (M)
3.90	1.3×10^{-4}
5.72	1.9×10^{-6}
7.05	8.9×10^{-8}
9.640	2.29×10^{-10}
11.38	4.2×10^{-12}
13.060	8.71×10^{-14}

4. To go from pH to [H$^+$] in "mol/L," use the same equations as in problem 3 above. But to convert from mol/L to mmol/L, multiply by 1000; to convert from mmol/L to mol/L, divide by 1000. Thus, the first row of the table gives [H$^+$] = 0.00245 M, which is equal to 2.45 mM.

In the second row, [H$^+$] = 0.0200 mM, which is the same as 2.00×10^5 M. The corresponding pH is 4.70.

pH	[H$^+$] (mM)
2.616	2.42
4.699	0.0200
7.00	1.0×10^{-4}
10.149	7.10×10^{-8}
12.27	5.4×10^{-10}
14.000	1.00×10^{-11}

5. The total mass is 721 g (0.721 kg). A 2.00 *m* solution contains 2 moles (360 g, 0.360 kg) of glucose for every kilogram of water present. Thus,

$$1 \text{ kg water} + 0.360 \text{ kg glucose} = 1.360 \text{ kg of solution}$$

Glucose accounts for 26.5% of the solution's mass:

$$\frac{0.360 \text{ kg of glucose}}{1.360 \text{ kg of solution}} \times 100\% = 26.5\%$$

The total mass of glucose, then, is 26.5% of 2720 g, or 721 g (0.721 kg):

$$0.265 \times 2720 \text{ g} = 721 \text{ g}$$

6.

Analyte	Your Result	Result in Requested Units
creatinine (112.3 g/mol)	6.4 mg/L	57 μM
folic acid (441.6 g/mol)	14 ng/mL	32 nmol/L
phenobarbital (230.8 g/mol)	15 μg/mL	65 μM
lead	4.2 μM	870 μg/L
phosphorus	1.62 mM	50.2 mg/L
iron	22.9 μmol/L	1280 μg/L
glucose	160 mg/dL	8.9 mmol/L
uric acid (168.1 g/mol)	77 mg/L	458 μM

Sample calculation, first row in the table.

$$\left(\frac{6.4 \text{ mg}}{L}\right)\left(\frac{g}{1000 \text{ mg}}\right)\left(\frac{mol}{112.3 \text{ g}}\right)\left(\frac{10^6 \text{ μmol}}{mol}\right) = 57 \text{ μmol/L} = 57 \text{ μM}$$

By the ratio method:

$$\left(\frac{1000 \text{ mg}}{1 \text{ g}}\right) = \left(\frac{6.4 \text{ mg}}{x}\right) \qquad x = 0.0064 \text{ g}$$

$$\left(\frac{112.3 \text{ g}}{1 \text{ mol}}\right) = \left(\frac{0.0064 \text{ g}}{x}\right) \qquad x = 5.7 \times 10^{-5} \text{ mol}$$

$$\left(\frac{1 \text{ mol}}{1 \times 10^6 \text{ μmol}}\right) = \left(\frac{5.7 \times 10^{-5} \text{ mol}}{x}\right) \qquad x = 57 \text{ μmol}$$

$$\frac{57 \text{ μmol}}{1 \text{ L}} = 57 \text{ μmol/L} = 57 \text{ μM}$$

7. Yes. The concentration is 0.62% (w/v).

$$\left(\frac{0.083 \text{ mol}}{L}\right)\left(\frac{74.44 \text{ g}}{mol}\right)\left(\frac{1 \text{ L}}{10 \text{ dL}}\right) = 0.62 \text{ g/dL} = 0.62 \text{ g/100 mL} = 0.62\% \text{ (w/v)}$$

By the ratio method:

$$\left(\frac{1 \text{ mol}}{74.44 \text{ g}}\right) = \left(\frac{0.083 \text{ mol}}{x}\right) \qquad x = 6.2 \text{ g} \quad \text{(in 1 liter, or 1000 mL)}$$

$$\frac{6.2 \text{ g}}{1 \text{ L}} = \frac{6.2 \text{ g}}{1000 \text{ mL}} = 0.0062 \text{ g/mL}$$

$$\left(\frac{0.0062 \text{ g}}{1 \text{ mL}}\right) = \left(\frac{x}{100 \text{ mL}}\right) \qquad x = 0.62 \text{ g/100 mL} = 0.62 \text{ g/dL} = 0.62\% \text{ (w/v)}$$

8. Calculate the factor that converts "mg/dL" to "mmol/L":

$$\left(\frac{1 \text{ mg}}{dL}\right)\left(\frac{g}{1000 \text{ mg}}\right)\left(\frac{mol}{40.08 \text{ g}}\right)\left(\frac{1000 \text{ mmol}}{mol}\right)\left(\frac{10 \text{ dL}}{L}\right) = 0.2495 \text{ mmol/L}$$

Your supervisor is correct.

By the ratio method:

$$\left(\frac{1000 \text{ mg}}{1 \text{ g}}\right) = \left(\frac{1 \text{ mg}}{x}\right) \qquad x = 0.001 \text{ g (in 1 dL)}$$

$$\left(\frac{40.08 \text{ g}}{1 \text{ mol}}\right) = \left(\frac{0.001 \text{ g}}{x}\right) \qquad x = 2.495 \times 10^{-5} \text{ mol (in 1 dL)}$$

$$\left(\frac{1 \text{ mol}}{1000 \text{ mmol}}\right) = \left(\frac{2.495 \times 10^{-5} \text{ mol}}{x}\right) \qquad x = 0.02495 \text{ mmol (in 1 dL, or 0.1 L)}$$

$$\left(\frac{0.02495 \text{ mmol}}{1 \text{ dL}}\right) = \left(\frac{0.02495 \text{ mmol}}{0.1 \text{ L}}\right) = 0.2495 \text{ mmol/L}$$

9. In order to answer this question, the result of 9.2 mmol/L must be converted to "mg/dL."

$$\left(\frac{9.2 \text{ mmol}}{L}\right)\left(\frac{1 \text{ mol}}{1000 \text{ mmol}}\right)\left(\frac{62 \text{ g}}{\text{mol}}\right)\left(\frac{1000 \text{ mg}}{1 \text{ g}}\right)\left(\frac{L}{10 \text{ dL}}\right) = 57 \text{ mg/dL}$$

Because the concentration is greater than 50 mg/dL, the patient is indeed a candidate for hemodialysis.

By the ratio method:

$$\left(\frac{1000 \text{ mmol}}{1 \text{ mol}}\right) = \left(\frac{9.2 \text{ mmol}}{x}\right) \qquad x = 0.0092 \text{ mol (in 1 L)}$$

$$\left(\frac{1 \text{ mol}}{62 \text{ g}}\right) = \left(\frac{0.0092 \text{ mol}}{x}\right) \qquad x = 0.57 \text{ g (in 1 L)}$$

$$\left(\frac{1 \text{ g}}{1000 \text{ mg}}\right) = \left(\frac{0.57 \text{ g}}{x}\right) \qquad x = 570 \text{ mg (in 1 L, or in 10 dL)}$$

$$\left(\frac{570 \text{ mg}}{1 \text{ L}}\right) = \left(\frac{570 \text{ mg}}{10 \text{ dL}}\right) = 57 \text{ mg/dL}$$

10. The answer is 2.8 mL. The target solution will contain 1 equivalent weight in every liter. For sulfuric acid (98.08 g/mol), an equivalent weight is half a mole, or 49.04 g. Thus, 100 mL of the dilute acid contains

$$100 \text{ mL} \left(\frac{L}{1000 \text{ mL}}\right)\left(\frac{49.04 \text{ g}}{L}\right) = 4.90 \text{ g}$$

The volume of concentrated acid that corresponds to this mass of 4.90 g is

$$0.97 \times \left(\frac{1.84 \text{ g}}{\text{mL}}\right) = 1.78 \text{ g}$$

Thus, each mL of the concentrated acid contains 1.78 g of H_2SO_4. The volume needed for dilution, then, is

$$4.90 \text{ g} \times \left(\frac{\text{mL}}{1.78 \text{ g}}\right) = 2.8 \text{ mL}$$

Glossary

Aqueous—of or pertaining to water; being based on, or dissolved in, water.

Concentration—an expression of the relative amounts of solute and solvent present in a solution.

Dissolve—to pass into solution.

Equivalent—one hydrogen ion in the formula of a chemical substance; one mole of positive or negative charges.

Equivalent weight—the amount of a substance that contains, theoretically combines with, or theoretically replaces 1 mole of hydrogen ions.

Immiscible—incapable of being mixed with something else.

Insoluble—incapable of dissolving in a given solvent.

Miscible—capable of being mixed with something else.

Molality—the amount of solute in solution per kilogram of solvent.

Molarity—the number of moles of a substance in 1 liter of solution.

Normality—the number of equivalent weights of a substance in 1 liter of solution.

pH—the negative logarithm of the hydrogen ion concentration; a measure of the acidity/alkalinity of an aqueous solution.

Soluble—capable of dissolving in a given solvent.

Solute—a solution component that is not the one present in the largest amount.

Solution—a homogeneous mixture of two or more substances that do not chemically react with each other.

Solvent—the component of a solution that is present in the largest amount.

Sparingly soluble—soluble in a given solvent, but only to a small degree.

Specific gravity—the ratio of the density of a solution to the density of water at 4°C.

v/v—the number of milliliters of solute in 100 mL of solution, expressed as a percentage.

w/v—the number of grams of solute in 100 mL of solution, expressed as a percentage.

w/w—the number of grams of solute in 100 grams of solution, expressed as a percentage.

Dilutions

Learning Objectives

At the end of this chapter, the student should be able to do the following:

1. Explain the nature, purpose, and strategy of dilution, as well as the general procedure for executing it
2. Use the dilution ratio, factor, and equation; plan a dilution for a target volume or concentration; and correct a raw test result on a diluted sample
3. Distinguish between simple and serial dilution and know when to use one over the other
4. Calculate and use the tube and sample dilutions in planning or interpreting a serial procedure

Key Terms

antibody titer
diluent
dilution factor
dilution ratio

sample dilution
serial dilution
tube dilution

In the clinical laboratory, we often need to carry out dilutions. In clinical chemistry, we most often make dilutions when the concentration of a given analyte is higher than the upper limit of the method we are using and when we prepare solutions for constructing a standard curve. The quality of test results, and therefore the quality of patient care, depends on how well the technologist pipets the solutions and carries out the calculations. In microbiology, we make dilutions in order to prepare liquid cultures for plating on agar, whereas in serology, we need dilutions to determine antibody titers.

SIMPLE DILUTIONS

To begin, consider the following scenario from a clinical laboratory. A physician suspects that a patient in the emergency department took an accidental overdose of carbamazepine, a drug used to prevent epileptic seizures. Life-threatening toxic effects sometimes occur when the plasma concentration of this drug exceeds 15 μg/mL. A technologist in the laboratory runs the test for carbamazepine on a blood sample from this patient, using a method that is reliable for drug concentrations from 2 to 20 μg/mL. The result for this sample, however, is 22 μg/mL, an unreliably high value. Therefore, the technologist must lower the carbamazepine concentration into the acceptable range (2–20 μg/mL) by diluting the sample, running the test again, and then correcting the result for the dilution.

For example, if she[1] mixes 100 μL of the undiluted sample with 100 μL of saline solution (the **diluent**), the total final volume is now 200 μL (Figure 1 ■). The drug is present in twice as much volume as it was before dilution, and its concentration is now one-half of its real value. In other words, the ratio of the initial volume (100 μL) to the final volume (200 μL) is 1:2, the same as the ratio of the final concentration to the initial concentration. Therefore, the **dilution ratio** is 1:2, and the resulting solution is a "1:2 dilution" (pronounced "1-to-2"):

EQUATION 1

$$\text{dilution ratio} = \frac{V_{initial}}{V_{final}} = \frac{C_{final}}{C_{initial}}$$

where V is volume and C is concentration. The technologist could have prepared a 1:2 dilution from any initial volume, provided the final volume satisfied Equation 1. For example, she might have diluted 234 μL of the patient sample to 468 μL with saline solution, or 1.3 mL of the sample to 2.6 mL.

The technologist then runs the same analytical test on the 1:2 dilution of the original sample. The result is 12 μg/mL (Figure 1), a value that is clearly reliable because it falls between 2 and 20. Nevertheless, she must correct this result for the fact that the test was carried out on a 1:2 dilution, in which the drug's concentration is only one-half of its real value. Thus, she multiplies the result by 2, giving a final carbamazepine concentration of 24 μg/mL, which she then reports to the physician. The value of 2 by which the technologist multiplied the result of 12—the **dilution factor**—is simply the reciprocal of the dilution ratio.

However, she might well have chosen to mix 100 μL of the original sample with some other volume of saline solution, say, 300 μL, in which case the total volume would be 400 μL and the resulting dilution would be 1:4. The drug would then be present in four times as much volume as it was before dilution, which decreases its concentration to one-fourth of the real value. Substitution of these volumes into Equation 1 confirms this. The result of the test on a 1:4 dilution of the original sample would be 6, which, when multiplied by the dilution factor of 4, gives 24 μg/mL. This is the same final carbamazepine concentration as the 1:2 dilution yields.

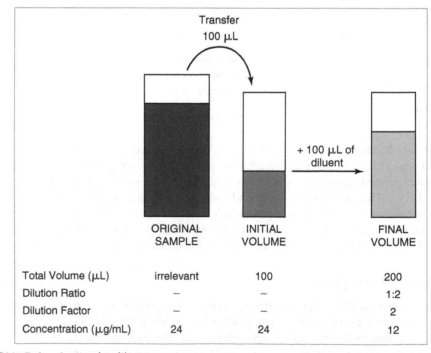

■ FIGURE 1 A simple dilution.

[1]Because English does not have a gender-neutral singular pronoun, this text alternates genders between scenarios.

For this patient, the consequences of a calculation mistake, of a pipetting error, or of simply forgetting to correct for the dilution, could be serious—even fatal. This is true for other analytes as well, underscoring the importance of making dilutions accurately and carrying out calculations correctly.

For the 1:2 dilution, the volume of sample before dilution (its "initial volume") was 100 μL, and the volume after dilution (its "final volume") was 200 μL. Furthermore, the carbamazepine concentration after dilution ("final concentration") was determined to be 12 μg/mL. The concentration before dilution ("initial concentration") was the target value—the result that the technologist calculated and reported to the physician: 24 μg/mL. Thus, the process of dilution increased the volume and decreased the concentration by the same factor of 2. This means, in turn, that the ratio of the final volume to the initial volume equals the ratio of the initial concentration to the final concentration:

$$\frac{V_{final}}{V_{initial}} = \frac{200 \ \mu L}{100 \ \mu L} = \frac{C_{initial}}{C_{final}} = \frac{24 \ \mu g/mL}{12 \ \mu g/mL} = 2$$

 EQUATION 2

It is clear from this equation that, if three of the variables are known, we can calculate the fourth. In this example, the technologist knew V_{final}, $V_{initial}$, and C_{final}, and from these three values she calculated $C_{initial}$, which corresponds to the undiluted sample. Simple algebraic rearrangement of Equation 2 isolates the target variable:

$$\frac{V_{final}C_{final}}{V_{initial}} = C_{initial}$$

EQUATION 3

Substitution into Equation 3 gives

$$\frac{(200 \ \mu L)(12 \ \mu g/mL)}{100 \ \mu L} = 24 \ \mu g/mL$$

We can apply Equation 3 to the 1:4 dilution on the same patient sample, giving the same result:

$$\frac{(400 \ \mu L)(6 \ \mu g/mL)}{100 \ \mu L} = 24 \ \mu g/mL$$

The general mathematical expression of this relationship becomes a useful tool in the laboratory:

$$V_{final}C_{final} = V_{initial}C_{initial}$$

EQUATION 4

For example, consider the use of Equation 4 in the following scenario. Your laboratory uses an analytical instrument for lead (Pb) that requires calibration with four standard solutions of lead at 5, 10, 20, and 50 μg/mL in 5% HNO_3. The manufacturer supplies a stock lead solution of 1000 μg/mL, which must be diluted to those four concentrations.

A technologist in your laboratory prepares the standard solutions by using Equation 4. His task is to determine the volume of stock solution to be diluted to a certain final volume with the diluent (5% HNO_3) in order to achieve the target concentrations. He decides to set the final volume of each standard solution at 50 mL because it is convenient to prepare and because it will provide enough solution to last many weeks. Next, he arranges Equation 4 to isolate the target variable, $V_{initial}$, which represents the volume of stock solution that must be diluted:

$$\frac{V_{final}C_{final}}{C_{initial}} = V_{initial}$$

 EQUATION 5

Thus, for the standard solution of 50 μg/mL,

$$\frac{(50 \ mL)(50 \ \mu g/mL)}{1000 \ \mu g/mL} = 2.5 \ mL$$

The technologist, therefore, will dilute 2.5 mL of the stock solution of lead to a final volume of 50 mL, using 5% HNO_3 as the diluent. The result is 50 mL of a lead solution at a concentration of 50 μg/mL; he can likewise use Equation 5 for each of the other three standard solutions.

1. If we dilute 10 μL of a sample up to 160 μL, what is the dilution ratio? What is the dilution factor?
2. A sample at 200 mM is diluted 1:6. What is the final concentration?
3. We mix 50 μL of a sample with 200 μL of diluent. If the concentration after dilution is 60 mg/dL, what was it before dilution?

    1. Dilution ratio $= V_{initial}/V_{final} = 1{:}16$. Dilution factor $= (\text{dilution ratio})^{-1} = 16$
    2. $C_{final} = C_{initial} \times (V_{initial}/V_{final}) = 200 \text{ mM} \times (1/6) = 33.3 \text{ mM}$
    3. $C_{initial} = C_{final} \times (V_{final}/V_{initial}) = 60 \text{ mg/dL} \times (250 \text{ μL}/50 \text{ μL}) = 300 \text{ mg/dL}$

SERIAL DILUTIONS

The two preceding scenarios, one involving an out-of-range test result and the other a set of standard solutions, show the two most common reasons for carrying out dilutions in the clinical laboratory, as the first paragraph of this chapter states. However, some special cases require dilution in several steps, rather than the single step used above.

Consider, for example, the case in which a procedure calls for a 1:8000 dilution. Performing such a large dilution in one step is impractical to the extent that it requires a vessel big enough to hold the large final volume and because a vessel containing 8 L of an aqueous solution weighs about 20 pounds. Also, if the vessel is glass, the combination of weight and breakability creates unnecessary risk for the technologist.

To avoid this problem, perform **serial dilutions**, a series of small dilutions that ultimately gives the same target ratio of 1:8000. Figure 2 ■ depicts the procedure. In this example, first perform a 1:20 dilution of the original sample, which in this case is at 200 mM; transfer 1 mL of this sample into another tube

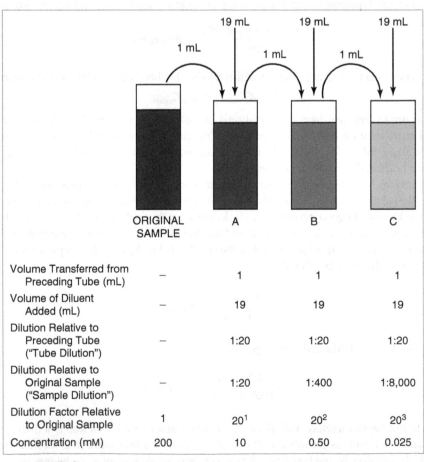

	ORIGINAL SAMPLE	A	B	C
Volume Transferred from Preceding Tube (mL)	–	1	1	1
Volume of Diluent Added (mL)	–	19	19	19
Dilution Relative to Preceding Tube ("Tube Dilution")	–	1:20	1:20	1:20
Dilution Relative to Original Sample ("Sample Dilution")	–	1:20	1:400	1:8,000
Dilution Factor Relative to Original Sample	1	20^1	20^2	20^3
Concentration (mM)	200	10	0.50	0.025

■ **FIGURE 2** A serial dilution.

("**A**") and dilute it to 20 mL. The resulting concentration is 10 mM. Then carry out a 1:20 dilution of solution **A** by transferring 1 mL into another tube ("**B**") and diluting it to 20 mL. The resulting concentration is 0.50 mM. Solution **B** is 20-fold less concentrated than solution **A**, which in turn is 20-fold less concentrated than the original sample. Therefore, solution **B** is 400-fold less concentrated than the original sample.

Lastly, dilute solution **B** 1:20 by transferring 1 mL into another tube ("**C**") and diluting it to 20 mL. Its concentration being only 0.025 mM, solution **C** proves to be a 1:8000 dilution of the original sample.

As Figure 2 shows, each of the solutions **A**, **B**, and **C** is 20 times less concentrated than the preceding solution; that is, the dilution factor of each tube is 20 times higher than that of the preceding tube. The corresponding dilution ratio is the **tube dilution**, which is usually constant from one tube to the next and which is calculated from this equation:

$$D_{tube} = \frac{V_{sample}}{V_{sample} + V_{diluent}}$$

where D_{tube} is the tube dilution, V_{sample} is the sample volume, and $V_{diluent}$ is the diluent volume. However, the dilution ratio of each tube relative to the starting solution is the **sample dilution**, and it reflects how much the original sample has been diluted up to that point in the sequence. In fact, because the tube dilution is the same for all tubes, the sample dilution forms a geometric series, which in this example is $1/20$, $1/400$, $1/8000$, or $1/20^1$, $1/20^2$, $1/20^3$. Thus, we can calculate the sample dilution for a given tube from this equation:

$$D_{sample} = (D_{tube})^N$$

> **EQUATION 6**

where N is the number of the tube in the sequence. For tube **C** in Figure 2, which is the third tube containing a dilution of the original sample, the sample dilution is $(1/20)^3$, or $1/8000$; the concentration of the sample in tube **C** is $1/8000$ of the original.

At this point, be sure to understand the difference between dilution ratio and dilution factor. As Equation 1 shows, the dilution ratio is the ratio of the concentration of a given dilution (the final concentration) to the concentration of the original sample (the initial concentration). In Figure 2, the concentration of solution **B** is $1/400$th the concentration of the original sample, making the dilution ratio 1:400. Therefore, the dilution factor is 400, the reciprocal of the dilution ratio; this is the number by which we multiply the concentration of solution **B** to yield the concentration of the original sample.

Equation 6 allows for the fast calculation of a sample dilution. For example, if there are 10 tubes in the series and if the tube dilution is $1/4$, then the sample dilution in tube #6 is $(1/4)^6$, or $1/4096$. The usefulness of this equation, however, goes even further.

Suppose a technologist is going to test the susceptibility of a bacterial strain to various antibiotics, and she receives from the supervisor a suspension of the bacteria at a concentration of about 6.0×10^7 cells/mL. In order to inoculate agar plates with the bacteria, she needs a suspension of cells at a concentration between 50 and 100 per mL. Therefore, she must achieve a dilution of the original sample between 600,000-fold and 1,200,000-fold, a very large factor that calls for a serial dilution.

Using Equation 6, the technologist sets the value of D_{sample} at $1/600,000$. After choosing a convenient tube dilution—say, 1:10—she calculates the number of tubes in the series necessary to bring the concentration of cells into the target range by substituting into Equation 6:

$$\frac{1}{600,000} = \left(\frac{1}{10}\right)^N$$

Algebraic manipulation of this equation gives

$$\frac{\log\left(\frac{1}{600,000}\right)}{\log\left(\frac{1}{10}\right)} = N$$

$$5.8 = N$$

Because 5.8 is close to 6, this result means that, if the technologist performs six dilutions in a series with a 1:10 tube dilution, the last tube should have a sample dilution in the target range of $1/600,000$ to

1/1,200,000. She confirms this expectation by substituting into Equation 6 the values of 1/10 for D_{tube} and 6 for N, which do indeed give a D_{sample} of 1/1,000,000.

Serology also employs the technique of serial dilution in the semiquantification of antibody titers. An **antibody titer** represents the amount of antibody present in serum against a certain antigen and is defined as the reciprocal of the highest sample dilution ratio at which antibody is detectable. This technique is used to screen patients for exposure to a pathogen or to evaluate a vaccination.

In short, the procedure is to prepare a dilution series with a tube dilution usually of 1:2, giving sample dilutions of 1:2, 1:4, 1:8, 1:16, 1:32, 1:64, 1:128, and so forth. Then antigen is added at a fixed volume to each dilution and the presence or absence of a reaction is noted. If, for example, there is a reaction in every dilution from 1:2 up to and including 1:32, then the antibody titer is said to be "32," which is the reciprocal of the highest dilution ratio at which there is reaction. This means that there was enough antibody in the serum to react visibly with antigen when diluted 32-fold, but there was not enough to react when diluted 64-fold or more.

The titer goes up with the concentration of antibody in the serum because the dilution factor necessary to make the antibody undetectable increases. In other words, a titer of 128 indicates a larger concentration of antibody than does a titer of 16 because rendering the reaction undetectable required an 8-fold higher dilution.

☑ CHECKPOINT 2

1. When is serial dilution preferable to simple dilution?
2. Consider the serial dilution of a sample at 50,000 ng/dL. If the tube dilution is 1:10, what is the concentration in the fourth tube?

    1. Serial dilution is preferred when the final volume required for a simple dilution would be inconveniently large.
    2. $D_{sample} = (D_{tube})^N = (1/10)^4 = 1/10,000$. Thus, the concentration in tube #4 is 5 ng/dL.

Summary

1. Common reasons for making dilutions are (a) to bring back into range a test result that exceeded the upper limit of the analytical method, (b) to prepare standard solutions at various concentrations, (c) to prepare a suspension of cells at a concentration suitable for plating, and (d) to semiquantify antibody titers.

2. In a simple dilution, add together a volume of the liquid sample (e.g., serum, urine, peritoneal fluid) and a volume of liquid *diluent*.

3. The extent of dilution is quantified by the *dilution ratio*:

$$\text{dilution ratio} = \frac{V_{initial}}{V_{final}} = \frac{C_{final}}{C_{initial}}$$

4. Identify a dilution by its ratio. If the ratio is 1/4, the dilution is "1:4" (pronounced "1-to-4").

5. The *dilution factor* is the value by which one multiplies the concentration of a dilution to give the concentration of the original sample. It equals the reciprocal of the dilution ratio.

6. This equation expresses the relationship among the volumes and concentrations before and after dilution:

$$V_{final}C_{final} = V_{initial}C_{initial}$$

7. For dilutions with very large factors—for example, > 1000—it may be more practical to perform serial dilutions than simple dilutions.

8. A serial dilution is a progressive series of dilutions in which each dilution is less concentrated than the preceding one by a constant amount. The *tube dilution* is the dilution ratio from one tube to the next, whereas the *sample dilution* is the dilution ratio of a given tube relative to the original sample.

9. Calculate the tube dilution from this equation:

$$D_{tube} = \frac{V_{sample}}{V_{sample} + V_{diluent}}$$

10. When the tube dilution is constant, the sample dilution forms a geometric series; one calculates it from this equation:

$$D_{sample} = (D_{tube})^N$$

where N is the number of the tube in the sequence.

Practice and Contextual Problems

1. (LO 2) For each of the following dilutions, calculate the dilution factor between the original liquid and the final solution.

   (a) 20 mL of solution Q is diluted to 100 mL.

   (b) 500 µL of solution X is diluted to 2.0 mL.

   (c) 150 µL of serum is added to 300 µL of saline solution, and 20 µL of the resulting solution is added to 180 µL of saline solution.

   (d) 25 mL of liquid W is diluted with solution Z to 75 mL and then to 750 mL with saline solution.

   (e) 0.10 mL of plasma is diluted to 1.0 mL, and the resulting solution is brought to a final volume of 4.0 mL with diluent.

   (f) 50 µL of urine is added to 0.150 mL of water.

   (g) 300 µL of cerebrospinal fluid is added to 2.70 mL of diluent, and 0.50 mL of the resulting solution is added to 2.0 mL of saline solution.

   (h) 5 mL of liquid K is added to 5.0 L of water.

   (i) 10 µL of urine is added to 90 µL of diluent, and the resulting solution is brought to a final volume of 0.50 mL with water.

   (j) 5 µL of whole blood is pipetted into 1.0 mL of diluent.

   (k) 0.040 mL of serum is added to 260 µL of saline solution, and 150 µL of the resulting solution is added to 1.35 mL of saline solution.

   (l) 13 mL of solution M is brought to a final volume of 100 mL with solution N.

   (m) 0.55 mL of plasma is mixed with 0.45 mL of diluent.

   (n) 1.0 mL of saline solution is mixed with 0.50 mL of water.

2. (LO 2) Complete the following table.

	Volume of Serum (µL)	Volume of Diluent (mL)	Dilution Factor
a	20		10
b		0.18	7
c	45	0.090	
d		240	4
e	50		10
f	100	0.400	
g		380	20
h	150		3
i	65	0.455	

3. (LO 1, 2, 4) Nine serum samples (a–i) appear in the table below. Each was diluted serially, into tubes A, B, and C. For each sample, provide the missing information about the serial dilution.

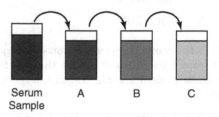

Serum Sample   A   B   C

4. (LO 2, 4) Propose a procedure for carrying out each of the following dilutions.

   (a) In one step, dilute 10 µL of solution 1:50 such that the final volume is 0.50 mL.

   (b) In one step, dilute 20 µL of serum 1:6 such that the final volume is 120 µL.

	Tube A			Tube B			Tube C			
	Volume of Serum (mL)	Volume of Diluent (mL)	Tube Dilution	Volume From Tube A (mL)	Volume of Diluent (mL)	Tube Dilution	Volume From Tube B (mL)	Volume of Diluent (mL)	Tube Dilution	Sample Dilution
a	0.20	1.800		0.20	1.800		0.20	1.800		
b	0.50	4.50		0.10	0.90		0.05	0.100		
c	0.10	0.40		0.05	0.45		0.10	4.90		
d	0.10	4.90		0.10	4.90		0.10	0.30		
e	0.01		1:25	0.01		1:10	0.01		1:3	
f	0.02		1:50	0.02		1:40	0.02		1:3	
g	0.01	0.50		0.01	0.50		0.01	0.10		
h	0.40		1:10	0.02		1:30	0.02			1:9000
i	0.025		1:20	0.025		1:20	0.025			1:12,000

(c) In one step, dilute 15 μL of urine 1:30 such that the final volume is 450 μL.

(d) In a serial dilution of two equivalent steps, achieve a sample dilution of 1:100 starting with 50 μL of solution and ending with a final volume of 0.50 mL.

(e) In a serial dilution of three equivalent steps, achieve a sample dilution of 1:8000 starting with 10 μL of plasma and ending with a final volume of 0.20 mL.

(f) In a serial dilution of two equivalent steps, achieve a sample dilution of 1:25 starting with 1.0 mL of serum and ending with a final volume of 5.0 mL.

(g) In a serial dilution of five equivalent steps, achieve a sample dilution of 1:100,000 starting with 0.20 mL of solution and ending with a final volume of 2.0 mL.

5. (LO 1, 2, 3, 4) If the pipets available to you have variable volumes over the range 20–1000 μL, explain how to prepare the following dilutions of a patient serum that has a total volume of 1.5 mL. So as not to waste diluent, keep the final volume of the dilution no greater than 1.0 mL.

(a) 1:3   (b) 1:20

(c) 1:100   (d) 1:201

6. (LO 1, 2) The method you use for analyte X gives a reliable result from 5 to 50 ng/dL. After the raw first result for a particular patient sample comes out 59, you dilute the sample 1:5.

(a) If the raw second result (for the diluted sample) is 54 ng/dL, the concentration of X in the original sample is greater than what value?

(b) If the raw second result (for the diluted sample) is 6.2 ng/dL, what is the concentration in the original sample?

(c) If you dilute the 1:5 dilution by a factor of 2, and if the raw result for this further dilution is 52 ng/dL, the concentration of X in the original sample must be greater than what value?

(d) If you add 30 μL of the 1:5 dilution to 90 μL of diluent, and if the raw result for this further dilution is 46 ng/dL, what is the concentration in the original sample?

7. (LO 1, 2) A technologist mixes 100 μL of patient sample with 300 μL of diluent and then multiplies the result by 3 in an attempt to correct for the dilution. Explain whether the corrected concentration is accurate, too high, or too low. If inaccurate, by what percentage is it too high or too low?

8. (LO 1, 2) A technologist adds 40 μL of whole blood to 1.0 mL of diluent and then multiplies the result by 25 in an attempt to correct for the dilution. Explain whether the corrected concentration is accurate, too high, or too low. If inaccurate, by what percentage is it too high or too low?

9. (LO 1, 2, 4) A technologist is given a broth culture of bacteria believed to have about 100,000 viable cells per mL. In an attempt to determine this number more accurately, he decides first to carry out four serial dilutions, then to

spread 0.10 mL from each dilution on an agar plate and let it incubate 24 hours, and finally to count the colonies.

He begins by adding 1.0 mL of the culture to tube **1**, which contains 9.0 mL of water; he mixes the resulting suspension well. From tube **1** he then transfers 1.0 mL to tube **2**, which also contains 9.0 mL of water. From tube **2**, in turn, he removes 1.0 mL and adds it to tube **3**, in which there is again 9.0 mL of water. From tube **3**, he transfers 1.0 mL into the 9.0 mL of water in tube **4**. Finally, from tube **4** he withdraws 0.10 mL, spreads it on an agar plate, and counts the bacterial colonies 24 hours later.

(a) If the original culture actually has bacteria at 92,300 cells/mL, what is their concentration in tube **3**?

(b) If tube **4** shows 190 cells/mL, what is their concentration in the original culture?

(c) If the original culture actually has bacteria at 5.2×10^5 cells/mL, which tube would give the technologist about 50 cells in 0.10 mL for spreading on an agar plate?

(d) Suppose the technologist mistakenly dispenses 10.0 mL of water, rather than 9.0 mL, into each of tubes **1–4**. What is the resulting sample dilution in tube **4**?

10. (LO 4) If the tube dilution is 1:3, how many tubes are required in a series to achieve a sample dilution of 1:243?

11. (LO 1, 2) A laboratory uses an automated analyzer for quantifying glucose in serum. The reportable range for the method is 20–600 mg/dL. The analyzer is programmed to dilute automatically any sample whose glucose result lies above that range and then to repeat the test on the diluted sample.

They receive a patient sample from the nephrology unit of the hospital. The analyzer reports the first (undiluted) result to be 1220 mg/dL. Because this lies beyond the method's reportable range, the analyzer automatically dilutes the sample 1:2 and repeats the test. Eight minutes later, the second (diluted) result comes out as 688 mg/dL.

A technologist takes the straight serum sample in hand and transfers 200 μL to another tube, to which he adds 800 μL of the proper diluent. After thoroughly mixing the manually diluted sample, he loads it on the analyzer for glucose quantification. Coming out eight minutes later, the result for the manually diluted sample is 275, which falls within the reportable range of 20–600.

(a) What is the corrected glucose concentration for this sample?

(b) The technologist notices something in the data that leads him to wonder whether the laboratory should extend the reportable range for this particular method beyond 600 mg/dL. Explain.

12. (LO 1, 2) For protein electrophoresis tomorrow, a technologist uses the technique of membrane dialysis to concentrate a urine sample from a patient who may have multiple myeloma. In this dialysis technique, she put the urine in contact with a semipermeable membrane, through which

the water, electrolytes, and small molecules pass from the urine. This gradually causes the volume of the urine to decrease and the protein concentration in the urine to rise. When the volume of the urine has decreased into the proper range, she transfers it to a fresh tube where it will remain until she uses it in the electrophoresis step tomorrow.

In this case, the protein concentration of the straight urine sample, that is, before membrane dialysis, is 86 mg/dL. The electrophoresis method she will use, however, requires the concentration to be 1.5–2.0 g/dL. Therefore, if the starting volume of the urine sample is 9.8 mL, what is the optimal range for the final volume?

13. (LO 1, 2) A laboratory uses a method for total serum protein that has a linearity range of 2.0–12.0 g/dL. After the serum for patient Z gives a result of > 12.0, a technologist dilutes 100 μL of the serum with 200 μL of the proper diluent and then repeats the test. The second result, uncorrected for dilution, is 3.0. After confirming the calculation, he immediately notifies his supervisor that something may be wrong with the instrument. What led him to raise this possibility?

14. (LO 1, 2) N-Telopeptide (NTx) is a product of bone resorption by osteoclasts, a process that normally occurs in balance with bone formation by osteoblasts. Released into the blood during resorption, NTx is specific to the degradation of type I collagen in bone. The quantification of NTx in urine is used in the diagnosis of osteoporosis, which can be caused by various diseases, hereditary conditions, and nutritional deficiencies.

A technologist's laboratory uses company Q's method for quantifying NTx in urine. When a sample's concentration is greater than 3000 nM BCE (bone collagen equivalents), he must dilute it and repeat the assay. The method calls for diluting a sample 1:5 with another urine sample of known BCE concentration that is between 200 and 500 nM.

One of the urine samples (sample A) has a BCE concentration greater than 3000 nM. The following problem refers to this sample.

He dilutes sample A 1:5 with another urine sample (sample B) having a BCE concentration of 331 nM. If the uncorrected concentration of sample A diluted with sample B is 1946 nM BCE, what is the BCE concentration in undiluted sample A?

15. (LO 1, 4) A commercial screening test for syphilis consists of the semiquantitative detection of a substance called "reagin" which is present in the serum of an individual infected with a treponemal pathogen. The technologist

places sample at a different dilution on each of five circles that have been drawn on a white card and then adds reagent to each and, after a few minutes of shaking incubation, inspects for the presence of black clumps (a positive result) against the white background. Clumping is the result of agglutination caused by the presence of reagin in the specimen. Here is the layout of the card:

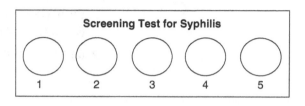

Procedure: Pipet normal saline solution (50 μL) onto each of circles 2–5. Next, place 50 μL of straight sample on each of circles 1 and 2. Then pump the mixture on circle 2 in and out of the pipet tip about 10 times. Of the resulting solution, transfer 50 μL onto circle 3 and repeat the procedure for mixing and diluting through the fifth circle. From the fifth circle, remove and discard 50 μL, equalizing the volumes on all five circles. Then add reagent to each circle, mix well the solution within each circle, and incubate the card for 10 minutes.

(a) Calculate the dilution ratio for each circle on the card.

(b) If the antibody titer in the patient's serum is so high that even the most dilute circle gives a positive result, then carry the dilution further on a new card. First, dilute 100 μL of sample into 1.50 mL of normal saline solution in a test tube. Then, use a pipet to put 50 μL of diluent onto each of circles 2–5. Next, dispense 50 μL of the diluted sample onto each of circles 1 and 2. Then pump the mixture in circle 2 in and out of the pipet tip about 10 times. Of the resulting solution, transfer 50 μL onto circle 3 and repeat the procedure for mixing and diluting through the fifth circle. From the fifth circle, remove and discard 50 μL, equalizing the volumes on all five circles. Then add reagent to each circle, mix the solution within each circle well, and incubate the card for 10 minutes. Calculate the dilution ratio for each circle on the card.

(c) Using only one card, outline an efficient serial dilution protocol that covers the range of 1:4 to 1:1024, with a constant dilution factor from circle to circle. After the serial dilution procedure and before addition of reagent, there should be no more than 75 μL of solution on each circle.

Answer Key

Practice and Contextual Problems

1. (a) 5　(b) 4　(c) 3 (1st), 10 (2nd), 30 (final)　(d) 30　(e) 40　(f) 4
(g) 10 (1st), 5 (2nd), 50 (final)　(h) 1001　(i) 50　(j) 201
(k) 7.5 (1st), 10 (2nd), 75 (final)　(l) 7.7　(m) 1.8　(n) 1.5

2. (a) 0.18　(b) 30　(c) 3　(d) 80　(e) 0.45　(f) 5　(g) 20　(h) 0.30　(i) 8

3.

	Tube A			Tube B			Tube C			
	Volume of Serum (mL)	Volume of Diluent (mL)	Tube Dilution	Volume from Tube A (mL)	Volume of Diluent (mL)	Tube Dilution	Volume from Tube B (mL)	Volume of Diluent (mL)	Tube Dilution	Sample Dilution
a	0.20	1.80	1:10	0.20	1.80	1:10	0.20	1.80	1:10	1:1000
b	0.50	4.50	1:10	0.10	0.90	1:10	0.05	0.100	1:3	1:300
c	0.10	0.40	1:5	0.05	0.45	1:10	0.10	4.90	1:50	1:2500
d	0.10	4.90	1:50	0.10	4.90	1:50	0.10	0.30	1:4	1:10,000
e	0.01	0.24	1:25	0.01	0.09	1:10	0.01	0.02	1:3	1:750
f	0.02	0.98	1:50	0.02	0.78	1:40	0.02	0.04	1:3	1:6000
g	0.01	0.50	1:51	0.01	0.50	1:51	0.01	0.10	1:11	1:28,611
h	0.40	3.60	1:10	0.02	0.58	1:30	0.02	0.58	1:30	1:9000
i	0.025	0.475	1:20	0.025	0.475	1:20	0.025	0.725	1:30	1:12,000

4. (a) Add the 10 μL to 490 μL of diluent.
(b) Add the 20 μL to 100 μL of diluent.
(c) Add the 15 μL to 435 μL of diluent.
(d) In each step, dilute 50 μL with 450 μL of diluent.
(e) In each step, dilute 10 μL with 190 μL of diluent.
(f) In each step, dilute 1.0 mL with diluent up to 5.0 mL.
(g) In each step, dilute 0.20 mL with 1.80 mL of diluent.

5. (a) Choose a convenient initial volume, say, 100 μL. The final volume, then, must be three times greater, or 300 μL. Therefore, mix 200 μL of diluent and 100 μL of sample. Any combination of volumes is acceptable if it meets the restrictions specified above and if the ratio of initial volume to final volume is 1:3.

(b) Because the dilution factor is 20, the initial volume must be 50 μL or less in order to keep the final volume at 1.0 mL or less. Therefore, add 50 μL of patient sample to 950 μL of diluent. Any combination of volumes is acceptable if it meets the restrictions specified above and if the ratio of initial volume to final volume is 1:20.

(c) Because the dilution factor is 100, a simple dilution is impossible. With the available pipets, there is no initial volume that can be diluted 100-fold in one step to a final volume of 1.0 mL or less. Therefore, a serial dilution is necessary. For example, two sequential 1:10 dilutions would succeed, such as adding 50 μL of sample to 450 μL of diluent. A 1:20 followed by a 1:5 would achieve the same goal, first by adding 20 μL of sample to 380 μL of diluent and then by mixing 100 μL of the resulting dilution into 400 μL of diluent. Another option is a 1:25 followed by a 1:4, done by adding 20 μL of specimen to 480 μL of diluent and then transferring 100 μL of the resulting dilution into 300 μL of diluent.

(d) With a dilution factor of 201, a simple dilution is impossible. With the available pipets, there is no initial volume that can be diluted 201-fold in one step to a final volume of 1.0 mL or less. Therefore, a serial dilution is necessary. For example, a 20.1-fold dilution followed by a 10-fold dilution would succeed. To do this, add 20 μL of specimen to 382 μL of diluent for the 20.1-fold dilution. Then, add 20 μL of the first dilution to 180 μL of diluent, giving the 10-fold dilution. Other combinations are possible. For example, execute a 40.2-fold and then a 5-fold dilution by adding 20 μL of specimen to 784 μL of diluent and then transferring 50 μL of the first dilution into 200 μL of diluent.

6. (a) 250 ng/dL. If the raw result for the second run had been 50 ng/dL, the corrected concentration would be 250 ng/dL. But, because the raw result is > 50, the real concentration must be > 250.

(b) 31 ng/dL. Simply multiply the raw result by the dilution factor of 5.

(c) 500 ng/dL. The overall dilution factor is 10 (5 $\times$ 2). If the third raw result had been 50 ng/dL, the corrected concentration would be 500 ng/dL. But, because the result is > 50, the real concentration must be > 500.

(d) 920 ng/dL. The sample dilution is 20-fold (5 $\times$ 4). Because the raw result of 46 ng/dL falls within the range of reliability, simply multiply it by the dilution factor of 20.

7. It is too low by 25%. The technologist should have multiplied the result by 4. Thus, the corrected concentration is only 3/4 of the real value or 1/4 less than it should be.

8. It is too low by 4%. The dilution is actually 26-fold.

9. (a) 92 cells/mL. Use the serial-dilution equation,

$$D_{sample} = (D_{tube})^N$$

where D_{tube} (the tube dilution) = 1:10 (1.0 mL + 9.0 mL) and N (the number of the tube in the sequence) equals 3. The sample dilution for tube **3** is 1/1000; divide the starting concentration (92,300 cells/mL) by 1000.

(b) 1.9 $\times$ 10^6 cells/mL. The sample dilution in tube **4** is 1:10,000. Therefore, multiply the concentration in tube **4** (190 cells/mL) by 10,000.

(c) The target concentration is 50 cells per 0.10 mL, or 500 cells/mL. This represents a sample dilution of about 1000-fold, which corresponds to tube **3**.

(d) The tube dilution in the series changes from 1:10 to 1:11 because 1.0 mL of specimen is added to 10.0 mL, giving a total volume of 11.0 mL. Therefore, the sample dilution (D_{sample}) in tube **4** is 1:14,600.

10. Solve the serial-dilution equation for N.

$$D_{sample} = (D_{tube})^N$$

$$\frac{1}{243} = \left(\frac{1}{3}\right)^N$$

$$\log\left(\frac{1}{243}\right) = N\log\left(\frac{1}{3}\right)$$

$$5 = N$$

Therefore the sample has been diluted 243-fold in the fifth tube.

11. (a) The raw result is "275 mg/dL," but it represents a 1:5 dilution because the technologist diluted 200 μL of the sample with diluent to a total volume of 1000 μL. Therefore, he must multiply the result by 5 to give the corrected concentration for the patient sample: 1375 mg/dL.

(b) The 1:2 dilution gave a raw result of 688 mg/dL, which yields a corrected result of 1376 mg/dL. Because this is effectively the same as the corrected result for the 1:5 dilution (1375 mg/dL), the value of 688 may have been reliable.

12. Rearrange the dilution equation to isolate V_{final}:

$$V_{final}C_{final} = V_{initial}C_{initial}$$

$$V_{final} = \frac{V_{initial}C_{initial}}{C_{final}}$$

Substitute the known values into the equation in order to give the target value, V_{final}:

$$V_{final} = \frac{(9.8 \text{ mL})(86 \text{ mg/dL})}{1500 \text{ mg/dL}} = 0.56 \text{ mL}$$

Thus, the optimal range for the final volume is 0.42–0.56 mL.

13. The result for the straight serum (>12.0) is greater than the result for the 1:3 dilution after correction (9.0). The corrected result should have given a number higher than 12.

14. There are two corrections to make on the raw concentration of 1946 nM BCE.

   1. From the total BCE, subtract the contribution of sample B in the mixture of samples A and B.

   2. Correct the concentration of BCE in diluted sample A for the dilution.

There are several approaches to solving these problems. Two of them follow

APPROACH 1

Consider the fact that the total number of moles of BCE from sample A is the sum of the number of moles from samples A and B:

Total moles BCE in mixture = moles BCE from A + moles BCE from B

To simplify the calculation, assume the mixture of A and B to have a final volume of 1.00 mL (1.00×10^{-3} L). Therefore, 0.20×10^{-3} L of A was diluted with 0.80×10^{-3} L of B. The total number of nanomoles of BCE in the mixture is 1.95 (1.00×10^{-3} L $\times$ 1946 nmol/L), and the number of nanomoles of BCE from sample B is 0.26 (0.80×10^{-3} L $\times$ 331 nmol/L). Substitute these values into the above equation:

1.95 nmol BCE in mixture = nmol BCE from A + 0.26 nmol BCE from B

Therefore,

1.95 nmol BCE in mixture − 0.26 nmol BCE from B = nmol BCE from A

1.69 = nmol BCE from A

What this means is that there are 1.68 nmol of BCE in 0.20×10^{-3} L, giving a concentration of 8400 nM for undiluted sample A.

APPROACH 2

Envision five test tubes, each containing 0.20 mL of sample B. If the contents of all five of the tubes are mixed, the concentration of the mixture is still 331 nM. Now, if a test tube containing 0.20 mL of A is substituted for one of the tubes containing B, then the final mixture is only 80% B; this means that the mixture's BCE concentration coming from sample B is not 331 nM but 80% of 331 nM, or 265 nM. Therefore:

BCE concentration in mixture = conc. coming from A + (80% of conc. coming from B)

1946 nM = conc. coming from A + 265 nM

1946 nM − 265 nM = conc. coming from A

1681 nM = conc. coming from A

Correcting this concentration for the 1:5 dilution gives 8405 nM.

15. (a) Because the sample on circle 1 is straight (undiluted), its dilution is considered 1:1. Here is a summary of the other four serial dilutions.

Circle	Starting Dilution	Dilution Relative to Preceding Circle	Sample Dilution
2	1:1	1:2	1:2
3	1:2	1:2	1:4
4	1:4	1:2	1:8
5	1:8	1:2	1:16

(b) Sample is diluted 1:16 at the start of this procedure (100 μL is added to 1500 μL, for a total volume of 1600 μL); this 1:16 dilution is what goes onto circle 1. Here is a summary of all five dilutions.

Circle	Starting Dilution	Dilution Relative to Preceding Circle	Sample Dilution
1	—	—	1:16
2	1:16	1:2	1:32
3	1:32	1:2	1:64
4	1:64	1:2	1:128
5	1:128	1:2	1:256

(c) Sample is diluted 1:4 at the start of this procedure (e.g., 100 μL + 300 μL of normal saline solution). Then, use a pipet to put 75 μL of diluent onto each of circles 2–5. Next, dispense 75 μL of the diluted sample onto circle 1 and 25 μL onto circle 2. Of the mixture on circle 2, transfer 25 μL to circle 3, and repeat this dilution procedure through the fifth circle. From the fifth circle, remove and discard 25 μL, equalizing the volumes on all five circles. Here is a summary of all five dilutions.

Circle	Starting Dilution	Dilution Relative to Preceding Circle	Sample Dilution
1	—	—	1:4
2	1:4	1:4	1:16
3	1:16	1:4	1:64
4	1:64	1:4	1:256
5	1:256	1:4	1:1024

Glossary

Antibody titer—the amount of antibody present in serum against a certain antigen, defined as the reciprocal of the highest sample dilution ratio at which antibody is detectable.

Diluent—a liquid (solvent or solution) used to dilute a solution.

Dilution factor—the value by which the concentration of a dilution is multiplied to give the concentration of the original solution. It equals the reciprocal of the dilution ratio.

Dilution ratio—the ratio of the initial volume to the final volume; the ratio of the final concentration to the initial concentration.

Sample dilution—in a serial dilution, the dilution ratio of a given tube relative to the original sample.

Serial dilution—a progressive series of dilutions in which each dilution is less concentrated than the preceding one, usually by a constant amount.

Tube dilution—in a serial dilution, the constant dilution ratio from one tube to the next.

An Introduction to Spectroscopy

Chapter Outline

1 INTRODUCTION: THE VIEW FROM ABOVE

In April 1999, NASA launched *Terra*, the first in a series of satellites that are now being used to make detailed studies of the life forms, land, oceans, and atmosphere of Earth. *Terra* is the size of a small school bus and contains several instruments for examining the radiation that is reflected by or absorbed by Earth. These instruments can then be used to obtain images of Earth (see Figure 1) and provide detailed information on its chemical and physical composition.[1,2]

The use of *Terra* and other satellites to provide such information is known as *remote sensing*. Remote sensing can be defined as the use of an analytical instrument to examine a distant sample, as occurs when a satellite records an image using light that is being reflected from the surface of Earth. In the case of *Terra*, there are five sets of sensors that are designed to measure different types of light. This information is used by scientists to learn about the distribution of plant life on Earth and the effects of climate change on the atmosphere, land, and sea.[3,4]

Remote sensing often involves measurements of light because light can interact in many ways with matter and can quickly travel across great distances. Many laboratory instruments also utilize light for chemical or physical measurements. The use of light to obtain information on the chemical or physical properties of a sample is a technique known as *spectroscopy*. In this chapter we will learn about the basic principles of spectroscopy and see how this method can be used in chemical analysis.

1A What Is Spectroscopy?

The term **spectroscopy** refers to the field of science that deals with the measurement and interpretation of light that is absorbed or emitted by a sample.[5] This type of analysis often involves the use of a **spectrum** (plural form, "spectra"), which is the pattern that is observed when light is separated into its various colors, or spectral bands.[5,6] Examples of some spectra are shown in Figure 2, which shows light that is emitted by the sun and the intensity of this light after it has passed through the atmosphere and interacted with the chemicals in air. Table 1 shows that there are various types of instruments and equipment used to collect such a spectrum. In this text we focus on the general type of instrument known as a **spectrometer**, which is designed to electronically measure the amount of light that occurs in a spectrum at a particular spectral band or group of bands.[5,6]

The x-axis of a spectrum indicates the type of light that is being measured or observed. For instance, in Figure 2 this axis distinguishes between the different types of light by using their "wavelengths," a term we will discuss in Section 2A. The y-axis of a spectrum shows the amount of light that is emitted by a particular source (such as the sun) or that interacts with a sample (Earth's atmosphere). A spectrum can provide both qualitative information on the chemical composition of a

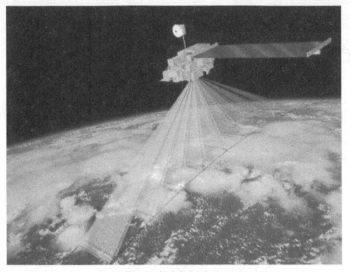

Terra (EOS AM-1)

FIGURE 1 An artist's view of the satellite *Terra* (officially known as EOS AM-1) and the use of the Multiangle Imaging SpectroRadiometer (MISR) instrument that is aboard this satellite. *Terra* is the flagship satellite of the Earth Observing System and is located in a 100 minute polar orbit at a height of 437 miles above Earth. Each day this satellite collects about 200,000 megabytes of information on our planet. (This image is reproduced with permission from NASA's Jet Propulsion Laboratory and is by S. Suzuki and E.M. De Jong.)

source or sample through the types of light that are detected and quantitative information on this composition based on the amount of light that is detected.

EXERCISE 1	Using a Spectrum to Learn About a Sample

According to Figure 2, what wavelengths of light have the most intense emission when given off by the sun? Which wavelengths of light are taken up by (or "absorbed") to the greatest extent by Earth's atmosphere?

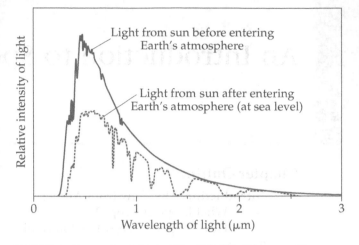

FIGURE 2 Spectra for light that is emitted by the sun and for sunlight that has passed through the atmosphere of Earth. The values on the upper graph with a solid line are related to the power or intensity of this light. The values on the lower graph with the dashed line show the percent of light that is transmitted at each wavelength. (These data are based on information in the American Society of Testing Materials Terrestrial Reference Spectra.)

SOLUTION

The upper graph in Figure 2 shows that the most intense emission of light from the sun occurs in the range of 0.5 μm (or 500 nm). From the lower graph we learn that at sea level there is an approximately equal intensity of light with wavelengths of 500 to 650 nm. (*Note*: These wavelengths are what give the sun its yellow color.) There is a decrease in intensity at several specific wavelengths after light from the sun has passed through the atmosphere. This decrease is a result of the uptake of light by gases such as water vapor, carbon dioxide, and ozone in the air and can be used to measure these chemicals in the atmosphere. The use of remote sensing to examine Earth's surface can be performed by selecting other wavelengths of light that can pass through the atmosphere, allowing this light to interact with this surface.

TABLE 1 General Types of Instruments Used to Perform Spectroscopy

Type of Instrument	Description[a]
Spectrometer	An instrument with an entrance slit and one or more exit slits, which makes measurements either by scanning a spectrum (point by point) or by simultaneous monitoring several positions in a spectrum; the quantity that is measured is a function of radiant power
Spectrophotometer	A spectrometer with associated equipment that is designed to furnish the ratio (or a function of the ratio) of the radiant power of two beams of light as a function of position in a spectrum
Spectrograph	An instrument with one slit and a wavelength selector that uses photography to obtain a simultaneous record of a spectrum
Spectroscope	An instrument with one slit and a wavelength selector, which forms a spectrum for visual inspection

[a]These definitions were adapted from "Guide for Use of Terms in Reporting Data: Spectroscopy Nomenclature," *Analytical Chemistry*, 62 (1990) 91–92; and from G. Maludzinska, Ed., *Dictionary of Analytical Chemistry*, Elsevier, Amsterdam, the Netherlands, 1990.

1B How Is Spectroscopy Used in Analytical Chemistry?

Spectroscopy is one of the most commonly used analytical tools for both qualitative and quantitative chemical analysis. One way spectroscopic methods can be classified is according to how these techniques are employed. For instance, the use of spectroscopy to identify a sample or measure chemicals in a sample is called *spectrochemical analysis*, while the use of spectroscopy to measure a spectrum is known as *spectrometry*.[5,6] Spectroscopic methods can also be subdivided according to the type of analytes they are examining or the types of light that they employ. As an example, the use of these methods to study analytes that are molecules is known as "molecular spectroscopy", and the study of atoms or elements by these methods is known as "atomic spectroscopy".

Probably the most common way of classifying spectroscopic techniques is according to the type of radiation they employ and the way in which this radiation interacts with matter. Many examples of this type of classification scheme are given in Table 2. These methods not only include those that use ultraviolet or visible light, but also methods that make use of infrared light, X rays, radio waves, and microwaves, among other types of interactions.

The types of interactions that can occur with matter and this radiation vary from low energy changes involving a change in spin state (as used in nuclear magnetic resonance [NMR] spectroscopy) to electronic transitions (ultraviolet/visible-absorption spectroscopy) and transitions in core shell electrons (X-ray fluorescence). We will discuss the principles and applications for many of these methods in the next two chapters.

Spectroscopy can be used alone for chemical analysis or it can be used in combination with other analytical methods. In this situation, the change in "color" (or the visually observed spectrum) for the indicator is used to help us determine when the end point has been reached in the titration. It is also sometimes possible during a titration to determine the end point by observing the change in color and spectrum for the analyte or titrant as they combine to form a product. Another way spectrometers are often used is as detectors for other analytical methods.

Color has been used since ancient times as a means for evaluating dyes and other commercial products, but the use of spectroscopy for chemical analysis is a more recent development. The area of spectroscopy began in 1672 when Sir Isaac Newton used a prism to separate a beam of white sunlight into such colors as red, orange, yellow, green, and blue (see Figure 3).[7,8] This ability made it possible for others to learn that the type of light that is emitted by a material is related to the sample's chemical composition. For example, in 1752 a Scotsman named Thomas Melville noticed that the addition of sea salt to a sample of alcohol produced a yellow color in a flame (an effect that we now know is due to the presence of sodium in sodium chloride).[8] In 1826, another Scotsman, William Henry Talbot, found that changing the types of salt that were added to samples created different colors in a flame.[7,8] These were the first examples of spectroscopy being used for chemical analysis. Modern chemists use spectroscopy for examining a large variety of materials and to obtain a wealth of information on the chemical composition of these materials.

2 THE PROPERTIES OF LIGHT

To understand spectroscopy, it is necessary to first learn about the properties of light and of how light interacts with matter. These properties and interactions can be

TABLE 2 Common Types of Spectroscopic Methods

Method[a]	Type of Radiation Employed[b]	Process Examined
NMR spectroscopy	Radio waves (λ = 100 cm to 10 m)	Change in nuclear spin
ESR spectroscopy	Radio waves (λ = 1 cm to 100 cm)	Change in electron spin
Microwave spectroscopy	Microwaves (λ = 100 μm to 1 cm)	Change in chemical rotation
Infrared spectroscopy	Infrared light (λ = 1 μm to 100 μm)	Change in chemical vibration
UV-visible spectroscopy	Ultraviolet and visible light (λ = 10 nm to 1 μm)	Change in electron distribution (outer-shell electrons)
X-ray spectroscopy	X rays (λ = 100 pm to 10 nm)	Change in electron distribution (inner-shell electrons)
Gamma ray spectroscopy	Gamma rays (λ = 10 nm to 1 μm)	Change in nuclear configuration

[a]*Abbreviations:* NMR, nuclear magnetic resonance; ESR, electron spin resonance; UV-visible, ultraviolet-visible.

[b]The wavelength regions given for each method and type of process are approximate and are based on values provided in C.N. Banwell, *Fundamentals of Molecular Spectroscopy*, 3rd ed., McGraw-Hill, New York, 1983, p. 7.

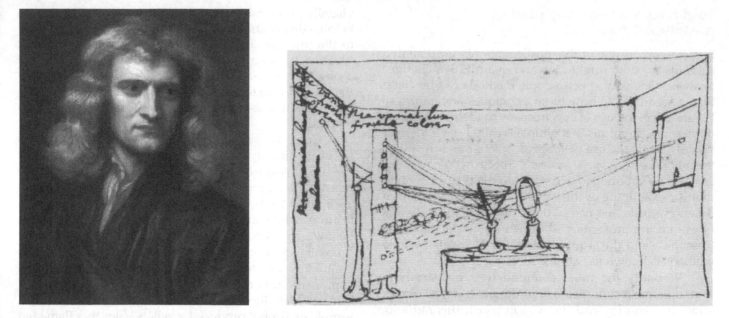

FIGURE 3 Sir Isaac Newton (1642–1727), and a sketch made by Newton in his notebook of an experiment in which he used a glass prism to separate a beam of sunlight into several distinct colors. In this experiment Newton first had the sunlight pass through a small slit in a window shutter, as shown on the right-hand side of the sketch. This beam of light was then passed through a lens and shown onto a prism, with the prism being used to separate the light into various color bands, which were observed on a screen. Newton also used a second prism (shown to the left of the sketch) to test whether one of the separated color bands (red, in this case) could be separated into further components. Newton called this work his "crucial experiment," or *experimentum crucis*, because he felt it would prove to even his many skeptics that white light was a mixture of many colors. (The image of Newton is from a 1689 painting by Godfrey Kneller.)

used for the design of spectrometers and for chemical analysis.

2A What Is Light?

An answer to the question "What is light?" has been sought by scientists for many centuries. Modern scientists define **light** as *electromagnetic radiation*, which is a wave of energy that propagates through space with both electrical- and magnetic-field components.[5,9–11] However, there are actually two ways in which we can describe light. One of these views looks at light as having the properties of a wave, while the second view considers light to be made up of distinct particles of energy. Together these two views make up what is called the "wave–particle duality" of light. Although it may seem odd at first that we can view light as both a wave and a particle, each of these views is necessary to adequately describe how light behaves and interacts with matter.[9,10,12]

The Wave Nature of Light. The first view of light is that of a wave of energy that moves through space. This wave can travel through a vacuum or in other transmitting media, such as air, water, or glass. Figure 4 provides a diagram of how light is pictured when using the wave model. In this model, a wave of light consists of an oscillating electric field that is perpendicular to an oscillating magnetic field. Like any other wave, these oscillating fields produce regular regions of high or

maximum intensity (called "crests") and regions of low or minimum intensity ("troughs"). The intensity of this wave, as measured by the height of the crests, is called the *amplitude*.[11] The idea that light acts as a wave was first suggested in 1678 by Christian Huygens, a Dutch mathematician and physicist. Our current mathematical description of light as electromagnetic radiation is the result of work by Scottish physicist James Maxwell in the middle of the nineteenth century.[9,10]

There are several properties that we can use to describe light as a wave. First, there is the velocity at which the light is traveling. Light has its fastest rate of travel in a true vacuum. This velocity is a physical constant represented by the symbol c, which in the SI system is equal to exactly 299,792,458 m/s. The velocity of light in a medium other than a vacuum is represented by the symbol "v." The ratio of these two velocities gives a parameter known as the **refractive index (n)**, also called the "index of refraction."[11]

$$\text{Definition of refractive index: } n = c/v \qquad (1)$$

Table 3 gives the refractive index of various common materials. Because the velocity of light through a medium other than a vacuum will be less than or equal to c, the result will be a refractive index for that medium that is greater than or equal to 1.000. (*Note*: Air has a typical refractive index of 1.0003, which allows us to use a rounded value of 3.00×10^8 m/s to describe the velocity of light in either a true vacuum or air.) The value of n does

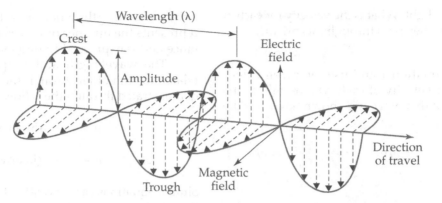

FIGURE 4 The wave model of light. In this model, light is viewed as being an oscillating wave with an electrical-field component (shown in this figure as moving from top to bottom) and a perpendicular magnetic-field component (shown here moving from left to right). The crest represents the maximum point of each wave, and the trough is the point at which the wave reaches its minimum. The height of the wave's crest is represented by the amplitude, and the distance between one crest and the next is known as the wavelength.

not have any units, but it does depend on the type of light that is being used for the measurement. The refractive index is highly characteristic of a material and will depend on the chemical concentration and composition of a sample. These properties make the refractive index useful in both chemical measurement and identification.

EXERCISE 2 **Relating the Velocity of Light to the Refractive Index**

Sir Isaac Newton separated sunlight into various colors by using a glass prism. The material used in one type of glass prism has a refractive index of approximately 1.61 for red

TABLE 3 **Values of the Refractive Index for Various Common Materials**

Type of Material or Medium		Refractive Index (n)[a]
Reference state	True vacuum	1.00000 (exact value)
Gases	Air	1.0003 (25°C, 1 atm)
	Helium	1.000036 (0°C, 1 atm)
	Carbon dioxide	1.00045 (0°C, 1 atm)
	Oxygen	1.00027 (0°C, 1 atm)
Liquids	Ethanol	1.36
	Water	1.333 (20°C)
	Sugar Solution (30%)	1.38
	Sugar Solution (80%)	1.49
Solids	Crown glass	1.52
	Diamond	2.417
	Glass	1.575 (light flint) – 1.89 (heaviest flint)
	Ice	1.309
	Polystyrene	1.55
	Quartz (fused)	1.46
	Ruby/sapphire	1.77
	Sodium chloride (salt)	1.544 (type 1) – 1.644 (type 2)
	Cellulose acetate (hard)	1.53

[a]These values for n were all determined using light from the sodium D line at 589 nm. The information in this table was obtained from D.R. Lide, Editor, *CRC Handbook of Chemistry and Physics*, 83rd ed., CRC Press, Boca Raton, FL, 2002.

light and 1.65 for blue light. What is the velocity for each of these types of light as they pass through this prism?

SOLUTION

We can rearrange Equation 1 and use the given values for n to solve for the velocity of each type of light in the prism. An example of this process is shown below for the red light.

Solving for v: $\qquad n = c/v \qquad \Rightarrow \qquad v = c/n$

Red light:

$$v = (3.00 \times 10^8 \text{ m/s})/(1.61) = \mathbf{1.86 \times 10^8 \text{ m/s}}$$

Blue light:

$$v = (3.00 \times 10^8 \text{ m/s})/(1.65) = \mathbf{1.82 \times 10^8 \text{ m/s}}$$

As this example indicates, the refractive index of a material (and the corresponding velocity of light in that material) will depend on the type of light that we are examining. It is this difference that allowed Sir Isaac Newton to use a glass prism for separating (or "dispersing") sunlight into red, blue, and other bands of color. The same effect is used in many modern analytical instruments to obtain a spectrum and to perform a chemical analysis using specific types of light.

A second property of light as a wave is the **frequency**, which is the number of waves (or "cycles") that occur in a specified amount of time.[6,11,13] The frequency of light is represented by the symbol ν (the Greek letter *nu*) and is given in units of cycles per second or hertz (Hz), where 1 Hz = 1/s. This frequency is a characteristic property of the light and is independent of its rate of travel or the medium in which the light is traveling. We will see later in this section that the frequency of light is *directly* related to its energy, where high-frequency light has a higher energy than low-frequency light.

A third and related property of light as a wave is the **wavelength**, which is the distance between any two neighboring crests in a wave.[6,11,13] The wavelength of light is represented by the symbol λ (the Greek letter *lambda*). Wavelength is measured in units of distance, such as meters, nanometers (nm), or micrometers (μm). Some older texts and resources also use the angstrom (Å) as a unit of distance to describe wavelengths, where 10 Å = 1 nm. The wavelength of light is *inversely* related to its energy, which means that light with a long wavelength will have lower energy than light that has a short wavelength. A closely related term that is directly proportional to energy is the *wave number* ($\bar{\nu}$, called "*nu* bar").[6,9] The wavenumber for any type of light is equal to the reciprocal of

light's wavelength, where $\bar{\nu} = 1/\lambda$. The wave number represents the number of waves that occur per unit distance and is expressed in units such as cm^{-1}.

The wavelength and frequency of light can be related to each other through the velocity of the light, as demonstrated through the following relationships.

$$\nu = c/\lambda \quad \text{(in a vacuum)}$$

$$\text{or} \qquad \nu = v/\lambda \quad \text{(in any medium)} \tag{2}$$

Similar equations can be written to relate the frequency of light to the wave number.

$$\nu = c\bar{\nu} \quad \text{(in a vacuum)}$$

$$\text{or} \qquad \nu = v\bar{\nu} \quad \text{(in any medium)} \tag{3}$$

These expressions can be used to find the wavelength or wave number of light that has a given frequency, or they can be used to find the frequency of light that has a known wavelength or wave number. The next exercise illustrates this process.

EXERCISE 3	Calculating the Wavelength and Frequency of Light

The most intense wavelength of light that reaches Earth from the sun has a wavelength of around 500 nm (see Figure 2). What is the frequency of this light in space? What is the wave number for this light?

SOLUTION

The velocity for this light in the vacuum of space will be equal to c. This information can be used with Equations 2 and 3 to find the frequency and wave number for light with a wavelength of 500 nm.

Conversion to Frequency:

$$\nu = c/\lambda$$

$$= [(3.00 \times 10^8 \text{ m/s})(1 \text{ s/Hz})]/[(500 \text{ nm})(10^{-9} \text{ m/1 nm})]$$

$$\therefore \nu = \mathbf{6.00 \times 10^{14} \text{ Hz}}$$

Conversion to Wave numbers:

$$\bar{\nu} = 1/\lambda$$

$$= 1/[(500 \text{ nm})(10^{-9} \text{ m/1 nm})(10^2 \text{ cm/1 m})]$$

$$\therefore \bar{\nu} = \mathbf{2.00 \times 10^4 \text{ cm}^{-1}}$$

It is interesting to note that if we had performed these same calculations for the light as it traveled through a glass prism, this light would have had the same frequency ($\nu = 6.00 \times 10^{14} \text{ s}^{-1}$), but the wave number and wavelength would have changed as the velocity of the light decreased. The wave number and wavelength would then return to their original values once the light had exited the prism and entered the surrounding air, which has a refractive index close to 1.000.

Figure 2 shows that sunlight is composed of light with many different wavelengths. Some of these wavelengths occur in a range that can be seen by the eye (the "visible range"), while others are above or below this range. Figure 5 shows the full range of electromagnetic radiation. Humans can see light with wavelengths that span from about 380 nm (violet light) to 780 nm (red light). There is, however, a *much* broader range of electromagnetic radiation that extends to both higher and lower wavelengths. Radiation with smaller wavelengths (and higher energies) than visible light include ultraviolet light, X rays, and gamma rays. Radiation with longer wavelengths (and lower energies) than visible light include infrared light, microwaves, and radio waves.[12,13] All of these wavelengths can be used in analytical chemistry but provide information on different chemical properties or types of matter (for instance, see Box 1).

The Particle Nature of Light.   A very different view of light from the wave model was first suggested by Sir Isaac Newton. Newton proposed that light was composed of small particles that moved at great speed.[7,8] Among the evidence for this "particle theory" of light

was work performed in 1905 by Albert Einstein, who found that electrons were ejected when "particles" of light hit the surface of certain materials (a phenomenon known as the *photoelectric effect*).[11,21] The term **photon** is now used to describe these individual particles of light.[11]

The energy of a single photon of light (E_{Photon}) can be related to its frequency (v, a wave property) by using *Planck's equation*.[11]

$$E_{Photon} = hv \qquad (4)$$

This equation is named after its discoverer, the German physicist Max Planck.[22] In this equation, the values of E_{Photon} and v are related to each other through a proportionality term known as *Planck's constant* (h). This constant has a value of approximately 6.626×10^{-34} J·s regardless of the type of light or photons that are being examined.[11]

Planck's equation is useful in determining the energy of a photon from its frequency or the frequency of light from its energy. In addition, this equation is the source of the symbol "hv" that is often used by scientists as an abbreviation for light. Equation 4 can also be combined with the expressions in Equations 2 and 3 to relate the energy of a photon to the wavelength and wave number of this light.

Relationships for a True Vacuum:

$$E_{Photon} = hc/\lambda \qquad (5)$$

$$E_{Photon} = hc\bar{v} \qquad (6)$$

Type of light	Wavelength range		Type of light	Wavelength range
Gamma rays	<0.1 nm		Violet	380–420 nm
			Blue-violet	420–440 nm
X rays	0.01 nm–10 nm		Blue	440–470 nm
Ultraviolet light	10 nm–380 nm		Green-blue	470–500 nm
			Green	500–520 nm
Visible light	380 nm–780 nm **Visible light**		Yellow-green	520–550 nm
			Yellow	550–580 nm
Infrared light	780 nm–0.3 mm		Orange	580–620 nm
Microwaves	0.3 mm–1 m		Red-orange	620–680 nm
Radio waves	>1 m		Red	680–780 nm

FIGURE 5   Various types of electromagnetic radiation, or "light." The approximate wavelengths are shown for each type of electromagnetic radiation, with the scale on the right showing an enlarged view of the wavelengths that make up visible light. (The wavelength ranges used in this figure are based primarily on those given in "Guide for Use of Terms in Reporting Data in Analytical Chemistry: Spectroscopy Nomenclature," *Analytical Chemistry*, 62 (1990) 91–92; the approximate ranges given for the colors of visible light vary slightly from one source to the next in the literature. A colored version of this figure, depicting the visible range of light, can be found in the center of this text.)

BOX 1
NMR: Tuning into Chemical Structure

Nuclear magnetic resonance spectroscopy (commonly known as "NMR spectroscopy") is a spectroscopic method that is valuable for determining the structure of molecules.[14,15] NMR makes use of the fact that the nuclei of some atoms possess a "spin." (*Note:* This is similar to the spin that is present for electrons.) The spin states for a given type of nucleus are of equal energy in the absence of a magnetic field, but differ by a small amount when the nuclei are placed in a magnetic field. This difference occurs in the range of energies that corresponds to electromagnetic radiation in the radio frequency (RF) range. The energy required for this transition is determined by the type of nuclei that are being examined and their local environments, including how an atom containing each nucleus is connected to other atoms. This feature results in an NMR spectrum in which a plot of the intensity of absorbed radiation versus the frequency of this radiation can be used to identify molecules and determine their structures (see Figure 6).

The practical use of NMR spectroscopy for chemical analysis was first reported in 1946 by American scientists Felix Bloch and Edward Purcell,[16,17] who were awarded the 1952 Nobel Prize in Physics for this work. The Nobel Prize in Chemistry was later awarded in 1991 to Swiss chemist Richard Ernst, who introduced the method of "Fourier transform NMR," and in 2002 to Swiss chemist Kurt Wüthrich for the use of NMR spectroscopy in three-dimensional studies of biological macromolecules such as proteins.[18] Modern NMR spectroscopy is now used in many fields, including organic chemistry, inorganic chemistry, analytical chemistry, and biochemistry. NMR spectroscopy is also commonly used for medical imaging under the name "magnetic resonance imaging" (MRI).[19,20]

A typical NMR spectrum is given in Figure 6, using a solution of ethanol dissolved in D_2O as an example. This spectrum shows the response measured for ^1H, which is found in most organic compounds and makes up 99.985% of all hydrogen in nature. The position of the peaks in this spectrum reflect the natural resonance frequency of the ^1H nucleus, as well the local environments of the ^1H nuclei in ethanol, which causes small differences in the locations of these peaks. This effect, known as "chemical shift," is why there are three groups of peaks in ethanol's ^1H NMR spectrum. These groups have relative areas of 1:2:3 and represent the -OH, $-CH_2-$, and $-CH_3$ portions of ethanol. It is possible from the splitting pattern in each group of peaks to determine how many ^1H atoms are on the neighboring carbon atoms in ethanol. The difference in energies between the individual peaks in each splitting pattern can be used to help determine which of the detected ^1H atoms are present on neighboring atoms. This information makes it possible to identify a molecule or determine its structure. A similar approach can be used with measurements based on the ^{13}C isotope of carbon (which makes up 1.11% of carbon in nature) or a combination of measurements looking at ^1H and ^{13}C (a method known as "2D NMR spectroscopy"), as well as methods using other isotopes (e.g., ^{15}N, ^{19}F, or ^{13}P). Although Figure 6 shows only a simple application of NMR spectroscopy, the same basic approach can be employed to study much more complex organic molecules and even large biological molecules such as proteins.[14,15]

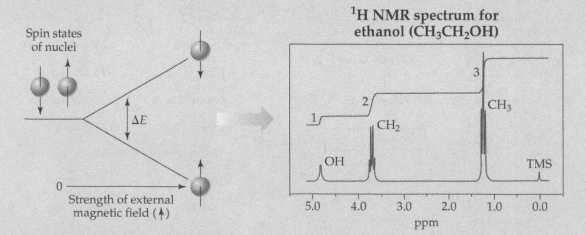

FIGURE 6 The effect of an external magnetic field on the difference in energy (ΔE) between the two spin states for a given type of nuclei, and an example of a typical ^1H NMR spectrum, using ethanol as an example. The positions of the peaks for the ^1H nuclei in the various portions of ethanol are shown in this spectrum along with the signal for the ^1H nuclei in trimethylsilane (TMS), which was added to the sample as a reference. The upper tracing in the ^1H NMR spectrum shows the results obtained when the detected peaks are integrated and represent the relative number of equivalent ^1H nuclei that are present at each of the indicated positions in ethanol.

Similar expressions can be written for other types of media by using the velocity v in place of c in Equations 5 and 6. The result is a series of relationships that we can use to easily convert between the energy of light and the properties such as its wavelength and frequency.

EXERCISE 4   Using Planck's Equation

  a. What is the energy of a photon that has a wavelength of 500 nm, if $n = 1.00$?
  b. What is the energy contained in one mole of photons with this wavelength?

SOLUTION

(a) We are told $n = 1.00$, which means the velocity of this light is approximately equal to c. We can then use the given wavelength of this light and Equation 5 to solve for E_{Photon}.

$$E_{Photon} = hc/\lambda$$

$$= \frac{(6.626 \times 10^{-34} \text{ J} \cdot \text{s})(3.00 \times 10^8 \text{ m/s})}{(500 \text{ nm})(10^{-9} \text{ m/nm})}$$

$$= \mathbf{3.98 \times 10^{-19} \text{ J}}$$

(b) We can find the energy (E_{Total}) contained in a mole of photons with a wavelength of 500 nm by taking the energy in a single photon and multiplying this value of Avogadro's number.

$$E_{Total} = E_{Photon} N_A$$
$$= (3.98 \times 10^{-19} \text{ J})(6.023 \times 10^{23} \text{ mol}^{-1})$$
$$= \mathbf{2.40 \times 10^5 \text{ J or } 240 \text{ kJ}}$$

The same process can be used to determine the energy contained in any amount of photons. This process is particularly valuable if we wish to examine how light will interact with matter, as will be considered in the next section.

2B Uptake and Release of Light by Matter

There are various ways in which light can interact with matter. One way these interactions can occur is if the light is either released by or taken up by matter. For instance, the *Terra* satellite makes use of light that is released by matter in the sun, with some sensors examining how this radiation is taken up by chemicals in the atmosphere or at Earth's surface (see Figure 7). The same processes are used in other types of chemical analysis to study the composition of samples.

Emission of Light. The release of light by matter is referred to as **emission**.[6] The emission of light occurs when matter such as an atom, ion, or molecule goes from an excited state to a lower-energy state. This process is illustrated in Figure 8. For atoms and other chemical species that emit light from the sun, this excited energy state is created by thermal energy. It is also possible to create an excited state in a chemical by other means, such as through the uptake of light (as occurs in "fluorescence") or through the input of energy from a chemical reaction (which occurs in "chemiluminescence"). When the excited state of this chemical relaxes to a lower energy state, it must release its extra energy. One way this energy can be released is by the chemical giving off a photon of light. The photon that is released will have an energy exactly equal to the difference in energy between the initial excited state of the chemical and its final lower-energy state.

EXERCISE 5   Determining the Energy and Wavelength of Emitted Light

One application of emission in remote sensing is in the detection of forest fires, as shown on the cover of this text. The *Landsat* satellite has a sensor that detects active fires by examining their emission in the wavelength region of 1.55 μm to 1.75 μm.

  a. What type of light (visible, ultraviolet, etc.) is being detected by this sensor?
  b. What are the energies for single photons of light at these wavelengths?

SOLUTION

(a) According to Figure 5, wavelengths of 1.55 μm to 1.75 μm are in the range expected for infrared light. This type of radiation represents some of the "heat" that is being emitted by the forest fire. (b) Equation 5 can be used to find the energy of single photons that have the given wavelengths, if we assume that the velocity of light in air is approximately equal to c.

For 1.55 μm light:

$$E_{Photon} = hc/\lambda$$

$$= \frac{(6.626 \times 10^{-34} \text{ J} \cdot \text{s})(3.00 \times 10^8 \text{ m/s})}{(1.55 \text{ } \mu\text{m})(1 \text{ m}/10^6 \text{ } \mu\text{m})}$$

$$= \mathbf{1.28 \times 10^{-19} \text{ J}}$$

The same approach gives a quantity of energy equal to **1.14×10^{-19} J** for 1.75 μm light. Both these energies are smaller than the result we found for shorter-wavelength light in the previous exercise (2.40×10^5 J at 500 nm, which represents visible light). This is the case because the processes that lead to the emission of visible light involve a larger change in energy than the changes that result in the release of infrared light.

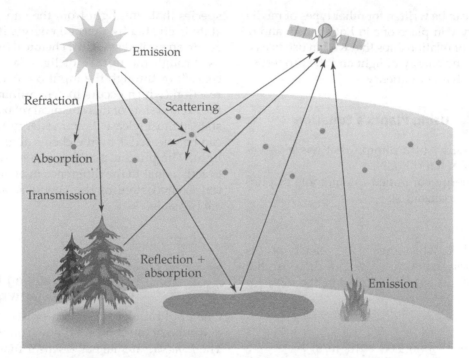

FIGURE 7 Interactions of sunlight with the atmosphere and Earth during remote sensing, including emission, absorption, transmission, reflection, refraction, and scattering. Emission also occurs during remote sensing as radiation is given off by the sun or by sources such as fire on Earth. This example is based on *passive remote sensing*, as performed by *Terra*, in which a satellite only makes use of radiation that originates from the sun or from Earth. It is also possible to perform *active remote sensing*, in which electromagnetic radiation (e.g., radio waves) are sent from the satellite to Earth and recorded once they have returned to the satellite.

A plot of the intensity of light that is emitted by matter at various wavelengths, frequencies, or energies is known as an *emission spectrum*.[6] One example of an emission spectrum was given earlier in Figure 2 for the light that is given off by the sun. We also saw in Exercise 1 that the wavelengths of visible light that are emitted by an object are what give that object a particular color (e.g., the yellow color of the sun). The difference in energy of a chemical as it goes from an excited state to a lower energy state is often a unique value for that chemical. This fact, in turn, means that we can use an emission spectrum and the measured energy, frequency, or wavelength of the emitted light to help us identify a chemical or material (e.g., as used to detect a forest fire). The amount of released light will be directly related to the amount of chemical that emitted this light. As a result, the intensity of this light can be used to determine how much of this chemical is present in a sample if we compare this emission to that obtained with standard samples.

Absorption of Light. A second way in which matter can interact with light is through absorption. **Absorption** can be defined as the transfer of energy from an electromagnetic field (as possessed by light) to a chemical entity (e.g., an atom or molecule).[6] The general process that occurs during light absorption is shown in Figure 9. Unlike emission, we now start with a chemical species that is in a low-energy state and move this species to a

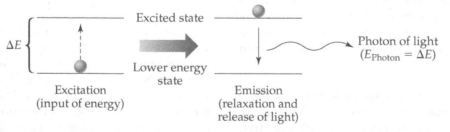

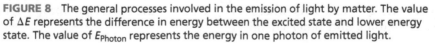

FIGURE 8 The general processes involved in the emission of light by matter. The value of ΔE represents the difference in energy between the excited state and lower energy state. The value of E_{Photon} represents the energy in one photon of emitted light.

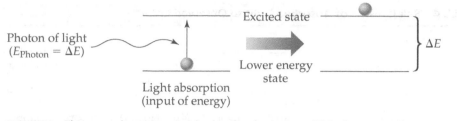

FIGURE 9 The general processes involved in the absorption of light by matter. The value of ΔE represents the difference in energy between the excited state and lower energy state. The value of E_{Photon} represents the energy in one photon of absorbed light.

higher energy state by having the chemical absorb a photon of light. This process again requires that the photon have an energy that is exactly equal to the difference in energy of the chemical in its original low-energy state and its final excited state.

The result of the absorption of light is that the intensity of this light after it leaves the sample will be lower than its original value at the energy or wavelength that was absorbed by the sample. The remaining light that passes through the sample is said to have undergone **transmission**,[5] which can be defined as the passage of electromagnetic radiation through matter with no change in energy taking place. The amount of light that is transmitted by a sample plus the amount that is absorbed by that sample will be equal to the total amount of light that originally entered the sample. A plot of the intensity of light that is absorbed (or transmitted) by a sample at various wavelengths, frequencies, or energies is called an *absorption spectrum*.[5,6] Figure 10 gives an example of this type of spectrum, as based on the uptake of light by chlorophylls *a* and *b* (i.e., the pigments that create the green color in plants and algae and that lead to the absorption of light for photosynthesis).

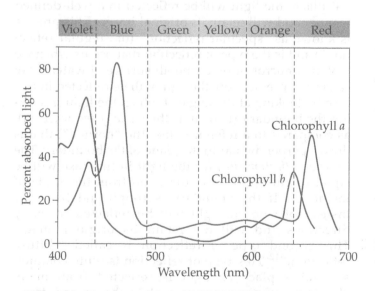

FIGURE 10 The absorption spectra for chlorophyll *a* and chlorophyll *b*. The scale at the top is shown as a reminder of the colors that are associated with various wavelengths of visible light.

| EXERCISE 6 | Using an Absorption Spectrum |

The interactions of light with chlorophyll are used in remote sensing to examine the plant and algae content of the land and sea.

a. What wavelengths of light in Figure 10 are the most strongly absorbed by chlorophyll *a* and *b*? What wavelengths are the most easily transmitted by these pigments?

b. Which wavelengths would you select if you wished to use light absorption to measure the chlorophyll *a* and *b* content of a sample? What types of light (visible, ultraviolet, etc.) would be present at these wavelengths?

SOLUTION

(a) The strongest absorption of light for chlorophyll *a* occurs at approximately 435 nm and 660 nm. The strongest absorption of light for chlorophyll *b* takes place at roughly 460 and 635 nm. Wavelengths between 500 and 600 nm have the greatest degree of transmittance by both chlorophyll *a* and *b*. Small differences in these wavelength ranges are present for these two types of chlorophyll because of their different chemical structures, which create slight differences in their energy levels and in the types of light they can absorb.

(b) If we ignore the effects of other chemicals in the sample, the measurement of chlorophyll *a* and *b* would be best performed by using the wavelengths at which these pigments have their strongest absorption of light (435 nm or 660 nm for chlorophyll *a*, and 460 or 635 nm for chlorophyll *b*, which represent visible light).

If you look closely at Figure 10, you will notice that it is the light that is not absorbed by chlorophyll *a* and *b* between 500 and 600 nm that gives these pigments and plants their green/yellow color. This last effect is quite common in nature, in which the color of an absorbing object is determined by the remaining types of light that are transmitted (or reflected) by the object. For instance, the passage of white light through a blue solution of copper sulfate indicates that blue light is being transmitted while its complementary color (orange, in this case) is being absorbed. Table 4 shows how other

TABLE 4   Relationship of Absorbed Light to Observed Color*

Absorbed light		Transmitted or reflected light and observed color[a]
Violet	(380–420 nm)	Yellow-green
Blue-violet	(420–440 nm)	Yellow
Blue	(440–470 nm)	Orange
Green-blue	(470–500 nm)	Red
Green	(500–520 nm)	Purple
Yellow-green	(520–550 nm)	Violet
Yellow	(550–580 nm)	Blue-violet
Orange	(580–620 nm)	Blue
Red-orange	(620–680 nm)	Blue-green
Red	(680–780 nm)	Green

White light
(all visible wavelengths)

*The listed wavelengths and color ranges are approximate and may vary in other sources.

[a]The color purple is created by a combination of red and violet. The color brown (not shown in this list) requires a combination of at least three colors, such as red, blue and yellow. An observed color of black is produced by the absence of any transmitted or reflected light in the visible range.

colors can be created through the absorption of specific types of visible light by a chemical sample. This information can be useful in estimating the wavelengths of light that are absorbed by an object based on its appearance.

2C Physical Interactions of Light with Matter

Besides being emitted or absorbed, it is possible for light to have other interactions with matter. In many cases, there are physical interactions that do not affect the energy or frequency of the light, but do affect such things as its velocity or direction of travel. These physical interactions are also important to consider in the use of light for chemical measurements. Examples of such interactions are refraction, reflection, some types of scattering, and diffraction.

Reflection.   The process of **reflection** occurs whenever light encounters a boundary between two regions that have different refractive indices, where at least part of the light changes its direction of travel and returns to the medium in which it was originally traveling (see Figure 11).[12] We make use of this process every time we look at a reflection in a mirror. The use of mirrors and reflection is also employed in analytical instruments to help control how light travels within the instrument. Reflection is also used in some types of

spectroscopy to obtain information about a sample. A good example in remote sensing is when the reflection of sunlight is used by satellites to obtain information on the structure and composition of Earth's surface.

There are several types of reflection. If the boundary between two regions that causes the reflection is a flat plane, the light will be reflected in a well-defined manner and will retain its original image. This process is known as "specular reflection" (or "regular reflection") and is the type of reflection that occurs when we look in a mirror or on a smooth surface of water.[12] We can easily predict how the light will be reflected in this case by looking at the angle at which the light is striking the boundary (known as the *angle of incidence, θ_1*), as compared to a reference line (the "normal") that is drawn perpendicular to the plane of the boundary. The *angle of reflection* (θ_{1r}) for the light in this case will be equal to but opposite in direction from the angle of incidence. If the boundary is rough and irregular instead of smooth, light will be reflected in many directions and will not retain its original image. This second type of reflection is called "diffuse reflection."[12] This type of reflection is quite common and takes place as light is reflected from many objects in our environment, such as the ground, trees, and buildings.

The degree to which light will be reflected at a boundary will depend on the relative difference in the

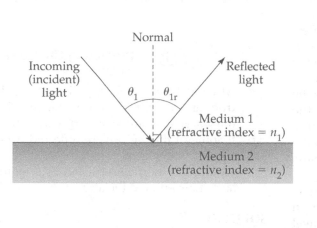

FIGURE 11 The process of reflection. The model on the left shows the expected angle of reflection (θ_{1r}) for light that approaches a planar boundary at an incident angle of θ_1 (versus the normal) and between two media with refractive indices of n_1 and n_2. This image on the right illustrates two types of reflection. Specular or "regular" reflection occurs for light that is reflected from still water, while diffuse reflection (involving an irregular surface) occurs for light that is reflected from the land and trees. Both types of reflection occur during remote sensing. (Photo by B.R. Hage.)

refractive indices for the two sides of the boundary. The larger this difference, the greater the fraction of the light that will be reflected. This idea is illustrated by Equation 7 (the *Fresnel equation*), which gives the fraction of light that will be reflected as it enters the boundary at a right angle. (*Note*: An expanded form of this expression is required for work at other angles.)[12]

$$\frac{P_R}{P_0} = \frac{(n_2 - n_1)^2}{(n_2 + n_1)^2} \tag{7}$$

The symbol P in this equation represents the *radiant power* of the light (in units of watts), which is defined as the energy in a beam of light that strikes a given area per unit time. (*Note*: Although the term "intensity" is often used interchangeably with "radiant power," these two terms do have different units and refer to slightly different aspects of light.)[13] The term P_0 in Equation 7 represents the original or "incident" radiant power of the light, and P_R describes the radiant power of the reflected light, while P_R/P_0 is the fraction of the original light versus the reflected light. For boundaries that have only a small difference in refractive index, such as between the vacuum in space and air, the fraction of reflected light will be small and most of the light will pass through the boundary and into the new medium. If a large difference in refractive index is present, as occurs between air or glass and the silver-coated surface of a mirror, a large fraction of light will be reflected.

EXERCISE 7   Working with Reflection

Some sensors on the *Terra* satellite make use of reflection patterns to map the surface of Earth.

  a. If a beam of light passes through air ($n = 1.0003$) and strikes the smooth surface of water ($n = 1.333$) at a right angle, what fraction of this light will be reflected by the water back into the air?

  b. If this beam of light strikes the water at an angle of 65.0°, what will be the angle of reflection?

SOLUTION

(a) The relative fraction of reflected light in this case can be found by using Equation 7 and the given values for n_2 (the refractive index of water) and n_1 (the refractive index of air).

$$\frac{P_R}{P_0} = \frac{(1.333 - 1.0003)^2}{(1.333 + 1.0003)^2} = \textbf{0.0203} \text{ (or 2.03\% reflection)}$$

(b) If the light is undergoing perfect regular reflection, it will be reflected at an angle of 65.0° on the other side of the normal from the incoming light. If the surface of the water is rough and diffuse reflectance instead occurs, the light will be reflected at many different angles.

Refraction. A second way in which light can be affected by matter is through refraction. **Refraction** is a process in which the direction of travel for a beam of light is changed as it passes *through* a boundary between two media having different refractive indices.[12] We learned earlier that light will have different velocities of travel for two media with different values for the refractive index, n. This change in velocity can also affect the angle at which the light is traveling. This idea is illustrated in Figure 12, which compares the angle of incidence for the incoming light versus the angle of refraction for the light in the new medium. Both of these angles are again being compared to the normal (i.e., a reference line drawn perpendicular to the boundary plane).

If the value of the refractive index for the new medium is larger than that for the original medium in which the light was traveling ($n_2 > n_1$), the angle of travel for the light will be bent toward the normal. Similarly, this angle is bent away from the normal if n_2 is less than n_1. It is easy to predict the size of these angles by using a relationship known as **Snell's law** (also known as "Descartes' law"),[11,12]

Snell's Law: $\quad n_2 \cdot \sin(\theta_2) = n_1 \cdot \sin(\theta_1)$

or $\qquad\qquad \sin(\theta_2) = \dfrac{n_1 \cdot \sin(\theta_1)}{n_2} \qquad (8)$

where n_1 is the refractive index for the medium in which the light is originally traveling, n_2 is the refractive index for the medium that the light is entering, θ_1 is the angle of incidence at which the light approaches the boundary on the side of medium 1, and θ_2 is the angle at which the light is refracted after it has passed through the boundary and entered medium 2. An example of how you can use this equation to examine light refraction is given in the next exercise.

<table>
<tr><td>**EXERCISE 8**</td><td>**Predicting the Refraction of Light**</td></tr>
</table>

a. At what angle would light be refracted if it passed from air ($n = 1.0003$) into water ($n = 1.333$), hitting the water at an angle of 45.0° versus the normal?
b. If some of this light were reflected back to the surface of water at an angle of 45.0°, at what angle would this light be refracted as it exited the water and again entered the air?

SOLUTION

(a) When the light goes from air to water, the value of n_1 in Snell's law will be equal to the refractive index for air and n_2 will be the refractive index for water. We also know that the angle of incidence (θ_1) is 45.0°, which makes it possible for us to solve for the angle of refraction (θ_2).

$$\sin(\theta_2) = \frac{(1.0003 \cdot \sin(45.0°))}{(1.333)}$$

$$\sin(\theta_2) = 0.531 \quad \text{or} \quad \theta_2 = \textbf{32.0°}$$

This result tells us that the beam of light is bent toward the normal, because water has a greater refractive index than air. (b) The refraction of light as it moves from the

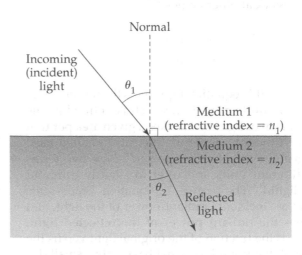

FIGURE 12 The process of refraction. The image on the left shows how refraction causes the image of a pencil to be bent as a result of the refraction of light as it passes between air and water. The model on the right shows the angle of refraction (θ_2) for light that strikes a planar boundary at an angle of θ_1 (vs. the normal) and that passes between two media with refractive indices of n_1 and n_2. The relationship between angles θ_1 and θ_2 is given by Snell's law (see Equation 8). (Photo by B.R. Hage.)

water back into the air can also be determined by using Snell's law. However, now the value of n_1 is the refractive index for water and n_2 is the refractive index of air. For the sake of comparison, the angle of incidence (θ_1) we are considering is again given as 45.0°. Under these conditions, the angle of refraction as the light moves from the water to the air would be found as follows.

$$\sin(\theta_2) = \frac{1.333 \cdot \sin(45.0°)}{(1.0003)}$$

$$\sin(\theta_2) = 0.942 \quad \text{or} \quad \theta_2 = 70.4°$$

This answer indicates that the direction of travel for light is bent away from the normal as this light moves from a medium with a higher refractive index than the medium that the light is entering.

We have seen that both refraction and reflection are created by a boundary between media with different refractive indices. This feature, in turn, means that the amount of light that is reflected will affect the amount that can be refracted, and then absorbed or transmitted by a sample. For instance, if 2% of the light is reflected as it travels through air and strikes a boundary with water, the other 98% of the light will be able to enter the water and undergo refraction. If we increase

the difference in the refractive index for our two media, the fraction of light that is reflected will increase and the amount that is refracted will decrease. It is even possible in some cases to have conditions in which 100% of the light is reflected. This situation can occur when there is a large difference in the refractive index across the boundary and when the light strikes this boundary at an appropriate angle that prevents it from crossing the boundary. This effect is employed in the design of optical fibers (see Figure 13) and can be valuable in controlling the travel of light within analytical instruments or to and from samples.[12]

Scattering. The term **scattering** is used in chemistry and physics to refer to the change in travel of one particle (such as a photon) due to its collision with another particle (e.g., an atom or molecule).[12] One common type of scattering is *Rayleigh scattering*, or "small-particle scattering" (see Figure 14). This type of scattering occurs when photons of light are scattered by particles such as atoms or molecules that are much smaller than the light's wavelength (particle diameter $< 0.05\ \lambda$). Rayleigh scattering results in light beams being redirected in a symmetrical pattern about the particles, but does not involve any change in the energy of the light. This process does depend on the wavelength of light, with short wavelengths being more effectively scattered than long wavelengths. This effect is

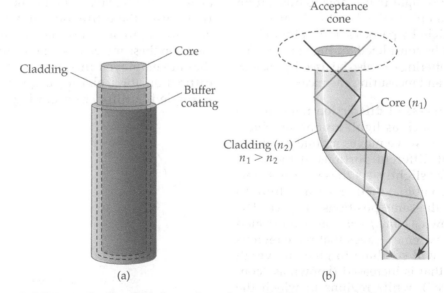

(a) (b)

FIGURE 13 The general design and use of an optical fiber. An optical fiber (a) contains at least two layers with different refractive indices. In the center of an optical fiber is the "core" (medium 1), which is a thin glass cylinder through which the light travels. Surrounding the core is the "cladding" (medium 2), a material that has a refractive index less than that of the core ($n_2 < n_1$) and that is used to keep light traveling within the core. There is also often an exterior buffer coating that protects the optical fiber from water and the outside environment. If light enters the optical fiber (b) at an appropriate angle (a range of angles known as the "acceptance cone"), this light can have an angle of refraction between the core and cladding that is at or exceeds 90° (versus the normal), a condition that causes all of the light to be reflected from the cladding back into the core. This effect is known as *total internal reflection* and is what allows optical fibers to carry light over great distances and through various paths without a large loss in intensity.

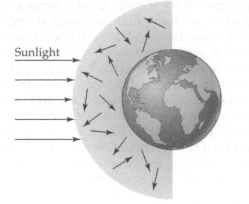

FIGURE 14 The scattering of sunlight by particles such as atoms and molecules in Earth's atmosphere. This process, which is based on *Rayleigh scattering*, is most effective for light with short wavelengths (such as blue light). This scattering is the reason why the sky appears to be blue during the daytime. This effect also explains why the sky at sunset is red, at which point we can better see the red light from the sun that is being transmitted through the atmosphere.

what creates the blue color of the sky because blue light has a shorter wavelength than other types of visible light and so is more effectively scattered by particles in the atmosphere.[12]

Scattering is important to consider in the measurement of light absorption or emission because this process will affect the amount of light that is able to travel from the light source and sample to the detector. As an example, the scattering of light by particles in the atmosphere is one factor that must be considered during remote sensing. The process of scattering can also be used by itself as a means for detecting and measuring chemicals.

Diffraction. The process of **diffraction** refers to the spreading of a wave, such as light, around an object (see Figure 15).[12] As the wave moves around an obstacle, the distance that different portions of the wave must travel will differ slightly. As these various portions of the wave recombine, their crests and troughs may no longer be in the same positions in space. The result is an effect known as *interference*, as is illustrated in Figure 16. At one extreme, waves that have regions with matched crests will combine to give an overall observed amplitude that is increased (known as "constructive interference"), while regions in which the crests of some waves combine with the troughs of others will give an overall observed amplitude that is decreased ("destructive interference"). This effect becomes particularly prominent as the obstacle that is encountered by the light approaches the same size as the wavelength of the light. The result is a pattern called a *diffraction pattern* that contains regions with either constructive or destructive interference.

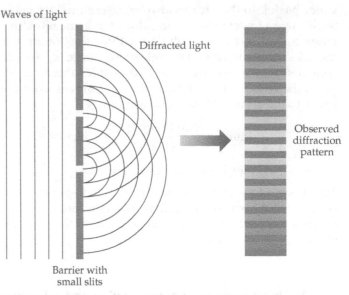

FIGURE 15 The production of a diffraction pattern as parallel waves of light strike a barrier with a series of small slits. The diffraction pattern is a result of constructive and destructive interference as the diffracted waves overlap. The position of the bands in this diffraction pattern will depend on the wavelength of light that is being diffracted and the spacing of the slits. A device that uses this effect to separate different wavelengths of light is called a *diffraction grating*.

Diffraction is used in several ways for chemical analysis. For instance, the method of X-ray crystallography uses the diffraction of X rays by chemicals in crystals to provide information on the arrangement of atoms in these molecules. There are also several devices that are employed in spectrometers that make use of diffraction for isolating a given type of light. One example is a diffraction grating, a simple example of

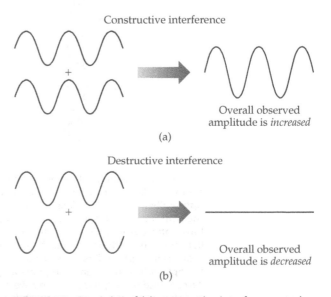

FIGURE 16 Examples of (a) constructive interference and (b) destructive interference for two overlapping waves. Various intermediate forms of constructive and destructive interference are also possible.

which is given by the two-slit system in Figure 15. This type of device gives an interference pattern in which different wavelengths of light will give regions of constructive interference at different locations around the device. It is then possible to select light from one of these regions (such as through the use of a slit) and to pass this light through a sample or onto a detector for use in an analysis.[5,12]

EXERCISE 9 — Diffraction of X Rays by a Crystal

It is possible to predict the angles at which constructive interference will be observed for X-ray diffraction by the atoms in a crystal. This can be achieved by using the *Bragg equation*,

$$n\lambda = 2d\sin(\theta) \qquad (9)$$

where λ is the wavelength of the X rays passed through the crystal, d is the interplanar distance (or "lattice spacing") between atoms in the crystal, and n is the order of diffraction for the observed constructive interference band (e.g., n = 1 for first-order interference). The term θ represents the specific angle at which the X rays will strike the crystal surface and produce, on the other side of the normal and at the same angle, a diffraction band for the given order of constructive interference.[12] If X rays with a wavelength of 0.711 Å are diffracted by a crystal of sodium chloride (d = 2.820 Å), at what angle will first-order constructive interference be observed for this crystal?

SOLUTION

We can rearrange Equation 9, as shown next, and solve for the angle θ by substituting in the known values for n, d, and λ.

$$\sin(\theta) = \frac{n\lambda}{2d} = \frac{(1)(0.0711 \text{ nm})}{(2)(0.2820)}$$

$$\therefore \sin(\theta) = 0.126 \text{ or } \theta = 7.24°$$

The same type of calculation predicts that additional bands of constructive interferences will be seen at angles of 14.6° (n = 2), 22.2° (n = 3), and so on for higher orders of interference.

3 QUANTITATIVE ANALYSIS BASED ON SPECTROSCOPY

3A Analysis Based on Emission

General Instrumentation. Figure 17(a) shows a simple spectrometer that could be used to examine the emission of a sample. This type of instrument consists of the following basic components: (1) the sample and a means for exciting chemicals in this sample, (2) a wavelength selector for isolating a particular type of light for analysis, and (3) a detector for recording this light. These are the same three components that were used by Sir Isaac Newton to study the emission of light by the sun (as shown earlier in Figure 3). For example, in Newton's work the sun was the "sample" and the high temperature of the sun was the means for exciting chemicals and allowing them to emit light. The wavelength selector in Newton's experiment was made up of the slit in the window, the lens, and the prism that were utilized to separate a beam of sunlight into various colored bands. The detector and recording device consisted of the screen that Newton used to allow him to see the separate bands of color.

Modern instruments are a bit more complicated and sophisticated than the equipment that was used by Newton, but the three basic components shown in Figure 9 still make up part of any spectrometer that measures light emission. When detecting forest fires by remote sensing, the fire and its heat would be the sample and excitation source, while the wavelength selector and detector would be present on a satellite such as *Terra*. A laboratory instrument for performing chemical analysis based on emission would also have all of these components, although on a small scale.

Emission and Chemical Concentration. The amount of light that is emitted by a sample will be directly related to the concentration of the atoms or molecules in the sample that are creating this emission. We can represent this relationship through the following equation,

$$P_E = kC \qquad (10)$$

where P_E represents the radiant power of the emitted light, C is the concentration of the species emitting this light, and k is a proportionality constant.[12] This equation can be used whether the excited state of the atom or molecule is produced by heat (as is the case for the sun) or by other methods (e.g., a chemical reaction).

Although it is necessary to correct for any background signal due to other sources of light, this type of correction can be made by preparing a calibration curve in which the emission of standard samples is used to determine the response that would be expected for the analyte in samples with a similar composition to that of the standards.

3B Analysis Based on Absorption

General Instrumentation. An illustration of a basic spectrometer for absorption measurements is shown in Figure 17(b). This instrument contains four main

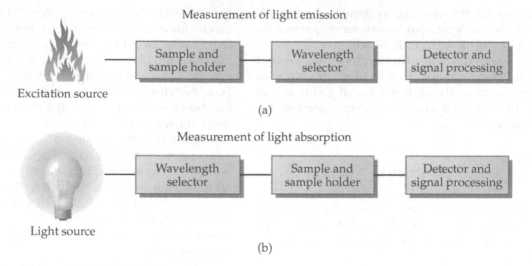

FIGURE 17 Design of a simple spectrometer for detecting (a) light emission or (b) light absorption.

components: (1) a light source, (2) a wavelength selector for isolating a particular type of light for use in the analysis, (3) the sample and a sample holder, and (4) a detector for recording the amount of light that passes through the sample.

The addition of the light source, when compared to the system for the emission spectrometer in Figure 17, is needed because now we are looking at how a sample absorbs or transmits light that is applied from an outside source rather than light that originates from the sample. The particular light source, wavelength selector, and detector that will be used in this system will depend on the type of light that we are examining. We will see some specific examples of these instruments later when we discuss the use of absorption measurements in molecular spectroscopy and atomic spectroscopy.

Absorption and Beer's Law. To measure the amount of light that is absorbed by a sample, we must compare the original amount of light that is applied to the sample and the amount that is transmitted by the sample. If the initial radiant power of this light is represented by P_0 and the power of this light after passing through a sample (or the "transmitted radiant power") is given by P, the fraction of transmitted light can be found by using a term known as T, the **transmittance**.[6,13]

$$T = P/P_0 \qquad (11)$$

A closely related value is the *percent transmittance* (% T), where % $T = 100 \cdot T$.

Although T and % T can easily be measured by using a spectrometer like the one in Figure 17(b), these values have an inherently nonlinear relationship with the concentration of an absorbing analyte. A term that is more convenient to relate to concentration is the **absorbance (A)**,

which is a measure of absorption that is found by taking the base-10 logarithm of the transmittance.[6,13]

$$A = -\log(T) = \log(P_0/P) \quad \text{or} \quad T = 10^{-A} \qquad (12)$$

Table 5 gives some typical values for the absorbance and transmittance, which helps demonstrate the logarithmic relationship between A and T. Like the transmittance, the absorbance for a sample has no units. In some older resources the absorbance is also known as the "optical density" of a sample.

The absorbance of a homogeneous sample can be related to the concentration of a dilute absorbing analyte through an expression called the "Beer–Lambert law," or simply **Beer's law** (see Box 2 and the derivation in Appendix A).[12,23]

$$\text{Beer's law:} \quad A = \varepsilon bC \qquad (13)$$

TABLE 5 Relationship Between Transmittance and Absorbance

Transmittance (T)	% Transmittance (% T = 100 T)	Absorbance = –log(T)
0.00010	0.010	4.00
0.0010	0.10	3.00
0.010	1.0	2.00
0.10	10	1.00
0.25	25	0.602
0.50	50	0.301
0.75	75	0.125
1.00	100	0.000

BOX 2
A Closer Look at Beer's Law

The equation we now call "Beer's law" or the "Beer–Lambert law" is a result of research that was performed by many scientists over the course of more than 100 years.[7,8] This process began in 1729 when a French scientist named Pierre Bouguer (1698–1758) noticed that the same relative fraction of light was absorbed for each additional unit of distance that light had to travel through matter. For instance, if half of the light was absorbed by one glass plate, then one-half of the remaining light (or one-quarter of the original amount) was absorbed by the next plate, and so on.[24] This same observation was later made by German physicist Johann Lambert (1728–1777), who in 1760 published a "law of absorption" in which he gave a mathematical description for this relationship between the amount of absorbed light and the distance of travel.[25] This same relationship is represented in our modern version of the Beer–Lambert law by the fact that the cell path length b is directly proportional to the absorbance A, where $A = -\log(P/P_0)$.

Another important development occured in 1852 when the description of light absorption was extended to solutions by the German scientist August Beer (1825–1863).[26] Beer found that the amount of light that was absorbed by an aqueous solution was proportional to the amount of an absorbing chemical that was present in that solution. (*Note*: This idea was also reported at about the same time by a French scientist named F. Bernard.)[27] We now represent this concept in the Beer–Lambert law by showing the absorbance A as being proportional to C, the concentration of the analyte. Beer also used a proportionality constant to relate the degree of absorbed light to analyte concentration.[7,8] We employ this same general approach in the modern version of the Beer–Lambert law when we use the molar absorptibity (ε) as a constant to relate the measured absorbance of a sample to an analyte's concentration and the cell path length.

Beer's law is useful for chemical analysis because it gives a linear relationship between the measured absorbance A for an analyte and the concentration of this analyte (C). This particular form of Beer's law has C as the molar concentration of the absorbing species (in units of M, or mol/L). The term b is the *path length*, or distance that the light must travel through the sample (in units of cm), and the term ε (the Greek letter *epsilon*) is the **molar absorptivity** (with units of L/mol · cm).[6] The molar absorptivity is a proportionality constant and will have a value that depends on the wavelength of light being used, the identity of the absorbing species, and the environment of this absorbing species. If units other than mol/L and cm are used for the concentration and path length, the proportionality constant in Beer's law will have units besides L/mol · cm and is then called the "absorptivity" (with recommended units of kg/m^3 or g/L) or the "extinction coefficient."[6,13]

EXERCISE 10	Calculating Absorbance and Using Beer's Law

Ozone is found not only naturally in the atmosphere but it is also used as a strong oxidizing agent in water treatment. One way to measure the ozone concentration in water is through its absorption of ultraviolet light. A solution of dissolved ozone in water gives a percent transmittance of 83.4% when measured at 258 nm and using a sample holder that has a path length of 5.00 cm. The molar absorptivity of ozone at 258 nm is known to be 2950 L/mol · cm.

a. What is the absorbance of this sample, and what is the concentration of ozone in the sample?

b. If no other absorbing species are present in the sample, what concentration of ozone would be expected to give an absorbance of 0.250 under these conditions?

SOLUTION

(a) The absorbance of this sample can be found by using Equation 12 and the measured transmittance, where $T = 0.834$ or % $T = 83.4\%$.

$$A = -\log(0.834) = \mathbf{0.0788}$$

If it is known that no other absorbing species is present in this sample, we can use the molar absorptivity for ozone along with Beer's law to determine the concentration of ozone.

Solving for C: $A = \varepsilon bC \Rightarrow C = A/(\varepsilon b)$

$$\therefore C = (0.0788)/[(5.00 \text{ cm})(2950 \text{ L/mol} \cdot \text{cm})]$$

$$= \mathbf{5.34 \times 10^{-6}\, M}$$

(b) The same approach as used to solve for the ozone concentration at $A = 0.0788$ can be used to estimate the absorbance that will be produced by this chemical at other concentrations if the wavelength and other conditions are kept the same.

Solving for C: $A = \varepsilon bC \Rightarrow C = A/(\varepsilon b)$

$$\therefore C = (0.250)/[(5.00 \text{ cm})(2950 \text{ L/mol} \cdot \text{cm})]$$

$$= \mathbf{1.69 \times 10^{-5}\, M}$$

This procedure can also be used to estimate the concentrations of ozone that give rise to other absorbance values, provided that these concentrations are not so large that they create deviations from the response that is predicted by Beer's law (a topic we examine in the next part of this chapter).

The preceding exercise indicates that it is sometimes possible to use Beer's law along with a measurement performed with a single standard to relate the absorbance of an analyte to its concentration. However, it is common for there to be more than one absorbing species in a solution or sample, which creates a "background" signal for the absorbance measurement. We can still use Beer's law in this situation by using several standards and making a plot of the measured absorbance for these standards versus their concentration for the analyte (see Figure 18). This type of graph is known as a *Beer's law plot*. This plot often has an intercept other than zero, as caused by the presence of species other than the analyte that might absorb light or cause the amount of transmitted light to be decreased (e.g., such as through light scattering).

The overall measured absorbance (A) for a sample that contains several absorbing species is the sum of the absorbance for each of these species (A_1, A_2, and so on). Equation 14 illustrates this relationship for two absorbing species,

$$A = A_1 + A_2$$
$$= \varepsilon_1 b C_1 + \varepsilon_2 b C_2 \tag{14}$$

where ε_1 and C_1 are the molar absorptivity and concentration for species 1, and ε_2 and C_2 are the molar absorptivity and concentration for species 2. (*Note*: The path length b is the same for both species because they are in the same sample.) If, however, we prepare a series of standards in which only the concentration of the analyte (species 1) is varied, the absorbance of the other component will be constant. The result will be a calibration curve like the one in Figure 18, in which a nonzero intercept is present, but that still provides a straight line that can be used to determine the concentration of an analyte in unknown samples with compositions similar to those of the standards. In next chapter we will also see how absorbance measurements made at several wavelengths can be used to determine the concentrations of multiple chemical species that have different molar absorptivity values at the given wavelengths.

Another factor to consider when we are measuring absorbance and transmittance is that several sources of random errors can limit the precision of these values. Some typical precision plots for absorbance spectrometers are shown in Figure 19. At a low absorbance (high transmittance) there is a loss in precision because it becomes more difficult for the spectrometer to differentiate the amount of light that is transmitted in the presence and absence of the sample (or P is close to P_0). At a high absorbance (low transmittance) there is a large difference between P and P_0, but P is now quite small, making this measurement subject to imprecision due to factors such as noise from the detector. The best precision for transmittance and absorbance measurements will occur at some intermediate value, which is indicated by the minimum in %RSD which is obtained at an absorbance of approximately 0.4 for the instrument in Figure 19(a). Fortunately, even simple absorbance spectrometers can be used over a relatively broad absorbance range and provide good precision (typically, A = 0.1 to 0.8). More sophisticated instruments, like the one in Figure 19(b) tend to provide good precision over an ever larger range of absorbance values.[12]

Limitations of Beer's Law. A big advantage of Beer's law is it can be used to relate concentration to the absorption of light for any type of light. It should be kept in mind, however, that there are several assumptions made in this equation that limit the circumstances under which it can be utilized (see Table 6).[12] The first assumption in Beer's law is that all of the absorbing species in the sample are acting *independently* of each other. This assumption makes Beer's law valid for only relatively

Methyl red conc. (mol/L)	Absorbance at 520 nm
0.00E+00	0.004
8.81E−06	0.262
2.06E−05	0.459
2.94E−05	0.758
4.40E−05	1.149
5.87E−05	1.495

Best-fit line	
Slope:	2.55E+04
Intercept:	0.0008
Corr. Coef.	0.9979

FIGURE 18 A Beer's law plot and a spreadsheet to prepare such a plot, as demonstrated for the measurement of methyl red in water.

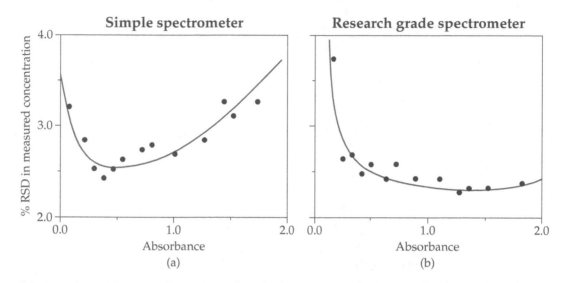

FIGURE 19 Precision curves for two UV-visible absorption spectometers. The curve in (a) is for a relatively simple instrument that is often used in teaching laboratories (the Spectronic 20), while the curve in (b) is for a more advanced instrument used in research laboratories (the Cary 118). The *percent relative standard deviation (% RSD)* values were calculated by using the formula % RSD = 100 (s_c/C), where C is the measured concentration and s_c is the standard deviation of this measured concentration. (These results are based on L.D. Rothman, S.R. Crouch, and J.D. Ingle, *Analytical Chemistry*, 44 (1972) 1375).

dilute samples (i.e., usually below 0.01 *M*). Deviations from this assumption will occur at higher concentrations as the distance between individual analytes becomes sufficiently small to allow the electric field around one analyte to affect the absorption of light by another. Similar effects occur if high concentrations of other species (particularly ions) are present in the solution. The result is a lower-than-expected absorbance for high concentration samples and standards, causing a negative deviation in a Beer's law plot.

Another way in which a high analyte concentration can lead to deviations from Beer's law is through the corresponding change in refractive index. This effect occurs because the molar absorptivity is dependent on the refractive index, and the refractive index is dependent on a sample's composition and concentration. Fortunately, it is possible to correct for this effect if the refractive index is known or measured for the sample. This correction is made by using $(\varepsilon n)/(n^2 + 2)^2$ in place of ε in Beer's law, but is not usually required for analytes with concentrations below 0.01 *M*.[12]

A second assumption made in Beer's Law is that the absorbance of the sample is being measured using only *monochromatic light* (that is, light that contains only one wavelength). There is really no such thing as perfectly monochromatic light, but modern spectrometers come quite close in providing such light for absorbance measurements. What these spectrometers actually provide is *polychromatic light* (or light containing a mixture of two or more wavelengths), where the range of these wavelengths is described by the term $\Delta\lambda$. The effects of polychromatic light on a Beer's law plot are shown in Figure 20. The presence of polychromatic light will not create significant deviations from Beer's law as long as the change in the molar absorptivity for the analyte ($\Delta\varepsilon$) is small over the wavelength range $\Delta\lambda$ that is present. A change in the molar absorbitivity of less than 1% ($\Delta\varepsilon/\varepsilon < 0.01$) is generally desired. It is for this reason that absorbance measurements are often performed at or near the top of a peak in an absorption spectrum, where ε is approximately constant. If a wavelength range is used on the side of a peak or $\Delta\varepsilon/\varepsilon$ does change due to the presence of polychromatic light, the result will be a curved Beer's law plot where a lower-then-expected absorbance is measured as the analyte concentration is increased.[12]

A third assumption made in Beer's law is that all light that is passed through the sample has the same distance of travel. This assumption requires that the path length *b* be a constant for the measurement of a given sample and is usually met by using a square sample cell and parallel rays of light that strike the sample cell at a perpendicular to the surface to the cell. If a round sample

---

TABLE 6 Important Assumptions Made in Beer's Law

(1) All absorbing species act independently of each other

(2) The light being used for the absorbance measurement is "monochromatic"

(3) All detected rays of light that pass through the sample have the same distance of travel

(4) The concentration of absorbing species is constant throughout the path of light in the sample

(5) The light that is being used to measure absorbance is not scattered by the sample

(6) The amount of light entering the sample is not large enough to cause saturation of the absorbing species in this sample

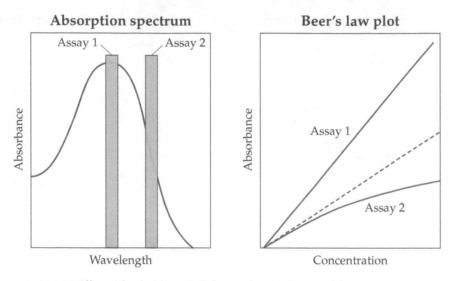

FIGURE 20 Effects of polychromatic light on plots made according to Beer's law.

cell is instead used (as can occur in some inexpensive instruments), curvature and negative deviations can appear at high analyte concentrations in a Beer's law plot.

There are several other inherent assumptions in Beer's law. For instance, a fourth assumption is that the concentration of the absorbing species is constant throughout the path length of light through the sample. Thus, we should make sure that we are working with a homogeneous sample when using Beer's law to relate the absorbance to analyte concentration in this sample. A fifth assumption in Beer's law is that all light entering the sample is either transmitted or absorbed. This assumption must be met if the relative difference in P versus P_0 is to be used to determine the absorbance and transmittance of light through the sample. Finally, a sixth assumption in Beer's law is that the amount of incoming light (as given by P_0) is not large enough to cause saturation of the absorbing species. This last requirement is needed to ensure that the measured value of P will increase in proportion to P_0 and that the value of P/P_0 will not be affected by the size of P. Deviations from this assumption can occur when using high-intensity light sources such as lasers.

Another situation in which curvature can occur in a Beer's law plot is if the absorbing species is involved in a chemical reaction that will alter the concentration of this particular species as its total analytical concentration is varied. This problem can appear in reactions that involve weak acids or weak bases. For instance, when the concentration of a solution of a weak acid in water is increased, the fraction of this acid in the dissociated form will decrease (i.e., the ratio of $[A^-]/[HA]$ decreases). If the molar absorptivity is different for the two species HA and A^-, a plot of the overall measured absorbance versus the total analytical concentration can give a curved relationship (see Figure 21). Similar effects can occur for reactions that involve dimer formations, ion pairing, and other types of equilibria.

There are some instrumental limitations that can also cause deviations in a Beer's law plot. For instance, light that reaches the detector without going through the sample (known as *stray light*) can cause errors in the measured absorbance.[12] This stray light (which can be

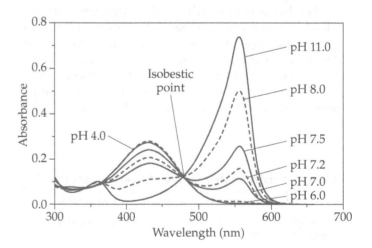

FIGURE 21 Change in absorbance spectrum for phenol red with a variation in pH. The observed change in these plots with pH is due to the conversion of phenol red from its acid form to its base form, which have different absorption spectra. This graph shows the location of an isobestic point at 480 nm. There are also two other isobestic points in these plots, which occur at 367 and 338 nm.

represented as having a radiant power of P_S) will add to values of both P and P_0, as shown in Equation 15. The net result is an observed absorbance (A_{Obs}) that is lower than the true absorbance of the sample.

Effect of Stray Light:
$$A_{Obs} = -\log\left(\frac{P + P_S}{P_0 + P_S}\right)$$

$$\approx -\log\left(\frac{P + P_S}{P_0}\right) \quad (\text{if } P_0 \gg P_S) \qquad (15)$$

The result of this scattering is an increase in the apparent amount of light that is transmitted (or a decrease in A_{Obs}), leading to *negative* deviations in a Beer's law plot.

The reflection of light off of surfaces of the sample cell will also create deviations to Beer's law due to the instrument. In this case, the reflections will result in light that goes through the sample but that does not reach the detector. This effect will decrease the observed absorbance according to the relationship shown in Equation 16,

Effect of Reflection:
$$A_{Obs} = -\log\left(\frac{P - P_R}{P_0 - P_R}\right)$$

$$\approx -\log\left(\frac{P - P_R}{P_0}\right) \quad (\text{if } P_0 \gg P_R) \qquad (16)$$

where P_R represents the power of the reflected light. This change, in turn, increases the apparent absorption of light and gives *positive* deviations in a Beer's law plot.

It is important to consider all of these possible sources of deviations when using Beer's law to perform a chemical analysis. Minimizing these effects will help to increase the linear range of a Beer's law plot. However, even if precautions are taken to reduce these effects it is important that we *always* carefully examine a Beer's law plot to determine whether this plot is or is not giving a linear response at the concentrations we wish to measure. This linearity can easily be examined by visually inspecting the Beer's law plot or by using such tools as a residual plot. If we wish to analyze a sample that has a concentration higher than this linear range, one common option is to dilute the sample until it has a concentration in this range.

Key Words

Absorbance	Frequency	Refraction	Spectroscopy
Absorption	Light	Refractive index	Spectrum
Beer's law	Molar absorptivity	Scattering	Transmission
Diffraction	Photon	Snell's law	Transmittance
Emission	Reflection	Spectrometer	Wavelength

Other Terms

Absorption spectrum	Emission spectrum	Percent transmittance	Remote sensing
Amplitude	Fresnel equation	Photoelectrical effect	Spectrochemical
Angle of incidence	Interference	Planck's constant	analysis
Angle of reflection	Monochromatic light	Planck's equation	Spectrometry
Beer's law plot	Nuclear magnetic	Polychromatic light	Stray light
Bragg equation	resonance	Radiant power	Wave number
Diffraction pattern	spectroscopy	Rayleigh scattering	
Electromagnetic	Path length		
radiation			

Questions

WHAT IS SPECTROSCOPY AND HOW IS IT USED FOR CHEMICAL ANALYSIS?

1. What is "spectroscopy"? What is a "spectrometer"? Explain how light is used by each of these two items.
2. What is "remote sensing"? What are some ways in which spectroscopy is used in remote sensing?
3. What is a "spectrum"? What information in used in plotting a spectrum? How can this information be used in chemical analysis?
4. Figure 22 shows a spectrum that was acquired for the complex $Fe(1,10\text{-phenanthroline})_3^{2+}$, which is often used to measure the concentration of iron in water samples. At what

wavelength does this complex have its strongest absorption of light? What wavelength(s) would you use to measure this complex in absorption spectroscopy?

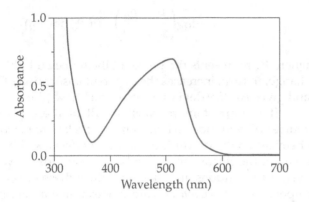

FIGURE 22 Spectrum for Fe(1,10-phenanthroline)$_3$$^{2+}$. This spectrum was acquired using a $6.26 \times 10^{-5}\,M$ aqueous solution of this complex and using a sample cell that has a path length of 1.00 cm.

5. The following data were obtained at various wavelengths for a $3.6 \times 10^{-4}\,M$ solution of permanganate held in a square cuvette with a path length of 1.00 cm.

Wavelength (nm)	% T	Wavelength (nm)	% T
400	89	575	50
425	92	600	82
450	83	625	86
475	60	650	88
500	27	675	93
525	15	700	96
550	29		

Plot a simple absorption spectrum for permanganate using these data. At what wavelength(s) in this spectrum does permanganate have the strongest absorption of light? At what wavelength(s) does it have the weakest absorption of light?

6. What is the difference between a "spectrochemical analysis" and "spectrometry"?

7. List two types of spectroscopy that are classified based on the types of analytes they examine. List two types of spectroscopy that are classified based on the type of light that they employ.

8. Briefly describe three different ways in which spectroscopy can be used for chemical analysis.

WHAT IS LIGHT?

9. Explain how "light" is defined by modern scientists. How does this definition differ from the common use of this term when referring to "visible light"?

10. What is meant by the "wave–particle duality" of light? Explain why this concept is essential in understanding the properties of light.

11. Define the following terms, as related to the wave model of light.
    (a) Crest
    (b) Trough
    (c) Amplitude
    (d) Frequency
    (e) Wavelength
    (f) Wave number

12. What is the value of constant c? What is the physical meaning of this constant?

13. What is the definition of the "refractive index"? How is this index related to the velocity of light?

14. Calculate the following values.
    (a) The velocity of 589 nm light in pure water ($n = 1.333$ at 25°C)
    (b) The velocity of 250 nm light in fused quartz ($n = 1.507$ at 25°C)
    (c) The refractive index of white light in $CO_2(g)$ ($v = 2.9965 \times 10^8$ m/s at 25°C and 1 atm)
    (d) The refractive index of 589 nm light in acetone ($v = 2.2063 \times 10^8$ m/s at 20°C)

15. A spectrometer has a path of 25 cm (roughly 1 ft) that must be traveled by a beam of light. Most of this travel occurs in air, which has an average refractive index of 1.0003 for the light. Approximately how long will it take the beam of light to cover this distance?

16. In 1999, a group of scientists used a special type of matter known as a Bose–Einstein condensate to slow a beam of light to a velocity of only 17 m/s (see Reference 8). What was the refractive index of this condensate?

17. Calculate the following values, using a velocity of c for light. In each case, indicate what type of electromagnetic radiation is present (e.g., visible light, ultraviolet light, etc.).
    (a) Frequency for 3.50 μm light
    (b) Wave number for 635 nm light
    (c) Wavelength for 2.1×10^{18} Hz radiation
    (d) Wave number for 5.5×10^{11} Hz radiation

18. A scientist wishes to study a chemical that has an energy transition that occurs at 4.5×10^{14} Hz. What is the wavelength (in nm) and wave number (in cm^{-1}) of the electromagnetic radiation that will be needed to study this transition? What general type of electromagnetic radiation (visible, ultraviolet, etc.) will be needed for this experiment?

19. An organic chemist uses both infrared and ultraviolet light to examine a newly synthesized chemical. This chemical is found to have strong absorption of light at both 2.5 μm and 400 nm. What general types of light are being absorbed at each of these wavelengths? How many photons of light at 2.5 μm are needed to give the same energy as one photon of light at 400 nm?

20. A chemist wishes to use a spectrometer that is capable of discriminating between light with a wavelength of 500 nm from light with a wavelength of 501 nm (when traveling through air at standard temperature and pressure [STP]). What is the difference in frequency for these two types of light? What is the difference in energy for a photon of light at each of these wavelengths?

21. The oxygen–oxygen bond in hydrogen peroxide contains 145 kJ/mol in energy. This bond can be broken if the hydrogen peroxide absorbs a photon that has the same amount of energy as is stored in this bond. What wavelength of light is needed to break this bond?

UPTAKE AND RELEASE OF LIGHT BY MATTER

22. Define "emission" as related to light. Describe the process of light emission by matter.

23. Sodium that is heated in a flame will emit light at 589 nm. This process is due to an electron falling from a 3p orbital to a 3s orbital.
    (a) Explain what is happening during this emission process, using the scheme in Figure 8 as a guide.
    (b) Light at 589 nm is the most intense emission that is observed for sodium. Use the transitions that are involved in this process to explain why this is the case.
24. Explain how the chemicals in a flame emit light, using the model in Figure 8 as an example.
25. What is an "emission spectrum"? How can an emission spectrum be used for chemical analysis?
26. What color and type of light would be associated with light that is emitted at each of the following wavelengths?
    (a) 475 nm
    (b) 250 nm
    (c) 675 nm
    (d) 1000 nm
27. What is meant by the terms "absorption" and "transmission" as related to light? Explain how these two terms are related.
28. How does light absorption differ from light emission?
29. What is an "absorption spectrum"? Discuss how this type of spectrum can be used for chemical analysis.
30. Based on the spectrum in Figure 2, over what ranges of wavelengths does sunlight have the greatest amount of absorption by Earth's atmosphere? Use this same figure to explain why the atmosphere is often said to be "transparent" to the visible range of sunlight.
31. Explain how the wavelengths of absorbed light are related to the color of a chemical.
32. What is the expected color of a solution if it strongly absorbs light from 450 to 500 nm? What is the expected color if the solution absorbs strongly at only 250–300 nm?
33. A pharmaceutical company develops a test for pregnancy in which a product is formed on a test strip that absorbs visible light and has a dark blue color. What wavelengths of visible light are probably absorbed by this colored product?

PHYSICAL INTERACTIONS OF LIGHT WITH MATTER

34. What is light "reflection"? What is needed for light reflection to occur?
35. Define the following terms.
    (a) Specular reflection
    (b) Diffuse reflection
    (c) Angle of incidence
    (d) Angle of reflection
36. What is the "Fresnell equation" and how is this equation used?
37. What factors determine the fraction of reflected light that will be reflected by a surface? Do you think this fraction of reflection will also be affected by the wavelength of light? Explain your answer.
38. Estimate the fraction of light that will be reflected in each of the following examples. In each case, you may assume that the light is striking the boundary at a right angle (90° to the plane of the boundary). (*Note*: You may assume that the light has a wavelength of 589 nm unless indicated otherwise.)
    (a) Light passing through air and striking a diamond
    (b) Light passing through water and striking ice
    (c) Light traveling from air to a surface made of hard cellulose acetate
    (d) Light passing through helium and striking a cuvette made of light flint glass

39. It is possible to estimate the amount of reflection that occurs for sunlight by Earth's atmosphere by using a model similar to that shown in Figure 8. In this model, we will assume there is a well-defined boundary between space and the atmosphere and that the atmosphere has an average refractive index of 1.0003 for visible light.
    (a) Calculate the fraction of reflection that would be expected for visible light at this boundary. Based on your results, do you think this reflection will play an important role during the use of sunlight for remote sensing?
    (b) The actual change from space to Earth's atmosphere is more gradual than the model in Figure 7, and the refractive index of air will change with altitude and other conditions. In general, how do you think these factors will affect the amount of visible light that is reflected by Earth's atmosphere?
40. What is light "refraction"? What is needed for refraction to occur?
41. What is "Snell's law"? What factors appear in this law?
42. At what angle would light be refracted if it passes from air ($n = 1.0003$) into glass ($n = 1.5171$) and hits the glass at an angle of 30° vs. the normal? How will this angle of refraction change if the light instead hits the glass at 45.0° or 60° vs. the normal?
43. Different types of glass will have different values for the refractive index of light. For instance, light with a wavelength of 589 nm has the following values of n for various types of glass: 1.51714 (ordinary crown glass), 1.52430 (borosilicate glass), and 1.65548 (dense flint glass).
    (a) Calculate the angle of refraction of 589 nm light as it passes from air into each of these glasses at an angle of 50.0° vs. the normal.
    (b) Repeat the calculation in Part (a), but now calculate the angle of refraction of 589 nm light as it passes from pure water into each glass at 50.0° vs. the normal.
    (c) Use the results in Parts (a) and (b) to rank the three types of glass based on their ability to refract 589 nm light. Which type of glass gives the largest change in direction of travel for this light? Which type of glass gives the smallest change due to refraction? Explain these results using Snell's law.
44. What is meant by light "scattering"? What is "Rayleigh scattering"?
45. Why is scattering important in chemical analysis?
46. Define the following terms. Explain how diffraction and interference are related.
    (a) Diffraction
    (b) Interference
    (c) Diffraction pattern
    (d) Constructive interference
    (e) Destructive interference
47. What are two ways in which diffraction is used for chemical analysis?
48. What is the "Bragg equation?" What terms appear in this equation?
49. A chemist wishes to use examine diffraction by a crystal of topaz that is exposed to X rays with a wavelength of 0.63 Å. If the interplanar distance of topaz is 1.356 Å, at what angle will a first-order constructive interference band be observed for this crystal?
50. Diffraction gratings are often used in place of prisms as wavelength selectors for ultraviolet-visible (UV-vis) spectroscopy. Typical gratings used in these devices have 300–2400 groves

per millimeter. If light approaches this grating at a right angle, the angle θ at which constructive interference will occur for the light is given by Equation 17,

$$d \sin \theta = n\lambda \qquad (17)$$

where λ is the wavelength of the light, d is the distance between adjacent grooves on the grating, and n is the order of diffraction for the observed constructive interference band.[12]

(a) At what angle will first-order constructive interference be observed for 600 nm light that hits at a right angle a grating that contains 1000 groves per mm?

(b) At what angle will first-order constructive interference be observed for 610 nm light when using the same grating as in Part (a)?

(c) If constructive interference bands are observed at a perpendicular distance that is 10.0 cm away from the grating, how far apart will be the first-order interference bands be at this location for the 600 and 610 nm light?

ANALYSIS BASED ON EMISSION

51. List the main components of a simple spectrometer for measuring light emission. Describe the function of each component.

52. Give a general equation that can be used to relate the amount of light emission to the chemical concentration of a sample. Describe each term that appears in this equation.

53. A series of calcium standards and two unknown calcium solutions are measured under the same conditions at 620 nm by flame emission spectroscopy. The following results are recorded. Determine the concentrations of Ca^{2+} in the unknown samples.

Concentration of Ca^{2+} (M)	Relative Measured Emission Intensity
0.000	0.0010
1.00×10^{-4}	5.02
2.00×10^{-4}	10.4
3.00×10^{-4}	16.1
5.00×10^{-4}	26.5
10.00×10^{-4}	51.3
Unknown no. 1	20.5
Unknown no. 2	57.0

54. The same system as in Problem 53 gives a signal of 127.6 for an unknown sample. (*Note*: This system is known to give a linear response up to a signal of roughly 150.) The student analyzing the sample takes a 10.00 mL aliquot, places it into a 50.00 mL volumetric flask, and fills the flask to the mark with deionized water. What approximate signal would be expected for the diluted sample? What is the concentration of Ca^{2+} in this sample?

ANALYSIS BASED ON ABSORPTION

55. List the main components of a simple spectrometer for measuring light absorption. Describe the function of each component.

56. Define "transmittance," "percent transmittance," and "absorbance." Show how these terms are related to each other.

57. Complete the following table, calculating all missing values.

Transmittance	% Transmittance	Absorbance
0.156	—	—
—	35.8	—
—	—	0.251
0.689	—	—
—	78.0	—
—	—	1.250

58. What is "Beer's law"? What terms appear in this law?

59. Calculate the molar absorptivity of an analyte if a $3.40 \times 10^{-4}\, M$ solution of this chemical is placed in a sample cell with a path length of 5.0 cm and is found to give a value for % T of 67.4 at 450 nm.

60. Calculate the concentration of an analyte in solution placed in a 1.00 cm wide sample cell if the measured absorbance of this sample is 0.367 and the analyte has a known molar absorptivity of $6.87 \times 10^3\, L/mol \cdot cm$.

61. In the presence of a solution that has a background absorbance of 0.050, a $1.0 \times 10^{-4}\, M$ solution of an analyte is found to give an overall absorbance of 0.350 ($b = 1.00$ cm). A similar solution that contains $3.0 \times 10^{-4}\, M$ of the same analyte gives an overall measured absorbance of 0.900. What is the molar absorptivity of this analyte at the wavelength that is used in these experiments?

62. What is a "Beer's law plot"? How is this plot used in chemical analysis?

63. A Beer's law plot is shown for the measurement of "protein A" at the end of this chapter. Based on this plot, what would be the expected concentration of this protein in an unknown sample that had an absorbance reading of 0.76? What would be the concentration in a sample that had a percent transmittance of 51%? Explain how you obtained your answers.

64. The following results were obtained by a clinical chemist when measuring morphine at 285 nm and using a 1.00 cm square cuvette as the sample holder.[28]

Morphine Concentration (M)	Absorbance
5.0×10^{-5}	0.229
1.0×10^{-4}	0.308
2.0×10^{-4}	0.467
5.0×10^{-4}	0.942

Prepare a Beer's law plot for these data. Use this plot to determine the concentration of morphine in an unknown sample that gives a measured absorbance of 0.615 in this assay.

65. Show how the overall measured absorbance for a sample will be affected by the presence of two or more analytes that absorb light at the same wavelength. Give an equation that describes this relationship.

66. What are some sources of random errors that can affect absorbance or transmittance measurements?

67. It was stated earlier that simple absorbance spectrometers tend to give the most reliable measurements for absorbance values between 0.1 and 0.8. Use Figure 19(a)

to explain this statement. Also explain why this range is not necessarily valid for all spectrometers that are used for absorbance measurements.

68. A pharmaceutical chemist wishes to determine the range at which both of the spectrometers in Figure 19 will provide a given level of precision for an absorbance measurement.
    (a) Over what range of absorbance values can the instrument in Figure 19(a) be used to provide a precision of 2.5% or better? Over what range of absorbance values will this instrument provide a precision of 3.0% or better?
    (b) Over what range of absorbance values will the instrument in Figure 19(b) give a precision of 2.5% or better? Over what range will the precision be 3.0% or better?

69. Explain why a Beer's law plot can show deviations from a straight line as the concentration of an analyte increases. Give two reasons why such deviations may occur.

70. Define the terms "monochromatic light" and "polychromatic light." Which type of light is assumed to be present when using Beer's law?

71. What happens to a Beer's law plot when there is an increase in the range of wavelengths that are used to make an absorbance measurement? Explain how selecting the proper wavelengths (e.g., those at the top of a peak in a spectrum vs. those on the side of a peak) can minimize this effect.

72. Based on the spectra in Figure 10, state how you would expect the slope and linear range to compare in Beer's law plots made for each of the following pairs of wavelengths.
    (a) 465 nm vs. 645 nm for chlorophyll *b*
    (b) 645 nm vs. 660 nm for chlorophyll *a*
    (c) 475 nm vs. 645 nm for chlorophyll *b*
    (d) 440 nm vs. 660 nm for chlorophyll *a*

73. What is "stray light"? How can stray light affect an absorbance measurement? How can stray light affect a Beer's law plot?

74. Discuss why reflection in a spectrometer can affect an absorbance measurement.

75. A sample is known to have an observed absorbance of 1.30, or % T = 5.0. What will be the apparent absorbance of this sample if stray light is present that has a radiant power equal to 1.0% of the incident radiant power (P_S = 0.010 P_0)? What will the size of the error be in this observed absorbance vs. the true absorbance of the sample?

76. What will the observed absorbance of the sample in Problem 72 be if there is no stray light, but there is reflection of light at a level that is equal to 1.0% of the light's initial radiant power (P_R = 0.010 P_0)? What will the size of the error in this observed absorbance be vs. the true absorbance of the sample?

CHALLENGE PROBLEMS

77. There are several different types of spectrometers used in analytical chemistry. One way these spectrometers can be classified is by the means with which they detect light. Use the Internet or resources like References 5 and 6 to determine how each of the following types of spectrometers is able to detect light.
    (a) Spectrophotometer
    (b) Spectrograph
    (c) Spectroscope

78. Locate the refractive index for each of the following materials by using the *CRC Handbook of Chemistry and Physics*[11] or other resources.
    (a) Benzene (sodium D light—589 nm, 20°C)
    (b) Rock salt (1.229 μm infrared light)

(c) 10% (w/w) aqueous solution of sucrose (sodium D light—589 nm, 20°C)
    (d) Polyethylene plastic (medium density, sodium D light—589 nm light)

79. The Heisenberg uncertainty principle sets certain limits on the precision with which certain pairs of physical parameters can be determined. Two such related parameters are the lifetime of atom or molecule in its excited state and the energy that is released as this excited state goes to a lower energy state. This relationship is represented by the following equation,

$$\Delta E \cdot \Delta t \geq h/4\pi \qquad (18)$$

where ΔE is the uncertainty in energy of this transition, Δt is the lifetime of the excited state, and h is Planck's constant. One outcome of this relationship is that it's impossible to have truly monochromatic light due to an emission process because Equation 18 states that the shorter the lifetime of the excited state, the greater the uncertainty in its energy and, hence, the greater uncertainty there will be in the wavelength of light that is emitted from this excited state.
    (a) Light with a wavelength 589.3 nm is often emitted by sodium atoms. If the lifetime of these sodium atoms in their excited state is 10 ns, what is the uncertainty in the energy of this emitted light?
    (b) What will the uncertainty in the wavelength of light that is emitted by the sodium atoms in Part (a) be? From this information, determine the range of wavelengths that are actually emitted by the sodium atoms as they give off 589.3 nm light.
    (c) According to Equation 18, what would be required to have the emission of truly monochromatic light (i.e., what happens if ΔE = 0)?

80. When light passes through a glass sample cell, it will encounter several boundaries between regions with different refractive indices. First, the light passes from air into the glass wall of the cell. This light then passes through the glass and onto the boundary between the glass and the sample. The light then travels through the sample until it reaches the other side of the glass sample cell. After reentering the glass, the light then passes onto the exterior of the sample cell, where the light goes back into the surrounding air and moves on to the detector.
    (a) At each of these boundaries a small amount of light will be lost due to reflection. Estimate the fraction of light that is reflected at each step of this process, assuming that the light is hitting each boundary at a normal angle (90° to the plane of the boundary).
    (b) What is the total fraction of light that is lost to reflection in this system? Which boundaries lead to the greatest loss of light due to reflection?

81. Molar absorptivity is not the only way we can describe the ability of a chemical to absorb light. Another closely related parameter is the *absorption cross section*, which can be calculated directly from the molar absorptivity by using unit conversions and dimensional analysis.[6,12]
    (a) What units are obtained from the value of ε when using the substitution 1 L = 1000 cm^3? What units are obtained when an additional substitution is made using Avogadro's number, where N_A = 6.023 × 10^{23} molecules/mol? Use your results to explain why the resulting value is referred to as an absorption "cross section."

(b) The absorption spectrum for benzene gives a peak with a molar absorptivity of 60,000 L/mol · cm at 184 nm.[29] What is the absorption cross section for benzene at this wavelength? How does this value compare with benzene's actual cross section of approximately 2.5×10^4 pm^2?

82. Any heated object will emit a continuum of wavelengths. This effect is known as "blackbody radiation" and is responsible for the broad range of wavelengths that are emitted by the sun.

(a) Equation 19 shows how the wavelength of maximum emission (λ_{max}) will change with temperature for a blackbody source,

$$\lambda_{max} = 2.879 \times 10^6/T \qquad (19)$$

where λ_{max} is given in units of nm, and T is the absolute temperature in units of Kelvin.[12] The sun is often modeled as a blackbody source with a temperature of 5900 K. What is the expected value for λ_{max} under these conditions? How does this value compare with the wavelength of maximum emission that was shown earlier in Figure 2?

(b) The amount of light that is given off at a given wavelength by a blackbody source will also depend on temperature. This relationship is described by Equation 20,

$$B = (2hc^2/\lambda^5)(1/e^{hc/\{\lambda kT\}} - 1) \qquad (20)$$

where B is the total radiance, a value that is proportional to the relative intensity of emitted light.[12] The other terms in this equation included the speed of light (c), the absolute temperature (T, in kelvin), the wavelength of light (λ, in meters), Planck's constant (h), and Boltzmann's constant (k). Use Equation 20 and a spreadsheet to plot the spectrum that would be expected between wavelengths of 0.1 and 3.0 μm for a blackbody source such as the sun at 5900 K. (*Note*: Be sure to use consistent SI units for all terms in Equation 20 when doing your calculations.) How do your results compare with the actual emission spectrum that shown in Figure 2?

83. Optical fibers are an efficient way to move light from one place to another. The composition of such a fiber consists of a transparent core with a refractive index of n_1. This core is surrounded with a cladding material that has a lower refractive index (n_2, where $n_2 < n_1$). Total internal reflection will occur for light if this light strikes the core/cladding interface at an angle equal to or greater than θ, where $\sin(\theta) \geq (n_2/n_1)$. The angle ($90° - \theta$), for the case in which θ is given in degrees, then describes the acceptance cone for the optical fiber, as shown earlier in Figure 13. One particular optical fiber has a core with a refractive index of 1.3334 and cladding with a refractive index of 1.4567. What range of angles make up the acceptance cone for this optical fiber?

84. The index of refraction for fused quartz, which changes at various wavelengths, is as follows: $n = 1.54727$ (202 nm), 1.53386 (214 nm), 1.46968 (404 nm), 1.46690 (434 nm), 1.45674 (644 nm), and 1.45640 (656 nm).

(a) A plot of refractive index vs. wavelength for a material is called a dispersion curve. Use the preceding data and a spreadsheet to prepare a dispersion curve for fused quartz.

(b) Use your spreadsheet to determine the angle at which each of the listed wavelengths will be refracted if light at these wavelengths were to pass through air and strike the surface of a fused-quartz prism at an incident angle of 45°. Make a plot that shows how this angle of refraction changes with the wavelength of light.

(c) Based on your results in Part (b), which wavelengths of light do you think will be the most easily separated based on their refraction by a fused/quartz prism? What colors of visible light will be the most easily separated by this prism?

85. The following data were obtained when using absorbance measurements to determine the amount of iron in a corrosion sample from a Civil War–era ship sunk in the ocean in the 1860s. A 0.0465 g portion of this sample was dissolved in acid and diluted to 100.00 mL. A 1.00 mL portion of this solution was then treated with 1,10-phenanthroline, hydroxylamine, and acetate buffer and diluted to a total volume of 100.00 mL. Several standard solutions were prepared from ferrous ammonium sulfate and treated in the same way. The following results were obtained after measuring the absorbances of these samples and standards at 510 nm.

Iron Concentration (mg/L)	Absorbance
0.000	0.002
0.359	0.077
1.198	0.127
2.995	0.256
5.990	1.090
8.985	1.556
Unknown sample	0.406

(a) Prepare a spreadsheet that uses these data to construct a Beer's law plot.

(b) Use your spreadsheet to examine the fit of a best-fit line to your Beer's law plot. What is the approximate linear range for this plot? What are the best-fit slope and intercept over this linear range?

(c) What is the concentration of iron in the unknown sample? What absorbance would have been expected if this sample had contained 4.15 mg/L iron? What would have been the approximate absorbance for a sample containing 15.7 mg/L iron?

86. Although a Beer's law plot is a popular way of plotting absorption data, another way of examining such data is to use a *Ringbom plot*. A Ringbom plot is prepared by plotting the transmittance of a sample vs. the concentration of an absorbing analyte in this sample.[30]

(a) Use a spreadsheet to calculate the transmittance for each sample and standard listed in Problem 85. Use these new values to prepare a Ringbom plot for these data. What type of response do you see in this plot?

(b) Use your Ringbom plot to determine the concentration of the unknown sample in Problem 85. How does your answer compare to the result that was obtained when using the Beer's law plot in Problem 85?

(c) Beginning with the definition of transmittance, derive an equation that shows how the transmittance for a sample containing a single absorbing analyte will be related to the concentration of this analyte. Use this derivation to explain the response that you saw for the Ringbom plot in Part (a).

TOPICS FOR DISCUSSION AND REPORTS

87. Locate more information on the area of remote sensing and its application. Discuss one specific example of remote sensing with your class. State how spectroscopy is being used in this application.
88. Obtain information on one of the following persons and explain who contributed to the field of spectroscopy or our current understanding of light.
    (a) James Clerk Maxwell
    (b) Heinrich Hertz
    (c) Max Planck
    (d) Robert Bunsen
89. Refractive-index measurements are often used to identify or confirm the identity of a relatively pure chemical compound. This type of measurement is performed by using an instrument known as a refractometer. Obtain more information on refractometers from the literature and manufacturers of these devices and learn about how they are used to measure refractive index. Discuss what you learn with other members of your class.
90. Visit a laboratory that has an instrument that makes use of NMR spectroscopy for chemical measurements. Describe how NMR spectroscopy is used in this laboratory and describe the types of equipment that are used to perform these studies.
91. NMR spectroscopy is also an important tool for the study of biochemical systems. Obtain a research article that used NMR spectroscopy to examine a biochemical system. Write a short report discussing how NMR spectroscopy was used in this article.
92. Obtain more information on one of the following methods. Report on how the method is performed, the types of chemicals it is used to examine, and the information that it provides on these chemicals.
    (a) Microwave absorption spectroscopy
    (b) Gamma-ray spectroscopy
    (c) Electron-spin resonance spectroscopy
93. Locate a recent research article in a journal like *Analytical Chemistry* in which optical fibers are used for chemical analysis. Describe the type of analysis that is being performed in this article and state how optical fibers were used to make this analysis possible.

References

1. National Aeronautics and Space Administration, *Terra: Flagship of the Earth Observing System*, Release No. 99-120, 1999.
2. M. Sharpe, "Focus Analyst in the Sky: Satellite-Based Remote Sensing," *Journal of Environmental Monitoring*, 2 (2000) 41N–44N.
3. T. M. Lillesand, R. W. Kiefer, and J. W. Chipman, *Remote Sensing and Image Interpretation*, 6th ed., Wiley, New York, 2007.
4. C. Elachi and J. Van Zyl, *Introduction to the Physics and Techniques of Remote Sensing*, 2nd ed., Wiley, New York, 2006.
5. G. Maludzinska, Ed., *Dictionary of Analytical Chemisty*, Elsevier, Amsterdam, the Netherlands, 1990.
6. J. Inczedy, T. Lengyel, and A. M. Ure, *Compendium of Analytical Nomenclature*, 3rd ed., Blackwell Science, Malden, MA, 1997.
7. F. Szabadvary, *History of Analytical Chemistry*, Pergamon Press, New York, 1966.
8. H. A. Laitinen and G. W. Ewing, *A History of Analytical Chemistry*, Maple Press, York, PA, 1977.
9. *The New Encyclopaedia Britannica*, 15th ed., Encyclopaedia Britannica, Chicago, IL, 2002.
10. H. D. Young, R. A. Freedman, A. L. Ford, and T. Sandlin, *University Physics*, Addison-Wesley, New York, 2007.
11. D. R. Lide, Ed., *CRC Handbook of Chemistry and Physics*, 83rd ed., CRC Press, Boca Raton, FL, 2002.
12. J. D. Ingle Jr. and S. R. Crouch, *Spectrochemical Analysis*, Prentice Hall, Upper Saddle River, NJ, 1988.
13. "Guide for Use of Terms in Reporting Data in Analytical Chemistry: Spectroscopy Nomenclature," *Analytical Chemistry*, 62 (1990) 91–92.
14. H. Geunther, *NMR Spectroscopy: Basic Principles, Concepts and Applications in Chemistry*, Wiley, New York, 1995.
15. J. W. Akitt and B. E. Mann, *NMR and Chemistry: An Introduction to Modern NMR Spectroscopy*, Thornes, London, 2000.
16. F. Bloch, W. W. Hansen, and M. Packard, "The Nuclear Induction Experiment," *Physics Review*, 70 (1946) 474–485.
17. E. M. Purcell, R. V. Pound, and N. Bloembergen, "Nuclear Magnetic Resonance Absorption by Hydrogen Gas," *Physics Review*, 70 (1946) 980–987.
18. The Nobel Prize Internet Archive, http://www.almaz.com/nobel/
19. C. Westbrook, C. K. Roth, and J. Talbot, *MRI in Practice*, Wiley, New York, 2007.
20. S. C. Bushong, *Magnetic Resonance Imaging: Physical and Biological Principles*, Mosby, Amsterdam, the Netherlands, 2003.
21. A. Einstein, "Heuristic Viewpoint on the Production and Conversion of Light," *Annalen der Physik*, 17 (1905) 132–148.
22. G. Gamow, *Thirty Years that Shook Physics: The Story of Quantum Theory*, Dover, Dover, DE, 1985.
23. L. D. Rothman, S. R. Crouch, and J. D. Ingle Jr., "Theoretical and Experimental Investigation of Factors Affecting Precision in Molecular Absorption Spectrophotometry," *Analytical Chemistry*, 47 (1975) 1226–1233.
24. P. Bougouer, *Essais d'Optique sur la Graduation de la Lumière*, Paris, 1729.
25. J. Lambert, *Photometria*, 1760.
26. A. Beer, "Bestimmung der Absorption des rothen Lichts in farbigen Fl" ussigketiten," *Annalen der Physik*, 86 (1852) 78–88.
27. D. R. Malinin and J. H. Yoe, "Development of the Laws of Colorimetry: A Historical Sketch," *Journal of Chemical Education*, 38 (1961) 129–131.
28. F. D. Snell and C. T. Snell, *Colorimetric Methods of Analysis, Including Photometric Methods*, Vol. IVAA, Van Nostrand Reinhold, New York, 1970.
29. D. A. Skoog, F. J. Holler, and S. R. Crouch, *Principles of Instrumental Analysis*, 6th ed., Brooks/Cole, Pacific Grove, CA, 2006.
30. A. Ringbom, "Accuracy of Colorimetric Determinations. Part 1," *Zeitschrift fur Analytische Chemie*, 115 (1939) 332–343.

Figure for Problem 63

A reading on the analog output of a Spectronic 20 absorbance spectrometer.

Selected Answers

4 510 nm

5 The strongest absorption occurs at 525 nm and the weakest absorption occurs at 700 nm.

14

  a. $v = 2.249 \times 10^8$ m/s   b. $v = 1.989 \times 10^8$ m/s

  c. $n = 1.0005$ d. $n = 1.3588$

15 $t = 8.3 \times 10^{-10}$ s

17

  a. 8.56×10^{13} s^{-1}, infrared light

  b. 1.57×10^6 m^{-1}, visible light

  c. 0.14 nm, X-ray

  d. 1.83×10^1 cm^{-1}, infrared light (far IR)

19 A wavelength of 2.5 μm is in the infrared range and 400 nm is in the visible range. The number of photons at 2.5 μm that would have the equivalent energy of one photon at 400 nm would be 6.25, but you can't have just a fraction of a photon, so at least 7 such photons would be need to supply at least as much energy as one 400 nm photon.

20 Difference in frequency $= 1.197 \times 10^{12}$ s^{-1}; difference in energy $= 7.93 \times 10^{-22}$ J

26

  a. 475 nm is in the green-blue region of visible light

  b. 250 nm is in the ultraviolet region

  c. 675 nm is in the red-orange region of visible light

  d. 1000 nm is in the infrared region

32 For the first solution, 450–500 nm light is blue to green-blue, so if this light is absorbed the object will appear as the complementary color, which is red-orange. If the solution absorbs 250–300 nm light, this light is in the ultraviolet and the object will appear colorless.

39

  a. $F = 2.25 \times 10^{-8}$; this fraction is far too small to be an important issue when using sunlight for remote sensing.

  b. Reflection of light by particulate matter in the atmosphere would be an important factor.

42 At 30°, $\theta_2 = 19.25°$; at 45°, $\theta_2 = 27.79°$; at 60°, $\theta_2 = 34.82°$

53 Concentration of Unknown #1 $= 3.94 \times 10^{-4}$ M; concentration of Unknown #2 $= 1.10 \times 10^{-3}$ M

57

Transmittance	%Transmittance	Absorbance
0.156	15.6	0.807
0.358	35.8	0.446
0.561	56.1	0.251
0.689	68.9	0.162
0.780	78.0	0.108
0.056	5.6	1.250

59 $\epsilon = 124$ L/mol·cm

60 $C = 5.34 \times 10^{-5}$ M

64 Unknown concentration $= 2.94 \times 10^{-4}$ M

68

  a. Approximately 0.3 to 0.4 for 2.5% and 0.1 to 1.3 for 3%

  b. Approximately 0.3 to more than 2.0 for 2.5% and 0.20 to more than 2.0 for 3%

72

  a. The absorbance at 465 nm is low and on the side of a peak, while 645 nm is a peak maximum; therefore, a plot made using data obtained at 645 nm will have a larger slope and better linearity than a plot made using data obtained at 465 nm.

  b. The absorbance at 645 nm is low but 660 nm is a peak maximum; therefore, a plot made using data obtained at 660 nm will have a larger slope.

75 The measured absorbance will be 1.23 instead of 1.30, which is a relative error of 5.4%.

Molecular Spectroscopy

Molecular Spectroscopy

Chapter Outline

1 INTRODUCTION: THE GOOD, THE BAD, AND THE UGLY

Cholesterol is often viewed as being an undesirable molecule. This view is true in that high levels of cholesterol in the diet have been associated with heart disease, which is a leading cause of death in the United States and in many industrialized nations.[1-3] As a result, the screening and measurement of cholesterol levels in blood is now a routine part of medical exams in these countries. Simply measuring the total cholesterol content of blood, however, only gives a partial picture of the role this molecule plays in heart disease.[2-4]

There are actually several "forms" of cholesterol in blood. These forms consist of different particles of proteins, phospholipids, triglycerides, and cholesterol or cholesterol esters that transport cholesterol throughout the body.[4] Two important types of these cholesterol-containing particles are low-density lipoprotein (LDL) and high-density lipoprotein (HDL) (see general structure given in Figure 1). LDL particles carry cholesterol and cholesterol esters that have been formed in the liver and deliver these chemicals to other parts of the body. A large amount of LDL can lead to the creation of plaque in arteries, making LDL represent the "bad cholesterol" in the circulation. HDL particles act to remove excess cholesterol from the body and to take this cholesterol back to the liver for excretion or recycling. This action has given HDL the label of "good cholesterol" because it helps prevent heart disease. The result of an imbalance in these two types of cholesterol-containing particles results in the "ugly" effects of cardiovascular disease.[2,4]

Spectroscopy is a valuable tool that is used in various ways by clinical laboratories to study and measure cholesterol, as well as many other molecules of interest in the diagnosis and treatment of disease. In this chapter, we examine a set of methods known as *molecular spectroscopy* that examine the interaction of light with an intact molecule.[5-7] Various approaches can be utilized in these measurements, including ultraviolet-visible (UV-vis) spectroscopy, infrared spectroscopy, and luminescence spectroscopy. We will also discuss in this chapter how each of these methods is carried out and learn about some typical applications and results for these measurements.

1A What Is Molecular Spectroscopy?

Molecular spectroscopy can be defined as the examination of the interactions of light with molecules.[5-7] Molecules can absorb light, emit light, and scatter light. All of these interactions can lead to chemical information. Absorption occurs when an analyte absorbs the energy of a photon, is raised to a higher energy level, and later emits light as the analyte

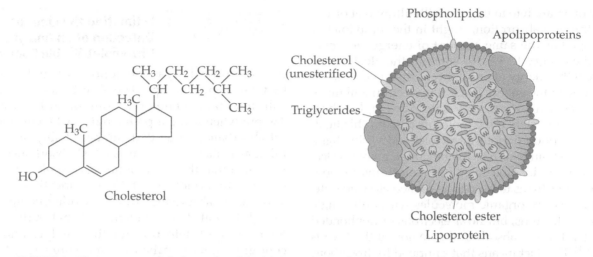

FIGURE 1 The structure of cholesterol and the basic structure of a lipoprotein, such as high-density lipoprotein (HDL) or low-density lipoprotein (LDL). Lipoproteins contain a nonpolar core of triglycerides and cholesterol esters that is surrounded by an outer coating of phospholipids, cholesterol, and special proteins known as "apolipoproteins." Lipoproteins are used in blood to help deliver and transport cholesterol, triglycerides, and other related agents throughout the body. (The diagram of a lipoprotein is courtesy of M. Sobansky.)

goes from the high energy level to a lower level. This absorption in molecules can involve a change in electronic energy levels, as well as a change in vibrational or rotational energy levels. This feature makes spectroscopy a valuable tool in providing both qualitative and quantitative information on molecules.

1B How Is Molecular Spectroscopy Used in Chemical Analysis?

Molecular spectroscopy has many uses in chemical analysis. UV-vis spectroscopy is used primarily for quantitative analysis or screening assays, while infrared spectroscopy is used primarily to identify molecular substances. Visible spectroscopy began with a technique called *colorimetry*.[6,7] In colorimetry, the analyte is combined with a reagent that will form a colored product. The color of this product is then compared to the color of standards, making it possible to determine the amount of analyte that is present in the sample or to simply see if the analyte is present above a certain level as part of a screening assay. One of the first known uses of colorimetry was by Pliny the Elder around A.D. 60 when he used an extract of gallnuts to test for the presence of iron in vinegar.[8] Colorimetry is still employed in modern chemical analysis, with common examples being the use of color-forming reactions in home kits sold for pregnancy detection or for monitoring blood cholesterol levels.[9]

In the 1830s and 1840s methods were developed to measure the concentrations of specific metal ions in slender tubes. This method was developed in 1846 by the Italian chemist Augustin Jacquelain for the analysis of Cu^{2+} in the presence of ammonia in water, giving $Cu(NH_3)_4^{2+}$ as a colored product.[8] The color of an unknown solution was compared with several standards by this approach to determine the concentration of the

unknown. Visual comparison colorimeters are still widely used for measurement of a wide variety of substances in field measurements (e.g., by environmental chemists) so that samples need not be returned to the laboratory for measurement. However, most quantitative measurements made by molecular spectroscopy are conducted in the laboratory using instruments that are designed to conduct more accurate and precise measurements of light absorbance or emission for chemical analysis.[7,10,11] We will see several examples of such instruments in Sections 2 and 4.

Spectroscopy can also be used to help identify chemicals and to provide information on their structure. Some information on chemical identity can be obtained by using the interactions of chemicals with ultraviolet or visible light, but infrared (IR) light is much more frequently utilized for this purpose. This is the case because an IR spectrum for a molecule often has many peaks instead of the one or two that are typically seen for the absorption of ultraviolet or visible light by molecules. In addition, the location, number, and intensities of the peaks in an IR spectrum form a useful fingerprint pattern for a molecule that can be used in identification or to determine the types of functional groups this molecule possesses.[7,10,11] The use of IR light and IR spectroscopy for this purpose is discussed in more detail in Section 3.

2 ULTRAVIOLET-VISIBLE SPECTROSCOPY

2A General Principles of Ultraviolet-Visible Spectroscopy

UV-visible spectroscopy (often called "UV-vis spectroscopy") is a common method for the analysis of molecules and other types of chemicals. This technique can be defined as a type of spectroscopy that is used to examine the ability of an analyte to interact with ultraviolet or visible light through absorption.[5] Light in the ultraviolet or visible range has the same amount of energy as occurs between the energy levels for some of the electrons in molecules. If the energy of this light exactly matches a difference in one of the energy levels, the electron will move from an orbital in a lower energy state to an empty orbital in a higher energy state if the molecule absorbs this light.

The absorption of both ultraviolet and visible light, especially in the range of 200–780 nm, often involves electronic transitions in molecules by π electrons or nonbonded electrons (n) as they go to an excited electron state, π^*. For this reason, organic molecules with only single bonds and σ electrons, but no π electrons or nonbonded electrons, tend to not absorb in this region of the UV-vis spectrum.[7,11] This fact means that saturated hydrocarbons can't be measured by routine UV-vis spectroscopy, because they contain only single bonds and σ electrons. However, a molecule like cholesterol that contains a number of carbon–carbon double bonds and oxygen atoms (which have nonbonding electrons) does have strong absorbance above 200 nm, as shown by the spectrum in Figure 2.

The portion of a molecule that has properties that allow it to absorb light is known as a *chromophore*.[5–7] A typical chromophore in an organic molecule will contain π bonds (such as those in double or triple bonds) and will often have extended conjugation (i.e., a large number of sequential double and single bonds) that tend to absorb ultraviolet or visible light efficiently. This absorption process can be described by using Beer's law. Table 1 shows some typical molar absorptivities for chromophores in organic molecules that absorb in the ultraviolet or visible range. The size of these molar absorptivities is sufficiently high to allow many organic compounds containing these chromophores to be measured at μM concentrations or less when using an appropriate detection wavelength and sample path length.

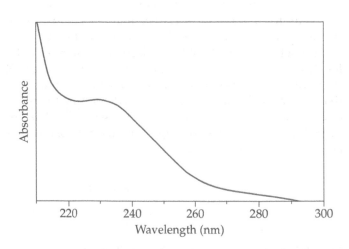

FIGURE 2 A typical Ultraviolet-visible (UV-vis) absorption spectrum, using the analysis of cholesterol as an example. This spectrum illustrates the broad absorption bands that are often seen with molecules for ultraviolet or visible light.

| EXERCISE 1 | **Estimating the Limit of Detection of an Analyte in Ultraviolet-Visible Spectroscopy** |

An unsaturated organic compound is to be examined by UV-vis spectroscopy. The absorbance of an aqueous solution that contains this compound is measured at 450 nm when using a path length of 1.0 cm. The smallest absorbance value that can be reliably measured by this particular instrument is 0.002 absorbance units. It is known that this compound has a molar absorptivity of 1.5×10^4 L/mol·cm at 450 nm and that there is no appreciable absorbance from any other components in its solution at this wavelength. What is the expected lower limit of detection for this analyte under these conditions if its absorbance is measured at 450 nm?

SOLUTION

We can find the lower limit of detection for the concentration of the analyte (C_{LOD}) by using Beer's law. This can be done by using the smallest reliable absorbance measurement ($A = 0.002$), along with the known molar absorptivity for the analyte ($\varepsilon = 1.5 \times 10^4$ L/mol·cm) and the path length of light through the sample ($b = 1.0$ cm).

Beer's Law: $\quad A = \varepsilon b C$

$$(0.002) = (1.5 \times 10^4 \text{ L/mol·cm})(1.0 \text{ cm}) C_{LOD}$$

$$\therefore \quad C_{LOD} = \frac{0.002}{(1.5 \times 10^4 \text{ L/mol·cm})(1.0 \text{ cm})}$$

$$= \mathbf{1.3 \times 10^{-7} \, M}$$

An even lower limit of detection would be expected for an analyte with a higher molar absorptivity. For instance, a molecule that has a 10-fold higher value for ε (1.5×10^5 L/mol·cm) would have a 10-fold lower limit of detection ($C_{LOD} = 1.3 \times 10^{-8} \, M$).

The absorption of light in the ultraviolet or visible range is also possible for transition metal ions as they undergo electronic transitions that involve d- or f-shell electrons.[7,11] This type of absorption is seen for the ions of most lanthanide and actinide elements in the periodic table. Chemical species that can undergo charge-transfer absorption are also quite important in many assay methods because of their large molar absorptivities and ease of measurement in UV-vis spectroscopy. This type of light absorption is seen for many inorganic complexes. A few common examples include the complex that is formed between Fe^{2+} and 1,10-phenanthroline, and the complexes that are produced when Fe^{3+} reacts with thiocyanate and phenol. This type of process is also responsible for CrO_4^{2-} and MnO_4^{-} having strong absorption of visible light.[7]

TABLE 1 Examples of Chromophores in Ultraviolet-Visible Spectroscopy for Organic Molecules*

Chromophore	Wavelength of Absorbance Maximum (nm)	Molar Absorptivity (L/mol·cm)
$\ce{C=C}$	182	25
	174	16,000
	170	16,500
	162	10,000
$\ce{-C#C-}$	172	2,500
$\ce{C=C-C=C}$	209	25,000
(benzene ring)	255	200
	200	6,300
	180	100,000
(naphthalene)	270	5,000
	221	100,000
$\ce{C=O}$	295	10
	185	Strong

*The data in this table are from J.D. Ingle Jr. and S.R. Crouch, *Spectrochemical Analysis*, Prentice Hall, Upper Saddle River, NJ, 1988. Futher examples of chromophores can be found in this reference.

A typical UV-vis absorption spectrum was given earlier in Figure 2, using cholesterol as an example. In this particular case, wavelengths up to only 300 nm are shown in the spectrum because cholesterol does not absorb at higher wavelengths between 300 and 800 nm. The x-axis for this type of spectrum is usually plotted in terms of the wavelength, which is commonly expressed in units of nanometers for ultraviolet or visible light. The y-axis is often plotted using the measured absorbance at a given wavelength. When working with analytes that are molecules, the bands in this type of spectrum tend to be quite broad. For instance, cholesterol has an absorption band that spans at least 30–40 nm from 225 nm to 260 nm in Figure 2. The reason for the width of these molecular absorption bands is that the electronic energy levels that are involved in these absorption processes also contain many smaller vibrational and rotational transitions. The result is many possible transitions in a molecule that have only small differences in energy, which creates the broad peak observed in the absorption spectrum. In addition, spectra that are acquired for a molecule in a solution are broad because of the rapid, repeated collisions each molecule undergoes with neighboring solvent molecules. These collisions shorten the lifetime of each vibrational/rotational state in the molecule to such a great extent that the Heisenberg uncertainty principle comes into play. This effect causes a loss in precision for the measured changes in energy due to light absorption, and in the wavelengths of absorbed light that are observed.[7]

2B Instrumentation for Ultraviolet-Visible Spectroscopy

Typical System Components. An instrument that is used to examine the absorption of light in UV-vis spectroscopy is known as a *UV-vis absorbance spectrometer*. An absorbance spectrometer has four basic components: a light source, a means for selecting a particular type of light for analysis, a sample container, and a detector. A UV-vis absorbance spectrometer has all of these components, but each of these components must be capable of working with ultraviolet or visible light.

A common light source for visible light is a *tungsten lamp*, as illustrated in Figure 3. In this device, a heated tungsten wire gives off a wide spectrum of light with both an intensity and wavelength maximum that depend on the temperature of the wire. This type of light emission is known as "blackbody radiation". Tungsten is used in this lamp because it can be heated hotter than any other metal without melting, making it possible to obtain strong-emission and high-emission wavelengths with this material. At a typical operating temperature (2000–3000 K), the wavelength of maximum emission is at about 1000 nm for a tungsten lamp, with a usable range that spans from 320 to 2500 nm.[7]

A modified form of this previous design is the *tungsten/halogen lamp*. In this device a small amount of iodine is also present inside the tungsten lamp. As the tungsten gets hot, small amounts of tungsten atoms will

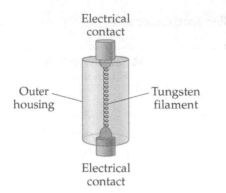

FIGURE 3 The general design of a tungsten lamp. A tungsten/halogen lamp has a similar design, but includes some I_2 in the chamber that surrounds the tungsten filament.

sublime off the surface and coat the interior of the lamp with a gray solid. The presence of iodine, however, will cause the gas-phase tungsten atoms to react and form tungsten(II) iodide, WI_2.

$$W + I_2 \rightarrow WI_2 \qquad (1)$$

WI_2 is stable at low temperatures, but if a WI_2 molecule hits the hot tungsten filament, it will decompose to put tungsten back onto the filament (the iodine atoms also recombine to form I_2 as part of this process). In this way, a more stable lamp is created that can be operated at a higher temperature (up to 3600 K) and with a greater intensity of light emission. This lamp can provide emitted light up to about 3000 nm.[7] Both the tungsten and tungsten/halogen lamps are mostly used in the visible region of the spectrum and emit almost all their radiation as infrared or visible light. As a result, a different type of light source is needed for work in the ultraviolet region in UV-vis spectroscopy.

The *hydrogen lamp* and *deuterium lamp* are two other light sources that can be used in UV-vis spectroscopy.[7,11] Both lamps consist of two inert electrodes across which a high voltage is imposed in a quartz bulb that is filled at a low pressure with either H_2 or D_2. The presence of the high voltage results in the excitation of H_2 or D_2 and their dissociation into H or D atoms plus with the emission of

light. A hydrogen lamp was used by Neils Bohr as he sought to understand the nature and electronic structure of the hydrogen atom. Bohr's interest was in the several bright lines of emitted light that corresponded to electrons falling from a higher orbital into the $n = 2$ orbital. This same type of lamp provides a continuous source of radiation in the ultraviolet region by using light that is emitted when an electron falls from a nonquantized energy level into the $n = 2$ orbital of what had been a gas-phase hydrogen ion. Hydrogen and deuterium lamps provide ultraviolet radiation as a continuous band that spans from roughly 180 to 370 nm. A deuterium lamp is more common in modern laboratories because it gives more intense light emission than a hydrogen lamp.[7]

The wavelength selector (or monochromator) in an absorbance instrument often consists of a narrow slit through which light enters, a device for separating this light into its various wavelengths, and another narrow slit through which a particular portion of this light is allowed to exit and pass onto the sample and detector. Instruments for absorption measurements in UV-vis spectroscopy often use a prism or grating to separate light. The use of a prism for this purpose is demonstrated in Figure 4. Prisms used in the visible region are made of glass. The difference in the index of refraction of glass as a function of wavelength creates a separation of light into its various colors. The bigger that this change in angle is with wavelength, the better the separation will be for light with wavelengths in this range of the spectrum.

There are two types of gratings that can be used as monochromators. A *transmission grating* is one in which diffraction is produced by having light pass through a grating consisting of a series of small slits that create constructive and destructive interference of the light. Different wavelengths of light will have different angles at which they will produce constructive interference, making it possible to then select these wavelengths for use in absorbance measurements. A *reflection grating* is more common in modern instruments. This type of grating uses a polished and reflective surface that has a series of parallel and closely spaced steps cut into its surface, as is also illustrated in Figure 4. When a beam of light is reflected from this surface, a pattern of constructive and destructive interference is again created in which certain angles have constructive interference for

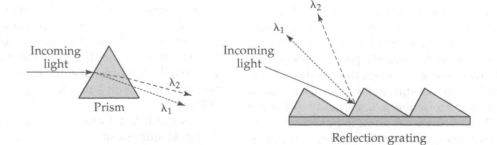

FIGURE 4 Use of a prism (left) or a reflection grating (right) for the separation of light containing various wavelengths.

particular wavelengths of light. Changing the orientation and sample angle of either a transmission or reflection grating can allow the desired wavelengths of light with constructive interference to strike an exit slit and pass onto the sample and detector for use in absorbance measurements.[7,11]

The sample holder in UV-vis spectroscopy is usually a cuvette into which a sample or standard solution can be placed. This cuvette must be transparent to the wavelengths of light that will be used for the measurement and have a well-defined geometry. Cuvettes for work with light in the visible region are typically made of glass or a clear plastic. For work with ultraviolet light, cuvettes made from quartz or fused silica are required, because glass or many types of plastics will absorb such light. Many modern spectrometers use cuvettes with a square cross section and with an internal path length of 1.00 cm. However, some instruments use cylindrical test tube-looking cuvettes and/or cuvettes with longer path lengths.[7]

Many detectors that are used to monitor ultraviolet or visible light make use of the photoelectrical effect (or "photoelectric effect"), which occurs when light strikes certain substances and causes the ejection of an electron from this surface. Such an effect can be used in a phototube or photomultiplier tube to detect the light (see Figure 5 for an example). Both of these devices are designed so that light can enter them and strike a photoactive substance. The result is the production of electrons and a current that is proportional in size to the number of photons that have struck the photoactive surface. The absorption of a greater number of photons by the sample will result in a lower flux striking the phototube and a decreased current measurment.[7,10,11]

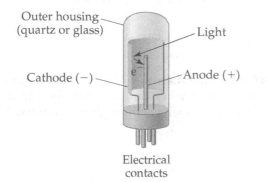

FIGURE 5   The basic components of a phototube. As light enters this device and strikes the cathode, electrons are given off by a photoemissive material on the cathode's surface. These electrons then travel to the more positive anode. This produces a current that is related to the intensity of light entering the phototube and striking the cathode. A photomultiplier tube has a similar design, but contains a series of intermediate electrodes between the cathode and anode that are each at a progressively more positive potential; this design results in a large number of electrons being produced for each collision of a photon with the cathode.

Single- and Dual-Beam Instruments.   Two common types of devices for UV-vis spectroscopy are "single-beam" and "double-beam" instruments. As its name implies, a **single-beam instrument** has a single path for the light to take through the instrument, as shown in Figure 6(a).[7,11] The light in this instrument originates from the source, a wavelength is selected by using the monochromator, this light is passed through the sample in a cuvette, and the intensity of the remaining light is measured by a detector. Because transmittance and absorbance are defined in terms of the ratio of light intensity that passes through the sample divided by the intensity of light that is entering the sample, there must be some way to measure both of these quantities in this device. In a single-beam instrument, the device is first adjusted so that it gives an output of 0% transmittance when a shutter is closed and no light reaches the sample (the "dark current"). The instrument is then set to read 100% transmittance (or $A = 0$) when a blank solution containing no analyte is in place. Next, the sample is introduced and its % transmittance (% T) or absorbance is measured. With older single-beam instruments, one must reset the dark current and 100% T current whenever wavelength is changed. With modern single-beam instruments, a computer remembers these settings during the collection of an entire spectrum. One possible problem with this process is that the intensity of the lamp or the response of the detector may change between the time the instrument is adjusted and the sample is analyzed. This type of change, if not corrected for, would give a systematic error in the final results.

A **double-beam instrument** in spectroscopy is a device in which the original beam of light is split so that half the light goes through a reference (or "blank") solution, while the other half passes through the sample.[7,11] This type of instrument, as shown in Figure 6(b), helps minimize errors that are caused by any drift in the lamp's intensity or in the detector's response. If either the lamp intensity or the detector response changes, this change will affect both the signal from the sample and from the blank, while the ratio of these signals will remain unchanged.

Related Devices.   Another design for a UV-vis spectrophotometer is one based on a **diode-array detector** (see Figure 7). This device differs from a standard spectrophotometer in that the monochromator has an entrance slit but no exit slit, which allows light of many wavelengths to enter the sample and to be detected simultaneously by an array of small diode detectors. Each diode in this array monitors a small range of wavelengths that have been separated *after* they have passed through the sample. This process allows the simultaneous measurement of an entire spectrum for a sample. These are single-beam instruments with a computer to remember the signal at all wavelengths for the dark current and the 100% T signal, as well as to monitor the light at each of the photodiodes in the array detector.[7,11–13]

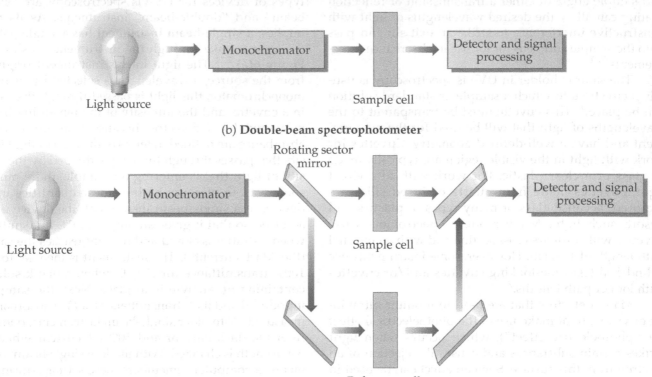

(a) Single-beam spectrophotometer

Light source → Monochromator → Sample cell → Detector and signal processing

(b) Double-beam spectrophotometer

Light source → Monochromator → Rotating sector mirror → Sample cell → Detector and signal processing

Reference cell

FIGURE 6 General design of (a) a single-beam instrument, or (b) a double-beam instrument for UV-vis spectroscopy.

Flow injection analysis (FIA) is a useful way in which UV-vis spectroscopy can be used to conduct a large number of routine analyses in a short period of time. In this approach, samples are injected sequentially into a flowing stream of a reagent, which then reacts with the contents of these samples to give a colored product.[14–15] After color development, the flowing stream passes through a spectrophotometer that is part of the FIA system (see Figure 8). The absorbance of the solution that results from the reaction of the analyte with the color-forming reagent is then measured, allowing the concentration of the analyte to be determined. The most desirable analyses for FIA are those in which the colored product forms rapidly, so that only a few seconds pass

between injection of the sample into the stream of reagent and the measurement of its absorbance. FIA is commonly used in laboratories where the same analytes are monitored on a regular basis in a large number of samples. A good example is the use of FIA and related flow-based devices to determine the concentration of cholesterol in blood samples in a clinical laboratory.[2,4]

2C Applications of Ultraviolet-Visible Spectroscopy

Direct Measurements. The most common use of spectrophotometry in chemical analysis is in the direct measurement of analytes through colorimetry. The term

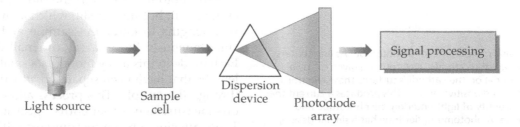

Light source → Sample cell → Dispersion device → Photodiode array → Signal processing

FIGURE 7 The general design of a diode array detector for UV-vis spectroscopy. Although this particular design shows a prism as the dispersing device for the sake of simplicity, gratings can also be used for light dispersion in this type of instrument.

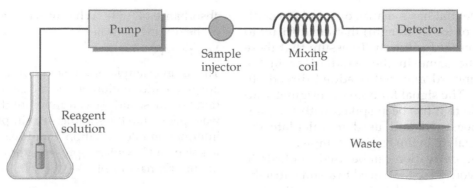

FIGURE 8 An example of a simple system for performing flow injection analysis (FIA). In this particular case, the sample is injected into a flowing stream of a reagent that results in the formation of a product that is monitored later at the detector. A mixing coil is present between the sample injector and detector to provide time for this reaction to occur. More advanced systems that use multiple reagents and flow streams and temperature control for the mixing chamber can also be developed based on this general design.

"colorimetry" is often used to describe the use of spectrometry in the visible region of the spectrum, where one can visually observe the color of a sample. This approach can also be use in the form of direct measurements made by instruments in the ultraviolet region. In this technique, the concentration of an analyte is determined by comparing the absorbance of an unknown concentration of a substance with the absorbance of a known concentration of the same material. Beer's law is then used to relate the measured absorbance of an analyte to its concentration.

If the molar absorptivity of the analyte is known and a sample has a known or negligible background absorbance, the concentration of the analyte can be determined directly by Beer's law. For instance, suppose the molar absorptivity of an analyte is 5.34×10^3 L/mol·cm at a particular wavelength. The same analyte gives an absorbance of 0.573 in a sample placed into a 2.00 cm sample holder, where a blank is used to correct for any background absorbance from the sample. One way the concentration of analyte in the sample can then be estimated is by rearranging Beer's law to give $C = A/(\epsilon b)$, or $C = 0.573/(5.34 \times 10^3$ L/mol·cm$)(2.00$ cm$)$ $= 5.36 \times 10^{-5}$ M. Although this single-point method is simple to do, it is often subject to errors if the sample and standard are not both in the linear response region of Beer's law or if there are differences in conditions, such as the solution pH or small changes in the detection wavelength, that were used to examine these solutions. A better approach is to use multiple standards and to prepare a Beer's law plot (see Figure 9), where these standards are measured under the same solution and wavelength conditions that will be used for the samples. The concentration of an analyte in a sample can then be determined by comparing the absorbance of this sample to the response of the plot.

Standard Addition Method. Another approach that can be used in UV-vis spectroscopy for analyte measurement is the **standard addition method**.[5-7] This is a technique that is used to determine the concentration of an

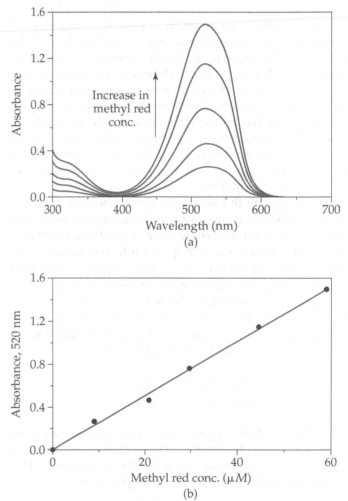

FIGURE 9 (a) A series of absorption spectra, and (b) a Beer's law plot for an analyte that is being examined by UV-vis spectroscopy, using methyl red as an example. These results were obtained for aqueous solutions of methyl red that were prepared in an acidic solution (pH < 4.4) and measured at 520 nm using a cuvette with a 1 cm path length. The same solutions of methyl red were used to acquire the spectra and to obtain the absorbance values that were used in the Beer's law plot.

analyte in a sample that has a matrix or solution conditions (such as pH or ionic strength) that are difficult to reproduce in a standard solution. To assure that these parameters are the same in the standard as in the unknown, the standard material is added directly to part of the sample. The signal for both the original sample and the sample that has been spiked with the standard are then measured and used to calculate the concentration of analyte in the original sample.

The following derivation can be used to illustrate how this method works. First, we need to assume that the signal we are measuring for either the sample or the standard will be proportional to the concentration of the analyte in each. We can represent this idea for absorbance measurements by the following relationships,

Absorbance of Original Sample: $\quad A_o = k\,C_o \quad$ (2)

Absorbance of Spiked Sample: $\quad A_{sp} = k\,C_{sp} \quad$ (3)

where C_o is the concentration of analyte in the original sample, C_{sp} is the total concentration of analyte in the sample that has been spiked with a known amount of the analyte, and k is a proportionality constant. (Note: $k = \varepsilon b$, for an absorbance measurement based on Beer's law.) We are assuming that the constant k is the same for both the original and spiked sample, which should be true if they contain the same matrix and we are working in the linear range of Beer's law. We are also assuming in this case that there is no background absorbance from the sample or its matrix.

Along with the measured absorbances of the original and spiked samples, we also know in this method (1) the original volume of the sample (V_o), (2) the volume of standard solution that we spiked into this sample (V_s), and (3) the concentration of analyte in this standard solution (C_s). This information can be combined to find the value of C_o, which is the goal of the standard addition method. To do this, we divide Equation 2 by Equation 3 to find the ratio of A_o/A_{sp} and substitute in the fact that $C_{sp} = (C_o V_o + C_s V_s)/(V_o + V_s)$.

$$\frac{A_o}{A_{sp}} = \frac{C_o\,(V_o + V_s)}{C_o V_o + C_s V_s} \qquad (4)$$

With this combined equation we can use the measured ratio A_o/A_{sp} to calculate the value of C_o because we know the values of all other terms in this expression. This process is illustrated in the following exercise.

EXERCISE 2 — The Standard Addition Method

A chemist performs a colorimetric assay that selectively measures iron. A 20.0 mL portion of the original sample gives an absorbance reading of 0.367 and a 20.00 mL portion of the same sample that has been spiked with 5.00 mL of a $2.00 \times 10^{-2}\,M$ iron solution gives an

absorbance of 0.538. What was the concentration of iron in the original sample?

SOLUTION

This is an example of the standard addition method. We are given information on the measured absorbance, solution volumes, and concentration of the iron solution that was spiked into the sample. We simply have to place this information into Equation 4 and rearrange this equation to solve for C_o, which represents the concentration of iron in our original sample.

$$\frac{0.367}{0.538} = \frac{C_o\,(0.02000\text{ L} + 0.00500\text{ L})}{C_o\,(0.02000\text{ L}) + (0.005000\text{ L})(2.00 \times 10^{-2}\,M)}$$

$$\Rightarrow\ 0.6822 = \frac{C_o\,(0.02500\text{ L})}{C_o\,(0.02000\text{ L}) + (1.00 \times 10^{-4}\,\text{mol})}$$

$$\Rightarrow\ (0.6822)[C_o\,(0.02000\text{ L}) + (1.00 \times 10^{-4}\,\text{mol})]$$

$$= C_o(0.02500\text{ L})$$

$$\Rightarrow\ (0.6822)(1.00 \times 10^{-4}\,\text{mol})$$

$$= C_o(0.02500\text{ L} - 0.02000\text{ L})$$

$$\therefore\ C_o = \frac{(0.6822)(1.00 \times 10^{-4}\,\text{mol})}{(0.02500\text{ L} - 0.02000\text{ L})}$$

$$= 0.01364\,M = \mathbf{0.0136\,M}$$

The previous equation shows how standard addition can be conducted when using only one spiked sample. It is also possible to use multiple spikes of a standard into the sample, with the assay response being measured for each spiked sample. The results of this assay would then be used to prepare a plot of $A_{sp}\,(V_o + V_s)$ on the y-axis and $C_s\,(V_s/V_o)$ on the x-axis (see the example in Figure 10). For absorbance measurements that are made in the linear region of Beer's law, the resulting plot should give a straight line where the value of the x-intercept is equal to $-C_o$, which provides the concentration of the analyte in the original sample.

Spectrophotometric Titrations. A common way in which UV-vis spectroscopy is employed in titrations is in the detection of visual indicators. For example, one acid–base indicator that we have already discussed is methyl red (see spectra in Figure 11). Methyl red is a "two-color indicator" which is red in an acidic solution and yellow in a solution with a basic pH. Both forms of methyl red are able to strongly absorb visible light but do so at different wavelengths, thus explaining why they have different colors. As the pH is changed during the course of a titration, we alter the relative amount of methyl red that exists in the acid or base form. This alteration in the relative amount

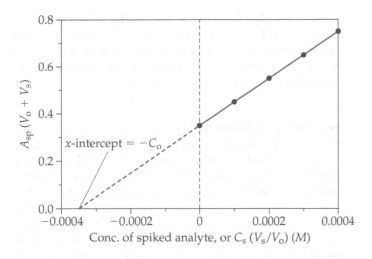

FIGURE 10 A plot for determining the concentration of analyte in a sample through the method of standard addition. The apparent amount of spiked analyte that corresponds to the negative value of the x-intercept is then determined, which provides a value that gives the amount of analyte in the original sample.

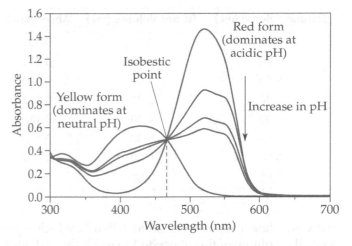

FIGURE 11 Absorption spectra obtained at several pH values for methyl red, a common visual indicator used for acid–base titrations. The pH range used here corresponds to the same range over which methyl red is used as an indicator, in which this chemical is red in an acidic solution (pH < 4.4) and yellow in a more basic solution (pH > 6.2). The approximate isobestic point for these acid and base forms occurs at 464 nm in these spectra.

of these two species is what leads to the observed change in color at the end point of the titration.

Besides using a visual indicator and our eyes to locate the end point of a titration, it is possible to use UV-vis spectroscopy to follow the course of a titration by measuring the absorbance due to an indicator, the analyte, the titrant, or the titration product. In the case of an indicator like methyl red, the end point could be detected by measuring the absorbance at a wavelength at which either the acid or base forms of the indicator have different molar absorptivities. Measurements at multiple wavelengths can also be used to determine the relative amounts of the different forms of the indicator at a given point during the titration (as is discussed in the next section). It is important during this type of analysis to select a wavelength at which the two forms of indicator have very different absorption spectra. This is not possible if we are using a wavelength at which the spectra for these two forms intersect (as occurs in Figure 11 at a wavelength of 464 nm). This point of intersection in the spectra for two absorbing species is called an *isobestic point* and represents a place where the two forms have an identical molar absorptivity.[5,6] Although an isobestic point should not be used if we are trying to differentiate between two absorbing species, this point can be valuable if we wish to measure the *total* amount of these species or want to work at a wavelength that will not give a change in absorbance as the relative fraction of these two species is altered.

Absorption spectroscopy can also be used to follow a titration if the analyte, titrant, or product of the titration reaction has any significant absorption of visible or UV light. In this case, we can use UV-vis spectroscopy to measure the absorbance at different points along the titration and use this information to locate the end point. This approach is called a **spectrophotometric titration**.[5–7] The actual shape of the titration curve in this type of

measurement will depend on the relative size of the molar absorptivities for the analyte, titrant, and titration product (see general examples in Figure 12 and a specific example in the center portion of this text). However, in each case there are a series of linear regions, and their point of intersection can be used to locate the end point. The reason why these titration curves have a linear form (rather than the nonlinear response we typically see when measuring pH or pM) is that the measured quantity of absorbance is directly related to the concentration of absorbing species through Beer's law. In contrast to this, values measured for pH or pM during an acid–base or complexometric titration (as well as E_{Cell} in a redox titration) are all related to a logarithmic function of an analyte's activity or concentration.

EXERCISE 3 | **Performing a Spectrophotometric Titration**

The following mixtures of a sample and titrant (with a concentration of 2.50×10^{-3} M) are placed with pipettes into a series of 25.00 mL volumetric flasks and diluted to the mark. The absorbance of each mixture is then measured. If the analyte and titrant are known to react in a 1:1 ratio, what volume of titrant is needed to reach the equivalence point for this titration? What was the concentration of analyte in the original sample?

SOLUTION

A titration curve can be prepared from these data by making a graph of the absorbance versus the volume of added titrant. This plot gives a linear region for the first five sample/titrant mixtures with a slope of 0.040 absorbance units per mL, followed by a region with no significant change in slope at absorbance = 0.170 for the last three sample/titrant mixtures. The intersection of

Sample Volume (mL)	Titrant Volume (mL)	Absorbance
5.00	0.00	0.000
5.00	1.00	0.040
5.00	2.00	0.080
5.00	3.00	0.120
5.00	4.00	0.160
5.00	5.00	0.170
5.00	6.00	0.170
5.00	7.00	0.170

these two linear regions occurs at 4.25 mL, which represents the volume of titrant needed to reach the end point. The concentration of the sample can then be calculated from this volume, the concentration of the added titrant, and the volume of the original sample.

Conc. analyte =

$$\frac{(2.50 \times 10^{-3} \, M \text{ titrant})(0.00425 \text{ L titrant})}{0.00500 \text{ L analyte}} \cdot$$

$$(1 \text{ mol analyte}/1 \text{ mol titrant})$$

$$= 2.125 \times 10^{-3} \, M = \mathbf{2.12 \times 10^{-3}} \, \boldsymbol{M}$$

Although a buret was not used in this particular analysis, this is still an example of a titration and volumetric method because it makes use of a measured volume and known titrant concentration to determine the concentration of an analyte in the sample.

Measuring Multiple Analytes. It is sometimes possible to use UV-vis spectroscopy to determine the concentration of several absorbing species (A, B, and so on) in a sample if these species have significantly different absorption spectra in the UV-vis range. This approach is performed by measuring the total absorbance of the sample at two wavelengths (ε_1 and ε_2), which have significantly different molar absorptivities for at least one of the absorbing species. We can then use Beer's law to relate these measured absorbance values (A_1 and A_2) to the concentrations of the two species (C_A and C_B) and the molar absorptivity of each species at the two wavelengths used in these measurements (ε_{A_1} and ε_{A_2} for species A, and ε_{B_1} and ε_{B_2} for species B).

Absorbance at Wavelength ε_1:

$$A_1 = (\varepsilon_{A_1} b C_A) + (\varepsilon_{B_1} b C_B) \tag{5}$$

Absorbance at Wavelength ε_2:

$$A_2 = (\varepsilon_{A_2} b C_A) + (\varepsilon_{B_2} b C_B) \tag{6}$$

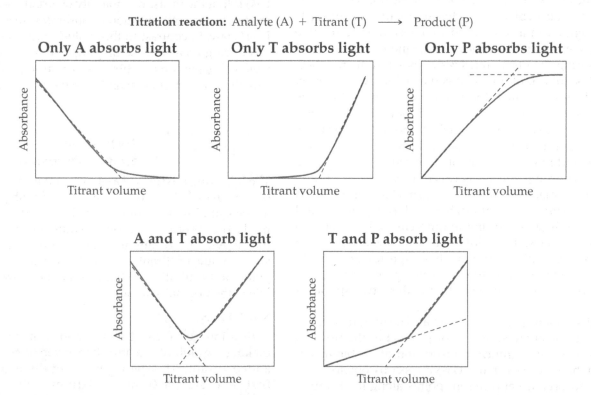

Titration reaction: Analyte (A) + Titrant (T) $\longrightarrow$ Product (P)

FIGURE 12 Example of general plots obtained for a spectrophotometric titration. These plots are for various types of analytes, titrants, and products in terms of their ability to absorb the light that is being used to follow the titration. An example of such a titration is provided in the color plates located in the center of this book.

If we measure A_1 and A_2 and know the values of b and the molar absorptivities (as obtained from the analysis of standards), we can rearrange Equations 5 and 6 to solve for both C_A and C_B. The same approach can be used to look at more than two sample components, as long as an equal or greater number of wavelengths is used for the corresponding absorbance measurements *and* these wavelengths have significantly different molar absorptivities for each of the given analytes.

EXERCISE 4   Spectroscopic Analysis of an Acid–Base Mixture

The two acid–base forms of methyl red present in the pH range over which it changes color are known to have the following molar absorptivities at 515 nm and 425 nm.

$\lambda_1 = 515$ nm	$\lambda_2 = 425$ nm
Acid form:	
$\varepsilon_{A_1} = 2.49 \times 10^4$ L/mol·cm	$\varepsilon_{A_2} = 2.04 \times 10^3$ L/mol·cm
Base form:	
$\varepsilon_{B_1} = 1.49 \times 10^3$ L/mol·cm	$\varepsilon_{B_2} = 1.06 \times 10^4$ L/mol·cm

A total concentration solution of $5.00 \times 10^{-5} M$ methyl red is placed into a sample and the absorbance of this mixture is measured in a cuvette with a 1.0 cm path length. An absorbance of 0.379 is measured at 515 nm and an absorbance of 0.419 is found at 425 nm. It is known from previous measurements that there are no other chemicals in the sample that absorb at these wavelengths. What are the concentrations of the acid and base forms of methyl red in this sample?

SOLUTION

This analysis is the same system represented by Equations 5 and 6, in which we have two equations and two unknowns (the concentrations of the acid and base forms of methyl red, C_A and C_B). To solve these equations, we can first rearrange Equation 5 to solve for C_A.

Absorbance at 515 nm (λ_1): $A_1 = (\varepsilon_{A_1} b C_A) + (\varepsilon_{B_1} b C_B)$

$$\Rightarrow \quad C_A = \frac{A_1 - (\varepsilon_{B_1} b C_B)}{(\varepsilon_{A_1} b)}$$

We can now substitute this equation for C_A into Equation 5 to get a combined expression that only has C_B as an unknown quantity.

Absorbance at 425 nm (λ_2): $A_2 = (\varepsilon_{A_2} b C_A) + (\varepsilon_{B_2} b C_B)$

$$\Rightarrow \quad A_2 = (\varepsilon_{A_2} b) \cdot \frac{A_1 - (\varepsilon_{B_1} b C_B)}{(\varepsilon_{A_1} b)} + (\varepsilon_{B_2} b C_B)$$

Next, we place our known values for the measured absorbances, molar absorptivities, and path length into this new equation and solve for C_B.

$$0.419 = (2.04 \times 10^3 \text{ L/mol·cm})(1.00 \text{ cm}) \cdot$$

$$\frac{0.397 - (1.49 \times 10^3 \text{ L/mol·cm})(1.00 \text{ cm}) C_B}{(2.49 \times 10^4 \text{ L/mol·cm})(1.00 \text{ cm})}$$

$$+ (1.06 \times 10^4 \text{ L/mol·cm})(1.00 \text{ cm}) C_B$$

$$\Rightarrow 0.419 = 0.0325 - (1.221 \times 10^2 \text{ L/mol}) C_B$$

$$+ (1.06 \times 10^4 \text{ L/mol}) C_B$$

$$C_B = \frac{0.419 - 0.0325}{(1.06 \times 10^4 \text{ L/mol}) - (1.221 \times 10^2 \text{ L/mol})}$$

$$= 3.69 \times 10^{-5} M$$

Placing our calculated value for C_B and our other known parameters back into Equation 5 then allows us to also calculate the concentration for the acid form of methyl red (C_A), or we can simply take the difference between the known total concentration of the methyl red and C_B to find C_A. Using either approach gives a concentration of $1.31 \times 10^{-5} M$ for the acid form.

3 INFRARED SPECTROSCOPY

3A General Principles of Infrared Spectroscopy

In UV-vis spectroscopy the absorption of visible or ultraviolet light can lead to an increase in the energy of the absorbing molecules due to *electronic transitions*. Molecules can also absorb other types of radiation, but these processes may involve different types of transitions than those that make use of a change in an electronic state. If a molecule absorbs infrared light (which has a lower energy than visible or ultraviolet light), this absorption is based on a change in the energy due to vibrations or rotations that are occurring in the molecule. A spectroscopic method that uses infrared light to study or measure chemicals is called **infrared spectroscopy** (or "IR spectroscopy").[5]

    The simplest kind of bond vibration involves stretching of a bond between two atoms. For example, water is often depicted as a triatomic, bent molecule with a bond angle of about 105° and bond lengths of roughly 96 pm. This model implies that a water molecule is a static object, but in reality a water molecule is always undergoing some changes in its bond angles and bond lengths (see examples of such processes in Figure 13). The static model merely depicts the *average* bond angle and bond length, which can have slightly higher or lower values at any given point in time. A better model is to view these bonds as acting as

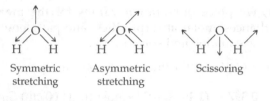

Symmetric stretching   Asymmetric stretching   Scissoring

FIGURE 13 The vibrational modes for water. The labels given below each of these vibrational modes are terms commonly used to describe these types of vibrations. Both these and alternative types of vibrations can occur in other types of molecules.

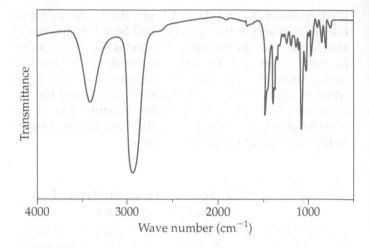

FIGURE 14 A typical IR absorption spectrum, using cholesterol as an example. In this type of spectrum the y-axis is often expressed in terms of transmittance or % transmittance rather than absorbance. The x-axis is often given in terms of the wave number of light instead of the light's wavelength.

small springs rather than fixed rods. Even at a temperature of absolute zero, molecules will vibrate as these bonds continue to contract and expand.

Energy absorption is required to cause a molecular vibration to occur more energetically, and the energy levels that describe these vibrations occur at distinct values (or are "quantized"). The differences in these vibrational energy levels are typically much smaller than the differences in energy present for electronic transitions. As a result, the energy for a photon that is needed to cause excitation in a vibration is also much smaller and is in the same range as is found for infrared light. Even smaller amounts of energy are needed to cause molecules to rotate more rapidly, corresponding to the energy present in microwave radiation. These small changes in rotational energies are often superimposed on the changes in vibrational energies that are seen in IR spectroscopy and lead to broadening of the observed absorption bands. This broadening occurs in a similar manner to the way in which vibrational and rotational transitions plus electronic transitions lead to broad absorption bands for molecules in UV-vis spectroscopy (see Section 2A).

Figure 14 shows a typical IR absorption spectrum, with cholesterol again being used as an example. We can see by comparing this spectrum with the spectrum for cholesterol in Figure 2 that the appearance of an infrared absorption spectrum is totally different from a UV or visible absorption spectrum. Most UV-vis absorption spectra exhibit one or two broad peaks, whereas IR spectra might have dozens of very narrow peaks. This is because only one or two electronic transitions often dominate a UV-vis spectrum, but each molecule can have many ways of undergoing vibrational transitions to produce an IR spectrum.

IR spectra are most commonly represented as a plot of % T versus wave number (in units of cm^{-1}), although some spectra are plotted in terms of % T versus wavelength (expressed in units of micrometers). This way of plotting a spectrum is in contrast to UV-vis spectra, which are usually plotted in terms of absorbance versus wavelength (in units of nanometers). The result is that an IR spectrum has a very different appearance from a typical UV-vis spectrum. The former

typically show a large number of peaks, each of which is quite narrow compared to the entire range of wavelengths in the spectrum. In contrast to this UV-vis spectra typically have only one or a few broad peaks for each analyte (see Box 1).

3B Instrumentation for Infrared Spectroscopy

Typical System Components. IR spectroscopy is similar to UV-vis spectroscopy in that it requires a source of light, a means for separating this light into different wavelengths, a sample holder, and a detector. However, the specific instrument components in IR spectroscopy are made of different materials and often operate on different principles than the devices that are used for UV-vis spectroscopy.

The source of light in IR spectroscopy is usually an inert rod that is heated to a much lower temperature than is used for light sources in visible spectroscopy. As a result, the maximum absorbance that is now obtained through blackbody radiation will occur in the infrared region. Glass and fused silica are opaque at wavelengths greater than 2.5 μm, so the glowing source must not be in a glass bulb or in a casing that is made of these substances. The heated material is either silicon carbide (SiC, giving a device called a *globar*), or is a mixture of rare-earth oxides (producing a device known as a *Nernst glower*).[7,10-11] The general construction of such a device, the Nernst glower, is shown in Figure 16 (see following pages). This design includes the material that is to be heated, a heating source, and a reflector to help pass the resulting radiation in the desired direction. The light that is produced by such a device closely matches what would be expected for blackbody radiation. For a globar heated at 1300–1500 K, usable light is provided at wavelengths of 0.4–20 μm. A Nernst glower that is heated

BOX 1
Raman Spectroscopy

IR spectroscopy is not the only way information can be obtained on vibrational transitions in a molecule. *Raman spectroscopy* is another method that provides information on such transitions. This technique is named after Sir Chandrasekhara Vancata Raman, a scientist from India who was awarded the 1930 Nobel Prize in Physics (see Figure 15). Sir Raman studied an effect in which the scattering of light by molecules sometimes involved a small change in the wavelength of the light. In this effect, the difference in energy between the light from the original source and the scattered light is equal to the difference in energy of vibrational levels in a molecule. Raman spectroscopy is a method that makes use of this phenomenon (known as "Raman scattering")[7,10,11] to study or measure chemicals.

The general process of Raman scattering is illustrated in Figure 15. In this effect, light is scattered as it interacts with a molecule. The amount of time that passes during this interaction is around 10^{-13} s. During this time, the molecule is temporarily raised to a higher energy level called a "virtual state," and the molecule returns to a lower energy state after the light is scattered. Most of these molecules return to their original energy level, which gives the incoming light and scattered light the same wavelength (a process known as "Rayleigh scattering"). However, occasionally a molecule will also undergo a change in vibrational level during the scattering process. This change means the scattered light and incoming light will now have a difference in energy that is equal to the energy involved in the vibrational transition. This effect provides these two types of light with slightly different wavelengths.[7,10]

These changes in wavelength are quite small and can only be seen when using incoming light that is monochromatic. Sir Raman conducted his experiments using an intense mercury discharge lamp, but modern instruments for Raman spectroscopy use a laser as the light source. Raman spectroscopy is similar to IR spectroscopy in that both techniques can be used for chemical identification or measurement by using spectroscopy to examine vibrational transitions in molecules. However, the ability to use a laser as a light source and to use visible light instead of infrared light for these measurements are two important advantages of Raman spectroscopy.[7,10,11]

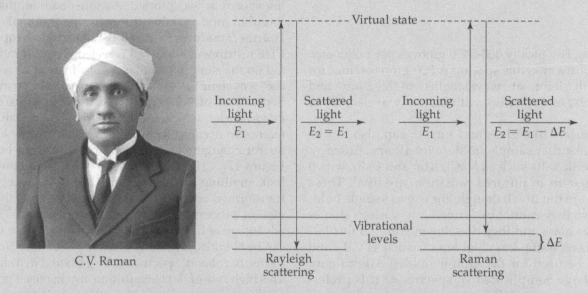

FIGURE 15 Sir C.V. Raman and an illustration of the types of energy transitions that occur in Rayleigh scattering vs. Raman scattering. In this example, a photon of incoming light in each type of scattering has an energy equal to E_1. In Rayleigh scattering, the scattered light has the same energy as the incoming light. In Raman scattering, the scattered light differs by a value of ΔE from the energy of the incoming light. The type of Raman scattering that is shown here, in which the molecule ends at a higher vibrational energy state and the light loses energy, is known as "Stokes scattering." It is also possible for a molecule to lose energy by ending at a lower vibrational state, in which case the scattered light gains energy; this process is known as "anti-Stokes scattering." (The photo of Sir Raman is by A. Bortzells Tryckeri and is provided courtesy of the AIP Emilio Segre Visual Archives, W.F. Meggers Gallery of Nobel Laureates.)

from 1200 to 2000 K produces adequate amounts of light at wavelengths ranging from 1 to 40 μm.[7]

A glass or quartz prism cannot be used as a part of a monochromator to separate light of different wavelengths in IR spectroscopy because of the absorbance of IR radiation by glass or quartz. Fortunately, a grating can still be used for this purpose. (*Note:* Another device that can be used for this purpose is an "interferometer," which will be discussed later in this section.) A grating in IR spectroscopy functions in the same manner as a grating that is used in UV-vis spectroscopy. However, the spacing of the lines in these gratings is different. For UV-vis spectroscopy,

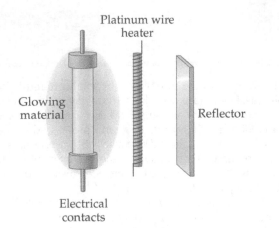

Platinum wire
heater

Glowing
material

Reflector

Electrical
contacts

FIGURE 16 The general design of a Nernst glower. The glowing element in this light source contains a semiconductor material that emits infrared light when a current is passed through the material and resistive heating occurs. This material must be preheated to achieve conductance, as is accomplished by using a separate platinum-wire heater. A reflector helps to collect and direct the radiation that is given off by this source in the desired direction for use.

this spacing is typically 300–2400 grooves per millimeter. In IR spectroscopy, this spacing is 300 grooves/mm for work with light at wavelengths of 2–5 μm and 100 grooves/mm for work with light at wavelengths of 5–16 μm.

Materials like glass and quartz can also not be used to construct sample holders for IR spectroscopy. Instead, ionic salts such as NaCl, KBr, and CsBr, which are transparent to infrared radiation, are used. These materials are not ideal, though, for use as sample holders because they cannot be formed into various shapes as easily as glass and they dissolve in water. If this last problem is an issue, less soluble salts such as CaF_2 and AgCl can be used for the sample holder. All ordinary solvents have complicated IR spectra, so it is preferable to measure spectra of pure substances rather than a solution, especially a dilute solution. As a result, a drop of a liquid sample is often simply put onto a flat plate of NaCl and another similar NaCl flat plate is put on top of it, clamped into place, and a spectrum taken of the resulting film. Solid samples can be mixed with dry KBr and pressed into a thin disk, which is put into the instrument for analysis.[7,11]

Finding suitable detectors for IR spectroscopy is another challenge because photons of infrared light do not have sufficient energy to dislodge an electron in a photomultiplier tube or phototube. Another problem with these latter devices is that they are surrounded with a casing made of glass or silica, which would absorb infrared light and prevent it from being

detected. Instead, most conventional scanning IR instruments utilize a heat sensing detector, such as a *thermocouple*. IR radiation heats the thermocouple by causing its atoms to move more rapidly. A thermocouple is a junction of two different conductors that generates an electrical voltage that depends on the temperature difference between the ends of two wires, one of which is maintained at a constant temperature. The intensity of IR radiation falling on this detector causes warming and a change in voltage, thus making it possible to detect the radiation.[7]

Scanning Instruments and Fourier Transform Infrared Spectroscopy. One difficulty in using IR spectroscopy is that CO_2 and H_2O in air both absorb IR radiation considerably and obscure the spectrum of the desired sample. For that reason, IR spectrophotometers are often double-beam devices in which the spectrum of air is subtracted from the spectrum of the sample, leaving only the spectrum of the desired sample.

Until recently, most IR instruments were double-beam scanning instruments. That is, the wavelength was changed gradually as % T was measured and the resulting spectrum was plotted. A more common instrument found in modern laboratories is one that makes use of **Fourier transform infrared (FTIR) spectroscopy.**[7,11] An FTIR instrument allows all wavelengths of IR radiation to fall on the sample simultaneously. Instead of separating the wavelengths in time or space, the wavelength dependence of % T is gained by use of a device called an *interferometer*, which causes positive and negative interference to occur at sequential wavelengths as a moving mirror changes the path length of the light beam (see Figure 17).[7] The initial output of the detector doesn't look anything like a spectrum, but this direct output is transformed into a spectrum by application of the mathematical process called a "Fourier transform." The major advantage of FTIR is in the speed with which a spectrum can be obtained, typically just a few seconds. This means a large number of spectra can be gathered in a short time. This high rate of data acquisition also makes it possible to combine a large number of spectra to help to remove random fluctuations in the signal, or "noise." The more spectra that are averaged, the better the signal-to-noise ratio will become. This approach, in turn, means that a good spectrum can be achieved for a small concentration of analyte and that a lower limit of detection for measurement of the analyte can be obtained.

3C Applications of Infrared Spectroscopy

IR spectroscopy is most frequently employed for qualitative identification of nearly pure compounds. Because each compound gives several peaks, an IR spectrum of a mixture is very difficult to interpret. The groups of atoms we call "functional groups" have characteristic vibrational energies and characteristic IR absorption wavelengths that can be used in this process.

Table 2 gives an example of a correlation chart that can be used to identify functional groups in a compound from its IR spectrum. For instance, cholesterol has an OH group that has absorption bands at 3300 and 1100 cm^{-1}. Cholesterol also has a large number of C—C single bonds (giving a band at 2900 cm^{-1}), a C=C double bond (with a band at 1650 cm^{-1}), and numerous C—H bonds (with a band near 3000 cm^{-1}). A chemist can learn a great deal about the structure of a compound from its IR spectrum. One can be even more certain as to the identity of a compound if its spectrum has been included in a library of IR spectra. A match between a measured spectrum of an unknown and a library spectrum is regarded as good evidence that the unknown substance is the same as the identity of the library spectrum. Modern IR instruments frequently come with a computer that contains a library of several hundred or thousand compounds that can be searched rapidly for agreement with a measured spectrum.

TABLE 2   Correlation Chart for Various Types of Organic Molecules in IR Spectroscopy*

Functional Group	Bond	Wave number(s), cm^{-1}	Relative Intensity
Acyl halide	C=O	1815–1770	
Alcohol	C–O	1200–1100	Strong, 3° > 2° > 1°
	O–H	3500–3200	Strong and broad
Aldehyde	C–H	2850–2700	
	C=O	1740–1685	Strong
Alkane	sp^3 C–H	2950–2850	Strong
	C–C	1200	
Alkene	sp^2 C–H	3100–3000	Medium, sharp
	C=C	1680–1620	
cis-Alkene	C=C	730–665	
trans-Alkene	C=C	980–960	
Alkyne	C≡C	2200–2100	
	sp C–H	3300	Medium–weak, sharp
Amide	C=O	1695–1616	Strong
Amide, Amine	N–H	3500–3350	Broad (with spikes)
Aromatic	C–H	3100–3000	
Carboxylic acid	O–H	3600–2500	Strong and broad
	C=O	1725–1665	Strong
	C–O	1350–1210	Medium–strong
Ester	C=O	1750–1730	Strong
	C–O	1310–1160	Strong
Ketone	C=O	1750–1660	Strong
Nitrile	C≡N	2280–2240	
Phenol	O–H	3500–3200	Strong and broad
	C–O	1300–1180	Strong

*The information in this table was obtained from F.A. Carey, *Organic Chemistry*, 6th ed., McGraw-Hill, Boston, 2006, and L.G. Wade Jr., *Organic Chemistry*, 7th ed., Prentice Hall, New York, 2010.

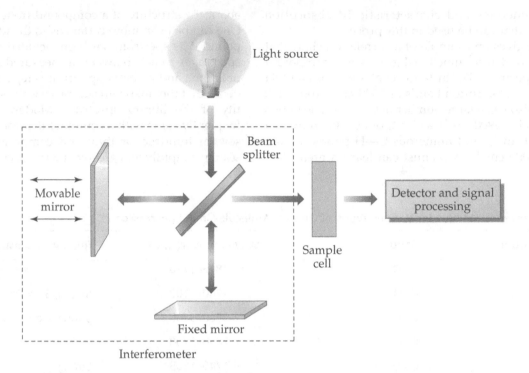

FIGURE 17 The general design of an instrument for FTIR spectroscopy. As one mirror is moved in this device, different wavelengths of light from the original source will have constructive interference and make it onto the sample. By moving this mirror it is possible to have different sets of wavelengths pass on to the sample. The absorption of light for each set of wavelengths and at each position of the mirror is measured and converted through the process of Fourier transform into a spectrum. A laser (not shown) is also used in this device to precisely record the position of the movable mirror. The section of the instrument that is in the dashed box and that is used for wavelength selection is known as an *interferometer*.

4 MOLECULAR LUMINESCENCE

4A General Principles of Luminescence

Luminescence is a general term that describes the emission of light from an excited-state chemical. There are three specific types of luminescence that we will consider: fluorescence, phosphorescence, and chemiluminescence. The use of these processes in spectroscopy to study molecules is sometimes known as *molecular luminescence spectroscopy*.

Fluorescence is a term used to describe light emitted by a sample after it has become electronically excited by absorbance of a photon, with the light emission being due to a "spin-allowed" transition (such as a singlet–singlet transition).[5,6] This type of process is illustrated in Figure 18. The emitted light in fluorescence is frequently in the visible region, while the original light absorbed by the analyte is often in the ultraviolet region but can also occur in the visible range. For low concentrations of a fluorescing compound, the relationship between fluorescence intensity and concentration is nearly linear. Fluorescence occurs rapidly, with the excited state usually lasting less than 10 nanoseconds. A method that uses fluorescence to characterize or measure chemicals is called **fluorescence spectroscopy**.[7,11]

Most molecules do not fluoresce efficiently. Instead of releasing most of the energy from their excited state in the form of light, much of this energy is lost as heat to their surroundings. Molecules that fluoresce usually have rigid structures that are often planar and have aromatic groups, as illustrated by the example if Figure 19. The efficiency of fluorescence by a chemical is described by using a *fluorescence quantum yield* (φ_F). This quantity is the ratio of the number of fluoresced photons that are produced divided by the number of absorbed photons. A chemical with perfect fluorescence will have all its absorbed photons lead to the emission of other photons by fluorescence, giving a maximum value for φ_F of 1.0. A chemical that absorbs light but does not undergo any fluorescence will have a value of zero for φ_F. The fluorescent quantum yield for other chemicals will be somewhere between these two limits, with compounds that have a degree of fluorescence that is appropriate for analysis typically having values for φ_F that are greater than 0.01.[5–7]

Phosphorescence also follows excitation of a molecule, but instead of immediately undergoing fluorescence, the excited electron first undergoes an intersystem crossing into a triplet state.[5–7] This means that the release of light from this excited state will now require a "spin-forbidden" transition from this triplet state to singlet state. This type of emission process is much less likely to occur and is a slower process than the singlet-to-singlet transitions that led to light emission in fluorescence. A spectroscopy technique that utilizes

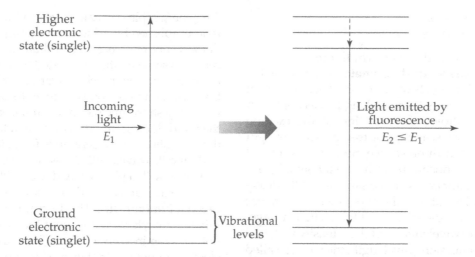

FIGURE 18 The basic processes that lead to light emission in fluorescence. After light has been absorbed by a molecule, some of this energy will be lost as heat through collisions as electrons move to the lowest vibrational level of the excited electronic state (a process known as "vibrational relaxation"). As the excited state of the molecule then emits light, these electrons in the excited electronic state may return to various vibrational states in the lower electronic state. The result is a series of emission wavelengths that are created when using even a single wavelength of light for excitation. Phosphorescence is a similar process, but also involves the conversion of the excited state electron from a singlet state to a triplet state before light emission takes place.

phosphorescence to characterize or measure chemicals is called **phosphorescence spectroscopy**.[7,11]

Phosphorescence is much more difficult to measure than fluorescence. A phosphorescence measurement usually requires the use of liquid nitrogen for work at low temperatures to provide a reasonable signal. The reason low temperatures are needed is that the lifetime of an excited triplet state is much greater than an excited singlet state (typically, $10^{-4} - 10^1$ s versus $10^{-9} - 10^{-8}$ s, respectively). This longer life time means the probability of energy loss through collisions and heat loss is also much greater in phosphorescence than in fluorescence. The use of a lower temperature for this measurement will minimize the degree of molecular motion around the analyte and make its collisions with the solvent or other sample components less likely to occur. This, in turn, increases the chance that the excited triplet state can instead give off its energy in the form of phosphorescence as it returns to the ground state.[7]

Chemiluminescence results from the emission of light by an excited state that is formed in a chemical reaction.[7,16,17] The term *bioluminescence* is sometimes also used when the chemical reaction is of biological origin. Fireflies and glowworms are well-known examples of bioluminescence. A good example of a nonbiological chemical that can undergo chemiluminescence is luminol (5-amino-1, 4-phthalazdione), which reacts with hydrogen peroxide to form the excited molecule shown in Figure 20, which quickly emits a photon to give blue light. The reaction for this process is given in Figure 20. The timescale for this process is mainly determined by the rate of the underlying chemical reaction and varies from one chemiluminescence reaction to the next. In some cases, this process is relatively fast, such as the burst of bioluminescence that occurs in fireflies. In other cases, this process can occur over several seconds or minutes, as takes place in glow sticks and in chemiluminescent reactions that are based on luminol.[16,17]

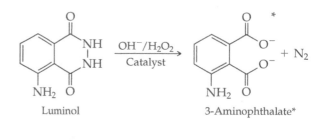

3-Aminophthalate* $\longrightarrow$ 3-Aminophthalate + light

FIGURE 20 The reactions involved in the production of chemiluminescence by luminol. The luminol is first reacted under basic conditions with the oxidizing agent H_2O_2 and in the presence of a catalyst. This reaction results in a product that is a molecule of 3-aminophthalate in an excited state. Some of this excited product releases its extra energy in the form of light.

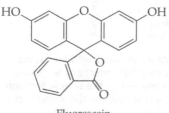

Fluorescein

FIGURE 19 The structure of fluorescein, a molecule that is often used as a fluorescent label in chemical assays.

4B Instrumentation for Luminescence Measurements

An instrument that is used to perform fluorescence spectroscopy is known as a **spectrofluorometer** (if it involves the use of sophisticated monochromator) or a *fluorometer* (if it makes use of simple filters for wavelength selection).[5–7] A spectrofluorometer allows the selection of the exciting wavelength and allows scanning of the spectrum of light that is emitted through fluorescence. Such an instrument has a light source, a monochromator before the sample, and another monochromator between the sample and the detector (see Figure 21). This allows the experimenter to choose optimum conditions for the analysis. If the excitation wavelength is fixed at one wavelength and the intensity is plotted as a function of the emission wavelength, the result is called an "emission spectrum." The other possibility is to fix the wavelength at which the fluorescence intensity is measured by varying the excitation wavelength. This results in an "excitation spectrum" and is similar to the absorption spectrum for the analyte that is undergoing fluorescence.[5,6]

The design of a fluorometer is simpler than that of a spectrofluorometer and uses only filters to select the wavelength of light that is used for excitation and that is analyzed for fluorescence. Although this design does not allow a fluorescence spectrum to be obtained, it does make it possible to measure the emission intensity at a given set of wavelengths for the quantitative analysis of a particular analyte that undergoes fluorescence at these wavelengths.[7,11]

An instrument designed for phosphorescence measurements is similar, but differs in two important respects.

First, the sample is usually kept at a low temperature, which is accomplished by using dry ice or liquid nitrogen. Second, fluorescence often occurs simultaneously with phosphorescence, so some method is needed to differentiate rapid fluorescence from the much slower phosphorescence. Usually, the excitation radiation is allowed to strike the sample only for a very short time (i.e., a few milliseconds at most). Then the rapid fluorescence dies away in a few nanoseconds and the phosphorescence continues for at least several milliseconds and its wavelength dependence is measured most conveniently with a photoarray detector.[7,11]

An instrument used to measure chemiluminescence is called a **luminometer**. This instrument includes a device to mix the analyte with a reagent that will lead to the formation of a luminescent product. The mixing device is placed close to a photomultiplier tube to measure the intensity of light given off by the excited product. A simple device merely measures this intensity, whereas a more complicated one passes the light through a monochromator to allow study of the wavelengths of the luminescence.[16]

4C Applications of Molecular Luminescence

Fluorescence, and to a smaller extent phosphorescence, is a valuable tool for measuring analytes at low concentrations. The more stringent requirements needed for solutes to undergo these processes also provide fluorescence and phosphorescence with greater selectivity and lower limits of detection than absorbance measurements for molecules.[7,10,11] It is also possible to use an approach based on fluorescence to examine many types of nonfluorescent

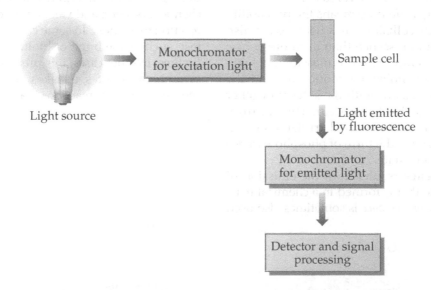

FIGURE 21 The general design of a spectrofluorometer. Two monochromators are used in this instrument. The first monochromator selects the wavelengths of light that will pass from the light source to the sample for excitation. The second monochromator selects the wavelengths that are emitted by the sample through fluorescence for measurement. If the wavelength in the first monochromator is varied and the wavelength setting in the second monochromator is held constant, the resulting plot of fluorescence intensity vs. wavelength is known as an "excitation spectrum." If the wavelength in the second monochromator is held constant and the wavelength setting in the second monochromator is varied, the resulting plot of fluorescence intensity vs. wavelength is known as an "emission spectrum" (or "fluorescence spectrum").

chemicals by first reacting these analytes with a reagent that converts them into a fluorescent form. A good example is the detection of amines and amino acids by fluorescence. Most amino acids that do not have significant fluorescence can be combined with the reagent o-phthaldialdehyde to yield a strongly fluorescent product. Similar reactions are available for chemicals that contain alcohol groups, aldehydes, or ketones as part of their structure.[7,11,18]

EXERCISE 5	Use of Fluorescence for Chemical Analysis

Estimate the concentration of glycine in the following unknown sample based on the fluorescence intensity that is measured for this sample and a series of standards that have each been reacted with an excess of o-phthaldialdehyde to create a fluorescent product.

Concentration of Glycine (μM)	Measured Fluorescence Intensity, I_F
0.00	0.10
0.20	3.4
0.40	6.9
1.00	17.1
2.00	34.3
5.00	83.2
10.0	152.
Sample	22.8

SOLUTION

A plot of the measured fluorescence intensity versus glycine concentration in the standards gives a linear response of the range of concentrations that were examined in this study (e.g., see the expected relationship between an emission signal and analyte concentration). The best-fit line for this graph has a slope of 15.3 μM^{-1} and an intercept of 1.77. Using this plot and fluorescence intensity obtained for the sample, the concentration of glycine in this sample is estimated to be **1.37 μM**.

Chemiluminescence can also be used as a selective means for the measurement of analytes in samples. For example, chemiluminescence can be used to measure nitric oxide (NO) in the atmosphere by first reacting NO with ozone (O_3).

$$\text{Step 1:} \quad NO + O_3 \rightarrow NO_2^* + O_2 \quad (7)$$

$$\text{Step 2:} \quad NO_2^* \rightarrow NO_2 + h\nu$$

In the first step of this process, an excited state molecule of NO_2^* is produced. This excited molecule then later returns to its ground state by emitting light that can be used for its detection. Examples of many other reactions that are based on chemiluminescence, and analytical applications of such reactions, can be found in References 16 and 17.

Key Words

Chemiluminescence	Fourier transform infrared spectroscopy	Phosphorescence spectroscopy	Standard addition method
Diode-array detector			
Double-beam instrument	Infrared spectroscopy	Single-beam instrument	UV-visible spectroscopy
Fluorescence	Luminometer	Spectrofluorometer	
Fluorescence spectroscopy	Molecular spectroscopy	Spectrophotometric titration	
	Phosphorescence		

Other Terms

Bioluminescence	Fluorometer	Luminescence	Thermocouple
Chromophore	Flow injection analysis	Molecular luminescence spectroscopy	Transmission grating
Colorimetry	Globar		Tungsten lamp
Deuterium lamp	Hydrogen lamp	Nernst glower	Tungsten/halogen lamp
Fluorescence quantum yield	Interferometer	Raman spectroscopy	UV-vis absorbance spectrometer
	Isobestic point	Reflection grating	

Questions

WHAT IS MOLECULAR SPECTROSCOPY AND HOW IS IT USED IN CHEMICAL ANALYSIS?

1. Explain what is meant by the term "molecular spectroscopy."
2. What are three ways in which molecules can interact with light?

3. What types of energy levels can be involved in the study or measurement of analytes by molecular spectroscopy? List one specific type of molecular spectroscopy that makes use of each of these changes in energy levels.

4. Describe the method of "colorimetry." Give one example of an early application that was developed for chemical analysis based on colorimetry.

5. Explain how molecular spectroscopy can be used for either the measurement or identification of a molecule. List one specific type of spectroscopy that is commonly used for each of these general applications.

GENERAL PRINCIPLES OF ULTRAVIOLET-VISIBLE SPECTROSCOPY

6. What is "UV-vis spectroscopy"? Explain why ultraviolet or visible light is useful in absorbance measurements for many types of organic molecules.

7. Define the word "chromophore." What are some typical features that are found in a chromophore of an organic molecule that can absorb ultraviolet or visible light?

8. Rank the following compounds in the order that you think will be easiest to measure by UV-vis spectrometry. Explain the reasons for the order of your ranking of these chemicals.
   (a) $CH_3-CH_2-CH_2-CH_2-CH_2-CH_3$
   (b) $CH_2=CH-CH_2-CH_2-CH_2-CH_3$
   (c) $CH_3-CH=CH-CH_2-CH=CH_2$
   (d) $CH_3-CH=CH-CH=CH-CH_3$

9. Explain why Beer's law is often used for the measurement of analytes in UV-vis spectroscopy.

10. An analyte that is to be measured by UV-vis spectroscopy has a molar absorptivity of 5.6×10^5 L/mol·cm at the wavelength that is chosen for its measurement. If the smallest absorbance that can be measured is 0.002 and the sample cuvette has a path length of 1.00 cm, what is the expected lower limit of detection for this analyte?

11. A solution has an analyte concentration of 5.7×10^{-3} M that gives a transmittance of 43.6% at 480 nm and when measured in a 5.00 cm cuvette. Calculate the molar absorptivity of the analyte. What is the expected lower limit of detection for this analyte if the smallest absorbance that can be measured by the instrument is 0.001.

12. What is the upper limit of the linear range for the analyte in Problem 11 if deviations for Beer's law are found to occur at an absorbance of approximately 1.00?

INSTRUMENTATION IN ULTRAVIOLET-VISIBLE SPECTROSCOPY

13. Describe the basic components of a UV-vis absorbance spectrometer. Give the function for each of these components.

14. Explain how a tungsten lamp works, including the basis for how this lamp emits light.

15. How does a hydrogen lamp work? How does a deuterium lamp differ from a hydrogen lamp?

16. What are two types of monochromators that are used in UV-vis spectroscopy?

17. What are some requirements for a sample holder in UV-vis spectroscopy? Describe the construction of a typical cuvette that is used for this purpose.

18. List two types of detectors for light that can be used in UV-vis spectroscopy. Describe how each of these detects the light.

19. What is the difference between a "single-beam instrument" and a "double-beam instrument"? What are some advantages and disadvantages for each of these instrument designs?

20. Explain what is meant by a "diode-array detector." How does this device differ from a single beam or double-beam instrument that is used for UV-vis spectroscopy?

21. Define "flow injection analysis" and explain how UV-vis spectroscopy can be used in this method.

APPLICATIONS OF ULTRAVIOLET-VISIBLE SPECTROSCOPY

22. Explain how direct measurements of an analyte can be made by UV-vis spectroscopy. Describe the role of Beer's law in such an analysis.

23. The complex of Fe^{2+} with 1,10-phenanthroline has a molar absorptivity of about 11,000 L/mol·cm in water at 510 nm. A 20.00 mL water sample thought to contain Fe^{2+} is mixed with an excess of 1,10-phenanthroline. Acetic acid, sodium acetate, and hydroxylamine are also added to buffer the solution and assure that all the iron is reduced to Fe(II). This mixture is diluted with distilled water to a total volume of 50.00 mL, and the final solution is found to give an absorbance of 0.762 at 510 nm when using a 1.0 cm cuvette.
   (a) If it is assumed that there are no absorbing species in this solution other than the Fe^{2+} complex with 1,10-phenanthroline, what was the concentration of Fe^{2+} in the original sample?
   (b) Discuss how the presence of other species that also absorb at 510 nm would have affected the accuracy of this measurement. Would a positive error or a negative error be obtained?

24. A geochemist wishes to estimate the volume of an irregularly shaped pool of water. This task is to be accomplished by placing a known amount of highly colored dye into this solution and then measuring the absorbance by this dye after it has been in the pool. To do this, the geochemist uses 1.00 L of a dye solution that has an absorbance of 0.768 when it is measured in a 1 mm cuvette at 450 nm. After all of this solution has been placed into the pool and allowed to mixed thoroughly, a sample of the pool water is taken and found to have an absorbance at 450 nm of 0.142 in a 10.00 cm cuvette. What is the volume of the pool? What assumptions are made during this analysis?

25. Four standard solutions and an unknown sample containing the same compound give the following absorbance readings at 535 nm when using 1.00 cm cuvettes. What is the concentration of the analyte in the sample?

Solution	Analyte Concentration (M)	Absorbance
Standard #1	0.00	0.005
Standard #2	2.5×10^{-3}	0.085
Standard #3	5.0×10^{-3}	0.175
Standard #4	25.0×10^{-3}	0.805
Unknown sample	?	0.465

26. The content of nitrate–nitrogen in water can be measured by evaporating a known amount of water (100.00 mL) to dryness. The resulting residue is then mixed with phenoldisulfonic acid and heated until all of the solid material has dissolved. This solution is diluted to a volume of 50.00 mL with water and ammonia, giving a solution with a yellow color that is related to the amount of the nitrogen–nitrate in the original sample. Absorbance of the sample and standards that are prepared in the same

manner is measured at 410 nm using a 1.00 cm cuvette. The follow data were obtained for a series of standards and an unknown sample that were examined by this method. What was the concentration of nitrate–nitrogen in the original sample?

Mass of Nitrate–Nitrogen in Sample/Standard (mg)	Absorbance
0.00	0.000
0.10	0.103
0.25	0.257
0.50	0.515
Unknown sample	0.318

27. What is the "standard addition method"? Under what circumstances is this method typically used for analysis?
28. A sample of coffee is analyzed to determine its caffeine concentration. Two portions of this sample are prepared for analysis. The first portion contains 50.0 mL of brewed coffee, to which is added 10.0 mL of water. The second portion contains 50.0 mL of brewed coffee that has been spiked with 10.0 mL of an aqueous solution that contains $1.0 \times 10^{-2}\ M$ caffeine. The first portion of the sample is found to give a measured absorbance of 243 units, and the second portion gives an absorbance of 387 units. What is the concentration of caffeine in the brewed coffee?
29. An aqueous sample containing Fe^{2+} is treated with 1,10-phenanthroline to form a colored complex for detection. This treated solution gives an absorbance of 0.367 when measured with a 1.00 cm long cuvette at 510 nm. Next, 5.0 mL of a $0.0200\ M\ Fe^{2+}$ solution is added to 10.0 mL of the unknown sample, treated with 1,10-phenanthroline in the same fashion as the previous sample, and found to give an absorbance of 0.538 at 510 nm. Based on this information, what was the concentration of Fe^{2+} in the original unknown?
30. Explain why a change in color occurs when an acid–base indicator is used for end-point detection. Use methyl red as an example to illustrate your answer.
31. What is a "spectrophotometric titration"? What is measured in this type of titration? How is the end point detected?
32. Explain why a linear response is typically seen in a spectrophotometric titration.
33. A spectrophotometric titration that is performed has the general reaction $A + T \rightarrow P$, where A is the analyte, T is the titrant, and P is the product of the reaction. Draw the titration curve that would be expected under each of the following conditions. Clearly indicate in each diagram the response that would be expected both before and after the equivalence point.

	ε_A	ε_T	ε_P
(a)	0	0	500
(b)	500	0	0
(c)	0	500	0
(d)	200	0	400
(e)	200	0	200

34. The following results were obtained for a spectrophotometric titration that was carried out at 600 nm to measure Cu^{2+} in a water sample by reacting Cu^{2+} with triethylenetetramine (trien) to form a colored complex, as shown below.

$$Cu^{2+} + trien \rightarrow Cu(trien)^{2+}$$

A 10.00 mL sample was used for this analysis, which was mixed with various volumes of a 0.0500 M solution of triethylenetetramine and distilled water to give a total final solution volume of 50.00 mL. The absorbance of each mixture was then determined, giving the following results.

Sample Volume (mL)	Volume Trien (mL)	Volume H_2O (mL)	Absorbance
10.00	0.0	40.0	0.005
10.00	2.0	38.0	0.217
10.00	4.0	36.0	0.428
10.00	6.0	34.0	0.643
10.00	8.0	32.0	0.750
10.00	10.0	30.0	0.750

(a) What was the concentration of Cu^{2+} in the original sample?
(b) Explain the shape of the titration curve that is obtained for this analysis. What does this curve tell you about the ability of the analyte, titrant, and product to absorb light at the wavelength that was used to follow this titration?
(c) Use the information provided to estimate the value of the molar absorptivities for the analtye, titrant, and product at 600 nm.
35. Explain how UV-vis spectroscopy can be used to examine several analytes in a sample by using absorbance measurements at multiple wavelengths. What requirements must be met for this approach to work?
36. A scientist wishes to measure three different analytes that all have significantly different spectra in the UV-vis range. How many absorbance measurements of the sample will be required for this analysis? What criteria should be used in selecting the wavelengths for these absorbance measurements?
37. What is an "isobestic point"? When should absorbance measurements at an isobestic point be avoided? When is an isobestic point useful in such measurements?
38. An unknown solution contains two absorbing species, P and Q, both of which are to be measured by UV-vis spectroscopy. Compound P has molar absorptivities of 570 L/mol · cm at 400 nm and 35 L/mol · cm at 600 nm. Compound Q has molar absorptivities of 220 L/mol · cm at 400 nm and 820 L/mol · cm at 600 nm. The unknown mixture of P and Q is placed in a 1.00 cm long cuvette and gives absorbance values of 0.436 at 400 nm and 0.644 at 600 nm. If no other absorbing species are present in this sample, what are the concentrations of P and Q?
39. The pH of the methyl red solution in Exercise 4 was 5.20. Based on the information given earlier in this exercise, determine the K_a value for the acid–base transition that was present under these conditions.

GENERAL PRINCIPLES OF INFRARED SPECTROSCOPY

40. What types of energy transitions in a molecule are involved in the absorption of light in IR spectroscopy? How are these energy transitions different from those that are used in UV-vis spectroscopy?

41. Describe what happens to the motions within a molecule when this molecule absorbs infrared radiation.

42. How is IR spectroscopy typically used for chemical analysis? How does the typical application of IR spectroscopy in chemical analysis differ from the applications of UV-vis spectroscopy? What are the reasons for these differences?

43. Describe the appearance of a typical IR spectrum, including the terms that are plotted on the x-axis and y-axis. How is this type of spectrum different from an absorbance spectrum that is used in UV-vis spectroscopy?

INSTRUMENTATION FOR INFRARED SPECTROSCOPY

44. How is the general design of an instrument for IR spectroscopy similar to one that is used in UV-vis spectroscopy? How are these two types of instrument different?

45. Describe a typical light source for IR spectroscopy. What are some special requirements for this type of light source?

46. What is a "Nernst glower"? What is a "globar"? How are each of these devices used in IR spectroscopy?

47. Explain why a glass or quartz prism cannot be used in IR spectroscopy.

48. How is a diffraction grating used in IR spectroscopy? How does a diffraction grating in IR spectroscopy differ from one that is used in UV-vis spectroscopy?

49. What types of materials are used for the sample holders in IR spectroscopy? What properties are desired for such materials?

50. Describe how you would prepare a liquid sample for analysis by IR spectroscopy? How would you prepare a solid sample for analysis by IR spectroscopy?

51. What problems are associated with finding a suitable detector for IR radiation? Give one example of a device that can be used in IR spectroscopy for this purpose.

52. Compare and contrast the design of a double-beam instrument in IR spectroscopy with the design of a more modern single-beam instrument.

53. What is meant by "Fourier transform infrared spectroscopy"? How is the measurement of an IR spectrum obtained in this method?

54. Describe how IR spectroscopy can be used for the identification of chemicals. What features of an IR spectrum are useful for this type of application?

55. What is a "correlation chart"? Explain how you can use this type of chart for chemical identification in IR spectroscopy.

56. A student receives an unknown organic compound that is either cyclohexane or cyclohexene. Explain how the student could use IR spectroscopy to tell which of these two compounds is present in the sample. Be as specific as possible in your answer.

57. A can of paint solvent that is found at the scene of an arson attempt is believed by a forensic laboratory to be either a mixture of hydrocarbons or acetone, $(CH_3)_2 C{=}O$. An IR spectrum for a sample of this solvent is found to show no appreciable absorbance in the region of 1700 cm^{-1}. Of the given possibilities, what is the most likely identity for this paint solvent?

58. A compound is known to have either a carbon–carbon double bond or triple bond in its structure. An IR spectrum for this chemical has a sharp peak at 2200 cm^{-1}, but

nothing at 1650 cm^{-1}. Determine whether a double or triple carbon–carbon bond is present in this compound.

59. Describe how computers and libraries of spectra can be used for chemical identification in IR spectroscopy.

GENERAL PRINCIPLES OF LUMINESCENCE

60. What is "fluorescence"? Describe the general process by which light is emitted during fluorescence.

61. What features are often found in molecules that undergo fluorescence?

62. Explain why the wavelength of light fluoresced by a molecule is longer than the exciting light, but light fluoresced by an atom is the same wavelength as the exciting light.

63. How is the intensity of light that is emitted by fluorescence related to the concentration of an analyte that is undergoing fluorescence?

64. What is "phosphorescence"? How is light emitted during this process?

65. How is phosphorescence similar to fluorescence? How are these two processes different?

66. How is the intensity of light that is emitted by phosphorescence related to the concentration of the analyte that is undergoing this phosphorescence?

67. What is "chemiluminescence"? Describe how light is emitted by this process.

68. What is "bioluminescence"? Give one example of a bioluminescence process.

INSTRUMENTATION FOR LUMINESCENCE MEASUREMENTS

69. Describe the general design of a spectrofluorometer. Explain the function of each major component in this design.

70. Describe the general design of a simple fluorometer. How does this design differ from that for a spectrofluorometer?

71. What is an "excitation spectrum" in fluorescence spectroscopy? What is an "emission spectrum"?

72. What are the differences in an instrument that is used to measure phosphorescence and an instrument that is used to measure fluorescence? How are these two types of instruments similar?

73. What is a "luminometer"? Describe how this type of instrument works.

APPLICATIONS OF MOLECULAR LUMINESCENCE

74. Riboflavin emits yellow-green light through fluorescence when this molecule is excited with ultraviolet light. The following data were obtained when measuring the fluorescence intensity of this analyte in a series of standards and a sample. Estimate the concentration of riboflavin in the sample.

Concentration (M)	Fluorescence intensity, I_F
1.0×10^{-5}	4.0
2.0×10^{-5}	8.0
4.0×10^{-5}	16.0
8.0×10^{-5}	32.0
16×10^{-5}	58.0
32×10^{-5s}	105
64×10^{-5}	170
Unknown sample	25.8

CHALLENGE PROBLEMS

75. What is the probable color of an aqueous solution that shows a maximum molar absorptivity at (a) 500 nm, or (b) 320 nm?

76. The most abundant substances in unpolluted air are nitrogen, oxygen, argon, carbon dioxide, and water. Explain why only CO_2 and H_2O are regarded as greenhouse gases.

77. The molar absorptivity has units of L/mol·cm. Given the fact that one liter is equal to a cubic decimeter, show how you can calculate the apparent cross section of a chromophore if you know its molar absorptivity.

78. A compound has a molar absorptivity of 15,460 L/mol·cm at 585 nm. The intensity of radiation at this wavelength that is incident upon a 2.40×10^{-4} M sample in a 5.0 cm cuvette is 450 lumens. What is the transmitted intensity of this light, in units of lumens?

79. The oxidation of lactic acid (LA) by NAD^+ to form pyruvic acid and NADH and H^+ is slow unless it is catalyzed by the enzyme lactic acid dehydrogenase (LDH). The overall reaction for this process is shown below.

$$\underset{\text{Lactic Acid}}{C_3H_6O_3} + \underset{}{NAD^+} \xrightarrow{\text{LDH}} \underset{\text{Pyruvic Acid}}{C_3H_4O_3} + NADH + H^+$$

The progress of this reaction can be monitored in a 1.0 cm cuvette at 340 nm, a wavelength at which NADH has an absorption maximum ($\varepsilon = 6{,}000$ L/mol·cm), but NAD^+ and the other reactants or products have essentially no light absorption. This reaction is first order with respect to both reactants and the catalyst. Suppose that the initial conditions in this reaction include a lactic concentration of 1.0×10^{-3} M and NAD^+ concentration of 2.0×10^{-5} M for a sample with an unknown concentration of LDH. The following absorbances are measured for this system as a function of time.

Time (s)	Absorbance
0	0.000
40	0.060
80	0.090
120	0.105
400	0.120

Find the concentration of the catalyst LDH if the fixed rate law for this process is Rate = k[LA][NAD^+][LDH] and the rate constant for this reaction is $k = 2.4 \times 10^6$.

80. A technique related to spectrophotometric titration is the method of continuous variation, also called Job's method. This procedure differs from the preceding in that the total concentration of both reagents remains the same instead of keeping the concentration of one species constant. The goal of Job's method is seldom to learn the concentration of an unknown, but rather to learn the stoichiometry of a color-forming reaction. An example of data for this method is given below for the reaction of U with R to form product P, which absorbs at the wavelength being used for the absorbance measurement.

Concentration of U (M)	Concentration of R (M)	Absorbance of P
0.000	0.008	0.000
0.001	0.007	0.250
0.002	0.006	0.500
0.003	0.005	0.750
0.004	0.004	0.950
0.005	0.003	0.750
0.006	0.002	0.500
0.007	0.001	0.250
0.008	0.000	0.000

Use the preceding information to prepare a plot of "Absorbance of P" vs. the concentration of U. What can you tell about the stoichiometry of the reaction between and U and R based on this plot?

TOPICS FOR DISCUSSION AND REPORTS

81. Visit a local clinical laboratory and obtain information on how methods such as UV-vis spectroscopy or fluorescence spectroscopy are used at the facility for chemical analysis.

82. Obtain a research article that uses flow injection analysis for chemical measurement. Write a report on your findings.

83. IR spectroscopy is commonly used as the basis for alcohol detection in breathalyzer devices. Obtain more information on this type of device and write a report on how it works.

84. Obtain more information on Raman spectroscopy and its use in chemical analysis. Discuss how this approach was used and the types of information it provided about the samples that were being examined.

85. Photoacoustic spectroscopy is another technique that can be used to measure and study various types of transitions in molecules. Locate some information on this method and how it is performed. Write a report on this method and describe some of its applications.

86. Use References 16 and 17 or related resources to obtain more information on the topic of chemiluminescence and bioluminescence. Describe one specific type of reaction that is based on these processes and that has been used in chemical analysis. Give an example of an application in which this type of analysis has been conducted.

References

1. W. J. Marshall, *Clinical Chemistry*, Elsevier, Amsterdam, the Netherlands, 2004.

2. C. A. Burtis, E. R. Ashwood, and D. E. Bruns, Eds., *Tietz Fundamentals of Clinical Chemistry*, 6th ed., Elsevier, Amsterdam, the Netherlands, 2007.

3. A. G. Gornall, Ed., *Applied Biochemistry of Clinical Disorders*, 2nd ed., J. P. Lippincott, New York, 1986.

4. W. Clarke and D. R. Dufour, Eds., *Contemporary Practice in Clinical Chemistry*, AACC Press, Washington, DC, 2006.

5. J. Inczedy, T. Lengyel, and A. M. Ure, *International Union of Pure and Applied Chemistry—Compendium of Analytical*

Nomenclature: Definitive Rules 1997, Blackwell Science, Malden, MA, 1998.

6. G. Maludzinska, Ed., *Dictionary of Analytical Chemistry*, Elsevier, Amsterdam, the Netherlands, 1990.

7. J. D. Ingle and S. R. Crouch, *Spectrochemical Analysis*, Prentice Hall, Upper Saddle River, NJ, 1988.

8. F. Szabadvary, *History of Analytical Chemistry*, Pergamon Press, New York, 1966.

9. J. Ross, "Home Test Measures Total Cholesterol," *The Nurse Practitioner*, 28 (2003) 52–53.

10. G. W. Ewing, Ed., *Analytical Instrumentation Handbook*, 2nd ed., Marcel Dekker, New York, 1997.

11. D. A. Skoog, F. J. Holler, and T. A. Nieman, *Principles of Instrumental Analysis*, 5th ed., Saunders, Philadelphia, 1998.

12. D. G. Jones, "Photodiode Array Detectors in UV/Vis Spectroscopy: Part I," *Analytical Chemistry*, 57 (1985) 1057A–1073A.

13. S. A. Borman, "Photodiode Array Detectors for LC," *Analytical Chemistry*, 55 (1983) 836A–842A.

14. J. Ruzicka and E. H. Hansen, *Flow Injection Methods*, 2nd ed., Wiley, New York, 1988.

15. S. D. Xoleve and I. D. McKelvie, Eds., *Advances in Flow Injection Analysis and Related Techniques*, Elsevier, Amsterdam, the Netherlands, 2008.

16. A. K. Campbell, *Chemiluminescence*, VCH Publishers, New York, 1988.

17. K. Van Dyke, Ed., *Bioluminescence and Chemiluminescence: Instruments and Applications*, CRC Press, Boca Raton, FL, 1985.

18. G. Lunn and L. C. Hellwig, *Handbook of Derivatization Reactions for HPLC*, Wiley, New York, 1998.

Selected Answers

8 In order from easiest to most difficult: d > c > b > a (not possible)

10 $C = 3.6 \times 10^{-9} M$

12 $C = 1.58 \times 10^{-2} M$

23

a. $[Fe^{2+}] = 1.73 \times 10^{-4} M$

b. If some other species absorbs at the given wavelength, the measured absorbance will be too high and will be interpreted inaccurately as a higher concentration of Fe^{2+}.

24 Volume = 541 L; it is assumed the dye is distributed uniformly throughout the pond and that no other solute in the pool absorbs significantly at 450 nm.

25 $C = 14.1 \times 10^{-3} M$

28 Concentration of caffeine in brewed coffee = $3.37 \times 10^{-3} M$

34

a. $[Cu^{2+}] = 3.53 \times 10^{-2} M$

b. The analyte by itself has a very small absorbance but the copper-trien complex absorbs quite strongly. Past the endpoint when only more trien is added, there is no increase in absorbance; this result means trien has no measurable absorbance at the given wavelength.

38 $[Q] = 7.65 \times 10^{-4} M$, $[P] = 4.69 \times 10^{-4} M$

56 Double bonds absorb at about 1650 cm^{-1} (6.0 μm); alkanes do not absorb here.

57

a. Ketones, such as acetone, show strong absorption near 1700 cm^{-1}. There is no such absorption present in this case, so the solvent must be the hydrocarbon mixture.

b. The absorption at 2950 cm^{-1} is due to a C-H stretch and the absorption at 1450 cm^{-1} is from a C-C stretch, which are present in both vegetable and mineral oil. The absence of a peak near 1720 cm^{-1}, which is characteristic of an ester group, shows that the sample can not be vegetable oil. Thus, it must be mineral oil.

74 $C = 6.45 \times 10^{-5} M$

Agglutination and Precipitation Reactions: The Unlabeled Immunoassays

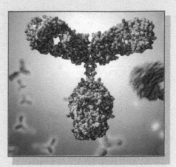

■ OBJECTIVES—LEVEL I

After this chapter, the student should be able to:

1. Define *precipitation*.
2. Discuss affinity and avidity and their influence on antigen-antibody reactions.
3. Explain how the prozone, postzone, and equivalence affect the amount of lattice cross-linked precipitates.
4. Compare and contrast the 2 optical-enhanced techniques: turbidity and nephelometry.
5. Interpret Ouchterlony immunodiffusion patterns.
6. Compare and contrast agglutination and precipitation.
7. Using what they have learned about agglutination and precipitation reactions, determine the effect of a hapten on a precipitation or an agglutination reaction.
8. Describe the physiologic conditions that can be altered to enhance agglutination.
9. Compare and contrast direct agglutination, passive agglutination, reverse passive agglutination, and agglutination inhibition.
10. Describe the direct antiglobulin test and evaluate situations to determine when it should be utilized.
11. Describe the indirect antiglobulin test and evaluate situations to determine when it should be utilized.
12. Describe the following instrument enhanced agglutination techniques: PETINA, PACIA, and QUELS.
13. Discuss conditions that must be met for optimal results in agglutination testing (equivalence, zeta potential).

■ OBJECTIVES—LEVEL II

After this chapter, the student should be able to:

1. Compare and contrast single diffusion and double diffusion.
2. Describe the principle of the kinetic (Fahey) and the endpoint method (Mancini) of radial immunodiffusion.
3. Define *zeta potential* and describe the effect of decreasing it on agglutination.

KEY TERMS

affinity
agglutination
avidity
direct agglutination
direct antiglobulin
    test (DAT)
double diffusion gel
    precipitation
equivalence
Fahey method
identity
indirect antiglobulin
    test (IAT)
lattice
Mancini method
nephelometry
nonidentity

partial identity
particle-counting
    immunoassay (PACIA)
particle-enhanced
    turbidimetric inhibition
    assay (PETINA)
passive agglutination
postzone
precipitation
prozone
quasi-elastic light scattering
    method (QUELS)
radial immunodiffusion (RID)
reverse passive
    agglutination
turbidometry
zeta potential

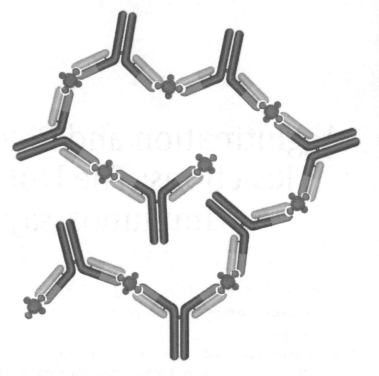

■ FIGURE 1 Antigen (dark green and orange) and antibody (blue and green) binding forming a complex.

► INTRODUCTION

In the unlabeled immunoassays, you can actually see part of the antibody molecules that have bound to antigen! The precipitation and agglutination reactions were the first immunoassays developed and rely on the fact that antibodies and most antigens have multiple binding sites. The multiple binding sites of the antibodies and antigens result in the formation of large complexes when antigens and antibody meet at appropriate concentrations (Figure 1 ■). Two types of reactions can result from the cross-linked structures that form: precipitation and agglutination reactions. **Precipitation** is the cross-linking of a soluble antigen to create an insoluble precipitate that is visible. **Agglutination** is the cross-linking of particulate antigens (bacteria, cells, or latex particles) to form larger complexes that are also visible. These assays are not very sensitive because a positive reaction of antibody and antigen is actually seen unamplified by the human eye. Using optics to register the differences between uncomplexed and complexed antigen and antibody results in some improvement of the sensitivity of agglutination and precipitation reactions. Two such optical techniques are turbidometry and nephelometry (1, 2, 3, 4).

All serologic reactions, whether unlabeled or labeled, rely on the affinity, avidity, and specificity of the antibody to bind to the antigen.

AFFINITY AND AVIDITY

Affinity is a measure of the strength of the binding of 1 Fab region with its corresponding epitope on the antigen. The affinity constant Ka is defined as follows:

$$Ka = \frac{[AbAg]}{[Ab][Ag]}$$

Where [AbAg] is the concentration of the complexed antibody and antigen, and [Ab] is the concentration of the free antibody, and [Ag] is the concentration of the free antigen.

From the preceding equation, we can see that the higher the affinity, the more of the antibody and antigen that is complexed in comparison to the amount that is free. Thus, the higher the affinity, the more sensitive is the reaction because more of the antigen and antibody will be in the complexed form, and this form will be visualized. **Avidity** is the number of binding sites times the affinity. So, IgG with its 2 binding sites has an avidity of 2 times the affinity, and IgM with its 10 binding sites has a theoretical avidity of 10 times its affinity constant. This increase due to the number of binding sites is particularly important for IgM reactions because IgM has, on average, a weaker affinity than IgG because IgG is usually produced after the somatic mutational events that improve affinity. One must also remember that steric hindrance can affect the binding of all binding sites and thus lower avidity. Steric hindrance affects the binding when the antigens bound are big enough to block binding by the other binding site(s) of the immunoglobulin molecule (1, 2, 3, 4, 5, 6).

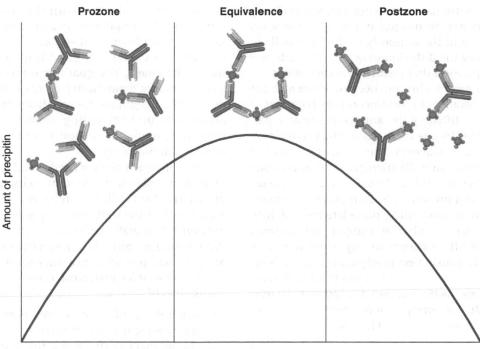

Amount of precipitin (y-axis)

Prozone   **Equivalence**   **Postzone**

Dilution of antibody (x-axis)

■ FIGURE 2   A depiction of the amount of precipitin that would form with different ratios of antigen and antibody. The prozone has antibody excess, and only small complexes with 2 antibody molecules and 1 antigen form. At equivalence, the number of paratopes roughly equals the number of epitopes, and the largest complexes form. The postzone has excess antigen, and the small complexes are formed of 2 antigens per antibody molecule.

EQUIVALENCE, PROZONE, AND POSTZONE

In the formation of antigen and antibody complexes, large complexes are formed when the antigen and antibody meet at a concentration in which the number of paratopes (antibody binding sites) approximately equals the number of epitopes; this part of the precipitation curve is called equivalence (Figure 2 ■). When there is too much antibody, 2 antibodies are bound to every bivalent antigen and there is no need for bridging of 2 antigen molecules by an antibody molecule. In this situation, little or no precipitate would form, which makes it appear that the patient does not have an antibody to the antigen when, in fact, he or she has too much antibody for the multiple bridging required for precipitation or agglutination reaction to occur. This part of the precipitation or agglutination curve is called the prozone. Most of the precipitation occurs when the ratio of antibody to antigen is just right (ie, the number of paratopes approximately equals the number of epitopes). When the amount of patient antibody is low so that each IgG antibody is bound by 2 antigen molecules, there is no bridging of 2 antibody molecules by the antigen, so little or no precipitation occurs. This situation is

called the postzone. In both the prozone and the postzone situations, the patient would appear negative for antibody to the tested antigen. In a prozone situation, the patient's serum can be diluted and tested again to reach equivalence. In the case of a postzone reaction, the patient's blood can be drawn again in 1 or 2 weeks to allow the patient to form more antibodies (an increase in titer) to bring the reaction to the zone of equivalence (1, 2, 3, 4, 5, 6).

> ✓ **Checkpoint! 1**
>
> *The patient really looks sick with an autoimmune disease that is caused by antibody; however, the agglutination reaction is negative. What should you do?*

▶ IMMUNODIFFUSION TECHNIQUES

Proof that an antibody is reacting with an antigen is at its simplest when you can actually see the precipitate that forms when the 2 interact, forming the lattice structure.

Precipitation, as a method of detecting antigen-antibody interactions, is a very easy technique; it usually involves just placing the antigens and the antibody in different wells in an agar plate, allowing the diffusion to occur, and analyzing the pattern of precipitation that results. However, this is the least sensitive serological technique because it requires the visualization of 2 substances in solution as they come out of solution. It is not amplified by the antigen being on a particle, nor is it amplified by any methods to link this reaction to another more visible reaction. The measuring limit of precipitation is approximately 20 microgram/ml of antibody and antigen. However, it is still a clinically important assay for fungal antigens and for some research purposes because it can give information concerning the relatedness of antigens and the minimum number of antigen and antibody pairs, which is difficult to garner in any other way. Two examples of immunodiffusion gel precipitation methods are **double diffusion gel precipitation** reactions, which are also called *Ouchterlony reactions* or *immunodiffusion (ID) reactions,* and single diffusion precipitation, which is also called **radial immunodiffusion (RID)** (1, 2, 3, 4, 5, 6).

OUCHTERLONY

In double diffusion gel precipitation, also known as Ouchterlony analysis, both the antibody and the antigen diffuse through agar or agarose. As they diffuse radially, their concentration diminishes (Figure 3 ■); at the point in the diffusion where the relative concentrations of antibody and antigen reach equivalence, a precipitin line appears, which is formed by the **lattice** (cross-linked) structure formed by the complexes. Double immunodiffusion gel precipitation analyses are unique in that they allow for determination of antigenic relatedness of an unknown test material with a known antigen. Specifically, double diffusion gel precipitation allows the determination of whether the unknown is identical, partially

identical, or nonidentical with the known antigen. Double diffusion gel precipitation is a *qualitative* procedure and is utilized clinically in the diagnosis of some fungal infections including coccidiomycosis and is used in research to determine relatedness. The qualitative procedure has also been used to analyze serum from patients with autoimmune disorders and to determine the specificity of antibodies found in antinuclear antibody testing. However, in the case of autoimmunity, immunodiffusion has largely been replaced by enzyme immunoassays.

To compare antigenic relatedness, 2 different antigen preparations are placed in different wells, and the antiserum is placed in a third well. The antigens and antibodies diffuse in a circle out of the well, and only some of the antibody and antigen will actually be in the reaction because much of it diffuses in the wrong direction. When the antibody and the antigen meet at equivalence, they form a precipitin line (Figure 4 ■). One of 3 patterns can occur when the precipitin line forms: lines of **identity, nonidentity,** or **partial identity.**

1. When the 2 different antigen preparations contain the same antigen, a line of identity will form (Figure 4(b)). The arc shape of this line is the result of the intersection of the circular shapes of the diffusion from each well so that the reagents react at equilibrium in an arc.

2. When the antigens are completely different (Figure 4(c)), 2 different lines of precipitation form, one made of 1 antibody and its antigen, and the other made of the second antibody and its antigen. In the figure, observe that the red antibody to "pink and purple" antigen can go through the wall formed by the blue antibody and "dark green and orange" antigen lattice. This happens because precipitin walls are permeable to everything except to the reagents of which they are composed. An additional blue antibody would not get through this wall because it would bind to the orange epitopes and make the wall thicker. Similarly,

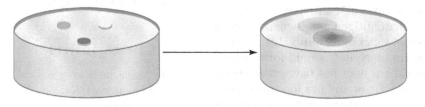

■ FIGURE 3   To illustrate how antibody and antigen diffuse from the wells, we depict colored dye diffusing from the wells. In diffusion of color from each well, the dye is most concentrated as it leaves the well, and as it goes farther, the concentration and the amount of color decreases. Where 2 colors meet a mixed color forms. In an antibody and antigen reaction where the two reactants met at appropriate concentrations the lattice precipitin product forms.

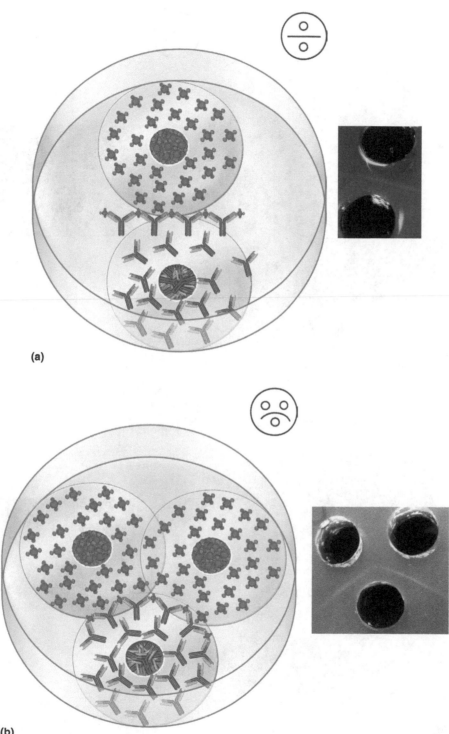

■ FIGURE 4   (a) An Ouchterlony double diffusion gel precipitation assay. The antigen and antibody solutions are most concentrated at the wells. When the Ag and Ab meet at equivalence, they form the lattice precipitin structure. (b) Two wells are filled with the same antigen, and when they diffuse to the antibody, they make a line of identity.

(continued)

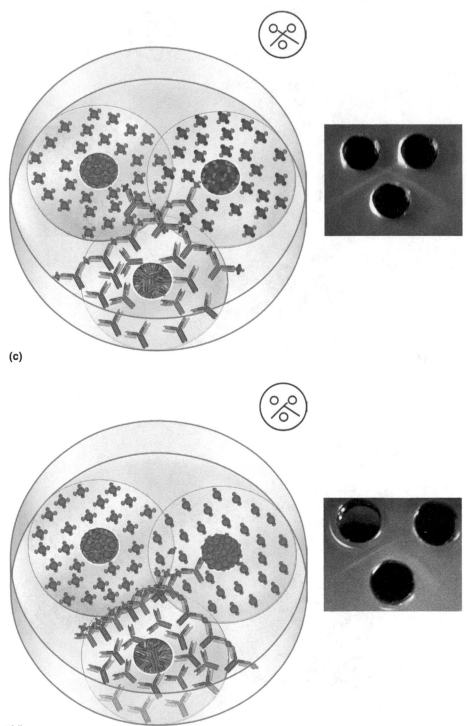

■ FIGURE 4 *(continued)* (c) Two wells are filled with different antigens and when they diffuse, they form lines that cross which is called a line of nonidentity. (d) Two wells are filled with related or partially identical antigens. The well on the left contains an antigen with an additional epitope when compared with the antigen in the well on the right. The precipitin line on the left is formed by the reaction of an antibody to the shared epiotpe, and this line continues on the right, as in a line of identity. Also in the line on the left is the reaction of an antibody to the unique epitope and the antigen with the unique epitope. This reaction line continues beyond the line of identity because the antibody to the unique epitope is not stopped as it comes to the line formed by the antigen without this epitope and antibody to the shared epitope. For simplicity, the antigen has been drawn with 2 to 4 epitopes, but proteins usually have more than this number of epitopes.

the orange and green antigen would not get through this wall but would bind to blue antibody and make the wall thicker.

3. When the antigens in the 2 wells are similar (Figure 4(d)) but the antigen in the well on the left contains an additional epitope (the pink piece), the antibody to the shared epitopes forms a line similar to a line of identity, but on the left, the antibody to the additional piece can also react. This antibody can also go through the wall made of the antigen without the pink epitope and its antibody, thus making a "spur" on the well on the left. The spur is made of antibody to the extra epitope and the antigen that contains the extra epitope. This line is called a *line of partial identity*. The spur always points to the simpler antigen.

Although the double diffusion gel precipitation reaction is qualitative rather than quantitative, it can be set up so that relative concentrations of the antigens can be determined. When the antigen and antibodies are diffusing from their respective wells, their concentration decreases as they move farther from the well, so when the antibody concentration in 2 wells is the same, the 2 wells containing the antigen opposite the 2 antibody wells would form precipitin lines in different places if their antigen concentrations are different. The antigen with the higher concentration would form a precipitin line closer to the antibody well because it would diffuse further before its concentration decreased to the level needed for equivalence (Figure 5 ■) (1, 2, 3, 4, 5, 6, 7).

RADIAL IMMUNODIFFUSION

Radial immunodiffusion utilizes an adaptation of the diffusion principle involving decreasing concentrations as one moves away from the source well to develop a quantitative immunoprecipitation technique. In radial immunodiffusion, single diffusion of the antigen takes place into a gel that already contains the antibody evenly distributed throughout (ie, the gel is poured with the antibody already mixed with it). Thus, as in Figure 5, the antibody concentration is held at a constant, and different concentrations of the antigen diffuse into it. Because the antigen is diffusing out of a circular well into the gel, the precipitation will be in a circle with its diameter reflecting the concentration of the antigen and with a more concentrated antigen traveling farther to become dilute enough for the precipitation to occur at equivalence (Figure 6 ■). A standard curve is prepared by using 3 different concentrations of the antigen in 3 different wells; the patient's results (ie, the diameter of the precipitation line from the patient's sample) are then compared to this standard curve, and an approximate concentration of antigen in the patient's sample is then obtained.

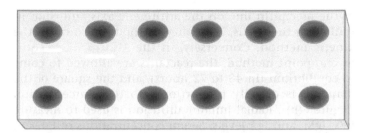

■ FIGURE 5 Concentration affects where the precipitin line forms. When 1 reactant is held at a constant concentration and the other reactant is varied in concentration, the place where the precipitin line forms changes in relation to the concentration.

Two slightly different methods are utilized for quantitating the results of radial immunodiffusion. The **Fahey method** allows the diffusion to proceed for 18 hours and the diameter is proportional to the log of the concentration. It is plotted using semilog paper with the diameter

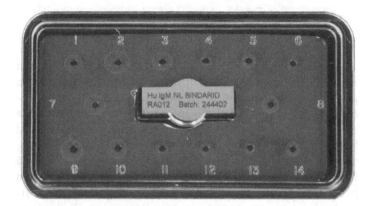

(a)

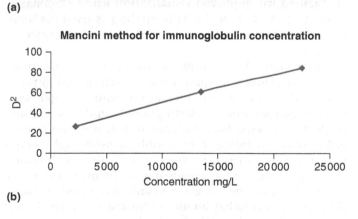

(b)

■ FIGURE 6 (a) A photograph of a radial immunodiffusion reaction for measurement of patient IgA concentrations. In this example the Ag concentration in well 2 is greater than that in well 3, or, well 5. (b) A plot of the Mancini method of determining immunoglobulin concentration.

of the precipitin line on the arithmetic axis and concentration on the y-axis. The Fahey method is also called the kinetic method. Conversely, in the Mancini method or end-point method, the reactants are allowed to come to equilibrium (in 48 to 72 hours), and the square of the diameter is directly proportional to the concentration (Figure 6(b)). Radial immunodiffusion is used to measure IgG, IgM, and IgA levels. Serum concentrations of IgE and IgD are not high enough to be read by this relatively insensitive method. These immunoglobulins are being measured as antigens, not as antibodies. The antibody in these commercial kits is anti-human immunoglobulin that is Fc specific. Concentrations of complement components are also determined this way.

✓ **Checkpoint! 2**

Should you use the Fahey method for RID or the Mancini method to get the patient's result faster?

Another method that utilizes immunoprecipitation is immunofixation electrophoresis. In this method a patient's serum proteins are separated as in serum protein electrophoresis 6 times in 6 different lanes. After the electrophoretic separation, each individual lane is overlaid with a different monospecific antisera, anti-IgG in 1 lane, and then anti-IgM, anti-IgA, anti-kappa, and anti-lambda in each subsequent lane. The sixth lane is treated with a protein fixative. After washing, the precipitated proteins are stained for improved visualization using Commassie blue (1, 2, 3, 4, 5, 6, 7). This method is used for identification of which immunoglobulin class is elevated in myeloma.

Other methods that utilize diffusion and electrophoresis were developed to speed up the reaction and improve sensitivity. These methods include immunoelectrophoresis, counter-current immunoelectrophoresis, and rocket immunoelectrophoresis. *Immunoelectrophoresis* is serum protein electrophoresis followed by double diffusion gel precipitation. *Counter-current electrophoresis* is the Ouchterlony technique enhanced and made quicker by using an electric current to bring the antigen and antibody together. *Rocket electrophoresis* is radial immunodiffusion using an electric current to bring the antigen into the antibody-containing gel. The shape of the precipitin line is the shape of a rocket. The height is proportional to the concentration of the antigen. None of these is used clinically any longer (1, 2, 3, 4, 5, 6, 7).

INSTRUMENTAL METHODS TO ENHANCE SENSITIVITY

Nephelometry and turbidometry use optical analysis methods to acquire and analyze antibody and antigen lattice formation. When antibodies and antigens are mixed in solution, the lattice structures begin to form and an initial cloudiness of the solution is followed by the lattice structures precipitating out of solution. In turbidometry, the initial cloudiness is measured by passing a light through the solution and determining the amount of light that comes directly across the solution into the detector. This is a measure of the amount of light that is lost due to scatter by the lattice structures. The amount of scatter is proportional to the concentration of the molecules in the lattice structures. Nephelometry is similar to turbidometry but does not measure the light directly across from the light source but at a 10° to 90° (70° typically used) angle from the light source. Both instrumental methods are much more sensitive than detecting precipitation with the naked eye and have been made more sensitive with the use of laser light as the light source. Nephelometry is more sensitive than turbidometry (Figure 7 ■). Immunoglobulin concentrations for IgG, IgM, and IgA as well as kappa and lambda light chains, complement proteins, and acute phase reactants are measured this way (7, 8, 9, 10).

✓ **Checkpoint! 3**

You were just hired, and the lab supervisor tells you to run an assay using the nephelometer. You have never seen one before and there are 2 instruments in the lab: One is a nephelometer and one is a turbidometer. You see that one of the instruments says that the light is detected at a 70° angle. A note on this instrument also gives the sensitivity range; it is more sensitive than the other instrument. Is this the correct instrument to use?

▶ AGGLUTINATION TECHNIQUES

HISTORY

The fact that serum from a patient could specifically agglutinate bacteria that caused an infection was discovered just before the 20th century. This discovery contributed evidence to the idea that the humoral (serum) part of the blood provided defense against infection. Soon after its discovery, bacterial agglutination was used to diagnose typhoid fever. Agglutination, the drawing together of particles that contain antigen to form a visible lattice or clump, is not very sensitive

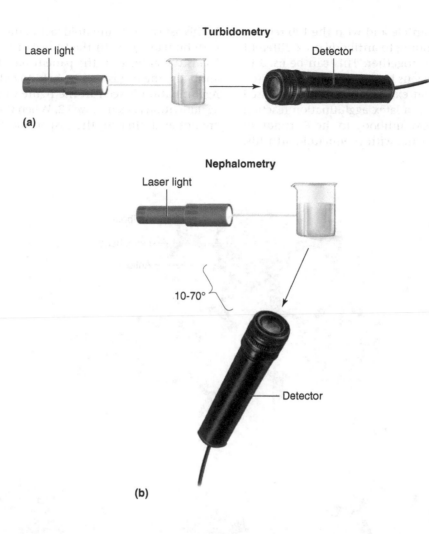

Turbidometry

Laser light

Detector

(a)

Nephalometry

Laser light

10-70°

Detector

(b)

■ FIGURE 7   (a) A turbidometry detector measures laser light directly across from the light source. The sample, the light source, and the detector are shown. (b) A nephelometry detector measures light at a 10° to 70° angle from the light source. The sample, the light source, and the detector are shown.

because nothing amplifies the actual antibody-antigen reaction. However, agglutination is more sensitive than precipitation because the larger antigen particles enhance visualization. Agglutination of particles that naturally have the antigen on their surface is called **direct agglutination.** The increased sensitivity of agglutination over precipitation was the reason for the development of **passive agglutination,** agglutination of particles that have been covalently coated with antigens (Figure 8(a) ■). Latex beads are the most commonly used particles for passive agglutination, although red blood cells that have been treated with tannic acid so that antigens will stick to them have also been used. Both direct and passive agglutination assays test for antibody that holds the antigen-coated particles together (1, 2, 3, 4, 5, 6, 7).

To test for antigen, different agglutination assays were developed. One of these is an inhibition agglutination assay. In this type of assay, agglutination is seen after mixing the antigen-coated particles from the kit and antibody supplied with the commercial kit. To determine if antigen is present in the patient's serum, the patient's serum is mixed with the kit antibody and if antigen is present in the serum it will bind to the kit antibody. Subsequent addition of the antigen-coated particles will not result in agglutination. So, in this inhibition assay, absence of agglutination is a positive result for antigen in the patient's serum (Figure 8(b)). Another type of agglutination assay that measures antigen is called **reverse passive agglutination.** In reverse passive agglutination, the particles have been coated with antibody (with the Fc regions down against the particle and with the Fab regions facing out), and antigen binding to antibody on 2 different particles holds the particles together. This can be used to detect bacterial or other antigens in solution; see Figure 8(c).

Refer to Figure 8(d) for an example of a clinically used agglutination reaction. This is a latex agglutination reaction for rheumatoid factor, an IgM antibody to the Fc region of IgG that is produced in patients with rheumatoid arthritis.

In this assay for rheumatoid factor, the latex beads are coated with human IgG with the Fc region facing out. This human IgG is the antigen. If the patient has the rheumatoid factor antibody, the beads will be held together and agglutinated. Agglutination is seen in the figure in wells 1, 3, and 4. No agglutination is seen in well 2. When the milky white particles are not agglutinated, the suspension looks like milk, while

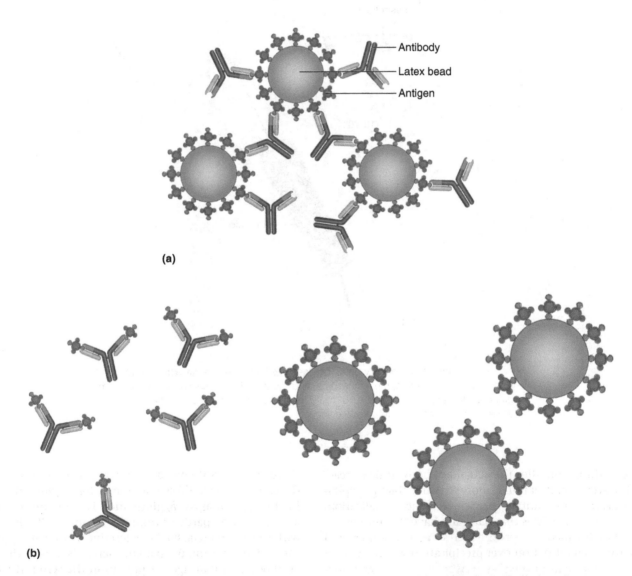

(a)

Antibody
Latex bead
Antigen

(b)

■ FIGURE 8   (a) An agglutination reaction. Antigen-coated latex beads are held together by antibody. In a direct agglutination reaction, the antigen is naturally part of the particle, but in passive agglutination, the antigen is attached to the particle. (b) An agglutination inhibition reaction. Commercial kit materials would create an agglutination reaction as seen in (a). If the patient's serum has antigen in it, mixing the patient's serum with the antibody first and then adding the antigen-coated beads would result in the reaction seen here. The antibody is bound by soluble antigen and no longer causes agglutination of the particles.

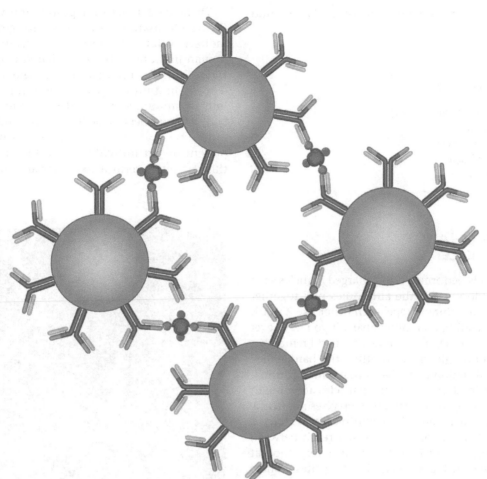

(c)

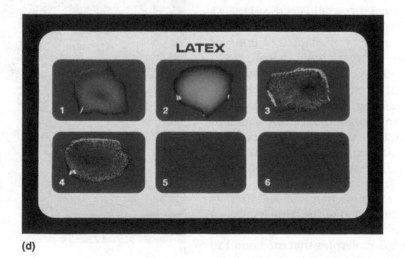

(d)

■ FIGURE 8 *(continued)* (c) A reverse passive agglutination reaction. The antibody is bound to the particles, and antigen in the patient serum or urine causes the particles to become agglutinated. (d) A latex agglutination reaction. This is an analysis for rheumatoid factor. Immunoglobulin is bound to the latex particles with the Fc facing out. For this disease, the Fc of immunoglobulin is the antigen that the patient makes antibody to. The patient's IgM to the Fc of IgG binds the particles together. A weak positive is seen in well 1, a negative control in well 2, and strong positives in wells 3 and 4.

agglutination looks gritty with a clearing of the background (1, 2, 3, 4, 5, 6, 7).

✓ **Checkpoint! 4**

Which of the following measures antibody?
A. *direct agglutination*
B. *reverse passive agglutination*
C. *agglutination inhibition*
D. *passive agglutination*

EFFECT OF A CHARGE ON THE PARTICLE

When agglutination is performed using charged particles such as bacteria or red blood cells, the antibodies pull together 2 particles that would naturally repel each other like 2 north poles of a magnet pushing each other apart. If you have ever held 2 north poles of a magnet together, you will remember that the closer you brought them together, the harder they pushed apart. Agglutination is similar in that with agglutination of charged particles, the closer the particles are brought together, the more they repel. This property results in the fact that IgM works much better for agglutination of charged particles than IgG because of the increased reach between the antigen-binding sites of IgM. IgM is also very good at agglutination because it has so many binding sites. Where the particle has a charge, the pH of the reaction is important because it affects the charge. The charge on the particle is called the zeta potential of the particle. If the charge or zeta potential increases, the apparent titer would decrease because it would take more immunoglobulin to hold these charged particles together. Methods have been adapted to improve binding of charged particles: using low ionic strength (LISS) media to decrease charge, using increased viscosity media to decrease the water of hydration, altering the temperature to improve antibody binding, treating the red cells with enzymes to decrease surface charge, and agitation or centrifugation to increase interaction. IgM antibodies agglutinate best between 4°C and 27°C, and IgG antibodies agglutinate best at 37°C. See Figure 9(a) ■ for IgM hemagglutination (agglutination of red blood cells) (1, 2, 3, 4, 5, 6, 7).

Because of the repulsive effect of charge, sometimes IgG antibodies do not cause agglutination of the particles; in this case, an anti-human immunoglobulin can be added to cross-link the Fc regions of the IgG molecules that are bound to the particle. The addition of the anti-human immunoglobulin increases the distance between the particles and allows agglutination to occur (1, 2, 3, 4, 5, 6). Figure 9(b) ■ shows IgG and anti-human immunoglobulin-mediated hemagglutination.

There are 2 types of agglutination with red blood cells (hemagglutination), the direct antiglobulin test and the indirect antiglobulin test. Both tests involve IgG and anti-human immunoglobulin-mediated hemagglutination (see Figure 9(b)). Anti-human immunoglobulin is antibody that is made in another species and binds to the Fc region of human immunoglobulin. It is used to detect human antibody in a number of reactions in the serology lab. The direct antiglobulin test (DAT) measures whether antibody is present on an individual's red blood cells. For example, this test can determine whether an infant's red blood cells

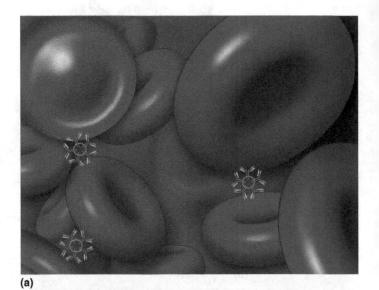

(a)

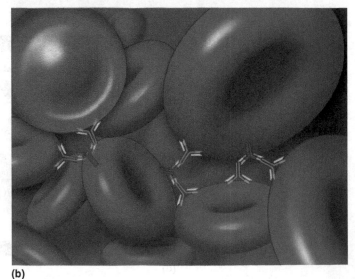

(b)

■ FIGURE 9 (a) Hemagglutination with IgM antibody. (b) Hemagglutination with IgG binding to the rbcs and an anti-human immunoglobulin added to bridge the IgG antibodies.

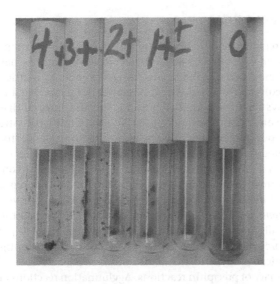

(c)

■ FIGURE 9 *(continued)* (c) A photograph of a hemagglutination reaction. In the tube labeled 0, there is no agglutination, in the tube labeled +/−, a small amount of agglutination is seen and as the numbers increase, there is progressively more agglutination. In the tube labeled 4+, you can see that the red blood cells are in 1 large clump.

have their mother's anti-Rh on their surface and whether a patient has an autoimmune hemolytic anemia, a transfusion reaction, or antibody to drug-sensitized red blood cells. Anti-human immunoglobulin is added directly to red cells from the patient which are then observed for agglutination. Using an **indirect antiglobulin test (IAT)**, the clinical laboratory looks for the presence of patient antibody to red blood cells. Compared with the previous example, this test would be used to see whether a mother has anti-Rh antibodies. It can also be used to test for transfusion compatibility. The patient's serum is added to the red blood cells and after incubation and washing, anti-human immunoglobulin is added. The cells are centrifuged and observed for agglutination. Figure 9(c) shows different degrees of hemagglutination from no agglutination to a 4+ agglutination reaction in which the cell button comes off the bottom of the tube in 1 clump (1, 2, 3, 4, 5, 6, 7).

INSTRUMENTAL METHODS TO ENHANCE AGGLUTINATION SENSITIVITY

Similar to the way the sensitivity of precipitation assays are enhanced using the optical-enhanced methods of nephelometry and turbidometry, agglutination assays are also enhanced with optical detection methods, including the **particle-enhanced turbidimetric inhibition assay (PETINA)**,

the **particle-counting immunoassay (PACIA)**, and the **quasi-elastic light scattering method (QUELS)**.

PETINA is used to determine the serum concentration achieved with administration of a therapeutic drug. The need for this monitoring of therapeutic drug concentration occurs because different individuals metabolize drugs differently and certain concentrations of the drug must be maintained but not exceeded for efficacy without toxicity. This *therapeutic drug monitoring* is particularly important with the anti-clotting drug Coumadin, but is important for many other drugs as well. In a PETINA for therapeutic drug concentration, the commercial kit comes with a specific drug linked to particles and an antibody to the drug. Mixing antibody with these particles will cause increased turbidity of the solution because it agglutinates the particles. When the patient's serum containing that particular drug is added to this mixture, it will bind the antibody, so no antibody is left to bind the particles. This drug in the patient's serum *inhibits* the cross-linking of the particles by the antibody because the antibody-binding sites are bound to the drug in the patient's serum and are not free to cross-link the particles. Therefore, no agglutination indicates the presence of the drug in the patient's sample. This is diagramed in Figure 8(b), the agglutination (or lack thereof) is detected using turbidometry and has enhanced sensitivity for measuring drug concentrations over nonoptically enhanced methods (7, 8, 9, 10).

In PACIA, an agglutination reaction occurs, but this reaction is observed by counting the residual nonagglutinating particles. They are measured by an optical cell counter calibrated to count single particles and to exclude aggregated particles according to size. The particles are brought through a detector and measured either by the change in conductance as the particles go through the detection path or they are measured as they go through a detector by light scattering. This assay is more sensitive than nephelometry because dimers are easily gated as agglutinated particles whereas most other techniques need agglutination of higher order before it is detected. These assays are much more sensitive than noninstrumental agglutination techniques, reaching down to 10^{-10} molar (9).

QUELS, or quasi-elastic dynamic light scattering method, measures changes that are related to diffusion coefficients. Diffusion coefficients, in turn, are related to particle size, shape, flexibility, and particle-to-particle interactions. Fluctuations in light intensity are measured after a laser light is shined on the sample. The amplitude of the scattered wave of light is proportional to particle size. For QUELS to be an accurate representation of aggregation of the particles, the sample must be dust free because dust will register as aggregated particles. This method works best when the light is scattered by a single particle, not by the light hitting multiple particles, so this method works best at low concentrations (10).

✓ Checkpoint! 5

Match the items 1 through 3 to the proper letter A through C.

1. PACIA
2. PETINA
3. QUELS

A. *uses inhibition*
B. *counts nonagglutinating particles*
C. *uses the fact that little particles and big particles scatter light differently*

Ⓔ CASE STUDY

You are working at a biotechnology company. Your supervisor asked you to improve the sensitivity of a latex agglutination assay. This assay has been especially designed to need no instrumentation because it will be used in third-world countries in laboratories. Currently, 20% of the patients with this disease do not test positive until they have already developed significant illness due to the infection. If they tested positive earlier, they would have received antibiotics and would not have become so ill.

1. To improve the sensitivity, a smaller amount of patient's immuno-globulin should agglutinate the particles. Latex particles are not charged. How can you design the agglutination assay to be more sensitive?

2. If the assay had been done with red blood cells (negatively charged particles), how could you increase the sensitivity of the assay in relation to charge?

SUMMARY

In precipitation and agglutination reactions, the complexes of molecules of antibody and antigen are visible with the naked eye. In these reactions, the key to the development of lattice (cross-linked) structures that we can visualize is the fact that antibodies always have more than 1 binding site and most antigens also have more than one binding site. To form these lattice structures, antibody and antigen must be at or near equivalence; too much antibody causes a false negative (prozone) and too much antigen causes a false negative (postzone) as well. The most commonly performed precipitin techniques are immunodiffusion plates also called *double diffusion gel precipitation reactions* or *Ouchterlony reactions*. Antibody and antigen detection for fungal infections are still sometimes performed with this technique. The pattern of the precipitin line allows one to determine whether antigens are identical, partially identical, or nonidentical. See Table 1 Ⓞ for a summary of precipitin reactions. Agglutination reactions are more sensitive than precipitation reactions because fewer of these larger particles are needed to form a visible reaction. Agglutination reactions can be direct assays, which are performed on an antigen that is naturally a part of the particle or they can be passive agglutination when the antigen is covalently attached to a carrier such as a latex bead. Direct and passive agglutination reactions are used to measure antibody, and reverse passive and agglutination inhibition assays are used to measure antigen. In testing to see whether a baby has received placentally transferred anti-RH antibodies from his or her mother, an agglutination assay is done with the baby's red blood cells. This assay measures whether antibody is bound to these red blood cells. Anti-human immunoglobulin is added to the red cells, and if this causes agglutination, the baby has this anti-RH antibody on his or her red blood cells. This is a direct antiglobulin test (DAT). To test whether a woman has anti-RH in her serum, it is mixed with RH+ red blood cells and

Ⓞ TABLE 1

Summary of Precipitation Reactions

Assay	Double Diffusion Gel Precipitation	RID	Nephelometry	Turbidometry
Step 1	Place antiserum in 1 well	Place antigen in well	Add antibody and antigen together, place in instrument	Add antibody and antigen together, place in instrument
Step 2	Place antigens in wells across from antiserum	Allow diffusion to occur	Visualize light that is scattered at a 10–90° (usually 70°) angle	Visualize light that is directly across from the light source
Step 3	Allow diffusion to occur	Visualize and interpret reaction	Create a standard curve	Create a standard curve
Step 4	Visualize and interpret reaction Document as number of lines present and pattern of identity, nonidentity, or partial identity	Draw standard curve using D^2 versus concentration for Mancini or Fahey on semilog paper with D versus concentration on the y-axis		

then anti-human immunoglobulin is added. This is an indirect antiglobulin test (IAT). Charged particles repel, so more antibody is needed to hold charged particles together. To increase the sensitivity of an agglutination assay with charged particles, the ionic strength of the media is reduced to lower particle charge. Refer to Table 2 ✪ for a summary of agglutination reactions. Media viscosity can also be increased to decrease charge, clinical laboratories do this by adding 22% bovine serum albumin to the reaction. Instrumental methods can be employed to increase the sensitivity of precipitation (nephelometry and turbidometry) and agglutination reactions (PETINA, PACIA, and QUELS) (1, 2, 3, 4, 5, 6, 7, 8, 9, 10).

✪ TABLE 2

Summary of Agglutination Reactions

Assay	Direct Agglutination	Passive Agglutination	Inhibition Agglutination	Reverse Passive Agglutination	Direct Antiglobulin Test	Indirect Antiglobulin Test
Step 1	Add patient's serum to red blood cells or bacteria	Add patient's serum to antigen-coated particles	Add patient's serum or urine to kit-supplied antibody	Add patient's serum or urine to antibody-coated particles	Draw red blood cells from newborn	Prepare RH+ red blood cells
Step 2	Mix	Mix	Add antigen-coated particles from the kit	Mix	Add anti-human immunoglobulin	Add patient's serum
Step 3	Visualize presence or absence of agglutination	Visualize presence or absence of agglutination	Mix	Visualize presence or absence of agglutination	Visualize presence or absence of agglutination	Add anti-human immunoglobulin
Step 4			Visualize presence or absence of agglutination			Visualize presence or absence of agglutination
Detects	Antibody	Antibody	Antigen	Antigen	Anti-RH on infant's red blood cells	Anti-RH in patient's serum

LABORATORY EXERCISE

INSTRUCTIONAL OBJECTIVES

At the conclusion of this lab, the student will be able to:

COGNITIVE DOMAIN

1. Define *precipitation*.
2. Discuss the principle of radial immunodiffusion (RID).
3. Compare and contrast the overnight (Fahey) and the endpoint (Mancini) methods of interpreting results.
4. Discuss several sources of error in quantifying immunoglobulins by RID.
5. Define *prozone*.
6. Describe the requirement for multiple epitopes and for a certain minimal molecular size for the antigen for a precipitation reaction to occur.
7. Discuss how initial concentration in the well of an RID or Ouchterlony plate affects where the precipitin line forms and equivalence occurs.

PSYCHOMOTOR DOMAIN

1. Identify and interpret the reactions of identity, partial identity, and nonidentity in an Ouchterlony double diffusion plate.
2. Perform and interpret the results of an IgG RID procedure.

3. Define *lattice formation* and be able to draw a molecular depiction to explain lattice formation in a precipitation reaction. Also define *prozone* and *postzone* and draw the effect of excess Ab or Ag on lattice formation.

4. Define *equivalence* in terms of the answer to Objective 3. In addition, draw the way that the concentration of the Ag and the Ab changes as the distance from the well of origin increases.

DOUBLE IMMUNODIFFUSION (OUCHTERLONY): LABORATORY PART 1

Double immunodiffusion allows the determination of antigenic relatedness of an unknown test material with a known antigen. This technique allows for determining whether the unknown is identical, partially identical, or nonidentical with the known. Double immunodiffusion is a *qualitative* procedure, largely a research tool, and used in the laboratory for analysis of serum from patients with autoimmune disorders.

You and a partner will prepare an Ouchterlony system, set up as follows:

1. Fill a Petri dish with 1% agarose in phosphate-buffered saline (PBS) with azide to a depth of 3 mm. Allow to cool.

2. Cut 3- to 4-mm holes in the agarose. Remove the plugs by suction.

3. Prepare an Ouchterlony reaction (one person should do the identity plate, and one the nonidentity) as follows:
   a. Label under the wells carefully with a sharpie. Do not get ink between the wells.
   b. Add 40 microliters of antibody of bovine serum to A wells.
   c. Add 40 microliters of albumin to wells labeled C (1–10 mg/ml).
   d. Add 40 microliters of bovine IgG (1–10 mg/ml) to the well labeled D on only one of the plates.
   e. Incubate overnight on a flat surface.
   f. Observe, draw, and interpret patterns.*

*The exact concentration of antigen required depends on the particular antiserum that you are using. Run a test immunodiffusion prior to using these concentrations in class.

Plate 1 Nonidentity

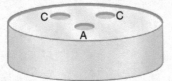

Plate 2 Identity

4. Interpret the following:

   a. Fusion: Identity of antigens

   b. Crossing over: Nonidentity

c. Spur formation: Partial identity

Variables in the double diffusion method include size of the antigen wells relative to the antibody well, concentration of antiserum, and time.

RADIAL IMMUNODIFFUSION: LABORATORY PART 2

MATERIALS

1. Bindarid™ RID plate from The Binding Site Ltd. Birmingham, UK (RN004.3, RN010.3, RN012.3, or RK002)
2. Serum samples for testing

PROCEDURE

1. Remove the RID plate from the foil pouch, remove the lid, and allow condensation to evaporate for 10 to 15 minutes.
2. Mix calibrators gently before using.
3. Fill wells with 5 microliters of the samples and calibrators. Do not leave the plate open for an extensive period of time.
4. Incubate the RID plate at room temperature (20° to 24° C) for 18 hours for the Fahey method or 48 hours for the Mancini method (72 hours for IgM; the larger molecular weight molecule takes a longer time to diffuse).
5. Measure the diameter of each precipitin ring from the back of the plate using the jeweler's eyepiece or the RID ruler. Measure the diameter to the nearest 0.1 mm and then square it.
6. Draw a standard curve on linear graph paper for the Mancini method (concentration on the x-axis; d^2 on the y-axis). This will give a straight line. Determine the immunoglobulin concentration of the sample by squaring the diameter, plotting it on the y-axis, and reading the concentration from the standard curve on the x-axis.
7. Plot the Fahey method as above, but the line will be curved. For a straight line for the Fahey method, use semilog paper with the diameter on the arithmetic axis and concentration on the y-axis.

REVIEW QUESTIONS

1. In an Ouchterlony plate, a precipitin line of identity forms between 2 Ags and an Ab, the 2 lines
   a. cross
   b. merge
   c. cross on 1 side only
   d. form 2 separate lines

2. A prozone effect
   a. occurs in agglutination and precipitin reactions when there is antigen excess
   b. occurs in agglutination and precipitin reactions when there is antibody excess
   c. occurs in agglutination but not in precipitation reactions
   d. occurs in enzyme immunoassay and fluorescent immunoassays when there is antigen excess

3. Which of the following describes agglutination?
   a. soluble Ag + soluble Ab
   b. particulate Ag + soluble Ab
   c. reaction that requires instrumentation to read
   d. reaction that requires covalent binding to the Ab molecule

4. Which of the following enhances agglutination of charged particles?
   a. increasing the ionic strength
   b. removing albumin from the reaction buffer
   c. decreasing viscosity
   d. decreasing ionic strength

REVIEW QUESTIONS (continued)

5. A direct agglutination reaction involves an
   a. antigen that is already part of the particle
   b. antigen that has been covalently attached to the particle
   c. antigen that has been attached with van der Waals forces to the particle
   d. antibody that has been covalently attached to the particle

6. Agglutination reactions involve all of the following except
   a. van der Waals, hydrophobic and hydrophilic interactions, electrostatic interactions, hydrogen bonding
   b. covalent attachment of something to an antibody molecule
   c. Ab and Ag reaction
   d. zones of equivalence

7. In radial immunodiffusion by the Mancini method, the
   a. concentration of the antigen is directly proportional to the ring diameter
   b. concentration of the antigen is inversely proportional to the ring diameter
   c. concentration of the antigen is directly proportional to the ring diameter squared
   d. time required is less than that for the Fahey method

8. A direct antiglobulin test
   a. measures the amount of antibody in the RH− mom that reacts with the RH+ fetal red blood cells
   b. determines whether anti-RH is already present on the newborn's red blood cells
   c. measures the amount of antibody produced by the fetus to the mother's red blood cells
   d. uses cross-linking antibodies of the IgD type

9. When a light shines directly through a solution and the amount of light that goes through the sample (directly across) is measured as the amount of complex formation, this is called
   a. nephelometry
   b. turbidometry
   c. spectrophotometry
   d. fluorescence

10. If a patient shows the signs and symptoms of severe rheumatoid arthritis but the 1:40 dilution of her sera did not show an agglutination reaction,
    a. we should use an enzyme immunoassay instead, because we need a more sensitive assay
    b. we should test for other forms of arthritis
    c. we should serially dilute the serum and run the test again
    d. we should report to the physician that she is negative for rheumatoid factor

11. A physician came into your laboratory and wants a stat result on the immunoglobulin level in a patient's sera. You have an RID commercial kit for immunoglobulin levels. How soon can you give the physician the results, remembering that the physician wants a stat, or fast, result?
    a. 18 hours by the Mancini method
    b. 18 hours by the Fahey method
    c. 48 hours by the Mancini method
    d. 48 hours by the Fahey method

12. If an Ouchterlony were repeated using twice as much total antigen concentration in the well as used originally, the precipitin line would be
    a. closer to the antibody well
    b. closer to the antigen well
    c. in the same place
    d. not enough information is available to decide between the above answers

REFERENCES

1. Bailey G. Ouchterlony double immunodiffusion. *The Protein Protocols Handbook.* 1996;part VII:749–752. doi: 10.1007/978-1-60327-259-9_135.

2. Saubolle MA. Laboratory aspects in the diagnosis of coccidioidomycosis. *Ann N Y Acad Sci.* 2007;1111(1).

3. Silverstein AM. Cellular versus humoral immunity. In: Silverstein AM, ed. *A History of Immunology.* 2nd ed. Elsevier, NY: 2009: chap 2.

4. Stevens CD. *Clinical Immunology and Serology: A Laboratory Perspective.* 3rd ed. Philadelphia, PA: F.A. Davis Co; 2009; chap 8.

5. Stevens CD. *Clinical Immunology and Serology: A Laboratory Perspective.* 3rd ed. Philadelphia, PA: F.A. Davis Co; 2009: chap 9.

6. Berzofsky JA, Berkower IJ, Epstein SL. Antigen-antibody interactions and monoclonal antibodies. In: Paul WE, ed. *Fundamental Immunology.* 6th ed. Philadelphia, PA: Wolters Kluwer/Lippincott Williams & Wilkins; 2008.

7. Kaplan LA, Pescoe A, Kazmierczak SC. Clinical chemistry: Theory, analysis, correlation. *Laboratory Techniques.* 4th ed. chap 12.

8. Bangs Laboratories, Inc. Tech Note 304 Light-Scattering Assays. April 2008. http://www.bangslabs.com/sites/default/files/bangs/docs/pdf/304.pdf

9. Beckman Coulter, Inc. The Chemistry Information Sheet Theophylline Kit. https://www.beckmancoulter.com/wsrportal/techdocs?docname=/cis/A18559/AG/EN_THE.pdf

10. Lomakin A, Teplow DB, Benedek GB. Quasielastic light scattering for protein assembly study. In: Sigurdsson EM, ed. *Methods in Molecular Biology*. Totowa, NJ: Humana Press; 2005:153–174. http://web.mit.edu/physics/benedek/ArticlesMore/Lomakin2005.pdf

ANSWERS TO REVIEW QUESTIONS

1. b
2. b
3. b
4. d
5. a
6. b
7. c
8. b
9. b
10. c
11. b
12. a

ANSWERS TO CASE STUDIES

1. After the antigen-coated beads are added to the patient's serum, you can add anti-human immunoglobulin to cross-link the human antibody bound to the antigen on the beads.
2. The pH of the reaction is important because it affects the charge. The charge on the particle is the particle's zeta potential. Decreasing the charge or zeta potential would increase the apparent titer because it would take less immunoglobulin to hold these less charged particles together. To improve binding of charged particles (1) use low ionic strength media to decrease charge (LISS), (2) use increased viscosity media to decrease the water of hydration, (3) alter the temperature to improve antibody binding, (IgM antibodies agglutinate best between 4° and 27° C, and IgG antibodies agglutinate best at 37° C.) (4) treat the red cells with enzymes to decrease surface charge, and (5) add agitation or centrifugation to increase interaction.

ANSWERS TO CHECKPOINTS

Checkpoint! 1
Repeat the assay with diluted serum to see whether the first reaction was negative because of a prozone reaction.

Checkpoint! 2
Fahey method

Checkpoint! 3
yes

Checkpoint! 4
A and D

Checkpoint! 5
1. B
2. A
3. C

GLOSSARY

Affinity measure of the strength of the binding of one Fab with its corresponding epitope on the antigen.

Agglutination cross-linking of particulate antigen (bacteria, cells, or latex particles) by antibody to form larger complexes that are also visible.

Avidity number of binding sites times the affinity.

Direct agglutination the agglutination of particles that naturally have the antigen on their surface.

Direct antiglobulin test (DAT) measures whether antibody is present on an individual's red blood cells. Anti-human immunoglobulin is added directly to red cells from the patient and the cells are observed for agglutination.

Double diffusion gel precipitation also known as *ouchterlony analysis*, both the antibody and the antigen diffuse through agar or agarose, and where they meet at equivalence form a lattice structure. It is a qualitative technique.

Equivalence when the antigen and antibody meet at a concentration in which the number of paratopes (antibody binding sites) approximately equals the number of epitopes; this part of the precipitation curve is where large complexes called *lattices* are formed.

Fahey method radial immunodiffusion method plotted using semilog paper with diameter on the arithmetic axis and concentration on the y-axis. In an antibody-antigen precipitation reaction that allows diffusion to proceed for 18 hours; diameter is proportional to the log of the concentration.

Identity the name of the arched reaction line which occurs when, in double diffusion gel precipitation reactions the antigens in the 2 wells are the same.

Indirect antiglobulin test (IAT) looks for presence of patient antibody to red blood cells. The patient's serum is added to the red blood cells and after incubation and washing anti-human immunoglobulin is added. The cells are centrifuged and observed for agglutination.

Lattice name of the cross-linked structure of antibody and antigen that forms in equivalence in either precipitation or agglutination assays.

Mancini method (also called *end-point method*) radial immunodiffusion method in which the reactants are allowed to come to equilibrium (24–72 hrs) and the square of the diameter is directly proportional to the concentration of the antigen.

Nephelometry uses optical analysis methods to acquire and analyze antibody and antigen lattice formation. Scattered light is measured at a 10 to 90° angle from the light source, usually at 70°.

Nonidentity is the name of the 2 crossed reaction lines when, in double diffusion gel precipitation reactions the antigens in the 2 wells are different.

Partial identity the name of the arched reaction lines with a spur that forms when, in double diffusion gel precipitation reactions the antigens in the 2 wells are share an epitope, but one of the antigens has an additional epitope. The "spur" points to the simpler antigen.

Particle-counting immunoassay (PACIA) an instrumentation enhanced agglutination method in which residual nonagglutinating particles are counted.

Particle-enhanced turbidometric inhibition assay (PETINA) an instrumentation enhanced agglutination method in which drug linked to particles and antibody to the drug cause increased turbidity of the solution when added to the particles. When the patient serum containing the drug is added to this mixture it will inhibit the cross-linking of the particles by the antibody.

Passive agglutination an agglutination reaction using particles that have been coated with the antigen. Latex particles are most often used.

Postzone exists when the amount of patient antibody is low so that each antibody is bound by 2 antigen molecules, resulting in no bridging of 2 antibody molecules by the antigen, so little or no precipitation occurs.

Precipitation the cross-linking of soluble antigen to create an insoluble precipitate that is visible.

Prozone is when, in a precipitation reaction, there is too much antibody, so that there are 2 antibodies bound to every bivalent antigen and there is no need for bridging of 2 antigen molecules by an antibody molecule. In this situation little or no precipitate would form, that makes it appear that the patient does not have antibody to the antigen, when, in fact, they have too much antibody for the reaction to occur.

Quasi-elastic light scattering method (QUELS) an instrumentation enhanced agglutination method in which light scattering changes are measured.

Radial immunodiffusion (RID) single diffusion of the antigen into a gel that already contains the antibody throughout. It is a quantitative technique.

Reverse passive agglutination   an antibody rather than antigen is linked to the particles, this method was developed to detect antigen in patient's fluids.

Turbidometry   turbidometry uses optical analysis methods to acquire and analyze antibody and antigen lattice formation. Light is measured directly opposite the light source.

Zeta potential   the charge on the particle involved in the agglutination reaction.

Labeled Immunoassays

From Chapter 7 of *Contemporary Clinical Immunology and Serology*, First Edition. Kate Rittenhouse-Olson, Ernesto De Nardin.

Labeled Immunoassays

■ OBJECTIVES—LEVEL I

After this chapter, the student should be able to:

1. Describe the creation of the first labeled immunoassay.
2. Describe the typical constituents of a labeled assay.
3. Identify standards that an antibody must meet to be used for immunoassay.
4. Distinguish between heterogeneous and homogeneous enzyme immunoassays.
5. Describe applications for homogeneous enzyme immunoassays.
6. Explain the principle of direct immunoassays.
7. Explain the priniciple of indirect immunoassays.
8. Explain the principle of sandwich or capture immunoassays.
9. Explain the principle of competitive immunoassays.
10. Compare and contrast enzyme immunoassay and radioimmunoassay as to ease of performance, shelf life, sensitivity, and clinical application.
11. Compare and contrast direct and indirect techniques.
12. Explain the principle of a Western blot assay.
13. Explain why it is sometimes important to perform a Western blot assay rather than an enzyme immunoassay to determine whether a patient has an antibody to a particular disease.
14. Relate the principle of fluorescence polarization immunoassay.
15. Discuss advantages and disadvantages of each type of immunoassay.
16. Compare and contrast the immunoassays in terms of sensitivity

■ OBJECTIVES—LEVEL II

After this chapter, the student should be able to:

1. Describe how a multiplex assay allows for the analysis of multiple antibody and antigen reactions at one time.
2. Describe assay-specific factors that may affect a particular immunoassay (substrate or enzyme effects).
3. Describe patient-specific factors that may affect an immunoassay.

KEY TERMS

anti-human immunoglobulin

chemiluminescence

colloid particles

competitive immunoassay

direct immunoassay

fluorescence

fluorescence polarization immunoassay

heterogeneous assays

homogeneous assays

human anti-mouse antibody (HAMA)

immunochromatographic sandwich assay

indirect immunoassay

multiplexed fluorescent microbead assays

optical immunoassays

recombinant immunoblot assay (RIBA)

rheumatoid factor

sandwich assay

spectrophotometer

steric hindrance

Western blot

▶ HISTORY AND INTRODUCTION

The unlabeled immunoassays have the advantage of ease of use and are still utilized when the concentrations of the reactants are high enough to visualize. However, relying on actually seeing the antibody and antigen reaction requires a large amount of the immune complex to be formed and is inherently insensitive. With the use of nephelometry and turbidometry, instrumentation improves the ability to visualize the reaction, but the sensitivity is still limited. The vast potential for earlier disease detection and for research applications inspired scientists to look for ways to increase the sensitivity of visualization of antibody and antigen reactions. As in the unlabeled immunoassays, the affinity and the specificity of the antibody utilized in the assay is a key component in any immunoassay. The first assay in which a marker or label was covalently attached to the antibody or antigen to increase the sensitivity of detection was the radioimmunoassay (RIA) developed in 1959 by Rosalyn Yalow who won the Nobel prize for this discovery (1). In this competitive RIA, antigen from the patient competed with radiolabeled antigen for binding to a fixed amount of antibody. Reactants were measured at concentrations that were not visible to the human eye. Yalow's assay, which was developed to help study the clearance of insulin, became the predecessor of many sensitive assays in which a detectable marker or label is attached to either an antibody or antigen. In these assays, the reaction of antibody and antigen complex formation is detected with a thousandsfold increase in sensitivity. Yalow compared the change brought about by this technique to viewing the sky with a powerful telescope compared to viewing it by eye alone (1).

✓ Checkpoint! 1

Who invented the labeled immunoassay?

✓ Checkpoint! 2

What was the first label used in a labeled immunoassay?

This enhanced view of immune reactions is not only brought about by radiolabels; antibody or antigen can alternatively be labeled with enzymes (enzyme immunoassays (EIA) or enzyme-linked immunosorbant assays (ELISA)), fluorescent compounds (fluorescent immunoassay (FIA)), chemiluminescent labels, and colloid particles. In the 1970s, Engvall and Perlman developed an enzyme label for the antibody-antigen reaction to use instead of a radioactive tag (2). In these immunoassay reactions, it is essential to be able to measure the amount of the label that is bound to the antigen-antibody interaction and to separate this bound label from the amount of label that is on unbound antigen or antibody. This is done most often by using a solid phase for the reaction and washing away unbound reactant. This type of assay, requiring separation of bound from free is called a heterogeneous assay. Homogeneous assays do not require a separation or washing step to separate the bound antigen and antibody molecules from the free ones. Homogeneous assays can be accomplished because the binding of an antigen to an antibody affects the activity of the label in such a way as to cause a measureable change.

✓ Checkpoint! 3

A patient's urine was applied to a chromatographic membrane and the reactants traveled up the membrane to the point where the Ag + Ab complexes bound to a spot on the membrane and the free Ab and Ag kept traveling. Is the reaction homogeneous or heterogeneous?

Radiolabels are detected by either gamma counters or liquid scintillation counters. Enzyme labels are detected by the addition of a substrate, which the enzyme changes to produce either (1) a color change that can be measured in a spectrophotometer, (2) fluorescence that can be measured fluorometrically, (3) a flash of light (chemiluminescence) that can be measured with a luminometer, or (4) a change in optical reflection in optical immunoassays (OIA). Fluorescent labels are detected in a spectrofluorimeter by detecting the amount of fluorescence at the emission wavelength after application of the excitation wavelength of light. The chemiluminescent assay is based on (1) labeling either an antigen or antibody with a chemiluminescent compound, (2) separating the bound from the free label, (3) activating the chemiluminescent compound with a "trigger" followed by (4) the subsequent measurement of the light in a luminometer or on employing a photomultiplier tube for maximal sensitivity.

In colloid immunoassays, colloid particles are detected by eye after separation in a process called *immunochromatography*. These large colored colloid particles must be attached to the antibody or antigen in a way that does not cause steric hindrance. The optical immunoassay is based on the changes in the reflection of light after antigen and antibody binding to a surface. The optical immunoassay is also visualized by eye. Because they do not require instrumentation, the colloid and the optical immunoassays are useful for point-of-care testing. The colloid immunoassay is frequently utilized in over-the-counter home diagnostic kits such as pregnancy tests. In colloid immunoassays, these tiny colloid particles allow visualization of the reaction.

▶ TYPES OF HETEROGENEOUS ASSAYS

Many permutations of heterogeneous assays are utilized in the clinical laboratory. Variations can include whether (1) the antigen or the antibody is labeled, (2) the antigen antibody complex is detected directly or, (3) a second anti-immunoglobulin antibody that is labeled is utilized, (4) the antigen or antibody is captured by a capture molecule to a solid phase and detected by a second molecule, and (5) if an inhibition step is performed in which labeled and unlabeled reactants compete. Most of these heterogeneous assays are performed using solid-phase attachment of one of the reactants to a microtiter plate, a slide, or a bead. The use of the solid phase allows the rapid separation of the bound molecules from the free ones by washing steps to remove free labeled reagent so that only the bound label is measured (2).

DIRECT IMMUNOASSAY

A direct immunoassay utilizes a labeled antibody binding to an antigen or a labeled antigen binding to an antibody. The direct immunoassay is typically used to detect an antigen in a cell preparation or biopsy sample. An example of the use of a direct assay is a direct fluorescent immunoassay in which antibody to anthrax is labeled with a fluorescent compound and the antigen source is a suspect skin lesion biopsy. The biopsy sample, which has been prepared, sectioned, and placed on a microscope slide, is incubated with a purchased fluorescently labeled antibody to anthrax. After a suitable incubation period, the slide is washed and observed under a fluorescent microscope. The wash step removes the fluorescently labeled antibody that has not bound to the anthrax antigen. This type of assay is used to find antigen in infected tissues and in cultured cells. See Figure 1 ■ for direct assays with an enzyme, a fluorescent, and a radiolabeled tag. Please note that the only differences between a direct enzyme immunoassay, a direct immunofluorescent assay, a direct radioimmunoassay and a direct chemiluminescent assay are the label that is conjugated and the method of detection used (Table 1 ✪).

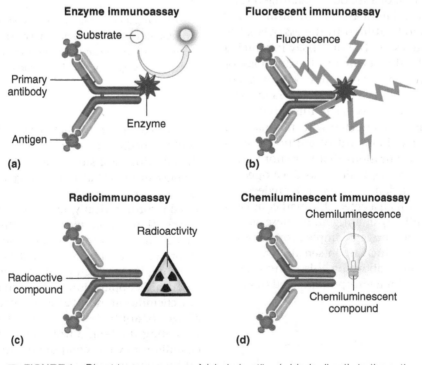

■ FIGURE 1   Direct immunoassays. A labeled antibody binds directly to the antigen. The label on the antibody can be (a) an enzyme, (b) a fluorochrome, (c) a radioisotope, or (d) a chemiluminescent compound.

○ TABLE 1

Direct Immunoassays				
Assay	A. Enzyme Immunoassay	B. Fluorescent Immunoassay	C. Radioimmunoassay	D. Chemiluminescent
Label	Enzyme	Fluorochrome	Radioactive molecule	Chemiluminescent compound
Detection method	Spectrophotometer/ Fluorimeter/ Luminometer	Fluorimeter	Gamma or scintillation counting	Luminometer

INDIRECT IMMUNOASSAY

An **indirect immunoassay** utilizes an unlabeled antigen, an unlabeled antibody, and a labeled antiglobulin to detect the reaction of the initial antibody and antigen complex. This immunoassay is generally used to measure a patient's antibody titer to a known antigen. An example of this type of assay is the use of an indirect enzyme immunoassay to measure a patient's titer or level of antibody to rubella (Figure 2 ■). A kit in which the rubella antigen is coated on wells in a microtiter plate is purchased, and the patient's sera is diluted and added to a well.

After an incubation period, the nonbinding antibody is washed off and then a second antibody, an anti-human immunoglobulin that is enzyme labeled, is added. After a suitable incubation and another wash step to remove the secondary antibody that has not bound, a substrate for the enzyme is added and incubated. Depending on the substrate, the enzyme reaction is subsequently read using a spectrophotometer, fluorimeter, or luminometer. This use of a labeled anti-human immunoglobulin was developed because it would not be practical nor would it create a very sensitive assay if each patient's immunoglobulin had to be purified and labeled before each assay for disease. The **anti-human immunoglobulin** step can be performed to detect either all immunoglobulins, IgM only (using a heavy chain-specific anti-human IgM), IgG only (using a heavy chain-specific anti-human IgG), or IgE only (using anti-human IgE). Because IgM is present in acute infections, this ability to detect a specific isotype can help determine whether the antibody that is present is due to a past or current infection. The use of IgG-specific immune conjugates can help determine immune status, and IgE-specific immune conjugates can help diagnose allergy. Any of the other labels could be used in an indirect immunoassay as well as the indirect enzyme immunoassay depicted here. An indirect fluorescent immunoassay, indirect radioimmunoassay, indirect chemiluminescent assay, indirect immunocolloid assay, and indirect optical immunoassay could all be performed. Once again, the only difference would be the label utilized and the method of detection. The ability to use any label type is consistent with all methods that will be discussed.

In a variation of an indirect assay, labeled protein A is used instead of a labeled anti-human IgG antibody. Protein A is isolated from *Staphylococcus aureus* and, like the anti-human immunoglobulin, binds immunoglobulin at the Fc region.

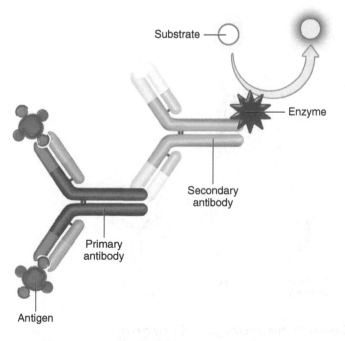

Substrate

Enzyme

Secondary antibody

Primary antibody

Antigen

■ **FIGURE 2**   Indirect enzyme immunoassay. A patient's antibody reacts with the antigen, which is detected with the addition of an anti-human immunoglobulin labeled with an enzyme. The enzyme reacts with a colorless substrate, which changes to a colored product.

✓ Checkpoint! 4

Do you think it would be a better idea just to label the patient's antibody instead of using the indirect immunoassay in which a labeled anti-human immunoglobulin is used to detect the patient's immunoglobulin?

SANDWICH OR CAPTURE IMMUNOASSAY

A **sandwich assay** usually captures antigen between 2 molecules of antibody, one of which captures the antigen to a solid phase while the other is labeled and used to visualize the reaction (Figure 3(a) ■). These assays are commonly performed on disposable membrane cassettes. An

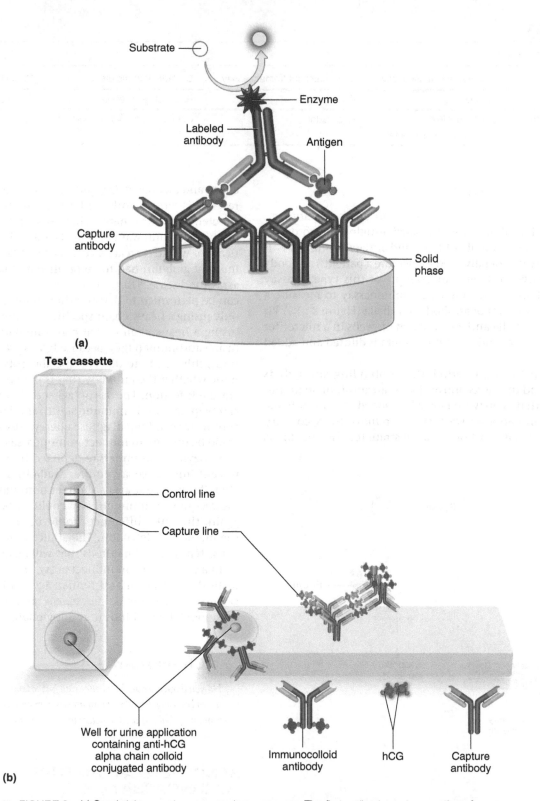

FIGURE 3 (a) Sandwich or capture enzyme immunoassay. The first antibody captures antigen from a body fluid (or from any sample), this is followed by the addition of the second labeled antibody, which also reacts with the antigen. The enzyme on the detecting antibody converts the substrate to a colored product. (b) Colloid-labeled immunochromatographic sandwich assay. The separating properties of chromatography facilitate a capture or sandwich assay. The detecting antibody reacts with the antigen and travels along the chromatographic membrane until it is captured by the capture antibody along the positive line of the test strip.

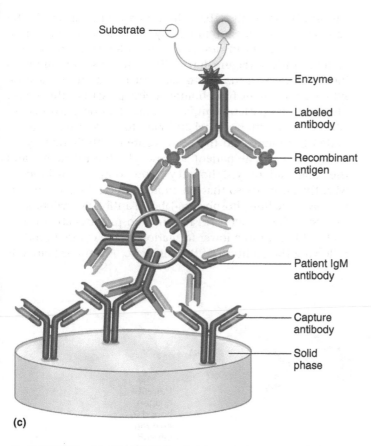

Substrate

Enzyme

Labeled antibody

Recombinant antigen

Patient IgM antibody

Capture antibody

Solid phase

(c)

■ FIGURE 3   *(continued)* (c) Sandwich or capture enzyme immuno-assay for patient IgM (double capture: IgM capture, Ag capture).

example of a sandwich assay is a pregnancy colloid labeled **immunochromatographic sandwich assay;** see Figure 3(b). In this assay, the 2 antibodies react with the 2 different subunits of human chorionic gonadotropin (hCG), a hormone produced by trophoblastic tissue and excreted in the urine. This capture assay allows for the detection and isolation of hCG, which is present at very low concentrations in the urine. The use of a capture assay increases the specificity of the reaction. The alpha subunit of hCG is nearly identical for luteinizing hormone, follicle-stimulating hormone, thyroid-stimulating hormone, and human chorionic gonadotropin, whereas the beta subunit has hCG-specific epitopes. hCG in the patient's urine is complexed with antibody to the α region of hCG attached to a red colloid. A second antibody, which is directed against an antigenic determinant on the β subunit, is immobilized on the membrane window. This second antibody will also attach to the urine hCG, forming a sandwich. Color capture on this line indicates a positive test. The capture antibody can also be attached to the membrane so that it forms a plus sign if the urine contains hCG (3). The control line is a second antibody capture line after the HCG capture line. This line shows that the reagents are working and that the applied sample is sufficient. See Figure 3(b). It is important

to note that the antigen must have more than 1 epitope to utilize a sandwich assay.

A capture assay can also be used to detect immunoglobulin by sandwiching immunoglobulin between a solid-phase antigen and a labeled antigen; an example of this is an assay for the IgM antibody. The antigen is coated on the solid phase, the patient's sera is added, and then after washing, a labeled antigen is added. Bound IgM will have ample binding sites left for reaction with the labeled antigen.

Adaptations have been developed to ensure that an assay for antibody is IgM specific. In many diseases, it is imperative for a prognosis to determine whether the infection responsible for the current illness is caused by a particular pathogen. IgG positivity may indicate only a past infection, so to determine whether the serologic positivity is related to the current illness, paired antibody titers early and late in the infection are compared. For quicker results, the presence or absence of IgM to the pathogen can be determined. IgM is usually present only in the first weeks of an infection and thus indicates an acute infection with this pathogen. However, IgM determinations can be negatively affected by the presence of IgG to the pathogen. When the patient's serum is diluted and incubated with antigen, the presence of IgG to the test antigen will block the binding of IgM to it. This is true even if IgG is present in lesser amounts because it usually has a higher affinity of binding to the antigen and thus would preferentially bind, causing a false negative reaction for the presence of IgM to the antigen (4).

A false positive reaction for IgM to the antigen can occur if the patient has IgG to the pathogen and has IgM rheumatoid factor. **Rheumatoid factor,** which is present in most patients with rheumatoid arthritis, is defined as antibody to the Fc region of the IgG immunoglobulin. It is usually, but not always, of the IgM class. The reason that the rheumatoid factor can cause a false positive is that it can bind to the Fc region of any antibody in the assay, including the capture antibody and the detecting antibody. An adaptation of the capture assay has been developed to detect pathogen-specific IgM without interference with serum IgG to the pathogen; in this example, the pathogen is West Nile virus (WNV). The solid phase is coated with anti-human IgM, the patient's serum is added, and the patient's IgM is attached to the solid phase. Next the antigen, a recombinant WNV Ag, is added. If the patient has IgM specific for this virus, the antigen will be captured. Then an enzyme-labeled mouse monoclonal antibody to the WNV antigen is added. After washing, a substrate is added. The amount of the patient's IgM to WNV will be proportional to the amount of color conversion; see Figure 3(c). In this adaptation, the anti-human IgM captures the IgM, and the antigen is captured between the IgM and the enzyme-labeled antibody to the antigen. Another adaptation that measures IgM specifically is the removal of the patient's IgG prior to the performing assay. To do this, the patient's sera is treated with anti-human IgG at precipitating concentrations to remove the IgG prior to incubation with the plated antigen (4).

COMPETITIVE ASSAYS

When an antigen is small and has either only one epitope or if binding to multiple epitopes would create steric hindrance, a capture immunoassay would not work, so a competitive assay would be utilized. *Steric hindrance* refers to a reaction that is inhibited because the bulk of the molecule is in the way of the reaction. In a **competitive immunoassay,** a test kit analyte competes for limited reagent with the analyte in the patient's sample. Antigen can compete for reaction with the antibody, or the antibody can compete for the antigen. An example of a competitive immunoassay for antigen used clinically is the measurement of total homocysteine, which is a risk factor for cardiovascular disease and can assist in the diagnosis of patients with hyperhomocysteinemia or homocystinuria. Homocysteine, at a molecular weight of approximately 138

daltons, is too small to be utilized in a capture assay. In the competitive enzyme immunoassay for patient plasma homocysteine levels, beads are coated with S-adenosyl-L-homocysteine antigen (Figure 4(a) ■). The patient serum sample is incubated with an enzyme to cause the formation of S-adenosyl-L-homocysteine from homocysteine present in the serum. The prepared patient sample and an alkaline phosphatase labeled mouse monoclonal antibody to S-adenosyl-L-homocysteine are added to the beads coated with S-adenosyl-L-homocysteine. The patient S-adenosyl-L-homocysteine and the tube S-adenosyl-L-homocysteine compete for binding with the antibody so that the more antigen the patient has, the fewer alkaline phosphatase-labeled antibodies will bind to the beads. The reduction in alkaline phosphatase-labeled antibody will result in a lower formation of the colored product following the addition of the substrate. A standard curve is

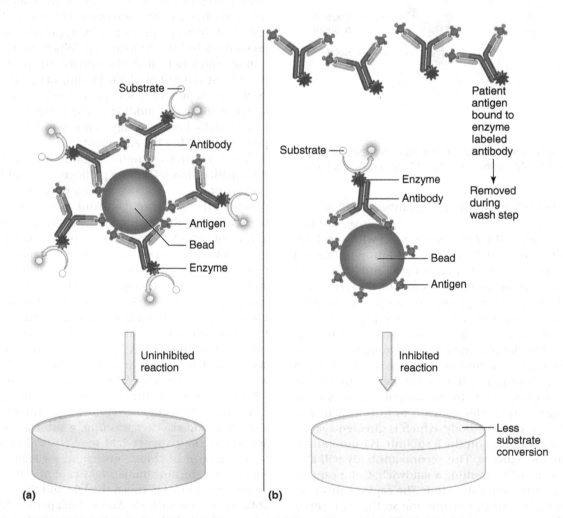

■ FIGURE 4   Competitive enzyme immunoassay. (a) Shows the uninhibited reaction and (b) shows the inhibited reaction, in which the binding of the labeled antibody to the patient's antigen in solution blocks the binding of the antibody to the well and results in a decrease in substrate conversion.

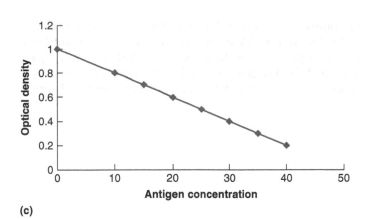

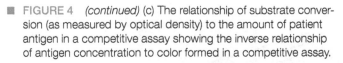

(c)

■ FIGURE 4 *(continued)* (c) The relationship of substrate conversion (as measured by optical density) to the amount of patient antigen in a competitive assay showing the inverse relationship of antigen concentration to color formed in a competitive assay.

utilized to relate the amount of enzymatic substrate conversion to the amount of homocysteine present in the sample; refer to Figure 4(b) (5). The pretreatment step for the conversion of homocysteine to S-adenosyl-L-homocysteine was utilized because of the difficulty in forming an antibody to an unmodified amino acid.

An example of a competitive assay for antibody is a microparticle enzyme immunoassay for antibody to hepatitis A antigens. In this assay, microparticles that have been coated with hepatitis A virus (HAV) antigens are incubated with the patient's sera, and then the microparticles are incubated with an enzyme-conjugated antibody to the HAV antigens. In this case, only

the antigenic sites that have not been bound with the patient antibody will be available to this enzyme-labeled antibody. The microparticles are washed and then incubated with the enzyme substrate. For this analysis, a standard curve is created with the amount of patient antibody inversely related to the amount of substrate conversion. (Table 2 ✪) (6).

WESTERN BLOT

A **Western blot** is an adaptation of an enzyme immunoassay. It is a technique that begins with the electrophoretic separation of proteins utilizing a sodium dodecyl sulfate polyacrylamide gel electrophoresis (SDS-PAGE) that separates proteins by their molecular weight. The next step utilizes a transfer of these proteins to nitrocellulose, which is a suitable solid phase for the final step of a direct or an indirect enzyme immunoassay. This more expensive and labor-intensive assay is performed when the diagnosis is either difficult or the appropriate diagnosis is critical, or both. An example of a clinically used Western blotting technique for diagnosis is the Western blot for HIV. In this assay, instead of using a solid phase coated with HIV antigens, the proteins from HIV-infected cells are electrophoretically separated using SDS-polyacrylamide gel electrophoresis. The proteins are transferred to nitrocellulose, then non-fat dried milk is added, to block the remaining nonspecific binding sites on the nitrocellulose. The nitrocellulose is cut into strips from top to bottom and each strip is used to test one patient's serum. These strips are sold in diagnostic test kits already prepared with the electrophoretically separated HIV antigens on them. In the clinical

✪ TABLE 2

Steps of the Heterogeneous Immunoassays

Assay	Direct	Indirect	Competitive Direct Immunoassay	Sandwich—Solid Phase Ab-Ag-Ab	Sandwich Ag-Ab-Ag	Western Blot
Step 1	Solid-phase Ag incubated with labeled Ab	Solid-phase Ag incubated with Ab	Labeled Ab mixed with patient antigen	Ab (capture Ab), incubated with Ag	Solid-phase Ag (capture Ag), incubated with patient Ab	Polyacrylamide gel electrophoresis of virus or bacterial proteins
Step 2	Wash	Wash	Add mixture to solid-phase antigen	Wash	Wash	Transfer to nitrocellulose
Step 3	Visualize	Add labeled Ab	Wash	Add labeled Ab	Add labeled Ag	Block nonspecific binding sites
Step 4		Wash	Visualize inverse relationship	Wash	Wash	Add patient Ab
Step 5		Visualize		Vsualize	Visualize	Wash
Step 6						Add labeled antihuman immunoglobulin
Step 7						Wash
Step 8						Visualize

laboratory, an indirect enzyme immunoassay is performed on the nitrocellulose strip. The patient's serum is added, incubated, and washed, and then an enzyme-conjugated anti-human immunoglobulin is added. After incubation and washing, the appropriate substrate is added. Diagnosis occurs by comparing the patient's nitrocellulose strip with a positive control strip. For HIV diagnosis, there must be an antibody to two of the major antigens, which include p24, p31, gp41, and gp120/160 (Figures 5 ■ and 6 ■) (7). This creates a high specificity for the assay, which gives no false positives because

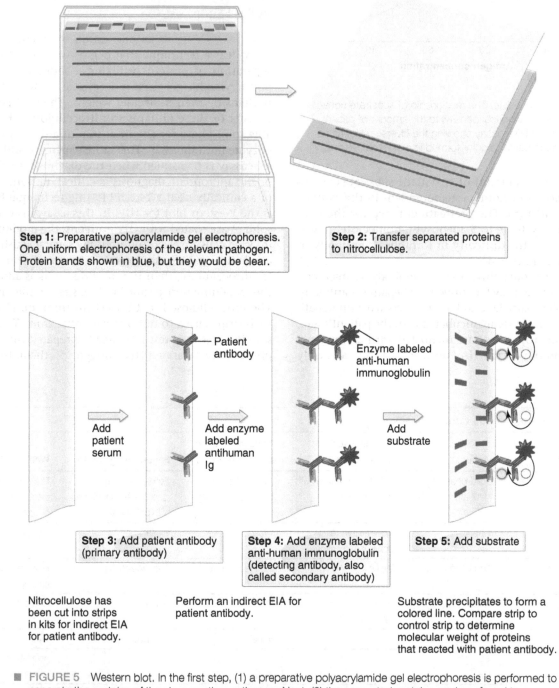

Step 1: Preparative polyacrylamide gel electrophoresis. One uniform electrophoresis of the relevant pathogen. Protein bands shown in blue, but they would be clear.

Step 2: Transfer separated proteins to nitrocellulose.

Add patient serum

Patient antibody

Add enzyme labeled antihuman Ig

Enzyme labeled anti-human immunoglobulin

Add substrate

Step 3: Add patient antibody (primary antibody)

Step 4: Add enzyme labeled anti-human immunoglobulin (detecting antibody, also called secondary antibody)

Step 5: Add substrate

Nitrocellulose has been cut into strips in kits for indirect EIA for patient antibody.

Perform an indirect EIA for patient antibody.

Substrate precipitates to form a colored line. Compare strip to control strip to determine molecular weight of proteins that reacted with patient antibody.

■ FIGURE 5   Western blot. In the first step, (1) a preparative polyacrylamide gel electrophoresis is performed to separate the proteins of the virus or other pathogen. Next, (2) the separated proteins are transferred to a nitrocellulose paper that binds protein well. The nonspecific binding sites of the nitrocellulose paper are blocked by the addition of nonfat dried milk. (3) The paper is cut into strips, and each strip is used to diagnose 1 patient. The next steps (3–5) are to perform an indirect enzyme immunoassay in which the patient sera containing the primary antibody to the viral proteins is added (3). After washing, (4) a secondary labeled antibody is added and after washing again, (5) the substrate is added.

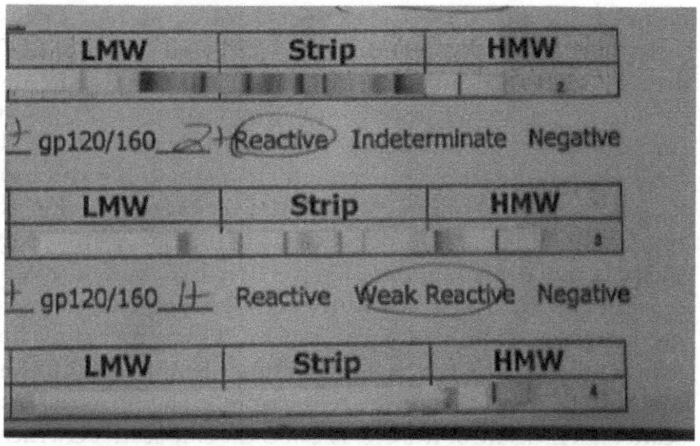

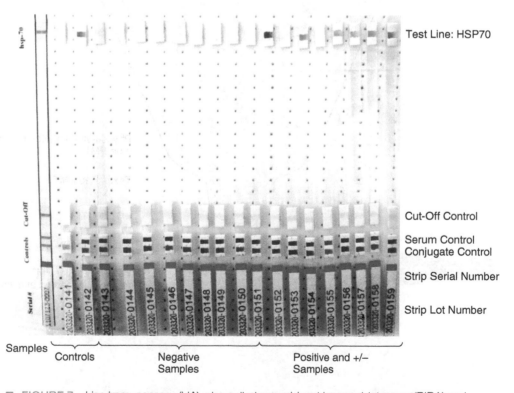

■ FIGURE 6 A Western blot for confirmatory HIV diagnosis. After an enzyme immunoassay has been performed and determined to be positive, a Western blot will be performed for confirmatory analysis. For this diagnosis, the specificity is increased due to the requirement for multiple lines to be present. At each line is a different HIV antigen and its corresponding patient antibody. A strongly positive reaction is seen in the line on the top, a weak but positive reaction is seen in the middle, and a negative reaction is seen on the bottom. *Source:* Rittenhouse-Olson K. HIV testing and confidentiality. ASCP TechSample. Chicago, IL: ASCP; 2004.

of the multiple reactions required to determine the assays's positivity and for the requirement for the binding to occur at the appropriate molecular weight.

For the diagnosis of hepatitis C, an assay called **recombinant immunoblot assay (RIBA)** has been developed. It is a strip immunoblot which has some but not all of the characteristics of a Western blot. A nitrocellulose strip is prepared by the manufacturer which has multiple purified viral antigens each placed on a different spot. An indirect immunoassay is performed by the clinical laboratory on the strip, testing for patient's antibody to the different antigens on the strip and comparing it to the control. The difference between the RIBA and a Western blot is in how the antigens are placed on the strip. In the RIBA the antigens are not electrophoretically separated, but are recombinant antigens and synthetic peptides bearing the important viral epitopes that were prepared, purified, and placed onto the strips in separate spots. Except for this initial step, the strip immunoblot proceeds like a Western blot (8).

This assay format is called RIBA, strip immunoblot, or a line immunoassay. It has recently been developed as a line immunoassay called Immco-stripe to test for auto-antibody to heat shock proteins 70 (HSP70) which has been linked to sensorineural hearing loss. This assay is shown in Figure 7 ■

■ FIGURE 7 Line immunoassay (LIA), also called recombinant immunoblot assay (RIBA) and Immuno-stripe, is similar to a Western blot in its membrane enzyme immunoassay format, but the antigens were not electrophoresed, but instead were made by recombinant methods and placed on the membrane. In this assay the test antigen, HSP70, is on the top, a cut-off control is next, then a control which will be positive if patient serum was added is next, followed by a control which will be positive if functional enzyme labeled anti-human antibody is added. *Source:* Immco Diagnostics, Inc. Buffalo, NY, USA with controls on every strip. At the top, the test antigen line contains recombinant HSP70, next is the cut-off control, then a control that contains anti-human immunoglobulin which will be positive if the patient's serum has been added, which is followed by a conjugate control that contains human immunoglobulin which will be positive if the conjugate has been added and is functional.

FLOW CYTOMETRY

Flow cytometry combines either a direct or an indirect immunofluorescent assay with a cell sampling and cell optics system that enables the analysis of the individual labeled cells or particles one at a time. Flow cytometry (Figures 8 ■ and 9 ■) is most commonly used for analysis of CD4/CD8 ratios for HIV patient monitoring. This assay is performed by a direct immunofluorescent assay. The patient's white blood cells are incubated with fluorescently labeled antibodies to CD45, CD3, CD4, and CD8, and each antibody is labeled with a different

color of fluorochrome. CD45 selects for white blood cells, antibody to CD3 ensures that the compared cells will be T cells, anti-CD4 and anti-CD8 are used to determine helper and cytotoxic T-cell numbers and ratio. After washing, the cells are introduced by vacuum into the flow cytometer in a sheath fluid that allows their movement in a single file through laser light. The laser light contains the excitation wavelength needed to excite the fluorochromes. Light is also scattered by the cells, and the amount scattered is used to identify the various cell types in the blood on the basis of their characteristic properties (9). From this point, several things, including the forward scatter, side scatter, and amount of emitted light from each of the fluorochromes, are measured. The forward light scatter is a measure of the cell size and the side scatter is a measure of the cell granularity. These 2 parameters are important to ensure the analysis of the correct cell population and to exclude cell aggregates. At this point in the analysis, the operator can elect to analyze further only those cells of the correct size and granularity and that are CD3 positive. The amount of each

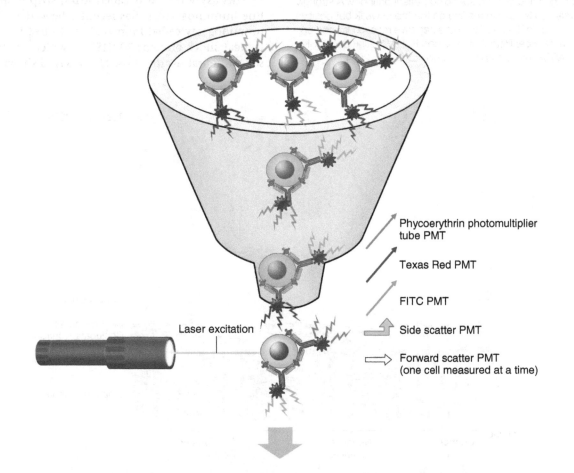

Phycoerythrin photomultiplier tube PMT

Texas Red PMT

FITC PMT

Side scatter PMT

Forward scatter PMT (one cell measured at a time)

Laser excitation

■ FIGURE 8   Flow cytometry. Cells expressing the surface markers CD4, CD8, and CD3 are labeled in a direct immunofluorescent technique with an antibody labeled with a fluorochrome. Anti-CD3 is labeled green with fluorescein isothiocyanate, anti-CD4 is labeled red with Texas Red, and anti-CD8 is labeled orange with phycoeryrthrin. Cells are processed single file and passed through an excitation wavelength and then through a detector that measures the amount of light at each emission wavelength. Also measured are forward scatter as a determination of cell size and side scatter as a determination of cell granularity.

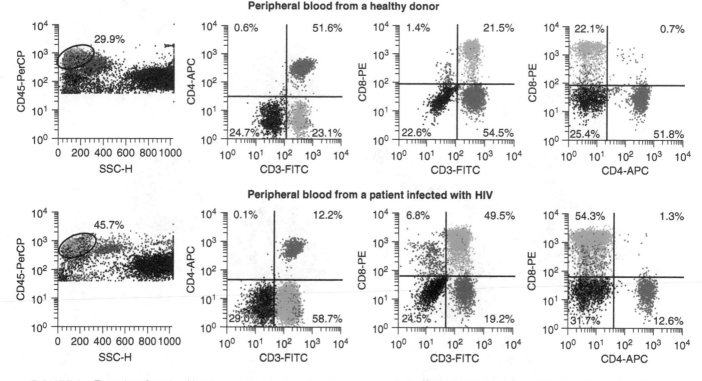

FIGURE 9 Flow data for a healthy donor (top panel) and a HIV positive patient. CD3 is a T-cell marker, CD4 is on helper T cells, and CD8 is on cytotoxic T cells. The number of CD3+ CD4+ dual positive cells is dramatically decreased in HIV patients. *Source:* Reprinted by permission of Paul Wallace and the Departmant of Flow Cytometry.

color emitted by the fluorochromes is measured by detectors and amplified to a digital signal using photomultiplier tubes (PMT). The data on the chosen cellular subset are presented as a 4-quadrant graph (Figure 9), which shows the percentage of the negative CD4 and CD8 cells, of dual positive CD4 and CD8 cells, and of those that are positive either for CD4 or CD8 but not both. Individuals without HIV (Figure 9 top) almost always have a CD4/CD8 ratio that is more than or equal to 1:1 whereas the ratio for HIV patients (Figure 9 bottom) is lower, and a drop in the ratio can indicate a worsening disease (9).

MULTIPLEXED FLUORESCENT MICROBEAD ASSAYS

Multiplexed fluorescent microbead assay is a new methodology that is an adaptation of flow cytometry which has recently been developed to respond to a need that is seen in some clinical diagnoses. In some cases, the clinical picture may indicate that several assays should be performed. For example, in autoimmune antibody screening, a positive antinuclear antibody result would indicate a need for follow-up (reflex) assays for antibody to the associated antigens SS-A, SS-B, Sm, RNP, Scl-70, Jo-1, dsDNA, centromere B, and histone. In infectious disease testing, multiple analyses performed simultaneously are important in testing for stage and prognosis of hepatitis B, as

screening for levels of hepatitis B surface antigen, hepatitis B e antigen, and antibodies to them are all relevant indicators. In allergy testing multiple analyses for IgE to a panel of respiratory allergens simultaneously can speed discovery and avoidance of the allergen (10).

These simultaneous tests can be performed using a modification of the direct immunofluorescent flow cytometry assay described. In a multiple analyte assay, tiny color-coded beads that have a discreet fluorescent color code associated with a particular surface antigen have been prepared. The assay is performed in microtiter plates. The patient's serum is added to the beads in microtiter plates and is incubated, and then the beads are washed. Next a fluorescently labeled anti-human immunoglobulin is added, and the beads are washed. Analysis occurs in an instrument that uses flow cytometric methodology. The beads are passed through a laser to excite the fluorochromes, and then both the bead's internal color-coded fluorescence and the presence or absence of surface fluorochrome due to the indirect fluorescent immunoassay (patient antibody and fluorochrome-conjugated anti-human antibody binding) are measured. A pattern determining which of the colored beads (with a particular surface antigen) have fluorescently labeled anti-human immunoglobulin conjugate attached is found. Thus, the amount of a patient antibody reacting to up to 100 antigens at a time can be determined in 1 assay (10) (Figure 10 ■).

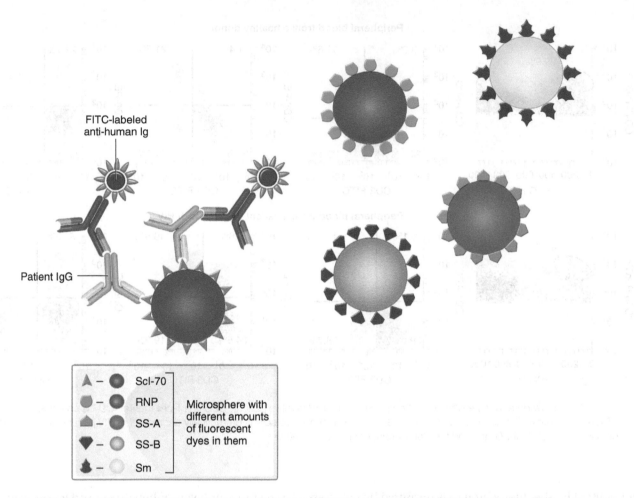

FITC-labeled
anti-human Ig

Patient IgG

▲ –	⬤	Scl-70
⬤ –	⬤	RNP
⬠ –	⬤	SS-A
▼ –	⬤	SS-B
✦ –	⬤	Sm

Microsphere with different amounts of fluorescent dyes in them

■ FIGURE 10   Multiplexed fluorescent microbead assays. Multiplex analysis for the ENA antigens, Sm, RNP, SS-A, SS-B, and Scl-70. Each antigen is attached to a bead with a different fluorescence. The patient's antibody is shown binding to the bead that has Scl-70 on its surface. The use of a FITC labeled anti-human immunoglobulin makes the presence of this binding apparent.

► LABELS FOR HETEROGENEOUS ASSAYS

Heterogeneous assays can be performed utilizing any type of labels. The choice of radioactive, enzyme, fluorescent, chemiluminescent, or colloid particle labels is based on many factors, including the equipment available, cost, ease of use, sensitivity, and personal preference. The details of the different methods are discussed next.

RADIOIMMUNOASSAY

Radioimmunoassays were the first labeled immunoassays developed and they were thought to be ideal because linking small radioactive molecules to either antigen or antibody causes no steric effects. However, it was later determined that the addition of enzymatic labels usually had little or no steric effect on the antigen and antibody reaction either (2).

The difficulties with radioactive waste disposal and the general safety issues when working with radiochemicals led to decreased use of these labels. In addition, assay stability was limited by the radioactive half-life of the label used. The radiolabel most often utilized was ^{125}I with a half-life of 59.6 days. Occasionally, hospital clinical laboratories use assays that require radiolabels because these assays are highly sensitive. For example, a competitive radioimmunoassay is currently available for testosterone, and a capture radioimmunoassay is available for CA-125, an ovarian cancer tumor marker. Additionally, assays utilized in specialty laboratories may require the use of radiolabels.

ENZYME IMMUNOASSAYS: ENZYMES AND SUBSTRATES

Enzymes are the most often used labels for labeled immunoassays. The most frequently used are horseradish peroxidase and alkaline phosphatase (11, 12, 13). Less commonly used enzymes include glucose oxidase, β-galactosidase, and glucose-6-phosphate dehydrogenase. Horseradish peroxidase (HRP) is chosen often because it is inexpensive, stable, and produces a good yield of chromogenic products. It catalyses the oxidation of a variety of substrates by hydrogen peroxide. Substrates commonly used with this enzyme in enzyme immunoassays include diaminobenzidine (DAB), 3,3′,5,5′-tetramethylbenzidine (TMB), 4-choloro-1-napthol, o-phenylenediamine (OPD), and 2,2′-azino-bis-(3-ethylbenzothiazoline sulfonate) (ABTS). DAB (a suspected carcinogen) is used in immunohistochemistry and yields an insoluble brown product. TMB (noncarcinogenic), which yields a blue product that is soluble in water and when acidified yields a yellow product, can be used in assays measured spectrophotometrically and creates a sensitive assay. In addition, because the blue product can also be precipitated on nitrocellulose or nylon membranes, it is utilized in Western blots; 4-choloro-1-napthol is also used for Western blots and strip immunoblots. OPD, which yields an orange-brown soluble product that becomes orange when the reaction is stopped with H_2SO_4, is less sensitive than TMB. ABTS yields a water-soluble green product and is the least sensitive of these water-soluble substrates but also yields a lower background (11, 12, 13).

Optical immunoassays are special adaptations of the peroxidase enzyme immunoassay that are visualized based more on a property of the solid phase of the reaction than on the substrate. Optical immunoassays are based on the change in the color of light reflected from the solid-phase polymer membrane when an antigen and an antibody are bound in comparison to the color when they are not bound. A silicon wafer is covered with an optical coating, which in turn is covered with a polymer coating that will absorb the antigen if present. An antibody-peroxidase conjugate and TMB are added, and the wavelength of light that is reflected through the complex is different from that of the unbound surface.

Horseradish Peroxidase

It is important to remember that HRP is sensitive to a number of inhibitors, so all buffers and solutions must be free of azides, sulfides, and cyanides. Substrate solutions are light sensitive, and many must be made just prior to use.

Alkaline Phosphatase

Alkaline phosphatase is also a commonly used enzyme label, it is inexpensive and stable, and produces a good yield of chromogenic product. Substrates commonly used in enzyme immunoassays with this enzyme include p-nitrophenyl phosphate (PNPP), which yields a soluble yellow product measured spectrophotometrically and 4-methylumbelliferyl phosphate, which yields a fluorescent product, 4-methylumbelliferyl. Nitroblue tetrazolium/5-bromo-4-chloro-3-indoylphosphate (NBT/BCIP) is used with an alkaline phosphatase conjugate to yield an insoluble dark blue product for Western blots (15, 16). A chemiluminescent substrate, adamantyl dioxetane, is available for use with alkaline phosphatase-labeled assays. Proprietary chemiluminescent substrates are also used. It is

important to review product inserts to determine whether both serum and plasma are suitable for the assay because anticoagulants used in the collection of plasma may adversely affect results with some substrates. Phosphates should be avoided in buffers for the alkaline phosphatase substrate and conjugate because their use can lower the assay's sensitivity. Cysteine, cyanides, arsenates, and divalent cation chelators can also impact the sensitivity of the alkaline phosphatase-labeled assay (11, 12, 13, 14).

FLUORESCENT IMMUNOASSAYS

Fluorescent labels are most often used for direct fluorescent immunoassays on tissues and cells, for flow cytometry, indirect immunoassays, autoimmunity and infectious disease testing, and multiplexed fluorescent microbead analysis. The direct fluorescent immunoassays are used for tissue biopsies or to look for viral antigens after patient samples have been added to tissue culture cells. The fluorochrome most often utilized is the apple green fluorescein isothiocyanate (FITC). Many different color fluorochromes are used for flow cytometry. Each different antibody is attached to a different colored fluorochrome so that the distinctive cell types can be identified through positivity for multiple color labels. Phycoerythrin (orange-yellow), PerCP (red), Texas Red (orange-red), and Alex-Fluor 488 (green) are a few of the many fluorochromes used in flow cytometry (9).

CHEMILUMINESCENT ASSAYS

Chemiluminescent assays are used for antibody or antigen detection. These assays use acridinium-labeled antibody or antigen conjugates (14). Various proprietary labels are used. These assays generally have lower background than colorimetric or fluorimetric assays and are sensitive with a large linear range of measurement. This assay is similar to the enzyme immunoassay with a chemiluminescent product, but the chemiluminescent product is directly linked to the antigen or antibody. Restrictions are that the conjugation step of the chemiluminescent compound to either antibody or antigen must not affect luminescence. Advantages are that fewer steps are involved and that endogeneous enzyme or enzyme inhibitors do not interfere with the analysis. The chemiluminescence is brought about by the addition of a trigger compound (14). Heparin can inhibit some of the chemiluminescent reactions, so it is important to observe the guidelines for the assay (15).

COLLOID IMMUNOCHROMATOGRAPHY

Colloid-labeled immunoassays are often used for immunochromatographic laboratory, point-of-care based, and home-based immunoassays. Their final reader is not a spectrophotometer, fluorimeter, or a gamma counter, but it is the human eye. However, in this assay, either the antibody or antigen is labeled with an easily visualized colloid or particle. Like all labeled immunoassays, colloid immunoassays have a sensitivity that is much improved from the early unlabeled assays that were visualized by eye. The immunochromatography method, which utilizes colloid labels, has already been described and pictured in Figure 3(b). The colloid labels utilized are simply described in the assay product inserts as either a red colloid or as immunocolloidal gold.

▶ TYPES OF HOMOGENEOUS ASSAYS

By definition, *homogeneous assays* do not require separation of bound analytes from free ones, so they are easier to perform than heterogeneous assays. The binding of an antibody to an antigen in homogeneous assays causes a change in the compound used for visualization that can be measured. These assays are used for small molecules such as drugs, including drugs of abuse and therapeutic drugs, to measure appropriate dose to reach therapeutic levels (14).

FLUORESCENCE POLARIZATION IMMUNOASSAY

In the **fluorescence polarization immunoassay,** a fluorescent label is placed on the small molecule that is the analyte. Small molecules rotate freely in solution, so when plane

polarized light is used as an excitation wavelength for a fluorochrome attached to a small molecule, this free rotation results in the emission of the fluorescent light in a variety of directions so that the light is no longer in 1 plane. However, if a relatively large antibody molecule has bound this small molecule, the rotation is retarded, and when the fluorochrome is excited by plane-polarized light, the emission remains polarized. The polarized emission can be measured using an appropriately placed detector. This assay is a competitive immunoassay; the unlabeled drug in the patient's serum competes with the labeled drug supplied in the assay for binding to antibody. In this assay, the more drug in the patient's serum, the lower the amount of plane-polarized fluorescence. The amount of drug in the patient's serum is determined by comparing the polarization units of the patient's sample with a standard curve prepared with known amounts of drug (Figure 11 ■) (9, 14).

ENZYME IMMUNOASSAY

In a homogeneous enzyme immunoassay, an enzyme bound to the drug analyte can perform its enzymatic function when the drug is free in solution. However, when an antibody binds to the drug-enzyme complex, the enzyme is sterically inhibited from having its enzymatic effect. As a specific example, the assay for amphetamine and methamphetamine includes these drugs labeled with glucose-6-phosphate dehydrogenase and monoclonal antibodies

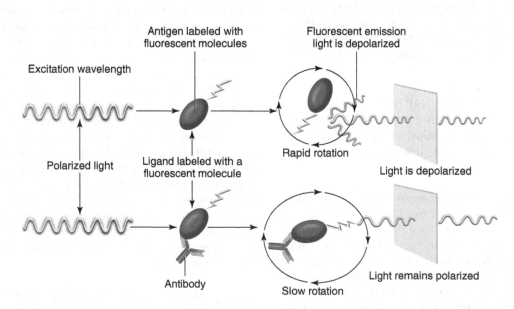

■ FIGURE 11   Flourescence polarization immunoassay. A florescently labeled analyte is excited with polarized light. When the analyte is bound to the antibody, the antibody rotates slowly, and the light is emitted in a polarized fashion. However, if the patient's serum contains the analyte, it competes for the antibody with the labeled analyte. Labeled analyte that is unbound moves freely in solution, so when the fluorochrome attached to it is excited, the emitted light is no longer polarized because of this free movement.

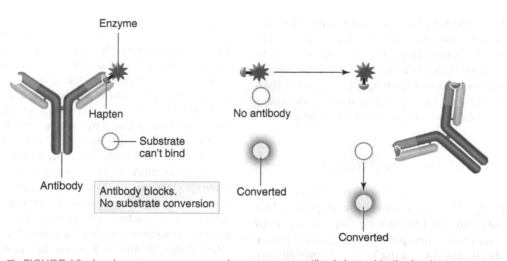

Enzyme

Hapten

Substrate can't bind

Antibody

Antibody blocks. No substrate conversion

No antibody

Converted

Converted

■ **FIGURE 12** In a homogeneous enzyme immunoassay, antibody bound to the hapten conjugated to the enzyme prevents enzyme function by blocking the substrate interaction. When the patient serum contains the antigen, the enzyme-labeled antigen and the patient antigen complete the binding to the antibody and the enzyme function increases.

to both drugs. The presence of drug in the patient's urine decreases the amount of antibody available to bind to the enzyme-labeled drug and thus increases the amount of enzyme activity visualized. In this homogeneous assay, the amount of drug is directly related to the amount of enzymatic activity (Figure 12 ■) (13).

▶ INTERFERING SUBSTANCES

Some substances can interfere with individual proprietary tests. Certain assays are affected by using plasma from EDTA or heparin tubes, so serum must be used. Other interfering substances are patient specific and thus can specifically affect the test results of certain patients. This type of interference is more difficult to identify. The presence of rheumatoid factor (RF), heterophilic antibodies, and human anti-mouse antibody (HAMA) are examples of patient-specific characteristics that can affect the results of enzyme immunoassays.

RHEUMATOID FACTOR

Rheumatoid factor is antibody to the Fc region of the IgG immunoglobulin. It is usually, but not always, of the IgM class. In capture assays in which the antibody is the capture molecule, rheumatoid factor can bind to the Fc region of the capture immunoglobulin, and then other binding sites on the IgM rheumatoid factor will bind the Fc region of the detecting labeled antibody. Thus, unless controlled for, the rheumatoid factor could result in a false positive reaction for any capture assay. To explain the possible effect of rheumatoid factor on diagnoses, let's first look at an unaffected indirect enzyme immunoassay for IgM for toxoplasmosis— a disease where many people have had past infections but a current infection could have severe effects on the fetus

in a pregnant woman. The patient's serum is added to the microtiter well which has the toxoplasmosis antigen on its surface. The patient's IgG that developed during a past infection binds and the labeled anti-human IgM antibody does not bind the patient's IgG and the test result is negative for IgM to toxoplasmosis. In a similar patient with rheumatoid factor, after their IgG bound to the antigen, their rheumatoid factor would bind to their IgG. Next, when the anti-human IgM was added it would bind to their rheumatoid factor and the result would look positive for IgM to the toxoplasmosis antigen, when in fact, the patient had IgG due to a past infection, not IgM due to a current infection. To correct for such misdiagnoses, indirect assays for IgM can be corrected for the rheumatoid factor effect by removing the patient's IgG prior to the assay. Some capture assays may control for rheumatoid factor by using a serum diluent that contains excess IgG that does not react to the test antigen but would bind to the rheumatoid factor. In the selection of test kits for laboratory use, it is important to determine whether rheumatoid factor affects the assays and, if so, what should be included in the analysis to control for this interfering substance. In all cases, results from immunoassays should be interpreted by considering the patient's entire clinical picture (15, 16).

HUMAN HETEROPHILIC ANTIBODIES

Human heterophilic antibodies binding to animal immunoglobulin can be present in individuals who work with or are exposed to animals. These antibodies can cause false positive reactions in sandwich antigen capture immunoassays by forming an antibody-heterophile antibody-labeled antibody complex rather than the antibody-antigen-labeled antibody complex expected. This reactivity occurs because immunoassays commonly employ animal (goat, mouse, sheep) antibodies as reagents. The presence of heterophilic antibody is hard to predict, but it is important to note that because they are low-affinity antibodies, assay adaptations can be performed to minimize their effect. Heterophile antibodies show some Fc specificity because they have little or no effect if the capture and labeled antibodies used in the kit are (Fab')$_2$ rather than whole antibody molecules (15, 16). Again, in all cases, results from immunoassays should be interpreted with the patient's clinical data.

HUMAN ANTI-MOUSE ANTIBODY

Human anti-mouse antibody (HAMA) is a special type of heterophilic antibody whose presence is easier to predict. This antibody is produced by the immune response of a patient who has been treated with therapeutic or diagnostic mouse monoclonal antibody. HAMA is usually of a higher affinity than other heterophile antibodies. Addition of the mouse immunoglobulin, which does not react with the antigen in question, may inhibit this reaction, but it is important to use the entire clinical picture involved with any immunoassay results in interpreting the patient's clinical data (15, 16).

▶ SENSITIVITY COMPARISONS

In any immunoassay, the affinities of the antibodies utilized are major determinants in the assay's sensitivity. All labeled immunoassays have assay sensitivity at least 1000 times higher than the unlabeled assays. Homogeneous assays are inherently less sensitive than heterogeneous assays. The detection limit of indirect assays is higher than the direct assays because the anti-human immunoglobulin binds to more than 1 site on the human immunoglobulin, thus amplifying the reaction. The detection limit of capture assays is higher than those of the competitive assays. In general, radioimmunoassays have higher sensitivity than colorimetric enzyme immunoassays but have lower sensitivity than the enzyme immunoassays with a fluorescent or chemiluminescent product, which are the most sensitive labels.

CASE STUDY

A physician in your hospital is seeing a patient who has a respiratory infection. The cultures are negative, so the physician asks you to do a respiratory infection panel for IgM. You run several capture assays for patient IgM to different respiratory pathogens with a setup like that shown in Figure 3(b). The results are positive for every pathogen you tested!

1. What could have happened?
2. What could be done to correct the problem?

SUMMARY

Labeled immunoassays have increased the sensitivity of the detection of antibody and antigen when compared to unlabeled immunoassays. The original labeled assay was a radioimmunoassay closely followed and now largely supplanted by enzyme, fluorescent, colloid, and chemiluminescent immunoassays. These assays can be heterogeneous—requiring a separation step—or homogeneous—not requiring a separation step. The basic types of these assays are direct, indirect, sandwich, and competitive immunoassays. Adaptations of the basic solid-phase heterogeneous techniques include Western blotting, flow cytometry, and multiplexed fluorescent microbead analysis. A variety of different enzymes and substrate combinations can be measured either by spectrophotometry, fluorimetry, with a luminometer, or by eye. Many different fluorochromes are available for fluorescent immunoassays. Multiplexing using different color-coded fluorescent beads with different antigens on their surfaces may be the wave of the future, allowing multiple analyses to be performed at the same time on a small sample volume. Chemiluminescent reagents are generally the most sensitive assays and are increasing in use. Although these assays allow excellent sensitivity and specificity, some factors can affect their validity, so that each assay must be evaluated with regard to the rest of the clinical picture of the patient.

✓ Checkpoint! 5

What is the difference between a direct enzyme immunoassay and a direct radioimmunoassay?

✓ Checkpoint! 6

Comparing the labeled immunoassays to the unlabeled immunoassays , do you think that the labeled assays will show a prozone effect and a negative result when there is too much antibody like the unlabeled assays do?

REVIEW QUESTIONS

1. Enzyme immunoassay uses all of the following *except*
   a. Ab and Ag reaction
   b. washing steps
   c. separation of bound from free
   d. measurement of radioactivity

2. Which of the following characterizes homogeneous enzyme immunoassays?
   a. they use an enzyme that has been isolated from the same species that produced the Ab
   b. they require no separation step
   c. they require 2 antibody incubation steps
   d. they are used for large Ags only

3. Which of the following steps are performed in a Western blot?
   a. an Ouchterlony followed by electrophoresis
   b. a polyacrylamide gel electrophoresis followed by blotting followed by an enzyme immunoassay
   c. an enzyme immunoassay followed by a polyacrylamide gel electrophoresis
   d. agarose electrophoresis followed by blotting and then an enzyme immunoassay

4. In an indirect assay,
   a. antibody is always coated on the plate as a capture molecule
   b. only one antibody is used
   c. an anti-immunoglobulin that is labeled is used
   d. none of the above

5. In a sandwich assay,
   a. antibody is coated on the plate as a capture molecule
   b. only one antibody is used
   c. an anti-immunoglobulin that is labeled is always used
   d. none of the above

6. In a fluorescence polarization assay,
   a. Ag and Ab are labeled and produce a new color fluorescence together
   b. binding increases fluorescence
   c. binding increases the degree of the polarization of the emitted fluorescence
   d. none of the above

7. Which is the most sensitive?
   a. Ouchterlony
   b. a homogeneous EIA
   c. a heterogeneous chemiluminescence assay
   d. a heterogeneous colloid immunoassay

8. Flow cytometry measures the size of the cell by
   a. CD4 rhodamine fluorescence
   b. CD3 FITC fluorescence
   c. side scatter
   d. forward scatter

9. An assay to determine whether a patient has HCG incubates the patient sample with an antibody-coated plate and then adds a detecting antibody is best described as a(n)
   a. indirect EIA
   b. direct EIA
   c. sandwich EIA
   d. prozone EIA

10. In an indirect EIA, would the amount of color at the end be higher or lower if you forgot the washing step between (1) the conjugate and the addition of substrate or (2) the primary antibody and the conjugate but remembered it between the conjugate and the substrate?
    a. (1) higher, (2) lower
    b. (1) lower, (2) higher
    c. (1) lower, (2) lower
    d. (1) higher, (2) higher

REFERENCES

1. Yalow R. Radioimmunoassay: A probe for fine structure of biologic systems. Nobel lecture presented at: Stockholm Concert Hall, Stockholm, Sweden; December 8, 1977. http://gos.sbc.edu/w/yalow/yalow.html#fig5. Accessed December 18, 2008.

2. Engvall E, Perlman P. Enzyme-linked immunosorbent assay, Elisa 3. Quantitation of specific antibodies by enzyme-labeled anti-immunoglobulin in antigen-coated tubes. *J. Immunol.* 1972;109(129).

3. Inverness Medical Professional Diagnostics. Clearview HCG Combo II. Product Insert. http://www.invernessmedicalpd.com/point_of_care/womens_health/acceava%c2%ae_hcg_urine_ii.aspx. Accessed April 7, 2011.

4. Focus Diagnostics. West Nile Virus IgM Capture DxSelect™. Product insert. http://www.focusdx.com/focus/packageInsert/EL0300M.pdf. Accessed April 7, 2011.

5. Siemens Medical Solutions Diagnostics. Homocysteine Immunolite 2500. Product manual. http://diagnostics.siemens.com/siemens/en_GLOBAL/gg_diag_FBAs/files/package_inserts/immulite_2500/Anemia_n/pil5kho-5_siemens.pdf. Accessed July 5, 2011.

6. Abbott AxSym System HAVAB. http://www.abbottdiagnostics.com/webapp/index.cfm?event=getPDF&controlNumber=696582. Accessed April 7, 2011.

7. Bio-Rad Human Immunodeficiency Virus Type I GS HIV-1 Western Blot. Package insert. http://www.qualtexlabs.org/assets/pdfs/assays/506100a%20GS%20HIV-1%20Western%20Blot-stamped.pdf. Accessed April 7, 2011.

8. US Food and Drug Administration Hepatitis C Virus Encoded Antigen (Recombinant/Synthetic)(RIBA). Product insert. http://www.fda.gov/cber/label/hcvchir021199LB.pdf. Accessed April 7, 2011.

9. BD Biosciences. Customer Training: Introduction to Flow Cytometry. http://bdbiosciences.com/immunocytometry_systems/support/training/online. Accessed April 7, 2011.

10. Luminex. About xMAP Technology. http://www.luminexcorp.com/technology/index.html. Accessed April 7, 2011.

11. Worthington Biochemical Corporation. Enzyme Manual. Peroxidase http://www.worthington-biochem.com/HPO/default.html. Accessed July 5, 2011.

12. Worthington Biochemical Corporation. Alkaline Phosphatase. Enzyme Manual. http://www.worthington-biochem.com/BAP/default.html. Accessed July 5, 2011.

13. Abbott AxSym System. Amphetamine/Methamphetamine. http://www.abbottdiagnostics.com/webapp/index.cfm?event=getPDF&controlNumber=344988R14. Accessed July 5, 2011.

14. Lumigen, Inc. Chemiluminescent Detection in Biomedical Assays. http://www.lumigen.com/documents/assays.shtml. Accessed April 7, 2011.

15. Chaitoff K, Armbruster D, Maine G, Kuhns, M. Abbott Learning Guide Immunoassay. http://www.abbottdiagnostics.com.au/viewFile.cfm?file=learning_immunoassay.pdf. Accessed April 28, 2012.

16. Bjerner J, Børmer OP, Nustad K. The war on heterophilic antibody interference. *Clinical Chemistry*. 2005;51:9–11

ANSWERS TO REVIEW QUESTIONS

1. d
2. b
3. b
4. c
5. a
6. c
7. c
8. d
9. c
10. a

ANSWERS TO CASE STUDIES

1. The patient may have rheumatoid factor. This antibody would bind the first antibody which captures IgM, and then although it did not bind the antigen, it bound the Fc of the enzyme labeled IgG to the pathogen. Then the enzyme reacted with the substrate and gave a positive result.
2. The patient's serum could be diluted with a solution that contains IgG that does not react with the pathogen. In this case, the rheumatoid factor would bind to the IgG in solution and would not become involved in the solid-phase assay.

ANSWERS TO CHECKPOINTS

Checkpoint! 1
Ruth Yalow in 1959

Checkpoint! 2
radioactivity

Checkpoint! 3
Heterogeneous, the chromatography along the membrane, separates bound from free.

Checkpoint! 4
No, it would not because each patient's immunoglobulin would have to be purified prior to labeling. This would be costly, and in purification steps some antibody would be lost, decreasing sensitivity. In addition, variations in the purification steps from patient to patient would yield erroneous results.

Checkpoint! 5

the way the antibody is labeled and the way the label is measured, the rest of the steps are the same

Checkpoint! 6

No, a lattice structure does not form for the labeled assays; a plateau may be seen with high amounts of antibody, but an apparent negative result would not occur.

GLOSSARY

Anti-human immunoglobulin antibody made in another species, usually rabbit or goat that reacts with human immunoglobulin. It is used to detect human immunoglobulin in indirect immunoassays. It can either react with all classes of immunoglobulin or be specific for one class of immunoglobulin.

Chemiluminescence emission of light as the result of a chemical reaction that produces no heat.

Colloid particle tiny particulate substance that contains one substance dispersed in another substance; allows visualization of the reaction in colloid immunoassays.

Competitive immunoassay assay in which a test kit analyte competes for limited reagent with the analyte in the patient's sample.

Direct immunoassay process that utilizes a labeled antibody binding to an antigen or vice versa to detect an antigen in a cell preparation or biopsy sample.

Fluorescence the emission of light from a substance that has absorbed light energy at a high wavelength to be emitted at a lower wavelength.

Fluorescence polarization immunoassay a homogeneous assay that places a fluorescent label on a small molecule that is the analyte; because small molecules rotate freely in solution, plane-polarized light as an excitation wavelength for the fluorochrome attached to these small molecules results in the emission of the fluorescent light in a variety of directions, so that, due to the free rotation, the light is no longer in 1 plane. However, if this small molecule has been bound by a relatively large antibody molecule, the rotation is retarded, and the emission remains polarized. The polarized emission can be measured utilizing an appropriately placed detector.

Heterogeneous assay are immunoassays that require a step to separate the bound from free antigen and antibody.

Homogeneous assays are immunoassays that do not require a separation or washing step to separate the bound from the free. These assays can be accomplished because the binding of antigen to antibody affects the activity of the label in such a way as to cause a measureable change.

Human anti-mouse antibody (HAMA) a special type of heterophilic antibody that is produced by the immune response of a patient that has been treated with therapeutic or diagnostic mouse monoclonal antibody. It can interfere with immunoassays, especially capture immunoassays.

Immunochromatographic sandwich assay an assay in which the bound antigen and labeled antibody is separated from free by migration along a chromatographic membrane, where it binds the capture antibody forming the labeled antibody-antigen-capture antibody sandwich.

Indirect immunoassay utilizes an unlabeled antigen, an unlabeled antibody and a labeled antiglobulin to detect the reaction of the initial antibody and antigen complex. This is usually done to measure a patient's antibody titer to a known antigen.

Multiplexed fluorescent microbead assays multiple analyte assays, in which color-coded beads have been prepared that have a discreet fluorescent color code associated with a particular surface antigen. These different color beads have been prepared bound with different surface antigens. The patient's serum is added, incubated and the beads are washed. Next a fluorescently labeled anti-human immunoglobulin is added, and the beads are washed. Analysis is in a Luminex instrument that uses flow cytometric methodology. The bead internal fluorescence and surface flourescence due to fluorochrome conjugated anti-human antibody binding are measured to determine multiple reactions at once.

Optical immunoassays special adaptations of the peroxidase enzyme immunoassay and are visualized based more on a property of the solid phase of the reaction than on the substrate. They are based on the change in the color of light reflected from the solid phase polymer membrane when antigen and antibody are bound in comparison to the color when antigen and antibody is not bound.

Recombinant immunoblot assay (RIBA) a strip immunoblot which has some but not all of the characteristics of a Western blot. A nitrocellulose strip is prepared by the manufacturer that has multiple viral antigens placed onto it, and an indirect enzyme immunoassay is performed by the clinical laboratory on the strip, testing for patient's antibody to the different antigens on the strip and comparing it to the control.

Rheumatoid factor present in most patients with rheumatoid arthritis, is defined as antibody to the Fc region of the IgG immunoglobulin. It is usually, but not always of the IgM class.

Sandwich assay this assay usually captures antigen between 2 molecules of antibody, 1 antibody captures the antigen to a solid phase and the other antibody is labeled and is used to visualize the reaction, sometimes antigen can capture antibody and labeled antigen is used to visualize the reaction but this is rarely used.

Spectrophotometer   the instrument used to make a quantitative measurement at a specific wavelength of the amount of light that is transmitted through a solution. Used with Beer's law to quantitate substances.

Steric hindrance   when the size or shape of the molecule interferes with the interaction. In antibody binding to antigen this occurs when the antigen is too large for the epitopes to be bound by 2 neighboring paratopes. In IgM reactions this can result in less than 10 antigens being bound, often with steric hindrance the binding ability of IgM is decreased to 5 epitopes.

Western blot   an adaptation of an enzyme immunoassay. This technique begins with electrophoretic separation of proteins utilizing a sodium dodecyl sulfate polyacrylamide gel electrophoresis (SDS-PAGE) which separates proteins by their molecular weight. The next step utilizes a transfer of these separated proteins to nitrocellulose, which is a suitable solid phase for the final step of a direct or an indirect enzyme immunoassay.

Chemical Activity and Chemical Equilibrium

Chapter Outline

1 INTRODUCTION: "AND THE LONG-RANGE FORECAST IS..."

In December 1997, delegates from over 150 nations met in Kyoto, Japan, to discuss the issue of global warming.[1] Of particular interest was the theory that an increase in the temperature of the Earth is occurring as result of a rise in carbon dioxide and other gases that can trap heat from sunlight. Part of the carbon dioxide entering the atmosphere is from natural sources and some comes from human activities, such as the burning of fossil fuels.[2-4] As a result of the 1997 meeting in Kyoto, a treaty was drafted calling for a dramatic reduction in human-related CO_2 production. The treaty took effect in February 2005,[5] but it has been a subject of continuing controversy related to how CO_2 emissions might be decreased and the expense of accomplishing this goal. There is also disagreement on how global warming will be affected by a change in emissions or how such a change might affect the Earth's climate.[3-9]

Analytical chemists have helped in this discussion by providing measurements of the past and present levels of CO_2 in the atmosphere (see Figure 1). These measurements are made at stations located throughout the world that have monitored the concentration of CO_2 in air for many decades. Carbon dioxide levels in the past are estimated by examining the content of this gas in ice core samples that are acquired at sites such as those located in Antarctica. These latter samples are useful because the ice at these sites never melts, giving an ongoing record of the CO_2 content in air. The results of these measurements are then compared to estimates of the average global temperature, allowing the effect of CO_2 on global warming to be examined.[3]

Based on such measurements, scientists have used computer models that incorporate data on past CO_2 levels and global temperatures to predict how Earth's climate will change in the future. This is an extremely complex problem in which scientists must consider how CO_2 is produced and circulated in the environment, along with the way in which sunlight interacts with the Earth, the degree of rainfall, and the circulation of water in the oceans.[9] Just as computer simulations can be used to help predict what the climate on Earth may look like in the future, we can use calculations on a smaller scale to develop or optimize a chemical analysis method, as well as to describe the composition of a sample or reagent. This type of work helps us understand the chemical reactions that are important for anyone who wishes to use such methods. In this chapter, we review several mathematical tools for describing the reactivity of chemicals and the extent to which chemicals react with other substances. We then move on in the next few chapters to see how these tools can be applied to specific reactions for the design and use of analytical methods.

1A Types of Chemical Reactions and Transitions

There are many types of reactions or transitions that a chemical may take part in within a sample or with a reagent. These processes are usually organized into

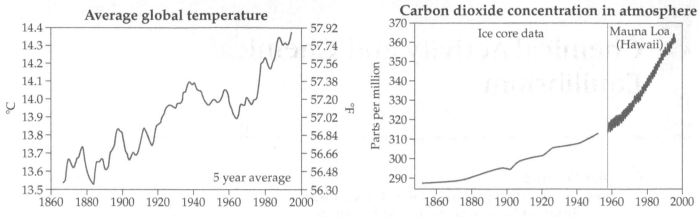

FIGURE 1 The average global temperature of the Earth since 1860, and measured levels of carbon dioxide in the atmosphere as determined from either ice core samples (before 1955) or direct measurements made at the Mauna Loa volcano in Hawaii (after 1955). The ice core samples were collected at sites like those in Antarctica (the South Pole station) or in Russia (the Siple station), where the ice within a given core layer is crushed to release the gas that is held in air bubbles in the ice. This released gas is then examined to measure its carbon dioxide content. (Based on data and graphs from NASA/Goddard Institute for Space Studies; the Office of Science and Technology Policy; and A. Neftel, E. Moor, H. Oeschger and B. Stauffer, "Evidence from Polar Ice Cores for the Increase in Atmospheric Carbon Dioxide in the Past Two Centuries," *Nature*, 315 (1985) 45–47.)

categories that have certain common features. Some of the more common types of reactions and transitions that are encountered in chemical analysis are shown in Table 1.

A *precipitation reaction* is one important process that is employed in analytical chemistry. This reaction takes place when the combination of two or more soluble chemicals leads to the creation of an insoluble substance, or *precipitate*. In the example shown in Table 1, carbonate ions and calcium ions in water form insoluble calcium carbonate, a solid that will drop out of the solution.

Another type of reaction that is often used in chemical analysis is an *acid–base reaction*, which can be defined in the classical sense as the transfer of a hydrogen ion from one compound (an acid) to another (a base)[10,11] An example is the transfer of a hydrogen ion from carbonic acid (H_2CO_3, formed when CO_2 combines with water) to water to give bicarbonate (HCO_3^-). This type of reaction is important whenever an acid or base is to be measured or controlled in a sample, such as in buffer preparation or in acid–base titrations.

Complex formation is another type of reaction that is important in chemical analysis. This reaction involves the formation of a reversible complex between two or more chemicals, such as a complex based on a coordinate covalent bond or on noncovalent interactions.[12] Many of these reactions involve the binding of a chemical that acts as an electron-pair donor (e.g., hemoglobin) with an electron-pair acceptor (O_2). However, other interactions can also be present, such as ionic forces and hydrogen bonds.

A fourth type of reaction that we will examine is an *oxidation–reduction reaction*.[11] An oxidation–reduction reaction occurs when there is an exchange of electrons between chemicals, in which one chemical has a net gain of electrons (or is *reduced*), while another has a net loss of electrons (or is *oxidized*). As shown in Table 1, the burning of fuels like octane and other carbon-containing substances is an example of an oxidation–reduction reaction; another example is respiration, in which food is "burned" by our bodies to generate energy.

A fifth set of important chemical processes are those that involve only a change in the *environment* of a chemical. One example is a *phase transition*, in which there is a change in the physical but not the chemical nature of a compound.[10] A few examples of phase transitions are the conversion of solid carbon dioxide into CO_2 gas (a process known as *sublimation*), the boiling of a liquid to form a gas, and the melting of a solid to give a liquid. A change in environment also occurs when we create a solution of one chemical in another (giving a *solubility equilibrium*),[12] or when we distribute a chemical between two or more separate chemical phases (a *distribution equilibrium*).[13] We will learn more about these processes later in this text when we discuss chemical solubility and the use of phase transitions and distribution equilibria in chemical separation methods.

1B Describing Chemical Reactions

Regardless of the type of chemical process we are studying, there are always certain questions we can ask about this process and how it takes place. Two such questions include "What amount of a chemical is

TABLE 1 Common Types of Chemical Reactions and Processes

Type of Reaction or Process	Examples
Precipitation reaction	Reaction of carbonate with Ca^{2+} to form solid calcium carbonate ($CaCO_3$), the main chemical in limestone $Ca^{2+} + CO_3{}^{2-} \rightleftharpoons CaCO_3(s)$
Acid–base reaction	Dissociation of carbonic acid (H_2CO_3) in water to give bicarbonate ($HCO_3{}^-$) $H_2CO_3 + H_2O \rightleftharpoons HCO_3{}^- + H_3O^+$
Complex formation	Binding of oxygen to hemoglobin (Hb) in blood $Hb + O_2 \rightleftharpoons Hb-O_2$
Oxidation–reduction reaction	Combustion of octane (C_8H_{18}) during the burning of this compound in fuel $2\,C_8H_{18} + 25\,O_2 \rightarrow 16\,CO_2 + 18\,H_2O$
Phase transition	Sublimation of dry ice to give carbon dioxide gas $CO_2(s) \rightleftharpoons CO_2(g)$
Solubility equilibrium	Dissolving of carbon dioxide gas in water $CO_2(air) \rightleftharpoons CO_2(aq)$

required in the reaction or process?" and "How much of this chemical is actually present?" When describing the chemical content of samples by using molarity, weight-per-weight, and related units, there are other questions about chemical processes that we have not addressed, such as "How does the ability of a chemical to react change as we alter its surroundings?" This question is addressed by using *chemical activity*, which refers to the actual amount of energy available from a chemical under the conditions used for a reaction or phase transition. As we will see later, the activity is closely related to the total amount of a chemical in a sample.

A second set of questions we can ask is "How far might the chemical process proceed?" or "How much energy will be given off or required by this process?" These questions are answered by using *chemical thermodynamics*,[12–15] which is the field of chemistry concerned with the changes in energy that take place during chemical reactions or phase transitions and the overall extent to which such processes can occur. To describe these properties, we will pay particular attention to a factor known as an *equilibrium constant*,[12] which we will learn about in Section 3.

A third question that can be asked is "How fast does a chemical process occur?" This issue is dealt with by using *chemical kinetics*, the field of chemistry that is concerned with the rates of chemical processes.[12,16,17] This information helps us determine the time required for a given process, which is related to the mechanism by which the reaction or transition takes place. An example of analysis that is based on chemical kinetics is given in Box 1. Later in this textbook we will see other examples of how the rate of a reaction can be used for chemical measurements.

2 CHEMICAL ACTIVITY

Before we discuss chemical reactions and transitions, we need to think about how we can describe the amount of each reactant or product in these processes. For example, if we were to place HCl into water, this chemical would dissociate to produce hydrogen ions and chloride ions. Although this process strongly favors the formation of such ions, to say this process is independent of concentration or that all these ions act independently of one another is just an approximation. Using this approximation can be a problem when we are dealing with a concentrated solution, because the total amount of the dissolved substances (especially ions) can alter the reactivity of chemicals and make their behavior different from what might be expected based on their total concentrations.

It is especially important to be aware of this relationship in analytical chemistry, where we often measure the apparent reactivity of a chemical with a reagent or method, but would really like to know the total concentration of the chemical. To help us describe this effect, we will use the term "chemical activity" (or simply "activity"). In this section we look at the definition of activity, see how it is related to the concentration of a chemical, and learn how to estimate or control activity in chemical measurements.

2A What Is Chemical Activity?

Definition of Chemical Activity. The chemical activity (*a*) is defined by Equation 1 as being related to the difference in energy μ for a chemical in a particular sample to the value $\mu°$ for the same chemical in its standard state.[12]

$$a = e^{(\mu - \mu°)/(RT)} \qquad (1)$$

BOX 1
Carbon-14 Dating

Along with thinking about chemical equilibrium and the extent to which a reaction might proceed, analytical chemists must also consider how quickly a reaction might occur. *Chemical kinetics* is the area of chemistry that is concerned with the speed of chemical reactions. An excellent example of the importance of kinetics in analytical chemistry is the method of *carbon-14 dating*.[18-20] This technique is commonly used in archaeology, geology, atmospheric science, and medicine for estimating the age of carbon-based materials. This method was developed in 1947 by a group of scientists led by U.S. Chemist William F. Libby, who won the 1960 Nobel Prize in chemistry for this work.[18]

Carbon-14 dating is based on the fact that there are three main isotopes of carbon in nature: carbon-12 and carbon-13, which are both stable, and carbon-14, which is radioactive and slowly converts into nitrogen-14 plus a high-energy electron known as a beta particle. Carbon-14 is unstable but is continually being replenished by the bombardment of nitrogen with neutrons, which are formed by cosmic radiation interacting with atoms in the atmosphere. This process results in the production of additional carbon-14 and causes a relatively consistent amount of carbon-14 to be present in air. This carbon-14 then enters other regions of Earth as part of the carbon dioxide in air goes into the oceans, is placed into sediments, or is incorporated into the food chain through photosynthesis.

The way in which this carbon-14 can be used for determining the age of a plant or animal sample is shown in Figure 2. While the plant or animal is living it is continually taking up carbon in food or eliminating it in waste, giving the organism an amount of carbon-14 that is in balance with the surrounding environment. Once the plant or animal has died, no new carbon is being added. The amount of carbon-14 in this sample (as well as in anything that is made from the plant or animal material) begins to decrease over time as the carbon-14 undergoes radioactive decay to form nitrogen-14. The time for half the carbon-14 to undergo this process (or its "half-life") is 5730 (±40) years. If it is assumed the original ratio of carbon-14 to carbon-12 is known, the date the plant or animal died can be estimated by comparing this ratio to the measured amount of carbon-14 vs. carbon-12 in the sample. This analysis is often made by burning a small portion of the sample to convert the carbon into carbon dioxide and then collecting and measuring the carbon-14 and total amount of carbon dioxide generated by the sample. The result is then used with the half-life of carbon-14 to determine the amount of time that has elapsed since the plant or animal that gave rise to the material in the original sample was alive.

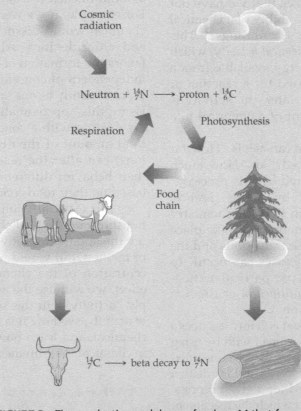

FIGURE 2 The production and decay of carbon-14 that forms the basis for carbon-14 dating. This figure shows how carbon-14 is formed in the atmosphere, followed by the uptake of this carbon-14 by plants and animals in the form of carbon dioxide. After the plant or animal dies, no more new carbon-14 enters this material and the remaining carbon-14 undergoes decay to form nitrogen-14.

In this equation, R is the ideal gas law constant and T is the absolute temperature of our system. This equation compares the *chemical potential* (μ) of the chemical (a measure of the energy available in one mole of this material)[12] to the *standard chemical potential* ($\mu°$) for the same material in some *standard state*. This comparison is needed so that we can judge whether the chemical is more or less reactive as we change its environment from a standard state, which is a pure form of the chemical (for example, a pure solid or pure liquid) or a solution that contains a well-defined concentration of this chemical (for example, an exactly 1 M solution). Table 2 lists the standard states that are commonly used for chemicals in this type of comparison.

Equation 1 indicates that the activity a of a chemical will be a number with no units and that simply reflects how much energy this chemical contains versus its standard state. Another way of looking at this equation is to say the activity and apparent reactivity of a chemical will change as the chemical's environment is changed. If a chemical is in its standard state, such as when we are working with the pure form of a solid or liquid, the value of μ will be the same as $\mu°$ and we will get an activity from Equation 1 of $a = 1.0$. If we are working with a dilute solution, the chemical potential will generally be much less than it is for the pure form of the same compound ($\mu < \mu°$), giving a value for a that is somewhere between 0 (the lowest possible value) and 1.0. There are also some situations in which a chemical can have more energy than its standard state. In this case, the chemical potential of the substance is greater than its standard state ($\mu > \mu°$) and gives a value for a greater than 1.0.

To illustrate this idea, let's see how the activity of HCl changes as we vary its total concentration in water (see Figure 3). At very low concentrations (that is, [HCl] < 0.01 M), the activities and concentrations for the hydrogen ions and chloride ions that are produced from HCl have similar values, differing by less than 10%. Under these conditions we have a solution that contains a large amount of solvent and only a small amount of dissolved ions. The result is a situation in which essentially all the ions are fully surrounded by the solvent and act independently from one another. Even at low HCl concentrations, however, there is a small difference between the activity of HCl and its total concentration. This difference is observed because the ions formed from HCl do have some influence over each other's behavior. For instance, the hydrogen ions and chloride ions can attract each other, while neighboring ions with like charges will repel each other (see Figure 4). This process becomes greater as we go to higher concentrations and it causes the activity to be lower than would be expected based on the total concentrations for H^+ and Cl^-.

As we move to even higher concentrations, other interactions also begin to alter the activity of the HCl solution. For instance, H^+Cl^- ion pairs may form, which will behave differently than individual H^+ or Cl^- ions. There also will be changes in the repulsion or attraction of these ions as they appear at levels high enough to alter the properties of the solution. In addition, the presence of large amounts of dissolved chemicals can affect the behavior of the solvent. In the case of the HCl solutions in Figure 3, the water used as the solvent will interact with ionic substances like H^+ and Cl^-. This

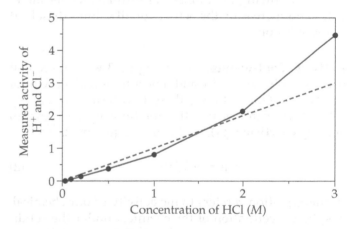

FIGURE 3 Change in the measured activity of H^+ and Cl^- in water as the total concentration of HCl is varied. The solid line and data points show the change in the measured activities. The dashed line is included as a reference and shows where the values of concentration and activity are equal. (This graph was generated using data from D.G. Peters, J.M. Hayes, and G.M. Hieftje, *Chemical Separations and Measurements: Theory and Practice of Analytical Chemistry*, Saunders, Philadelphia, PA, 1974, p. 46.)

TABLE 2 Standard States of Various Substances

Type of Substance	Standard State (where $a = 1$)
Solid	Pure form of the solid[a]
Liquid	Pure form of the liquid
Gas	Pure form of gas at 1 bar[b]
Solution of a dissolved chemical	One molar (1 M) solution of the chemical

[a]For solids with more than one form, the standard state is the most stable form of the solid.

[b]It is necessary to define the pressure and temperature of a gas in the standard state because the volume, and thus amount of gas per unit volume, will depend on both these factors. A pressure of 1 bar (formerly 1 atmosphere) and a temperature of 0°C (273.15 K) are often used for this purpose, although other temperatures can also be chosen. This combination of conditions is commonly referred to as the *standard temperature and pressure*, or *STP*.

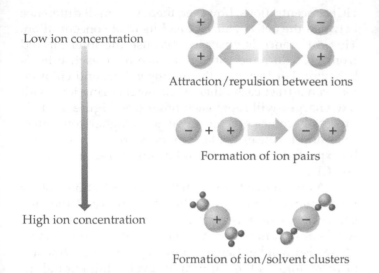

Low ion concentration

Attraction/repulsion between ions

Formation of ion pairs

High ion concentration

Formation of ion/solvent clusters

FIGURE 4 Examples of nonideal effects that can occur in a solution containing ions.

interaction forms large species like H_3O^+, $H_5O_2^+$, or $H_9O_4^+$, reducing the number of ordinary water molecules and increasing the activity of all solutes dissolved in the solution.

Activity Coefficients. From Figure 3 we can see that even though the activity and concentration of a chemical are two different things, these two terms are closely related. We can describe this relationship by using an **activity coefficient (γ)**, as shown in Equation 2.[11,12,21]

$$a = \gamma (c/c^\circ) \qquad (2)$$

In this equation, a refers to the activity of our chemical, c is the concentration of the chemical under the conditions we are examining, and c° is the concentration of the same chemical under some reference conditions (for instance, a concentration of exactly 1.00 M, when we are using molarity to describe the chemical content). Sometimes the subscript "c" is added to the activity coefficient in Equation 2 (written as "γ_c") to indicate that this is a "concentration"-based value. Similar relationships can be used to relate the activity of a chemical to its molality or other measures of chemical content.[12] Like activity (a), the activity coefficient for a chemical is a number with no units. This is the case because the concentration c in Equation 2 is divided by c°, allowing us to eliminate the units that are present in both these terms. Because c° is chosen to be equal to one, it is often not shown and Equation 2 is replaced with the simpler relationship $a = \gamma \cdot c$. Although c° will not be shown in the rest of this text, keep in mind that it is still present when using dimensional analysis to check the units in activity calculations, as illustrated in the following exercise.

EXERCISE 1   Determining Activity Coefficients

A sample of seawater has activities for bicarbonate and carbonate ions of 9.75×10^{-4} and 4.7×10^{-6}, respectively, at 25°C and one atmosphere pressure.[7] The concentrations of these same chemicals are 0.00238 M for HCO_3^- and 0.000269 M for CO_3^{2-}. What are the activity coefficients for these ions?

SOLUTION
The activity coefficient for bicarbonate can be determined from Equation 2, where the values of a and c are given and the value of c° is assigned a value of exactly 1.000 M.

$$a = \gamma (c/c^\circ)$$
$$9.75 \times 10^{-4} = \gamma (0.00238\ M/1.000\ M)$$
$$\therefore \gamma = 0.410$$

Using the same approach, the activity coefficient for carbonate is found to be **0.017**. In both cases the activity coefficients are much less than one, which reflects the fact that the activities for bicarbonate and carbonate were lower than the total concentrations of these ions. Although these are both dilute solutes, this difference in activity versus concentration is caused by the presence of other ions (e.g., Na^+ and Cl^-) that affect the overall properties of this solution.

As we can see from the last exercise, both the activity and activity coefficient for a solute will be affected by the presence of other substances in a solution. When we are dealing with very dilute solutions, there are few interactions that take place between individual solutes, making the activities and concentrations essentially the same and giving activity coefficients close to one. As we move to more concentrated solutions, more solute–solvent and solute–solute interactions take place and γ will usually be quite different from one. This effect is important to consider when work is being performed with concentrated solutions, reagents, or samples. We will come back to this problem later when we consider various strategies for dealing with the differences between activity and concentration in analytical measurements.

Ionic Strength. We have already seen two main effects that cause chemical activities to be different from chemical concentration: solute–solvent interactions and solute–solute interactions. Solute–solvent interactions tend to occur only at moderate to high concentrations and are often (but not always) negligible for many of the samples examined in analytical chemistry. Solute–solute interactions are a bigger problem because they occur at even reasonably low analyte levels. To help us identify and control this effect, it is necessary to have some way of describing such interactions. This is particularly true for ions in that their charges can give them an influence over other charged substances over relatively long distances.

In predicting the extent of these interactions, we need to consider the charge and concentration of every type of ion in the solution. This task is accomplished by determining the **ionic strength (I)** of the overall solution,[12]

$$I = \frac{1}{2}(c_1 z_1^2 + c_2 z_2^2 + \cdots + c_n z_n^2)$$

or

$$I = \frac{1}{2}\Sigma\,(c_i z_i^2) \tag{3}$$

where c_i is the concentration of a particular type of ion in solution, and z_i is the charge on that ion (for instance, "+1" for H^+, "−1" for Cl^-, and "+2" for Cu^{2+}). From Equation 3, we get a concentration-based ionic strength, which is sometimes written as "I_c."[12] The fact that the z-terms are all squared gives a positive $c_i z_i^2$ value for all ions, regardless of whether the ions are negative or positive. The result is that the value of I will always be positive. These squared terms also ensure that multiply-charged ions have a greater impact on chemical activities than singly charged ions.

EXERCISE 2	The Ionic Strength of Sea Water

A chemist wishes to mimic the effects of sea water on a reaction by preparing a solution that contains 0.500 M sodium chloride (NaCl) and 0.050 M magnesium chloride (MgCl₂). If these salts completely dissolve and no other substances are present, what is the ionic strength of this mixture?

SOLUTION

To find the ionic strength, we simply need to place the individual concentrations and charges for each of the ions in our solution (Na^+, Cl^-, and Mg^{2+}) in Equation 3. In this case, the total concentration for Cl^- is 0.600 M, which is the sum of what is produced from NaCl (giving 0.500 M Cl^-) and MgCl₂ (which gives $2 \cdot 0.050 = 0.100$ M Cl^-).

$$I = \frac{1}{2}[(0.500\ M\ Na^+)(+1)^2 +$$
$$(0.600\ M\ Cl^-)(-1)^2 +$$
$$(0.050\ M\ Mg^{2+})(+2)^2] = \mathbf{0.650\ M}$$

Notice that the ionic strength is larger than the concentration of any single type of ion in our solution, even for the ion with the highest concentration (Cl^- in this case). This result occurs because I is a measure of the overall influence of all ions on chemical activity.

Although ionic strength can be used to describe the composition of a reagent or sample, it differs from a chemical concentration in several ways. For instance, Equation 3 indicates that the value of I depends only on the charge and concentration of the ions in a solution,

and (at least to a first approximation) not on the specific types of ions present. As a result, a solution of 0.10 M NaCl (dissociating into Na^+ and Cl^- ions) will have the same ionic strength as a 0.10 M solution of HNO₃ (forming H^+ and NO_3^-) when both chemicals completely dissociate in water. Also, the concentrations of nonionic solution components are not considered in calculating the ionic strength, because such substances generally interact only with solute or solvent molecules very close to them and do not usually have any appreciable effect on the activity of other chemicals in a solution.

2B Chemical Activity in Analytical Methods

Because one of the most common applications of analytical chemistry is the measurement of chemicals, it is important to consider how the difference between chemical activity and concentration will affect these measurements. In such an analysis we generally have a series of standards and reagents that contain known amounts or concentrations of the chemicals we wish to use or study. However, when we use these reagents or samples, the results we obtain will often be based on the activity of the analyte in these samples. This fact means the conversion from activity to concentration is often an inherent part of an analysis. We will now look at several approaches for dealing with this issue, including methods for estimating or controlling chemical activity.

Estimating Activity. We would ideally like for a chemical analysis to directly measure the activity of an analyte and to relate this activity back to the amount of analyte in our sample. Many of the techniques we use in analytical chemistry do give a response that is related to chemical activity (for example, gravimetric analysis, titrations, chromatography, and electrochemical methods). Unfortunately, this direct approach is complicated by the fact that any experimental measure of activity gives a weighted average for the activities of both negatively and positively charged ions in solution (because one is always present with the other). This weighted average is represented by a term known as the *mean activity coefficient* ($\gamma_\pm$).[12] The following equation shows how activities of individual ions (γ_A and γ_B for ions A^{n+} and B^{m-}) are related to the mean activity coefficient for a strong electrolyte $A_m B_n$ (that is, a chemical where one mole dissociates to produce m moles of A^{n+} and n moles of B^{m-}).[22]

$$(\gamma_\pm)^{m+n} = (\gamma_A)^m \cdot (\gamma_B)^n \tag{4}$$

We have already seen one use of this value in Figure 3, where the measured activity for HCl was actually the mean activity of both H^+ and Cl^-, as described by the mean activity coefficient $(\gamma_{\pm HCl})^2 = (\gamma_{H+})^1 \cdot (\gamma_{Cl-})^1$.

If it is necessary to know the activity of a chemical and we do not have the time or ability to measure this value, another option is to use one of several equations that have been developed to estimate activity coefficients. Although this approach is not as reliable as using a measured value, it usually provides a reasonably good approximation for dilute solutions. The most famous relationship used for this purpose is the **extended Debye–Hückel equation**.[11,12,22]

$$\log(\gamma) = \frac{-A \cdot z^2 \cdot \sqrt{I}}{1 + a \cdot B \cdot \sqrt{I}} \qquad (5)$$

This equation, derived by Peter Debye and Erich Hückel in 1923 (see Figure 5),[23,24] relates the activity coefficient for an ion to the ionic strength of its solution (I), the charge on the ion (z), and three adjustable parameters: a, A, and B. The first of these adjustable parameters is an ion-size term a, which represents the closest distance the ion can approach another ion. Table 3 gives values for this term for many common inorganic ions in water. The other two adjustable parameters in Equation 5 are A and B,

which represent the effects of temperature and solvent on the activity coefficient.[22]

In water at room temperature (25°C, the condition often used during chemical analysis), the value of A is approximately 0.51 and B (when a is given in picometers) is roughly 3.28×10^{-3}, or $1/(305)$. Putting these values into Equation 5 gives the following version of the extended Debye–Hückel equation.[22]

In Water at 25°C:
$$\log(\gamma) = \frac{-0.51 \cdot z^2 \cdot \sqrt{I}}{1 + (a \cdot \sqrt{I})/305} \qquad (6)$$

If we are working with an even more dilute solution, Equation 6 can be further simplified to give an expression known as the *Debye–Hückel limiting law (DHLL)*, where $\log(\gamma) = -0.51 \cdot z^2 \cdot \sqrt{I}$. This latter equation is much more limited in use than Equations 5 and 6, so we will instead use these more complete equations throughout the rest of this chapter. (*Note*: In some texts you will see only the term $1 + \sqrt{I}$ in the denominator of Equation 6; this assumes you are working with an ion

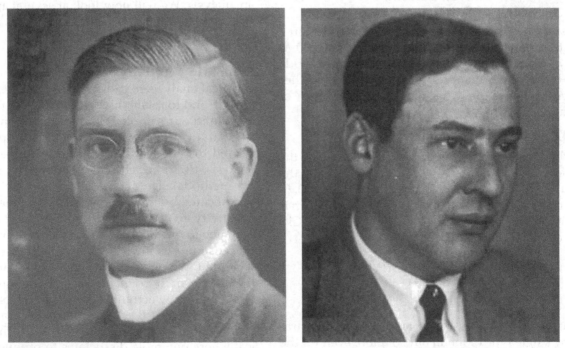

Peter Debye

Erich Hückel

FIGURE 5 Peter Debye (1884–1966) and Erich Hückel (1896–1980). Debye was a Dutch physicist who studied the behavior of ions in solution. Hückel was born in Germany and was Debye's assistant in Zürich, where in 1923 they together developed their famous equation for describing the activity coefficients of ions in solution. In earlier work with Swiss scientist Paul Scherrer, Debye showed that the powders of crystalline solids could be examined with X rays to determine the chemical structures of these solids, a technique now known as powder X-ray diffraction. Debye won the 1936 Nobel Prize in chemistry for his work, and moved to the United States near the beginning of World War II, continuing his studies at Cornell University. The unit of measure for a dipole moment, the *debye* (D), is named in his honor. After working for Debye, Hückel entered the area of quantum mechanics and briefly worked with Neils Bohr. Hückel later became a professor of physics in Marburg, Germany, until his retirement.

TABLE 3 Estimated Individual Activity Coefficients for Inorganic Ions in Water at 25°C[*]

Type of Ion	Ion Size Parameter a (pm)	Activity Coefficient at Ionic strength I (M)							
		I = 0.0005	0.001	0.002	0.005	0.01	0.02	0.05	0.10
Charge = +1 or –1									
H^+	900	0.976[a]	0.967	0.955	0.934	0.913	0.889	0.854	0.825
Li^+	600	0.975	0.966	0.953	0.930	0.907	0.878	0.833	0.795
Na^+, ClO_2^-, IO_3^-, HCO_3^-, $H_2PO_4^-$, HSO_3^-, $H_2AsO_4^-$, $[Co(NH_3)_4(NO_2)_2]^+$	400–450[b]	0.975	0.965	0.952	0.928	0.902	0.870	0.817	0.773
OH^-, F^-, SCN^-, OCN^-, HS^-, ClO_3^-, ClO_4^-, BrO_3^-, IO_4^-, MnO_4^-	350	0.975	0.965	0.951	0.926	0.900	0.867	0.811	0.762
K^+, Cl^-, Br^-, I^-, CN^-, NO_2^-, NO_3^-	300	0.975	0.965	0.951	0.925	0.899	0.864	0.806	0.753
Rb^+, Cs^+, NH_4^+, Tl^+, Ag^+	250	0.975	0.965	0.951	0.924	0.897	0.862	0.801	0.745
Charge = +2 or –2									
Mg^{2+}, Be^{2+}	800	0.906	0.872	0.829	0.756	0.689	0.616	0.516	0.444
Ca^{2+}, Cu^{2+}, Zn^{2+}, Sn^{2+}, Mn^{2+}, Fe^{2+}, Ni^{2+}, Co^{2+}	600	0.904	0.870	0.824	0.747	0.675	0.595	0.482	0.400
Sr^{2+}, Ba^{2+}, Cd^{2+}, Hg^{2+}, Ra^{2+}, S^{2-}, $S_2O_4^{2-}$, WO_4^{2-}	500	0.904	0.868	0.822	0.743	0.668	0.583	0.464	0.376
Pb^{2+}, CO_3^{2-}, SO_3^{2-}, MoO_4^{2-}, $[Co(NH_3)_5Cl]^{2+}$, $[Fe(CN)_5NO]^{2-}$	450	0.903	0.868	0.821	0.740	0.664	0.577	0.454	0.363
CrO_4^{2-}, Hg_2^{2+}, HPO_4^{2-}, SO_4^{2-}, $S_2O_3^{2-}$, $S_2O_6^{2-}$, $S_2O_8^{2-}$, SeO_4^{2-}	400	0.903	0.867	0.820	0.738	0.660	0.571	0.444	0.350
Charge = +3 or –3									
Al^{3+}, Ce^{3+}, Cr^{3+}, Fe^{3+}, In^{3+}, La^{3+}, Nd^{3+}, Pr^{3+}, Sc^{3+}, Sm^{3+}, Y^{3+}	900	0.801	0.737	0.659	0.539	0.442	0.348	0.241	0.178
$[Co(NH_3)_6]^{3+}$, $[Co(NH_3)_5H_2O]^{3+}$, $[Cr(NH_3)_6]^{3+}$, $[Fe(CN)_6]^{3-}$, PO_4^{3-}	400	0.795	0.726	0.640	0.505	0.393	0.283	0.161	0.094
Charge = +4 or –4									
Ce^{4+}, Sn^{4+}, Th^{4+}, Zr^{4+}	1100	0.678	0.587	0.485	0.347	0.251	0.172	0.098	0.062
$[Fe(CN)_6]^{4-}$	500	0.667	0.568	0.457	0.304	0.199	0.116	0.046	0.020

[*] This table is based on data provided in J. Kielland, "Individual Activity Coefficients of Ions in Aqueous Solutions," *Journal of the American Chemical Society*, 59 (1937) 1675–1678.

[a] The last number to the right and underlined in each activity coefficient is a guard digit.

[b] The activities coefficients given for a ± 1 charge and a = 400–450 are the averages of the values obtained at a = 400 and a = 450.

with a size term a of roughly 300 pm, making $a/305$ equal to about 1.0.)

One way we can use the extended Debye–Hückel equation is to predict how the activity coefficient for an ion will change with the ionic strength of its solution.

An example is shown in Figure 6, where the actual activity coefficients observed for HCl are compared to those calculated with Equation 6. The way these values were obtained is illustrated in the following exercise.

EXERCISE 3 Estimating Activity Coefficients for Ions

Using Equation 6, what activity coefficients would be expected for H^+ and Cl^- at 25°C in an aqueous HCl solution with an ionic strength of 0.010 M? What is the mean activity coefficient predicted for HCl and how does this compare to the measured values in Figure 3?

SOLUTION

In Table 3 the ion size parameters for H^+ and Cl^- are given as being 900 pm and 300 pm. By placing these values in Equation 6 along with the given ionic strength of 0.010 M, we get the following estimates for the activity coefficients for the individual H^+ and Cl^- ions.

For H^+ at $I = 0.010$ M:

$$\log(\gamma_{H^+}) = \frac{-0.51 \cdot (+1)^2 \cdot \sqrt{0.010\ M}}{1 + (900\ pm) \cdot \sqrt{0.010\ M}/(305\ pm)}$$

$$\therefore\ \gamma_{H^+} = 0.91\underline{3} = \mathbf{0.91}$$

For Cl^- at $I = 0.010$ M:

$$\log(\gamma_{Cl^-}) = \frac{-0.51 \cdot (-1)^2 \cdot \sqrt{0.010\ M}}{1 + (300\ pm) \cdot \sqrt{0.010\ M}/(305\ pm)}$$

$$\therefore\ \gamma_{Cl^-} = 0.89\underline{9} = \mathbf{0.90}$$

This same answer could have been reached by interpolating between the activity coefficients given for these ions in Table 3 at similar ionic strengths.

Now that we have estimated the activity coefficients for our separate ions, we can combine these values using Equation 4 to get the mean activity coefficient for HCl.

$$(\gamma_{\pm HCl})^{1+1} = (\gamma_{H^+})^1 \cdot (\gamma_{Cl^-})^1$$

$$(\gamma_{\pm HCl})^2 = (0.91\underline{3})^1 \cdot (0.89\underline{9})^1$$

$$\therefore\ \gamma_{\pm HCl} = 0.90\underline{6} = \mathbf{0.91}$$

In looking back to Figure 3, we can see that this calculated number agrees fairly closely with the expected value at $I = 0.010$ M for HCl in water.

One problem with the extended Debye–Hückel equation is that it only gives good agreement with experimental activity coefficients up to an ionic strength of about 0.10 M (for instance, see Figure 6). This difference occurs because the extended Debye–Hückel equation only considers how the activity coefficients for ions are affected by simple attraction and repulsion between neighboring ions. At higher ionic strengths, other effects like ion pair and ion/solvent cluster formation also become significant. This situation requires more advanced equations to estimate activity coefficients (see the problems at the end of this chapter).

Although ions are the main types of chemicals affected by changes in ionic strength, noncharged compounds are also affected to a small extent by these changes. This phenomenon, known as the *salting-out effect*, is usually seen as a slight decrease in the solubility

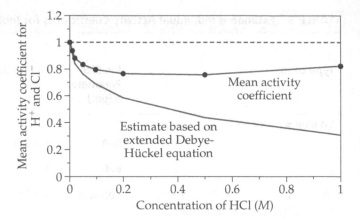

FIGURE 6 Actual and predicted mean activity coefficients for HCl based on the extended Debye–Hückel equation. (The experimental results are based on data from D.G. Peters, J.M. Hayes, and G.M. Hieftje, *Chemical Separations and Measurements: Theory and Practice of Analytical Chemistry*, Saunders, Philadelphia, PA, 1974, p. 46.)

of neutral compounds as the ionic strength is increased. This effect can be viewed as an increase in the activity of a neutral agent, causing it to have a higher effective concentration and come out of the solution more easily. Such an effect can be represented by the following equation,

$$\log(\gamma) = k \cdot I \tag{7}$$

where γ is the activity coefficient for the neutral compound, I is the ionic strength of the solution containing this compound, and k is a constant for the compound known as its *salting coefficient*.[22] The value of k is between 0.01 and 0.10 for most noncharged compounds, which means these compounds will have an increase in activity from 1.00 to 1.02–1.26 as we increase I from 0 to 1.0 M. For low ionic strengths ($I < 0.10$ M), this effect causes less than a 2.5% change in activity and is usually insignificant. Thus, the activity coefficient for a neutral compound in such solutions is approximately equal to one. However, the salting coefficient does need to be considered when working at higher ionic strengths.

EXERCISE 4 Estimating the Activity Coefficient for a Neutral Compound

The salting coefficient for H_2CO_3 in seawater is about 0.075. If a seawater sample has an ionic strength of 0.70 M, what is the activity coefficient for H_2CO_3?

SOLUTION

We can estimate the activity coefficient for H_2CO_3 by placing $k = 0.075$ and $I = 0.70$ M into Equation 7 and solving for γ.

$$\log(\gamma_{H_2CO_3}) = (0.075) \cdot (0.70\ M)\ \therefore\ \mathbf{\gamma_{H_2CO_3} = 1.13}$$

Under these conditions, H_2CO_3 will have an activity that is 13% higher than would occur if this same chemical were present in water without added salts.

Factors That Affect Activity. Besides allowing us to estimate activity coefficients, we can use relationships like Equations 5 through 7 to help us see what factors are most important in affecting the activity of chemicals. We already know that the ionic strength of a solution is important in determining the activity coefficients for both charged and neutral compounds. As a result, we should always try to match the matrix of a sample to that of our standards so that they will have similar ionic strengths. One way this can be done is by adding a fixed excess of a salt to all of our samples and standards to avoid any major changes in the ionic strength due to changes in the concentration of the analyte or the sample composition. For instance, a change in Ca^{2+} concentration from 0 to 10 μM for samples prepared in a 0.10 M NaCl solution will have an insignificant effect on the ionic strength during the measurement of Ca^{2+} levels.

The type of solvent used to prepare a solution is also important in determining chemical activity. One way the solvent can affect activity coefficients is through changes that occur in the *dielectric constant* (ε), which will alter both the A and B terms in the Debye–Hückel equation. The dielectric constant can be thought of as a measure of the degree to which a solvent or material will allow an electrostatic force from one charged body (such as an ion) to affect another.[15] The dielectric constant can also be used as a rough indicator of a chemical's "polarity." In general, it will be easier for dissolved ions to influence each other through attraction or repulsion when these ions are present in a polar solvent like water (which has a high dielectric constant of $\varepsilon = 78.54$ at 25°C) versus less polar solvents like methanol (CH_3OH, $\varepsilon = 32.63$) or ethanol (CH_3CH_2OH, $\varepsilon = 24.30$).

Equations 5–7 also show how the properties of a solute will determine the extent to which a change in ionic strength will affect its activity. The charge (z) on a solute is one item that appears in the Debye–Hückel equation. If we compare solutes with similar sizes, those with the largest charge will also be affected the most by changes in ionic strength and have the greatest difference between their chemical activity and concentration. The effective size of the solute is also important to consider. If we compare the calculated activity coefficients in Table 3 for hydrated ions with the same charge but different values for a, we see that in going from Rb^+ ($a = 250$ pm) to H^+ ($a = 900$ pm), the activity coefficient at $I = 0.10$ M changes from 0.75 to 0.83. However, this effect is much smaller than what is seen when increasing the charge on an ion and is often ignored when working at low ionic strengths.

You may have noticed that the ion size parameters in Table 3 do not follow the trend that might be expected based on the periodic chart. In moving down the left column of the periodic table from H^+ to Li^+, Na^+, and K^+, you would initially expect these ions to increase in size because they are adding greater numbers of electrons, protons, and neutrons. This trend is actually just the opposite of what you see when comparing the size parameters in Table 3. The reason for this difference is

that the ion size parameter in the Debye–Hückel equation is actually a measure of the size of an ion plus the shell of solvent that surrounds it. When we are using water as the solvent, this shell is called the *hydration layer*, and the resulting size of the ion plus this solvent is known as the *hydrated radius*. As shown in Figure 7, small ions like Li^+ (and also H^+) have a small region of concentrated charge that tends to attract a large amount of solvent and form a large hydrated radius. Larger ions like K^+ and Na^+ have a less concentrated charge, causing them to have smaller hydration layers, even though the ion itself is much larger.

Although most analytical chemists do not think about chemical activity as they go about their daily work, they do deal with this issue on a routine basis through the methods and reagents they use for chemical measurements. In most analytical techniques, this issue is handled by generating a calibration curve, in which the measured response (related to chemical activity) is plotted against the concentration or content of standards that contain known amounts of the chemical of interest. If the analysis method has been designed so that samples are treated in the same way as these standards, and therefore have similar relationships between their activity and content, this calibration curve can be used to determine the amount of the analyte in unknown samples. One example of this approach is the graph we saw in Figure 3, in which the measured activity for HCl was plotted against its total concentration in solution. Based on this graph, we could measure the activities of other HCl solutions and relate these activities back to the concentrations of HCl in these samples.

3 CHEMICAL EQUILIBRIUM

So far in this chapter we have discussed various types of chemical processes and have examined the concept of chemical activity. In this section we will learn about yet another factor, the equilibrium constant, which can be used to help us describe reactions used in analytical techniques.

3A What Is a Chemical Equilibrium?

To understand what is meant by a "chemical equilibrium," we can go back to our opening example of CO_2 production and uptake within the ocean. Carbon dioxide and related compounds in the ocean (such as carbonate ions, CO_3^{2-}) come from several sources, two of which are the air above the ocean and materials on the bottom of the ocean. To simplify this picture, we can focus on the events taking place near the ocean floor. On the ocean floor is calcium-containing debris from dead single-celled sea life. One compound found here is calcium carbonate, $CaCO_3$. As solid calcium carbonate comes into contact with water, it dissociates to a small extent to form calcium ions and carbonate ions dissolved in water.

$$CaCO_3(s) \rightarrow Ca^{2+} + CO_3^{2-} \qquad (8)$$

203

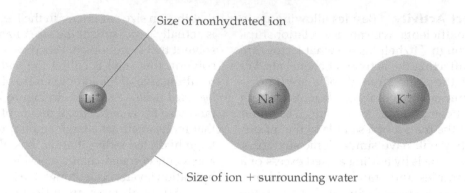

FIGURE 7 A comparison of the effective diameter of Li$^+$, Na$^+$, and K$^+$ in water versus the size of these same ions in the absence of water.

At the same time, some of the calcium ions in the surrounding water combine with carbonate ions to form new calcium carbonate that settles back on to the ocean floor.

$$Ca^{2+} + CO_3{}^{2-} \longrightarrow CaCO_3(s) \qquad (9)$$

Both processes happen at the same time but proceed in opposite directions, resulting in an ongoing process. To describe the overall reaction, we can combine these processes and use a double arrow $\rightleftarrows$ to indicate that the reaction is proceeding in both the forward and reverse directions.

$$CaCO_3(s) \;\rightleftarrows\; Ca^{2+} + CO_3{}^{2-} \qquad (10)$$

The same type of reaction can take place in a self-contained system, such as a beaker of water containing solid calcium carbonate. Given enough time, this reaction will reach a point where the rate at which calcium carbonate dissolves exactly equals the rate at which new calcium carbonate is formed. This situation, which occurs when the forward and reverse rates of a reaction are equal, is known as a **chemical equilibrium** and is represented by the symbol " $\rightleftharpoons$ ".[11,21]

At Equilibrium: $\;CaCO_3(s) \rightleftharpoons Ca^{2+} + CO_3{}^{2-} \qquad (11)$

A chemical equilibrium is important in analytical chemistry because it represents the furthest extent to which an overall reaction will proceed. Knowledge of this feature can be quite useful when you are preparing reagents or designing a method to obtain the maximum amount of a product for measurement.

Definition of an Equilibrium Constant. When a reaction has reached the point of equilibrium, the overall chemical activity of each product and reactant will be a constant. One way of describing this situation is to look at the relative amount of each reactant and product that exists under these conditions. This is accomplished by using a ratio known as an **equilibrium constant**, which is represented by the general symbol K.[12,21]

To illustrate this idea, suppose we have a reaction that involves the combination of m moles of reactant A with n moles of reactant B to give r moles of product C and s moles of product D.

$$mA + nB \rightleftharpoons rC + sD \qquad (12)$$

If this system is at equilibrium (as is implied by the symbol $\rightleftharpoons$), the equilibrium constant for this reaction is given by the following ratio of chemical activities (a_A, a_B, a_C, and a_D) for the reactants and products, in which each activity is raised to a power equal to the stoichiometric amount of its corresponding chemical in the reaction (that is, a_A is raised to the power m, a_B is raised to the power n, and so on).

$$K° = \frac{(a_C)^r (a_D)^s}{(a_A)^m (a_B)^n} \qquad (13)$$

Because we are using only activities in this particular case, the result is a special ratio known as a *thermodynamic equilibrium constant*, $K°$.[12,22] For example, we would use the following ratio to give the thermodynamic equilibrium constant for the calcium carbonate reaction in Equation 16.11.

$$K° = \frac{(a_{Ca^{2+}})\,(a_{CO_3{}^{2-}})}{(a_{CaCO_3})} \qquad (14)$$

It is important when we are writing an equilibrium constant expression to use a *balanced* chemical reaction, as we have done for the example in Equations 11 and 14. This practice is essential because each reaction or product in the reaction will have a term in the equilibrium constant, and the number of moles of these reactants or products that take part in the reaction (that is, the reaction **stoichiometry**)[11,21] will determine the powers that appear on these terms.

One way we can use an equilibrium constant is to determine the activities of all products and reactants in a reaction at equilibrium, as we will see later in this chapter. If we know the final activities of our reactants and products, we can also calculate the equilibrium constant for a reaction. This approach is illustrated in the next exercise. In addition, once we have calculated or measured an equilibrium constant, we can use it to predict how the same reaction will behave when we combine other amounts of products and reactants.

EXERCISE 5	Calculating the Value of an Equilibrium Constant

A beaker sitting at room temperature (25°C) contains an aqueous solution of calcium ions and carbonate ions in direct contact with solid calcium carbonate. The activities of the calcium ions and carbonate ions are both found to be 7.0×10^{-5}, and it is known that the activity of the solid calcium carbonate is equal to 1.0. If these chemicals are at equilibrium, what is the equilibrium constant for this reaction?

SOLUTION

The reaction taking place here is the same as given in Equation 11.

$$CaCO_3(s) \rightleftharpoons Ca^{2+} + CO_3^{2-}$$

To solve this problem, we simply need to place the activities for each of our chemicals into the equilibrium constant expression for this reaction, as given in Equation 14.

$$K° = \frac{(7.0 \times 10^{-5})(7.0 \times 10^{-5})}{1} = 4.9 \times 10^{-9}$$

Notice there are no units given for the value of $K°$ because it is based on chemical activities, which are also numbers with no units. Later we will see how equilibrium constants can also be written in terms of product and reactant concentrations.

Using Equilibrium Constants. One way we can use an equilibrium constant is to determine the actual extent to which a reaction will proceed toward the formation of products. A large equilibrium constant will be obtained for a reaction in which product formation is favored, while a small value for K will occur if the reaction creates only a small amount of products (or favors the presence of the reactants). As an example, in Exercise 5 the equilibrium constant for dissolving solid calcium carbonate and forming calcium and carbonate ions was found to be 4.9×10^{-9}. This result tells us this reaction highly favors the formation of calcium carbonate from calcium and carbonate ions or of solid calcium carbonate staying in its present form.

Another way we can use an equilibrium constant is to obtain information on the change in energy that accompanies a reaction. We can do this because an equilibrium constant is directly related to the change in standard Gibbs free energy ($\Delta G°$) that occurs as we go from the reactants to products. The actual relationship between $K°$ and $\Delta G°$ is as follows.

$$\Delta G° = -RT \ln K° \qquad (15)$$

where T is the absolute temperature at which the reaction is occurring and R is the ideal gas law constant.[11,22] The relationship in Equation 15 is the basis for the way in which we write equilibrium constant expressions, like those shown in Equations 13 and 14. Further information on this relationship can be found in the problems at the end of this chapter.

EXERCISE 6	Relationship Between an Equilibrium Constant and the Energy of a Reaction

What is the change in standard Gibbs free energy for the reaction we considered in Exercise 5?

SOLUTION

In Exercise 5 we determined that the thermodynamic equilibrium constant for the dissolving of calcium carbonate in water was 4.9×10^{-9} at 25°C (or 298 K). We can then place these numbers into Equation 15 along with a value for R of 8.314 J/(mol · K).

$$\Delta G° = -RT \ln K°$$
$$= -(8.314 \text{ J/mol} \cdot \text{K}) \cdot (298 \text{ K}) \cdot \ln(4.9 \times 10^{-9})$$
$$\therefore \Delta G° = 4.74 \times 10^4 \text{ J/mol or } 47.4 \text{ kJ/mol}$$

Figure 8 shows how the values of $K°$ and $\Delta G°$ are related at room temperature. As we can see, a value of $K°$ that is greater than 1.0 will result in a negative value for $\Delta G°$, which means such a reaction will release energy as it goes from reactants to products. A reaction with an equilibrium constant less than 1.0 will give a positive value for $\Delta G°$, indicating it requires added energy to go from the desired reactants to products. Furthermore, as $K°$ becomes much smaller or larger than 1.0, the amount of free energy given off or taken up by the reaction will increase.

We can also use equilibrium constants to predict the direction in which a reaction will tend to proceed when we start with any given amount of reactants or products. It is often possible for a chemist to generally predict which direction a reaction might proceed by using **Le Châtelier's principle**.[11,21] This principle states that when a change or "stress" is placed on a system at equilibrium (such as a change in reactant or product concentrations), the system will respond to partially relieve this stress (for instance, by creating more products or reactants). We can also examine this shift in a more quantitative manner by putting the activities (or concentrations) of these chemicals into the same type of ratio that we use to give the value for $K°$ at equilibrium, but now using the *nonequilibrium conditions*. When we do this, the ratio we calculate is known as the **reaction quotient (Q)**.[12,22] If this reaction quotient is greater than $K°$, it means we have too much product and the reaction will proceed to form reactants

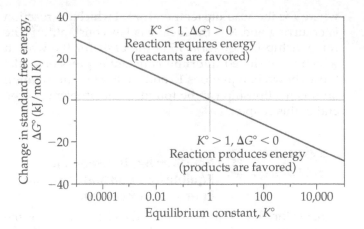

FIGURE 8 Relationship between the thermodynamic equilibrium constant ($K°$), the associated change in standard free energy ($\Delta G°$) for a reaction, and temperature. This plot was prepared using Equation 15.

until an equilibrium is reached. In this situation the "products," which are the chemicals written on the right side of the equation, are really acting as the "reactants" that give rise to other chemicals. If Q is less than $K°$, there is an excess of the reactants and more products will be formed until the reaction reaches equilibrium. As we will see later, this approach can also be used to predict the amount of each reactant and product that will be present at equilibrium.

EXERCISE 7	Predicting the Direction of a Chemical Reaction

A small amount of solid calcium carbonate is placed into water at room temperature along with calcium and carbonate ions that have initial concentrations of $1.0 \times 10^{-4}\,M\,Ca^{2+}$ and $1.0 \times 10^{-4}\,M\,CO_3{}^{2-}$. If we assume that the activities of all our dissolved chemicals are approximately the same as their concentrations, will this mixture react to form more calcium and carbonate ions or more calcium carbonate?

SOLUTION

The reaction we are considering for this mixture is the same as the one examined in Exercises 5 and 6, which has an equilibrium constant of 4.9×10^{-9} at 25°C. To solve this problem we simply need to use our starting activities to calculate Q and compare this value to $K°$.

Under Nonequilibrium Conditions:

$$Q = \frac{(a_{Ca^{2+}})\,(a_{CO_3{}^{2-}})}{(a_{CaCO_3})}$$

$$= \frac{(1.0 \times 10^{-4})(1.0 \times 10^{-4})}{1}$$

$$\therefore Q = 1.0 \times 10^{-8}$$

The value of Q is greater than $K°$ for this reaction ($1.0 \times 10^{-8} > 4.9 \times 10^{-9}$), so there is more product initially present than would be expected at equilibrium. Thus, for equilibrium to be established in this system some of the calcium ions and carbonate ions must combine to form calcium carbonate, which will lower the value of Q until it equals $K°$.

Concentration-Based Equilibrium Constants. Up to this point we have used chemical activities to describe the amount of each reactant and product at equilibrium. As we learned earlier, an equilibrium constant expressed this way is called a *thermodynamic equilibrium constant* ($K°$). Although these constants do depend on temperature and pressure, they are independent of ionic strength and other effects that could cause deviations from the expected behavior of ideal solutions. This feature makes these values popular for use in reference tables that provide equilibrium constants for chemical reactions. However, as we saw in Exercise 7, it is often convenient to use concentrations when calculating equilibrium constants or reaction quotients. For example, an equilibrium constant for the general reaction in Equation 12 could be written as shown below.

$$K = \frac{[C]^r\,[D]^s}{[A]^m\,[B]^n} \tag{16}$$

This type of relationship gives a value we will call a *concentration-dependent equilibrium constant.*[22] In this text we will sometimes use "apparent" units based on molarity in writing this type of equilibrium constant for solution-phase chemicals, but other concentration units can also be used (such as molality or mole fractions). When dealing with gas-phase chemicals in reactions, units such as partial pressures can also be employed. For any solid substance that takes part in a reaction, it is customary to use chemical activities instead of concentrations to describe this chemical in an equilibrium constant expression. We do this for solids because, as we saw in Table 2, the chemical activity for a solid is defined as a standard state and has an assigned chemical activity of exactly one. This is a useful feature when working with calculations and reactions that involve such materials.

Concentration-dependent equilibrium constants are convenient to use when such values have been determined under the same set of temperature, pressure, and solution conditions that we will actually be using in an analysis or experiment. It is important to keep in mind, though, that concentration-dependent equilibrium constants will depend on the ionic strength and type of mixture being examined, because concentrations for individual species are also affected by these factors. A concentration-dependent equilibrium constant (K) is only approximately equal to the thermodynamic equilibrium constant ($K°$) for a reaction when we are working with dilute solutions (that is, when chemical activities and concentrations are similar in value). This feature can create a problem if we want to study a reaction at higher chemical concentrations and are using thermodynamic equilibrium constants provided in tables. To tackle this problem, we need to know exactly how K and $K°$ are related to one another. This relationship can be found by going back to Equation 2 (which we will represent here as $a = \gamma c$), which shows that the activity for a chemical is related to its concentration through its activity coefficient. Based on this equation, we can show that the concentration-dependent and thermodynamic equilibrium constants are related as follows.

$$K° = \frac{(\gamma_C\,[C])^r\,(\gamma_D\,[D])^s}{(\gamma_A\,[A])^m\,(\gamma_B\,[B])^n} \qquad (17)$$

$$K° = K \cdot \frac{(\gamma_C)^r\,(\gamma_D)^s}{(\gamma_A)^m\,(\gamma_B)^n} \qquad (18)$$

An illustration of the differences between $K°$ and K is given in Table 4 for the dissociation of calcium carbonate into calcium ions and carbonate ions. As this table shows, the values for $K°$ and K are quite close at low ionic strengths, but become very different for even moderately concentrated solutions. The size of this difference will depend on such things as the ionic strength, the charge on each ion, and its effective size in the solvent. It will also depend on the number of ions involved in the reaction and whether these ions are present as both products and reactants, because these items will affect the value of the activity coefficient ratio in Equation 18. The more this ratio deviates from one, the greater $K°$ and K will differ under a given set of reaction conditions.

Equation 18 indicates that if we know the thermodynamic value $K°$ for a reaction and can estimate the activity coefficients for each product and reactant at a given ionic strength, we can also estimate K for the reaction under these conditions. This process is what was done in determining the values of K shown in Table 4. We can also use the relationship in Equation 18 in the opposite manner to go from a concentration-dependent equilibrium constant to a thermodynamic equilibrium constant by using the ionic strength of the solution to estimate the activity coefficients of the products and reactants. The following exercise illustrates this idea.

EXERCISE 8 Converting Between $K°$ and K

Write an expression that gives the concentration-dependent equilibrium constant for the dissociation of calcium carbonate into calcium ions and carbonate ions. What is the expected value for K if this reaction is conducted in a solution where $\gamma_\pm$ for Ca^{2+} and CO_3^{2-} is 0.80?

SOLUTION

The value of K for this reaction is given by the following equation.

$$K = \frac{[Ca^{2+}][CO_3^{2-}]}{1}$$

where an activity of one is given for the solid calcium carbonate in the denominator. By replacing activities with concentrations in the thermodynamic equilibrium expression we wrote for this same reaction in Equation 14, we can show that $K°$ and K for this reaction are related as follows.

$$K° = \frac{(\gamma_{Ca^{2+}})[Ca^{2+}](\gamma_{CO_3^{2-}})[CO_3^{2-}]}{1}$$

or

$$K° = K \cdot (\gamma_{Ca^{2+}})(\gamma_{CO_3^{2-}})$$

Using Equation 4, we estimated $\gamma_{Ca^{2+}}$ and $\gamma_{CO_3^{2-}}$ by using the fact that $(\gamma_\pm)^2 = (0.80)^2 = (\gamma_{Ca^{2+}})^1(\gamma_{CO_3^{2-}})^1$, giving a value of 0.894 for $\gamma_{Ca^{2+}}$ and $\gamma_{CO_3^{2-}}$. We also know the value for $K°$ in this reaction (4.9×10^{-9} at 25°C), so we can use the preceding relationship to obtain the expected size of K under the given reaction conditions.

$$K° = K \cdot (\gamma_{Ca^{2+}})(\gamma_{CO_3^{2-}})$$
$$4.9 \times 10^{-9} = K \cdot (0.894)(0.894)$$
$$\therefore K = 6.13 \times 10^{-9} = \mathbf{6.1 \times 10^{-9}}$$

We have already learned that thermodynamic equilibrium constants have no units because they are based on activities. A related question is "What are the units on a concentration-based equilibrium constant?" It is actually acceptable to write a concentration-dependent equilibrium constant either with or without units, depending on how such a constant is being used. For instance, the value of K in Exercise 8 for the reaction of Ca^{2+} with CO_3^{2-} should have apparent units of molarity raised to the second power (M^2) based on the terms that appear in the numerator and denominator of this equilibrium constant expression. (*Note:* These units will differ for other reactions and types of equilibrium constants.) It is convenient to show these units when we are using an equilibrium constant to calculate the amount of a chemical in a given reaction, which can help when we use dimensional analysis to see if we have obtained a reasonable answer.

There are also times when it is useful to "eliminate" the units on a concentration-dependent equilibrium constant. This type of situation occurred in Equation 18 when we related the values of $K°$ to K. In this case neither $K°$ nor activity coefficients have units, so Equation 18 would imply that K also does not have units. However, what really took place was that each concentration term in the expression for K was being divided by a reference concentration with a value of exactly 1.00 (e.g., a value of $1\,M$ for a concentration that is expressed in molarity). This is the same approach we discussed in Equation 2 for relating activity to chemical concentration and acts as

TABLE 4 Thermodynamic and Concentration-Based Equilibrium Constants ($K°$ and K) for the Reaction $H_2CO_3 \rightleftharpoons HCO_3^- + H^+$ in Water at 25°C

Ionic Strength	Activity Coefficients[a]			Activity Coefficient Ratio	Equilibrium Constants[b]	
	$\gamma_{H_2CO_3}$	γ_{H^+}	$\gamma_{HCO_3^-}$	$(\gamma_{H^+})(\gamma_{HCO_3^-})/\gamma_{H_2CO_3}$	$K°$	K
0.000	1.000	1.000	1.000	1.000	4.5×10^{-7}	4.5×10^{-7}
0.001	1.000	0.967	0.965	0.933	4.5×10^{-7}	4.8×10^{-7}
0.005	1.001	0.934	0.928	0.865	4.5×10^{-7}	5.2×10^{-7}
0.010	1.002	0.913	0.902	0.822	4.5×10^{-7}	5.5×10^{-7}
0.050	1.009	0.854	0.817	0.691	4.5×10^{-7}	6.5×10^{-7}
0.100	1.017	0.825	0.773	0.627	4.5×10^{-7}	7.1×10^{-7}

[a]The activity coefficients for H^+ and HCO_3^- were taken from Table 3. The activity coefficients for H_2CO_3 were calculated using Equation 7 with a salting coefficient of $k = 0.075$.

[b]The value of K was determined by using the relationship $K = K°/$(Activity Coefficient Ratio), as obtained by rearranging Equation 18.

a conversion factor to remove any units from K during the calculation. To remind us of this feature, whenever any units are given later in this text for a concentration-dependent equilibrium constant K, we will refer to these as "apparent" units.

3B Solving Chemical Equilibrium Problems

We learned earlier that many types of reactions are used in analytical chemistry. We also learned that an understanding of the fundamental basis for these reactions is important in helping us to use and predict how these reactions will perform in such methods. Being able to predict what reaction conditions will be needed for a particular analysis often involves using calculations that involve chemical equilibria. For instance, we might use information on the expected concentration range for an analyte to determine the optimum composition of a reagent that should be used for measuring an analyte. Let's now discuss some questions and approaches that can be used in dealing with such calculations.

General Strategy. In solving any type of chemical problem, it is important to first ask several questions about the reaction. A summary of these questions is given in Table 5. To illustrate this process, suppose we have a reaction that involves the dissociation of carbonic acid in water, where we are told to prepare a 0.00500 M solution of carbonic acid in water at 25°C. We will now see how we can estimate the concentration of hydrogen ions in this solution.

The first question that needs to be asked in this problem is "Which reactions are the most important to the problem at hand?" To answer this question, we need to consider both the main reaction and any side reactions that might take place in the system. In our example, the main reaction

is the ionization of carbonic acid to give bicarbonate and hydrogen ions, as shown in Equation 19.

$$H_2CO_3 \rightleftharpoons HCO_3^- + H^+ \quad (19)$$

However, there are other reactions that can also produce H^+, our product of interest. One is the further dissociation of the bicarbonate to form more hydrogen ions (Equation 20); the second is the dissociation of water to produce H^+ and hydroxide ions (Equation 21).

$$HCO_3^- \rightleftharpoons CO_3^{2-} + H^+ \quad (20)$$

$$H_2O \rightleftharpoons H^+ + OH^- \quad (21)$$

Another possible reaction that might be important is the combination of dissolved carbon dioxide with water to form more H_2CO_3, giving what is known as a *hydration reaction*.

$$CO_2 + H_2O \rightleftharpoons H_2CO_3 \quad (22)$$

Although it would be important to consider this latter reaction for an open system, as would be done when modeling global warming, in our particular example we will assume we are working with a closed system in which the concentration ratio of CO_2 and H_2CO_3 is constant. This assumption, in turn, makes it possible for us to focus on the solution-phase reactions in Equations 19–21 for the remainder of this chapter.

Once we have identified the reactions we need to consider, the next question to ask is "What is already known about the reaction?" In answering this question, we need to think about both the reactions and conditions in the system we are studying. With regard to our system, we know the

TABLE 5 Questions to Consider When Solving Chemical Equilibrium Problems

Which reactions are the most important to the problem at hand?

What is the main reaction of interest?

Are there any side reactions that must be considered?

What is already known about the reaction?

How much of each reactant or product is there at the beginning and/or end of the reaction?

How are the reactants and products related to each other (reaction stoichiometry)?

What other chemicals are present that might affect this reaction?

What is known about the amounts of these other chemicals?

What are the conditions for the reaction (temperature, solvent, etc.)?

What is the equilibrium constant for the reaction?

Are there any simplifying assumptions that I can make about these reactions?

What degree of accuracy and complexity will be required in the calculation?

Can concentrations be used instead of chemical activities?

Can any reactions be ignored or their effects treated using constants?

Are there any reactants or products whose concentrations will not change significantly during the reaction?

What equations can I use to describe my reaction?

What are the equilibrium expressions for this reaction?

What are the mass balance equations for this reaction?

What is the charge balance equation for the system?

Are there enough equations to obtain an answer?

What mathematical approach should be used to solve these equations?

Can a simple linear equation or quadratic equation be used?

Is it necessary to use successive approximations?

Will a spreadsheet or other computer-based tool be required?

Does my final answer make sense?

Are all of the concentrations (or activities) that were obtained of a reasonable size?

Do the results provide an adequate solution to each equation that was used to describe the reaction?

total amount of carbonic acid originally placed in solution was 0.00500 *M*. We also know the reaction is taking place in water at 25°C. It is further implied that no other substances are present in significant amounts, such as other sources of carbonate or bicarbonate. In addition, we know how the chemicals in our solution will react and the stoichiometry between the reactants and products. Finally, it is helpful to see what is known about the equilibrium constants for these reactions. In this case, the values of K for the reactions in Equations 19–21 in water and at 25°C can be found from the literature to be 4.5×10^{-7}, 4.7×10^{-11}, and 1×10^{-14}, respectively.

Another question to now ask is *"Are there any simplifying assumptions that can be made about the system?"* A few simplifications can make an equilibrium problem much easier to solve, but the number of assumptions and simplifications that are made will also affect the accuracy of the final answer. In this case, we have already assumed that we are working with a closed system, which allows us to ignore the effects of the reaction in Equation 22. We might also assume that the ionic strength of our

reaction mixture is low enough to allow the use of concentrations instead of chemical activities and use our known value for $K°$ in place of K. This second approximation is a good one in this case because (as shown in Table 4) even if all of the carbonic acid dissociated to form bicarbonate and hydrogen ions, the resulting ionic strength of 0.00500 *M* would give a difference of only 15% between the values for K and $K°$. This approximation would not be valid, however, if we needed results in which greater accuracy was required for our calculations.

We can now begin to set up the equations we need to solve our problem. We also need to see how many variables must be considered and identify at least as many equations as this number of variables to allow us to get a solution. If we assume that chemical activities and concentrations are approximately the same (or that K and $K°$ are roughly equal) and if we do not make any further assumptions about this system, then we have five variables to deal with in our problem. These variables include the hydrogen ion concentration, the main factor of interest. In solving for the hydrogen ion concentration, we must also obtain the concentrations for H_2CO_3, HCO_3^-, CO_3^{2-}, and OH^-, because these will all affect the value of $[H^+]$ through the reactions taking place in the system. The last remaining component in these reactions is water (see Equation 21), but we can safely assume its activity is one because it is the solvent and is in a large excess versus the other chemicals.

Fortunately, we already have three of the five equations we need to get at these five variables. These three equations are the equilibrium expressions for the three reactions in Equations 19–21, which are as follows when written in terms of concentration-based equilibrium constants.

For Reaction 6.19: $K_1 = \dfrac{[HCO_3^-][H^+]}{[H_2CO_3]} \approx 4.5 \times 10^{-7}$ (23)

For Reaction 6.20: $K_2 = \dfrac{[CO_3^{2-}][H^+]}{[HCO_3^-]} \approx 4.7 \times 10^{-11}$ (24)

For Reaction 6.21: $K_w = \dfrac{[H^+][OH^-]}{1} \approx 1.0 \times 10^{-14}$ (25)

If we also wish to include apparent units along with these equilibrium constants for use in later calculations, these units would be M for K_1 and K_2 and M^2 for K_w. At this point we have three unique equations that describe our reactions, but we still have five unknown concentrations. This means we must find two more equations to describe our system. The way we get these two other equations is by using the methods of mass balance and charge balance, as we will discuss in the following section.

Mass Balance and Charge Balance. One way that we can get additional equations to help us solve an equilibrium problem is to use *mass balance*. Mass balance is simply an application of the law of conservation of mass, which means that we cannot create or destroy matter as a result of an ordinary chemical reaction. One useful aspect of this concept when we are solving an equilibrium problem is that the total mass (or moles) of each element we place into a system must be equal to the sum of the masses (or moles) of all the individual forms of that element after equilibrium has been reached.

Mass balance is a particularly helpful tool when we are dealing with a set of reactions that involve many different forms of the same chemical. An example would be the reaction of carbonic acid to form bicarbonate and then carbonate ions, as is shown in Equations 19–21. In this particular case we often do not know the concentrations of each form of carbonate, but we do know the total amount of carbonic acid we initially placed into solution. We can use this information to write a **mass balance equation**, which is an equation that shows how the total concentration of a chemical is related to the concentrations of its various species. The mass balance equation for carbonate in our particular example would be as follows.

$C_{Carbonate} = [H_2CO_3] + [HCO_3^-] + [CO_3^{2-}]$ (26)

In this equation the term $C_{Carbonate}$ is also known as the **analytical concentration** for carbonate. The analytical concentration for a chemical is equal to the total concentration of that chemical in a solution, regardless of the final form or number of species for the chemical. In writing Equation 26 for carbonate, we have not introduced any new variables because we know the total concentration of carbonic acid placed into the initial solution, 0.00500 M. You may have also noticed that this relationship is written in terms of concentrations rather than chemical activities. The reason for this format is that we are now looking at the content of this chemical, rather than its reactivity. Thus, mass balance equations are always written in terms of mass, moles, or concentration rather than chemical activity.

There are several key things to remember when you are writing a mass balance equation. First, make sure you are considering all significant reactions that might involve substances in your mass balance equation. If you are not sure whether or not a particular reaction should be included, it is best to consider it until you learn more about your system and have determined whether the reaction can be safely ignored when you later make assumptions that can simplify your calculations. Second, it is important when you are writing a mass balance equation to always use *balanced* chemical reactions. This practice will provide you with the correct stoichiometry for each reactant and product, which, in turn, will ensure that your mass balance equation properly relates the amount of each form of your given chemical to that of its other possible forms.

Another resource we can use in helping solve equilibrium problems is a **charge balance equation**. Charge balance is an approach for solving chemical equations that makes use of the fact that the sum of all positive and negative charges in a closed system should be zero. For this situation to be true, the concentrations of all cations and anions must be balanced so their ionic charges cancel to give a net neutral charge to their solution. A simple example of a charge balance equation can be obtained by looking at water. As we have noted, even pure water will contain some charged species because water will dissociate to form hydrogen ions and hydroxide ions. However, we also know that the number of positive and negative charges must be equal so that the overall system has a net neutral charge. Pure water can have only two charged species present (H^+ and OH^-), which means we must have equal concentrations of these ions ($[H^+] = [OH^-]$) to obtain this net neutral charge.

In the case of pure water, the charge balance equation is the same as the mass balance equation (i.e., each mole of water that dissociates forms one mole of H^+ and one mole of OH^-, or $[H^+] = [OH^-]$). However, these equations are not necessarily the same for more complex solutions. For instance, if we were to also add sodium chloride to water (giving Na^+ and Cl^- ions), the mass balance equation between the hydrogen and hydroxide ions would still be $[H^+] = [OH^-]$, but the new charge balance equation would now be $[Na^+] + [H^+] = [OH^-] + [Cl^-]$.

Equation 27 gives a general relationship that can be used to write the charge balance equation for any chemical system.

$$(1) [C_1{}^{1+}] + (2) [C_2{}^{2+}] + \cdots + (n) [C_n{}^{n+}] =$$
$$(1)[A_1{}^{1-}] + \cdots + (2) [A_2{}^{2-}] + \cdots (n) [A_n{}^{n-} \cdots] \quad (27)$$

In this expression, $[C_1{}^{1+}]$, $[C_2{}^{2+}]$ and so on, refer to the concentrations of all cations in the solution, with absolute values for their charges of +1, +2, etc. Similar terms are used to represent the concentrations of all anions ($[A_1{}^{1-}]$, $[A_2{}^{2-}]$, ...) and their charges. Thus, for a solution of sodium chloride in water, the charge balance would be $(1) [Na^+] + (1) [H^+] = (1) [OH^-] + (1) [Cl^-]$. Additional practice with charge balance equations is given for you in the next exercise.

EXERCISE 9   Writing a Charge Balance Expression

Write a charge balance expression for the combined reactions in Equations 19–21 concerning the production of hydrogen ions from carbonic acid and water. How does this expression compare to the mass balance equation for all chemicals that produce hydrogen ions in this system?

SOLUTION

There is only one type of cation in this system (H^+), but there are several different anions ($HCO_3{}^-$, $CO_3{}^{2-}$, and OH^-). When we put these terms into Equation 27, we get the following result.

$$[H^+] = [HCO_3{}^-] + 2 [CO_3{}^{2-}] + [OH^-] \quad (28)$$

In this specific case, the charge balance equation is also the mass balance equation for hydrogen ions, because there is only one type of cation present in these reactions. However, if there were additional types of cations (such as Na^+ from sodium chloride), the charge balance and mass balance equations would not be the same for any of these ions. This situation would give us an additional equation that could be used to solve an equilibrium problem that involves such ions.

Other Tools. At this point we now have enough equations to solve our carbonic acid problem. These equations include three equilibrium constant expressions (Equations 23–25), one mass balance expression (Equation 26) and one charge balance equation (Equation 28). The next question we must address is *"What mathematical approach should be used to solve this problem?"* In this text, we will see several ways in which a final answer to such a problem can be obtained. We will also see that the particular tool we choose to solve a problem will depend on the complexity of this problem and the number of variables that must be considered.

The simplest chemical problem to solve is one that involves only a single reaction and one or two variables. An example is the reaction and calculations shown in Table 6, where we start with a known total amount of carbonic acid, and the dissociation of this acid is assumed to be the only source of hydrogen ions. All that is now needed to solve this problem is to take the concentration terms from Table 6 and place them into the equilibrium expression for the reaction. (*Note:* Units have been included here on K_1 for use in dimensional analysis.)

$$K_1 = \frac{[HCO_3{}^-][H^+]}{[H_2CO_3]}$$

$$4.5 \times 10^{-7} M = \frac{(x)(x)}{(0.00500 M - x)} \quad (29)$$

where $x = [HCO_3{}^-] = [H^+]$. Next, we can rearrange this equation so that all terms containing our unknown (x) appear on the same side.

$$0 = x^2 + (4.5 \times 10^{-7} M) x - (4.5 \times 10^{-7} M) \cdot$$
$$(0.00500 M) \quad (30)$$

This relationship is now written as a **quadratic equation**,[11] which is an equation where the highest-order term for "x" is x^2. The specific quadratic equation just shown is written in the general form

$$0 = Ax^2 + Bx + C \quad (31)$$

where A, B, and C are the constants that appear in front of the x^2, x, and constant terms of this equation. For instance, in Equation 30 the value of A is 1, B is $4.5 \times 10^{-7} M$ and C is $-(4.5 \times 10^{-7} M)(0.00500 M)$. It is useful to rearrange a quadratic equation into this form because the values of A, B, and C can then be used

---

TABLE 6   Use of Mass Balance in Solving a Simple Equilibrium Problem*

Reaction	H_2CO_3	$\rightleftharpoons$	$HCO_3{}^-$	+	H^+
Initial concentrations:	0.0050 M		0 M		0 M
Change in concentrations:	−x		x		x
Equilibrium concentrations:	0.0050 − x		x		x

*This type of table is also known as an *ICE table* because it lists the "initial," "change," and "equilibrium" concentrations for each reactant and product.

to solve for x by using the **quadratic formula**, as given below.[11]

$$x = \frac{-B \pm \sqrt{B^2 - 4AC}}{2A} \quad (32)$$

The "$\pm$" symbol in this equation means that there will always be two answers, or "roots," for x, one obtained when you use $-B + \sqrt{B^2 - 4AC}$ in the numerator and the other when you use $-B - \sqrt{B^2 - 4AC}$. In most chemical problems, however, only one of these roots will give a realistic answer to the problem (i.e., a value that is within the range of concentrations or values that may actually occur in your system).

EXERCISE 10   Using the Quadratic Equation

Based on the quadratic equation, what are the possible values for x in Equation 30? Based on these results, what are the approximate concentrations of carbonic acid, bicarbonate, and hydrogen ions that should be present at equilibrium for the system in Table 6?

SOLUTION

We have already seen that the values of A, B, and C in our particular example are $A = 1$, $B = 4.5 \times 10^{-7} M$, and $C = -(4.5 \times 10^{-7} M)(0.00500 M) = -2.25 \times 10^{-9} M^2$. When we substitute these values into the quadratic equation, we get the two possible answers for x.

$$First~x~value = \frac{-(4.5 \times 10^{-7}~M) +}{2(1)}$$

$$\frac{\sqrt{(-4.5 \times 10^{-7}~M)^2 - 4(1)(-2.25 \times 10^{-9}~M^2)}}{2(1)}$$

$$= 4.\underline{72} \times 10^{-5}~M$$

$$Second~x~value = \frac{-(4.5 \times 10^{-7}~M) -}{2(1)}$$

$$\frac{\sqrt{(-4.5 \times 10^{-7}~M)^2 - 4(1)(-2.25 \times 10^{-9}~M^2)}}{2(1)}$$

$$= -4.\underline{77} \times 10^{-5}~M$$

Although both of the values we obtained for x in the preceding equations make sense mathematically, from a chemical viewpoint only $x = 4.72 \times 10^{-5} M$ is reasonable, because we cannot have a negative value for $x = [HCO_3^-]$ or $[H^+]$. When we use this result with Table 6, we get the following final answers for our equilibrium concentrations when we round to the correct number of significant figures.

At Equilibrium: $[H_2CO_3] = 0.00500 - x = \mathbf{0.00495~M}$

$$[HCO_3^-] = x = \mathbf{4.7 \times 10^{-5}~M}$$

$$[H^+] = x = \mathbf{4.7 \times 10^{-5}~M}$$

In checking these results, you can see that all of the final concentrations are within a reasonable range (in this case, between 0 and 0.00500 M, because the reaction has a 1:1 stoichiometry between each reactant and product). Also, if we plug these concentrations back into the equilibrium expression for this reaction, we get back the expected equilibrium constant of 4.5×10^{-7} M.

It is possible on occasion that you may get an answer of $x = 0$ when you are using the quadratic equation to solve for the concentration or content of a chemical in an equilibrium. If this situation happens, the answer does not mean that there is none of the chemical present. You cannot have an equilibrium without having some of *both* the reactants and products present, even if they are present in only a small amount. What an answer of $x = 0$ in this case does mean is that the estimated amount of the chemical is quite small compared to other concentrations and terms in your calculation and cannot be distinguished from a value of zero with the number of digits that are being used to express this answer. There are several ways around this problem. First, see if you can use more digits (whether they are significant figures or guard digits) in your calculation; this will help to avoid problems due to rounding errors. Second, you can use the new information that you have (that the value of "x" is small compared to other values in your equations) to go back and simplify your equations. This simplification should then lead to a usable answer to your calculation.

If a reaction system is too complex to solve directly by using the quadratic formula, another approach must be used. As an example, suppose that we did not ignore the production of H^+ from water or from the dissociation of bicarbonate, as was done in Exercise 10. Instead of working with only one reaction, as illustrated in Table 6, we now must consider all of these reactions by combining the equilibrium expressions in Equations 19–21 with the mass balance and charge balance expressions derived in Equations 26 and 28. The result is the following relationship between $[H^+]$ and the other known factors (K_1, K_2, and $C_{Carbonate}$) that describe this system.

$$[H^+] = C_{Carbonate} \cdot \frac{K_1 [H^+] + 2K_1 K_2}{([H^+]^2 + K_1 [H^+] + K_1 K_2)} + \frac{1.0 \times 10^{-14} M^2}{[H^+]} \quad (33)$$

We will see in the next chapter exactly how this type of combined equation was obtained. For now, we will focus on how we can solve for the value of $[H^+]$. The quadratic equation cannot be used because we will not be able to get this expression into a form needed for this approach to work. One alternative approach that can be used in this case is to use the "solver function" found on many modern calculators. Another approach is to use a technique known as **successive approximations**.[22]

To perform successive approximations, begin by placing into your equation a rough estimate of what the concentration for the reagent or product of interest might be. In the carbonic acid example, suppose we guess that one-fifth of

TABLE 7 Example of an Equilibrium Problem Using Successive Approximations

Estimated [H$^+$], M	Calculated [H$^+$], M	Strategy for the Next Step[a]
0.001000	0.000002	Calculated value is much higher than estimate; use a smaller estimate
0.000100	0.000022	Calculated value is still much higher than estimate; decrease estimate further
0.000050	0.000045	Calculated value is slightly higher than estimate; decrease estimate slightly
0.000045	0.000050	Calculated value is slightly smaller than estimate; increase estimate slightly
0.000047	0.000047	Calculated value and estimate are the same—You have your answer!

[a]Another strategy would be to use each calculated value as the new estimated value. This approach often works well, but in this particular example this method takes a much larger number of cycles to converge on the final answer.

our 0.00500 M carbonic acid dissociates to give hydrogen ions, or [H$^+$] = 0.0010 M. As shown in Table 7, we then place this value into the right-hand side of Equation 33 and calculate the value of [H$^+$] on the left, which instead gives us a result of 0.000002 M. Because our initial guess and this calculated value for [H$^+$] are not the same, we then make a new estimate, place it into the right-hand side of Equation 33 and repeat the process. Each time we do this process, the value we calculate for [H$^+$] should hopefully get closer to our estimate until they approach the same value. At this point, the overall equation is balanced and we have arrived at our final answer, 4.7×10^{-5} M. Although this approach can take several cycles to get to a final answer, it does have the advantage of being able to work with complex equations that cannot be solved by other methods.

A third option for solving chemical equilibrium problems is to use computers to find possible answers for each calculation. This approach is used in modeling extremely complex systems, like when scientists use computers to study the fate of carbon dioxide in the atmosphere and to predict the consequences of changes in carbon dioxide levels. This approach involves the use of a program that is specially designed to solve multiple equations, such as the built-in "polynomial" or "solver" feature of a calculator. Another way computers can be employed in equilibrium calculations is by using a spreadsheet program to describe the reactions of chemical processes of interest.[22] An example of this method is shown in Figure 9, where a spreadsheet was used to determine how the concentrations of H_2CO_3, HCO_3^-, CO_3^{2-}, and

Concentrations for H_2CO_3 and related species in 0.100 M carbonic acid at various values for [H$^+$]

[H$^+$], M	K_{a1}	K_{a2}	[H$_2$CO$_3$], M	[HCO$_3^-$], M	[CO$_3^{2-}$], M
1.00E+00	4.45E−07	4.69E−11	1.00E−01	4.45E−08	2.09E−18
1.00E−01	4.45E−07	4.69E−11	1.00E−01	4.45E−07	2.09E−16
1.00E−02	4.45E−07	4.69E−11	1.00E−01	4.45E−06	2.09E−14
1.00E−03	4.45E−07	4.69E−11	1.00E−01	4.45E−05	2.09E−12
1.00E−04	4.45E−07	4.69E−11	9.96E−02	4.43E−04	2.08E−10
1.00E−05	4.45E−07	4.69E−11	9.57E−02	4.26E−03	2.00E−08
1.00E−06	4.45E−07	4.69E−11	6.92E−02	3.08E−02	1.44E−06
1.00E−07	4.45E−07	4.69E−11	1.83E−02	8.16E−02	3.83E−05
1.00E−08	4.45E−07	4.69E−11	2.19E−03	9.74E−02	4.57E−04
1.00E−09	4.45E−07	4.69E−11	2.14E−04	9.53E−02	4.47E−03
1.00E−10	4.45E−07	4.69E−11	1.53E−05	6.81E−02	3.19E−02
1.00E−11	4.45E−07	4.69E−11	3.95E−07	1.76E−02	8.24E−02
1.00E−12	4.45E−07	4.69E−11	4.69E−09	2.09E−03	9.79E−02
1.00E−13	4.45E−07	4.69E−11	4.78E−11	2.13E−04	9.98E−02
1.00E−14	4.45E−07	4.69E−11	4.79E−13	2.13E−05	1.00E−01

Formulas:

$$[H_2CO_3] = (0.100*[H^+]^2)/([H^+]^2 + K_{a1}*[H^+] + K_{a1}*K_{a2})$$

$$[HCO_3^-] = (0.100*K_{a1}*[H^+])/([H^+]^2 + K_{a1}*[H^+] + K_{a1}*K_{a2})$$

$$[CO_3^{2-}] = (0.100*K_{a1}*K_{a2})/([H^+]^2 + K_{a1}*[H^+] + K_{a1}*K_{a2})$$

FIGURE 9 Spreadsheet results predicting the change in concentration of carbonic acid and related species in an aqueous solution prepared with an initial concentration of 0.10 M carbonic acid and containing various fixed concentrations of hydrogen ions. The terms K_{a1} and K_{a2} are the equilibrium constants for the release of the first and second hydrogen ions from carbonic acid.

OH^- will change as the concentration of H^+ is fixed at various values in a solution with an analytical carbonate concentration of 0.010 M. We look at this type of system in the next chapter, and later in this text we see several other examples of how spreadsheets can be used in chemical calculations.

Key Words

Activity coefficient	Equilibrium constant	Le Châtelier's principle	Reaction quotient
Analytical concentration	Extended Debye–Hückel	Mass balance equation	Stoichiometry
Charge balance equation	equation	Quadratic equation	Successive
Chemical activity	Ionic strength	Quadratic formula	approximations
Chemical equilibrium			

Other Terms

Chemical kinetics	Debye–Hückel limiting	Mean activity coefficient	Standard state
Chemical potential	law	Salting-out effect	Thermodynamic equilib-
Chemical	Dielectric constant	Salting coefficient	rium constant
thermodynamics	Hydration layer	Standard chemical	
Concentration-dependent	Hydrated radius	potential	
equilibrium constant	Mass balance		

Questions

TYPES OF CHEMICAL REACTIONS/TRANSITIONS AND DESCRIBING CHEMICAL REACTIONS

1. What types of chemical reactions are commonly used in analytical chemistry? What are some examples of their applications?
2. What are some general factors to consider when describing a chemical reaction?
3. What is meant by "chemical thermodynamics" and "chemical kinetics"? Why are these terms important in describing chemical reactions?

WHAT IS CHEMICAL ACTIVITY?

4. Define "chemical potential" and "chemical activity." How are these terms related?
5. What is meant when we say a chemical is in its "standard state"? What is the activity of a chemical when it is present in its standard state?
6. What are the standard states for each of the following samples?
   (a) Oxygen gas
   (b) Sodium chloride crystals
   (c) Methanol as a solvent
   (d) Sodium chloride dissolved in water
   (e) Methanol dissolved in water
   (f) Helium as a trace component of air
7. What are some effects that can cause the activity for a chemical to differ from the activity for its standard state? Illustrate these effects using a solution of NaCl in water as an example.
8. Explain why water is often assigned an activity of 1.0 for an aqueous solution. Under what circumstances might the activity of water in this solution not be equal to 1.0?

9. What is an "activity coefficient"? What are the units on an activity coefficient?
10. A 0.10 molal solution of $AgNO_3$ in water that completely dissolves is found to produce an activity of 0.0734 for Ag^+ and NO_3^-. What are the activity coefficients for each of these ions?
11. If the K^+ and I^- ions in a completely dissolved sample of 0.20 molal KI each have an activity of 0.155, what are the activity coefficients for these ions?
12. Why is it important to consider the differences between chemical activity and concentration when using or creating an analytical method? What problems might arise if these differences are not considered?
13. Sodium perchlorate, $NaClO_4$, is a salt that has a high solubility in water. What is the ionic strength of an aqueous solution prepared by adding 0.20 g of this salt to 1.00 L water?
14. What is the ionic strength of a 0.100 M solution of NaCl in water? What is the ionic strength of a 0.100 M solution of Na_2SO_4 in water? Compare these ionic strengths and explain any differences in their values.
15. Determine the ionic strength for each of the following mixtures. In each case, assume that all of the salts completely dissolve and dissociate into their respective ions.
   (a) 0.10 M NaCl plus 0.20 M KI
   (b) 0.050 M $MgSO_4$ plus 0.050 M Na_2SO_4
   (c) 0.050 g KBr plus 0.100 g KCl in 1.00 L water

CHEMICAL ACTIVITY IN ANALYTICAL METHODS

16. What is the difference between a "mean activity coefficient" and a "single-ion activity coefficient"? How are these two items related to one another?

17. A solution of NaCl produces a mean activity coefficient of 0.85. If it is assumed the Na^+ and Cl^- ions have the same individual activity coefficients, what are the values of these activity coefficients?

18. A solution of K_2SO_4 has a mean activity coefficient of 0.75. What are the individual activity coefficients for K^+ and SO_4^{2-} in this solution?

19. What is the extended Debye–Hückel equation? What information is required when using this equation to estimate ion activity coefficients?

20. What form of the extended Debye–Hückel equation is used when working with a solution in water at 25°C? Under what conditions is it no longer suitable to use the extended Debye–Hückel equation?

21. Use the extended Debye–Hückel equation to estimate each of the following activity coefficients. Assume in each case that the given chemical completely dissolves to form the listed ions.
    (a) Activity coefficients for H^+ and NO_3^- in a 0.0050 M HNO_3 solution
    (b) Activity coefficients for K^+ and OH^- in a 0.020 M KOH solution
    (c) Activity coefficients for Ba^{2+} and Cl^- in a 0.010 M $BaCl_2$ solution

22. What are the expected mean activity coefficients for the solutions in Problem 21?

23. What is the Debye–Hückel limiting law (DHLL)? Use this equation to recalculate the activity coefficients in Problem 21. How do these results compare to those obtained with the extended Debye–Hückel equation?

24. How is the activity of a neutral compound altered by a change in ionic strength? How does this compare to the effect of ionic strength on activity for an ionic substance?

25. What is the "salting-out effect"? What is a "salting coefficient"?

26. Acetic acid has a salting coefficient of 0.066 in the presence of NaCl in water. What is the approximate activity coefficient for acetic acid in a 1.0 M NaCl solution under acidic conditions (where most of the acetic acid is in its original neutral form)?

27. A chemist wishes to have the activity of a neutral compound be within 1% of its concentration. If this compound has a salting coefficient of 0.15 in the presence of KNO_3, what is the maximum ionic strength that can be present in this solution for such a condition to be met?

28. Describe the following effects on activity coefficients based on the extended Debye–Hückel equation.
    (a) Charge effects
    (b) Size effects
    (c) Ionic strength effects

29. Explain how the use of a known excess of a salt such as sodium chloride could be used to maintain a constant ionic strength in a sample or reagent.

30. What is a "hydrated radius"? How is this value related to the ion size parameters used for the extended Debye–Hückel equation?

31. Explain how a calibration curve can be used by an analytical chemist to deal with changes in chemical activity.

WHAT IS A CHEMICAL EQUILIBRIUM?

32. What is meant by "chemical equilibrium"? Why is chemical equilibrium important to consider in analytical chemistry?

33. What is an "equilibrium constant" and how is this used to describe a chemical equilibrium?

34. Write equilibrium constant expressions (in terms of activity) for each of the following reactions.
    (a) $H_2SO_4 + H_2O \rightleftharpoons H_3O^+ + HSO_4^-$
    (b) $Zn^{2+} + NH_3 \rightleftharpoons Zn(NH_3)^{2+}$
    (c) $PbCl_2(s) \rightleftharpoons Pb^{2+} + 2\ Cl^-$

35. Write equilibrium constant expressions in terms of concentrations for each of the reactions in Problem 34. (*Note*: when dealing with a solid like $PbCl_2$, continue to use the activity of the given chemical in such an expression.)

36. A chemist is studying the acid dissociation of formic acid in water, as represented by the following net reaction: $HCOOH \rightleftharpoons H^+ + HCOO^-$. It is determined at 25°C that the activities of HCOOH, H^+, and $HCOO^-$ at equilibrium are 2.0×10^{-4}, 1.0×10^{-4}, and 3.6×10^{-4}. What is the equilibrium constant for this reaction under these conditions?

37. The reaction of Cd^{2+} with S^{2-} to form solid CdS is found to give a saturated solution that has activities of 8.4×10^{-14} for Cd^{2+} and S^{2-} and 1.00 for CdS. What is the equilibrium constant for this reaction?

38. How is the equilibrium constant for a reaction related to the change in standard Gibbs free energy for that reaction?

39. The reaction of aspartic acid with Ca^{2+} at 25°C has an equilibrium constant of 40. What is the change in standard Gibbs free energy for this reaction?

40. The binding of a drug with a protein is found to have an equilibrium constant of 2.3×10^5 at 37°C. What is the change in standard Gibbs free energy for this reaction?

41. What is a "reaction quotient"? How is a reaction quotient similar to an equilibrium constant? How is it different?

42. When solid silver chromate, $Ag_2CrO_4(s)$, is placed into water, some of this solid will dissolve to form Ag^+ and CrO_4^{2-} ions according to the following reaction.

$$Ag_2CrO_4(s) \rightleftharpoons 2\ Ag^+ + CrO_4^{2-}$$

This reaction has a known equilibrium constant of 2.4×10^{-12} at 25°C. If solid silver chromate is placed into a solution that contains $1.3 \times 10^{-4}\ M\ Ag^+$ and $6.3 \times 10^{-5}\ M\ CrO_4^{2-}$, what will be the reaction quotient for this process? Based on this value, in what direction will this reaction proceed as it approaches equilibrium (i.e., will it move to form more solid or to create more dissolved ions)?

43. The following reaction has an equilibrium constant of 7.1×10^2 at 25°C.

$$H_2(g) + I_2(g) \rightleftharpoons 2\ HI(g)$$

Predict the direction this reaction will shift (toward the left or right) when beginning with each of the following sets of reagents and products. Assume in each case that the chemical activities are approximately the same as the concentrations for these listed chemicals.
    (a) $[H_2] = 0.81\ M$ $[I_2] = 0.44\ M$ $[HI] = 0.58\ M$
    (b) $[H_2] = 0.078\ M$ $[I_2] = 0.033\ M$ $[HI] = 1.35\ M$
    (c) $[H_2] = 0.034\ M$ $[I_2] = 0.035\ M$ $[HI] = 1.50\ M$

SOLVING CHEMICAL EQUILIBRIUM PROBLEMS

44. What questions should you consider when setting up and solving a chemical equilibrium problem?

45. What is a "mass balance equation"? What is an "analytical concentration"? How can these tools be used to help solve a chemical equilibrium problem?

46. When phosphoric acid (H_3PO_4) is dissolved in water it can undergo a series of acid–base reactions to produce $H_2PO_4^{-}$, HPO_4^{2-}, and PO_4^{3-}. Write the mass balance equation for all species related to phosphoric acid in such a solution.

47. A 0.010 M solution of Cu^{2+} combines with a 0.030 M solution of NH_3 to form several complex ions of copper that have formulas ranging from $Cu(NH_3)^{2+}$ to $Cu(NH_3)_4^{2+}$. What are the mass balance expressions for copper and ammonia in this solution?

48. What is a "charge balance equation"? How can this be used to help solve a chemical equilibrium problem?

49. A solution is prepared by adding 0.05 M $CaCl_2$, 0.10 M $NaCl$, and 0.10 M $MgCl_2$ to water. If all of these salts completely dissolve in water, what is the charge balance equation for this solution?

50. Placing hydrogen fluoride (HF) in water results in the partial conversion of this chemical into hydrogen ions (H^+) and fluoride ions (F^-). At the same time, some of the water itself will form hydrogen ions and hydroxide ions (OH^-). Write the charge balance equation for this system.

51. What is the "quadratic formula"? It what type of situation is this formula a useful tool in solving a chemical equilibrium problem?

52. Use the quadratic formula to solve for x (reporting both possible answers) in each of the following equations.
   (a) $0 = 8x^2 + 3x + 0.10$
   (b) $8.3 \times 10^2 x^2 = 1.5 \times 10^2 - x$
   (c) $3.4x = 1.5x^2 - 2.0x + 0.8$
   (d) $2.8 \times 10^1 x^3 = 9.1 \times 10^2 x^2 + 4.5x$

53. Use the quadratic formula to solve the unknown concentration in each of the following equations.
   (a) $0 = [H^+]^2 + (2.5 \times 10^{-4})[H^+] - (3.0 \times 10^{-6})(1.0 \times 10^{-3})$ where $x = [H^+]$
   (b) $(1.0 \times 10^{-4})/[OH^-] = 5.5 \times 10^{-4} + [OH^-]$ where $x = [OH^-]$

54. What is the "method of successive approximations"? Describe how this method can be used to help solve chemical equilibrium problems.

55. Solve each of the following using the method of successive approximations.
   (a) $0 = 2x^3 + 4x^2 + x + 0.5$
   (b) $(2.5 \times 10^{-3} + x)/x = 1.0 \times 10^{-4} x^2$
   (c) $9.5x^3 = 0.25x^2 - 1.37x + 5.3$
   (d) $3.0 \times 10^3 x^2 = 4.1 \times 10^2 x^3 + 18.0$

56. Use the method of successive approximations to solve the unknown concentration for each of the equations given in Problem 53. How do these results compare to those obtained when using the quadratic formula?

CHALLENGE PROBLEMS

57. The Davies' equation (shown below) is an empirically modified version of the extended Debye–Hückel equation that can be used up to ionic strengths of approximately 0.2 M.[22]

$$\log(\gamma) = z^2 \cdot [0.15 \cdot I - \frac{0.51 \cdot \sqrt{I}}{1 + \sqrt{I}}]$$

$$= z^2 \cdot I' \quad \text{where} \quad I' = [0.15 \cdot I - \frac{0.51 \cdot \sqrt{I}}{1 + \sqrt{I}}] \quad (34)$$

(a) Use Equation 34 to estimate the individual ion activity coefficients for and in solutions of NaCl in water that range in concentration from 0 to 0.2 M.

(b) Make a plot of the values obtained in Part (a) and compare them to the results obtained with the extended Debye–Hückel equation. Under which conditions do these two equations give similar results? Under which conditions do they differ? Which approach is more accurate at moderate-to-high ionic strengths?

58. Another approach that is sometimes used to estimate the size of $K°$ from K or K from $K°$ is to take the logarithm of both sides and combine the resulting expression with the simplified Debye-Hückel expression in Equation 35.[19]

$$\log(K°) = \log(K) + [rAz_C^2 + sAz_D^2 + nAz_B^2]$$
$$\cdot (-0.51 \cdot \sqrt{I})/(1 + \sqrt{I}) \quad (35)$$

Use this equation to calculate the values for the concentration-dependent equilibrium constant in Table 4. When are the results similar? When are they different? Explain any differences you observe.

59. When chloride ions are added to a solution of silver ions the result is the formation of solid silver chloride, followed later by the formation of several soluble complexes as a large excess of chloride is added.

$$Ag^+ + Cl^- \rightleftharpoons AgCl(s)$$

$$AgCl(s) + Cl^- \rightleftharpoons AgCl_2^-$$

$$AgCl_2^- + Cl^- \rightleftharpoons AgCl_3^{2-}$$

$$AgCl_3^{2-} + Cl^- \rightleftharpoons AgCl_4^{3-}$$

Using moles as your unit of chemical content, write mass balance equations for both the silver- and chloride-containing compounds in this mixture.

60. The following formula can be used to estimate the age of an object that contains plant or animal material when this material is examined carbon-14 dating.

$$t = t_{1/2} \cdot -\frac{\ln(N_t/N_0)}{0.693} \quad (36)$$

In the equation, t is the estimated age of the sample, $t_{1/2}$ is the half-life of carbon-14, N_t is the relative amount of carbon-14 versus carbon-12 in the sample being studied, and N_0 is the relative amount of carbon-14 versus carbon-12 in a living plant or animal. The half-life of carbon-14 is 5730 years, and the relative amount of carbon-14 vs. carbon-12 in a living plant or animal is known to be approximately 1.3×10^{-12}.

(a) An ancient basket made from plant reeds is analyzed by carbon-14 dating and found to contain a ratio for carbon-14 vs. carbon-12 that is equal to 0.42×10^{-12}. What is the approximate age of this sample?

(b) The particular analysis method that is used in Part (a) can determine dates as far back as 60,000 years. This range is set by the limit of detection for carbon-14 vs. carbon-12 in the sample. What ratio of carbon-14 vs. carbon-12 will be present for a 60,000-year-old sample?

TOPICS FOR DISCUSSION AND REPORTS

61. Contact a meteorologist at a local television station, radio station, or newspaper. Discuss with him or her how chemical and physical measurements (such as pressure, humidity, and so on) are performed and used in weather forecasting. Write a report that discusses your findings.

62. There are many other general types of reactions besides those that were listed in Table 1. One example we saw briefly in this chapter was a hydration reaction, in which water will combine with a chemical to form a new "hydrated form." Below is a list of other classes of reactions. Obtain more information on one or more of these reactions and discuss how they occur. Also, try to find an example of where your reaction is used in a chemical analysis method.
    (a) Photochemical reaction
    (b) Enzymatic reaction
    (c) Ionization reaction (gas phase)
    (d) Polymerization

63. The field of paleoclimatology—the study of past climates—makes use of many techniques to look at how the composition of the atmosphere and the global temperature have changed over time. This field uses radiometric methods such as carbon-14 dating and the careful analysis of the fossil or chemical content of samples collected from the oceans, polar ice caps, or other regions of the Earth. Write a report that describes one analytical tool that is used in this field. Describe the type of information that can be gathered by the technique. Also discuss the advantages and limitations of the method.

64. Several precautions must be taken and assumptions made for carbon-14 dating to provide an accurate estimate of age for a sample. For instance, the ratio of carbon-14/carbon-12 does vary with different environments, such as air vs. the ocean. Obtain more information on carbon-14 dating and discuss the types of errors that can be present in this method. How do these errors affect the reliability of the method, and what steps must be taken to avoid or minimize these errors?

65. The use of computers in chemistry has given rise to many recent advances in our study of chemical interactions. Examine recent issues of journals such as *Scientific American*, *Science*, or *Nature* and locate an article in which computers played a major role in understanding a chemical reaction. Report on your findings.

66. One area of chemistry that frequently uses computers is research into the structures of proteins and other large biological molecules. Some researchers have used the Internet and volunteered time on many home computers to help in these efforts. Obtain information on this type of research effort. Describe, in general, how this method works and the types of chemical problems that have been examined by this approach.

67. Use Reference 25 or other sources to learn about the history behind the concept of ionic strength. Discuss how this concept was developed, and describe how it has been used over the years to characterize and study chemical reactions.

68. Learn more about the original development of the Debye–Hückel equation.[26] Describe how this equation originated and state how it has been used by chemists to help them understand chemical reactions.

References

1. P. Passell, "Global Warming Plan Would Make Emissions a Commodity," *New York Times*, October 24, 1997, p. D1.
2. Frederick K. Lutgens and Edward J. Tarbuck, *The Atmosphere: An Introduction to Meteorology*, 10th Ed., Pearson Prentice Hall, Upper Saddle River, NJ, 2007, Chapter 2.
3. *Climate Change: State of Knowledge*, Executive Office of the President, Office of Science and Technology Policy, Washington, DC, 1997. (Available on-line at http://www.usgcrp.gov/usgcrp/Library/CC-StateOfKnowledge1997.pdf)
4. C. Suplee, "Unlocking the Climate Puzzle," *National Geographic*, 1998 (193) 38–71.
5. M. Landler, "Mixed Feelings as Kyoto Pact Takes Effect," *New York Times*, February 16, 2005, p. C1.
6. A.C. Revkin, "New Warnings of Climate Change," *New York Times*, January 20, 2007, p. A7.
7. J. Haley, Ed., *Global Warming: Opposing Views*, Greenhaven Press, San Diego, CA, 2002.
8. S.G. Philander, *Is the Temperature Rising? The Uncertain Science of Global Warming*, Princeton University Press, Princeton, NJ, 1998.
9. A.C. Revkin, "Computers Add Sophistication, but Don't Resolve Climate Debate," *New York Times*, August 31, 2004, p. F3.
10. *IUPAC Compendium of Chemical Terminology*, Electronic version, http://goldbook.iupac.org
11. *The New Encyclopaedia Britannica*, 15th Ed., Encyclopaedia Britannica, Inc., Chicago, IL, 2002.
12. J. Inczedy, T. Lengyel, and A. M. Ure, *Compendium of Analytical Nomenclature*, 3rd ed., Blackwell Science, Malden, MA, 1997.
13. H. M. N. H. Irving, H. Freiser, and T. S. West, *Compendium of Analytical Nomenclature: Definitive Rules—1977*, Pergamon Press, New York, 1977.
14. B.E. Smith, *Basic Chemical Thermodynamics*, Oxford University Press, Oxford, 2004.
15. B.J. Ott and J. Buerio-Goates, *Chemical Thermodynamics—Principles and Applications*, Academic Press, New York, 2000.
16. J.H. Espenson, *Chemical Kinetics and Reaction Mechanisms*, McGraw-Hill, New York, 1981.
17. M.R. Wright, *Introduction to Chemical Kinetics*, Wiley, Hoboken, NJ, 2004.
18. E.C. Anderson, W.F. Libby, S. Weinhouse, A.F. Reid, A.D. Kirshenbau, and A.V. Grosse, "Radiocarbon from Cosmic Radiation," *Science*, 105 (1947) 576–577.
19. J.R. Arnold and W.F. Libby, "Age Determinations by Radiocarbon Content: Checks with Samples of Known Age," *Science*, 110 (1949) 678–680.
20. W.F. Libby, "Accuracy of Radiocarbon Dates," *Science*, 140 (1963) 278–280.

21. D. R. Lide, Ed., *CRC Handbook of Chemistry and Physics*, 83rd ed., CRC Press, Boca Raton, FL, 2002.

22. H. Frieser, *Concepts & Calculations in Analytical Chemistry: A Spreadsheet Approach*, CRC Press, Boca Raton, FL, 1992.

23. P. Debye and E. Hückel, "The Theory of Electrolytes. I. Lowering of Freezing Point and Related Phenomena," *Physikalische Zeitshrift*, 24 (1923) 185–206.

24. P. Debye and E. Hückel, "The Theory of Electrolytes. II," *Physikalische Zeitshrift*, 24 (1923) 305–325.

25. M.E. Sastre de Vicente, "The Concept of Ionic Strength Eighty Years After Its Introduction in Chemistry," *Journal of Chemical Education*, 81 (2004) 750–753.

26. B. Naiman, "The Debye-Hückel Theory and its Application in the Teaching of Quantitative Analysis," *Journal of Chemical Education*, 26 (1949) 280–282.

Selected Answers

6

  a. Pure oxygen gas at a pressure of one bar (formerly 1 atm)

  b. Pure sodium chloride crystals

  c. Pure liquid methanol

  d. A 1.00 M solution of NaCl in water

  e. A 1.00 M solution of methanol in water

  f. Pure helium gas at a pressure of one bar (formerly 1 atm)

10 Activity coefficients = 0.734

13 $I = 0.00163\ M$

14 I for NaCl solution = 0.100 M; I for Na_2SO_4 solution = 0.300 M

17 The individual activity coefficients for Na^+ and Cl^- are both approximately 0.85 in this case.

21

  a. Activity coefficient for H^+ = 0.93; activity coefficient for NO_3^- = 0.92

  b. Activity coefficient for K^+ = 0.86; activity coefficient for OH^- = 0.87

  c. Activity coefficient for Ba^{2+} = 0.53; activity coefficient for Cl^- = 0.84

22

  a. Mean activity coefficient = 0.92$\underline{5}$

  b. Mean activity coefficient = 0.86$\underline{5}$

  c. Mean activity coefficient = 0.61$\underline{8}$

26 $\gamma = 1.16$

34

  a. $K° = (a_{H_3O^+})(a_{HSO_4^-})/(a_{H_2SO_4})(a_{H_2O})$

  b. $K° = (a_{Zn(NH_3)_2+})/(a_{Zn^2+})(a_{NH_3})$

  c. $K° = (a_{Pb^2+})(a_{Cl^-})^2/(a_{PbCl_2})$

35

  a. $K = [H_3O^+][HSO_4^-]/[H_2SO_4]$

  b. $K = [Zn(NH_3)^{2+}]/[Zn^{2+}][NH_3]$

  c. $K = [Pb^{2+}][Cl^-]^2$

36 $K = (3.6 \times 10^{-4})(1.0 \times 10^{-4})/(2.0 \times 10^{-4}) = 1.8 \times 10^{-4}$

39 $\Delta G° = -9{,}140\ J/mol$

42 $Q = 1.1 \times 10^{-12}$; this value is smaller than the equilibrium constant, so some of the solid will dissolve to form more aqueous ions.

46 $C_{Phosphoric\ acid} = [H_3PO_4] + [H_2PO_4^-] + [HPO_4^{2-}] + [PO_4^{3-}]$

49 $2\ [Ca^{2+}] + [Na^+] + 2\ [Mg^{2+}] = [Cl^-]$

52

  a. Roots for x, $-0.33\underline{8}$ and $-0.037\underline{0}$

  b. Roots for x, $0.42\underline{4}$ and $-0.42\underline{6}$

  c. Roots for x, $3.3\underline{4}$ and $0.15\underline{5}$

  d. First divide all terms by x, and then obtain the roots for x, $32.\underline{5}$ and $-0.0049\underline{4}$

55

  a. $x = -1.8$

  b. $x = -2.5 \times 10^{-3}$

  c. $x = 0.77$

  d. $x = 0.0779$

An Introduction to Electrochemical Analysis

From Chapter 14 of *Analytical Chemistry and Quantitative Analysis*, First Edition. David S. Hage, James D. Carr. Copyright © 2011 by Pearson Education, Inc. Published by Pearson Prentice Hall.

An Introduction to Electrochemical Analysis

Chapter Outline

1 INTRODUCTION: GETTING A BRIGHTER SMILE

In the 1940s it was found that children in some regions of the world had fewer cavities and less tooth decay than children from other areas. This difference was eventually found to be due to the presence of fluoride in the drinking water. Many public drinking-water systems in the United States now either contain fluoride as a natural component or have fluoride added to the water to prevent cavities. This practice has been listed by the U.S. Centers for Disease Control as one of the ten greatest public health achievements of the twentieth century[1,2] (see Figure 1).

It is important when fluoride is being added to drinking water (or to products such as toothpaste) to ensure that just the right amount of this chemical is present. This means water-treatment facilities must regularly measure the level of fluoride that is present in drinking water. Such a measurement is now carried out using an electrode that can selectively measure fluoride ions.[3] Prior to the development of this electrode, the measurement of fluoride in water was based on a time-consuming, colorimetric assay. However, this measurement can now be easily made on a routine basis or even in a continuous manner by measuring the electrical potential that is formed between the fluoride-selective electrode and a reference electrode in the presence of drinking water or the desired sample.

The study of electrochemical reactions and their applications is a field known as "electrochemistry." In this chapter we refer to the use of electrochemistry for the analysis of chemicals as **electrochemical analysis**. There are many types of methods that can be employed for electrochemical analysis. For instance, the approach used with the fluoride electrode is a method known as *potentiometry*. In this chapter we will learn the basic concepts and terms that are used in the field of electrochemical analysis. We will then look in more detail at the method of potentiometry, including a discussion of how pH, fluoride ion activities, or concentrations and other chemical measurements can be made by this technique.

1A Units of Electrical Measurements

Before we begin to look at potentiometry and other techniques for electrochemical analysis, we first need to consider several important quantities that are measured or used in these techniques. Table 1 provides a summary of fundamental SI units and derived SI units that are used in electrochemical measurements.[4,5] One property that is commonly used, measured, or controlled in electrochemical methods is **charge**. The term "charge" is defined in this type of application as being equal to the integral of electrical current over time.

FIGURE 1 The analysis of fluoride as a means to monitor and control fluoridation in drinking water in public water systems in the United States. The instrument shown on the right is designed for the continuous analysis of fluoride in water by using a fluoride ion-selective electrode to measure this analyte. (The photo on the left is provided courtesy of the U.S. Centers for Disease Control; the photo on the right is provided courtesy and with permission from Thermo Fisher.)

Charge is represented by the symbol Q and is described in the SI system by using a unit known as the coulomb (C).

The smallest quantity of an elementary charge (represented by the symbol e) is the "+1" charge that is associated with a single proton or the "−1" charge that is present on a single electron.[6] The presence of a large number of charged particles can be described in terms of coulombs, where one mole of electrons is equal to a charge of 96,485 C. This particular value of 96,485 C/mol is called the *Faraday constant* (F), and exactly one mole of electrons is sometimes called one "Faraday."[6] The value of the Faraday constant can be used to determine moles of electrons (n_e)

that are needed to provide a certain charge, as shown by Equation 1.

$$Q = n_e F \tag{1}$$

Based on this equation, the charge on one electron can be written as $Q = (1 \text{ mol}/6.023 \times 10^{23}) \cdot (96,485 \text{ C/mol}) = 1.602 \times 10^{-19}$ C.

Another property that is often used or measured in electrochemical methods is current. **Current**, which is represented by the symbol I, is a measure of the amount of electrical charge that flows through a conducting medium in a given amount of time. The fundamental SI unit for current is the ampere (A, or "amp"). Many electrochemical

TABLE 1 SI Units and Derived SI Units for Electrochemical Measurements

Measured Quantity (symbol)	Unit (symbol)	Relationship to Other SI Units
Electric current (I)	ampere (A)	Fundamental SI unit[a]
Electric charge (Q)	coulomb (C)	$1 \text{ C} = 1 \text{ A} \cdot \text{s}$
Electric potential (E)	volt (V)	$1 \text{ V} = 1 \text{ W/A} = 1 \text{ J/A} \cdot \text{s}$
Electric resistance (R)	ohm (Ω)	$1 \Omega = 1 \text{ V/A}$
Time (t)	second (s)	Fundamental SI unit[b]
Frequency	hertz (Hz)	$1 \text{ Hz} = 1/\text{s}$

[a]One ampere is defined as the constant current that produces a force of 2×10^{-7} newton per meter of length when maintained in two straight parallel conductors of infinite length and negligible circular cross section that are placed one meter apart in a vacuum.

[b]One second is defined as the amount of time equal to 9,192,631,770 periods of the radiation corresponding to the transition between the two hyperfine levels of the ground state of cesium-133.

techniques involve small currents, so the related units of milliamps ($mA = 10^{-3}$ A) and microamps ($\mu A = 10^{-6}$ A) are often used in these methods.[5–7]

Current is related to charge and the amount of time (t) it takes this charge to pass through a system. This relationship for a system with a constant current is as follows,

$$I = Q/t \quad \text{or} \quad Q = I \cdot t \tag{2}$$

where the expression on the right is a reminder that charge is really the integral of current over time.[6–8] Based on the preceding equations, the current for an electrochemical measurement is sometimes given in units of coulombs per second (C/s), where 1 A = 1 C/s. Alternatively, it can also be said from the expressions in Equation 2 that $1\,C = 1\,A \cdot s$.

EXERCISE 1 — Relating Current and Charge

An electrochemical cell has a constant current of 250 μA that is allowed to flow through a wire for 220.0 s. What is the charge (in units of C) that was allowed to pass through this system? How many moles of electrons must have passed through the wire to produce this current and charge?

SOLUTION

We can first find the charge that passed through this system by using the known current and time of current flow along with the right-hand expression in Equation 2. (*Note:* To obtain a final answer for charge with units of "coulombs" it is necessary to make sure the current is expressed in units of amps and the time is given in seconds.)

$$Q = I \cdot t$$
$$= (250 \times 10^{-6}\,A)(220.0\,s) = \mathbf{5.50 \times 10^{-2}\,C}$$

We can then determine how many moles of electrons were needed to produce this change by using Equation 1 and the Faraday constant.

$$n_e = Q/F$$
$$= (5.50 \times 10^{-2}\,C)/(96{,}485\,C/mol)$$
$$= 5.70 \times 10^{-7}\,\text{mol electrons}$$

The preceding exercise and Equation 2 indicate that time is another important parameter in many types of electrochemical measurements. In this chapter, we represent time by the symbol t and use the fundamental SI unit of the second (s) to describe this parameter. A closely related term to time is *frequency*, which is a measure of how many cycles of an event occur per unit of time. Frequency is expressed in the SI system in units of hertz (Hz), where 1 Hz = 1/s.

Another factor that is controlled or measured in electrochemical methods is *electrical potential* (or the "potential"). Electric potential defined as a measure of the work that is required to bring a charge from one point to another. The difference in electrical potential between two points (E) is expressed in the unit of volts (V) in the SI system. Recall the use of the differences in electrical potential to describe electrochemical cells. This definition is reflected in Table 1 by the way in which the unit of volt is related to other SI units, where 1 volt is equal to 1 watt of power per ampere. A term that can be used in place of potential in an electrochemical cell that has no appreciable current flowing is the *electromotive force*, or "emf." In each of these situations, the electrical potential represents the driving force behind the movement of electrons through a conducting medium.[4–8]

Whenever there is an electrical potential that creates a flow of current, there will also be some resistance to this flow of current. This **resistance (R)** is expressed in a unit called the "ohm," as represented by the capital Greek letter omega (Ω, where $1\,\Omega = 1\,V/A$). The reciprocal of resistance ($1/R$) is known as the *conductance*, a value that is commonly given in units of the "mho" (Ω^{-1}, where $1\,\Omega^{-1} = A/V$) or the siemen (S).

The potential, current, and resistance for an electrochemical system are all related through **Ohm's law**, which is shown in the following formula.

$$Ohm's\ law:\quad E = I \cdot R \tag{3}$$

With Ohm's law it is possible to directly relate the potential of an electrical system to the current and resistance to current flow. This relationship makes Ohm's law valuable in finding one of these three factors if the other two parameters in Equation 3 are already known. Such a relationship can be quite valuable in the design and description of systems for electrochemical analysis.

EXERCISE 2 — Using Ohm's Law

If the resistance of the wire in Exercise 2 was 1000. ohms, what electric potential must have been present to create a constant current of 250. μA?

SOLUTION

We know the current (250×10^{-6} A) and the resistance in this case, so we can use Ohm's law to also find the electric potential.

$$E = I \cdot R$$
$$= (250. \times 10^{-6}\,A)(1000.\,\Omega) = \mathbf{2.50 \times 10^{-2}\,V}$$

Notice in this calculation that a value with units of volts is obtained if I is given in units of amps and R is given in ohms (Ω). We can show that this should be the case through dimensional analysis by using these units for I and R, because $(1\,A)(1\,\Omega) = (1\,A)(1\,V/A) = 1\,V$.

There are two types of current that can be used in electrical systems and in methods for electrochemical analysis. If the direction of electron movement and the current always proceed in the same direction, the current is called a *direct current* (*DC*). Most of the electrochemical methods discussed in this text make use of this type of current, but there are other methods that instead use an *alternating current* (AC).[9,10] In a system with an alternating current, the direction of the movement of electrons reverses at a regular rate. Batteries are examples of power supplies that produce a DC current, while the electricity used in most houses is based on an AC current, in which the direction of the current is alternated with a sinusoidal frequency of 60 Hz, or 60 cycles per second.

1B Methods for Electrochemical Analysis

There are many methods for electrochemical analysis. Table 2 summarizes several of the main types of electrochemical analysis techniques and lists the methods that we discuss in this text. The first of these methods is potentiometry. **Potentiometry** is a technique for electrochemical analysis that is based on the measurement of a cell potential with essentially zero current passing through the system.[7–10] This measured potential is related to the chemical composition of the two electrodes and the solutions into which they are placed. Potentiometry is the type of electrochemical method that forms the basis for use of the fluoride electrode and the pH electrode. This is also the technique we will focus on in the remainder of this chapter.

A special subcategory potentiometry is a *potentiometric titration*. This approach utilizes a potential measurement to follow the course of a titration as various amounts of titrant are combined with the analyte.[7,8] We have already seen several examples of potentiometric titrations, where we discussed the use of a pH meter to follow the course of an acid–base titration.

Two additional and related methods for electrochemical analysis are the techniques of amperometry and voltammetry. In **amperometry**, the current passing through an electrochemical cell is measured at a fixed potential. In **voltammetry**, the current is also measured but the potential is now varied over time.[7–10] The cell potential can be changed in a variety of ways, which creates a large number of subcategories for methods that all involve the use of voltammetry. Some examples of these subcategories that we will consider include DC voltammetry, anodic stripping voltammetry, and cyclic voltammetry.

A third type of method for electrochemical analysis is **coulometry**. This technique uses the measurement of charge for chemical analysis.[7,10] For example, the amount of current that is needed to completely reduce a particular analyte can be measured under conditions in which no other material undergoes reduction. The number of moles of electrons needed to produce this current is then calculated and used to find the moles of analyte that have been reduced. The same type of approach can be used to look at the oxidation of a chemical.

2 GENERAL PRINCIPLES OF POTENTIOMETRY

2A Cell Potentials and the Nernst Equation

Any chemical analysis that is carried out by using potentiometry will involve the measurement of a difference in potential between two electrodes in an electrochemical cell. Figure 2 shows a general cell that could be used in potentiometry. These components include the same basic features for other electrochemical cells. This type of system includes at least two electrodes, identified here as an indicator electrode and a reference electrode, which act as the cathode and anode. Each electrode is in contact with either the sample (in the case of the "indicator electrode") or a reference solution (in the case of the "reference electrode"). There is also usually some type of salt bridge present to provide contact between these two parts of the electrochemical cell. The circuit is completed by making an electrical contact between the two electrodes, which also provides a means for measuring the difference in potential across the cell.

It is important to remember from the definition of potentiometry that measurements in this method are made under conditions in which essentially zero current

TABLE 2 Examples of Methods for Electrochemical Analysis

Method	Definition[a]
Potentiometry	A method in which cell potential is measured, and used for chemical analysis, under conditions giving essentially zero flow of current
Amperometry	A method in which current is measured, and used for chemical analysis, at a constant cell potential
Voltammetry	A method in which current is measured, and used for chemical analysis, as the cell potential is varied
Coulometry	A method in which charge is measured and used for chemical analysis

[a]These definitions are based on those found in J. Inczedy, T. Lengyel, and A.M. Ure, *International Union of Pure and Applied Chemistry—Compendium of Analytical Nomenclature: Definitive Rules 1997*, Blackwell Science, Malden, MA.

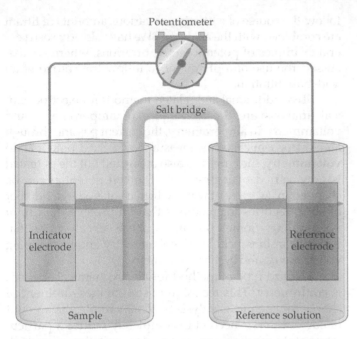

Potentiometer

Salt bridge

Indicator electrode

Reference electrode

Sample

Reference solution

FIGURE 2 The general components of an electrochemical cell for potentiometry. In many types of electrodes for potentiometry, several of these components are combined in the electrode design. For example, the salt bridge is often present as a porous frit on the side of the indicator electrode. In other cases, both electrodes and the salt bridge are used as part of a "combination electrode," as discussed in Section 3A.

is flowing through this system. This means that although an oxidation–reduction reaction may have the potential to go from reactants to products, the resistance of the electrical circuit that is used to measure this potential is high enough to prevent this reaction from occurring to any significant extent during the measurement.

The potential for each electrode in an electrochemical cell can be described in terms of the standard electrode potential for the half-reaction occurring at that electrode and the activities or concentrations of the species that are involved in this half-reaction. This relationship for a reversible half-reaction like the one in Equation 4 at 25°C is given by the Nernst equation in Equation 5.

General Half-Reaction:
$$Ox + n\,e^- \rightleftarrows Red \qquad (4)$$

Nernst Equation at 25°C:
$$E = E° - \frac{0.05916\ V}{n} \log\left[\frac{a_{Red}}{a_{Ox}}\right] \qquad (5)$$

If we use the Nernst equation to find the expected potentials at both the cathode and anode in an electrochemical cell, the difference in potential measured between these electrodes will be given by Equation 6 if essentially no current is present.

$$E_{Cell} = E_{Cathode} - E_{Anode} \qquad (6)$$

The **indicator electrode** in an electrochemial cell for potentiometry is the electrode that is in contact with the sample and gives a potential related to the activity and concentration of the analyte. The reference electrode provides a fixed potential against which the potential of the indicator electrode can be measured. By convention, the reference electrode is initially assigned the role of the "anode" in an electrochemical cell used for potentiometry and the indicator electrode is assigned the role of the "cathode." This assignment means that Equation 7 can also be written in the following form during a measurement that is performed by potentimetry,

$$E_{Cell} = E_{Ind} - E_{Ref} \qquad (7)$$

where E_{Ind} and E_{Ref} are now the potentials present at the indicator electrode and reference electrode, respectively, and E_{Cell} is the difference in potential that is measured between these electrodes.[7,10]

Measurements in potentiometry deal with galvanic cells, in which we are measuring the potential of a cell as it approaches equilibrium by undergoing a spontaneous oxidation–reduction reaction. This type of cell should have a value for E_{Cell} that is either positive (indicating it has not yet reached equilibrium) or zero (indicating that equilibrium is present in the cell). A cell potential that is determined by potentiometry to give a "negative" value for E_{Cell} simply means that the roles of the two electrodes are actually the opposite of those that have been assigned to them (i.e., the indicator electrode is actually the anode and reference electrode is actually the cathode), or that the overall oxidation–reduction reaction for this cell will occur in the opposite direction to that in which it is currently written.

2B Cell Components in Potentiometry

Reference Electrodes. The reference electrode that is used in potentiometry plays the same role that it does in any type of electrochemical cell. This purpose is to provide a reproducible, known, and constant potential against which the potential of another electrode can be measured. Although the standard hydrogen electrode (SHE) is the ultimate reference electrode against which all other potentials are compared, the SHE is far too inconvenient for general use. This problem is due to the reaction components that are needed for the SHE, as indicated by the following half-reaction for this electrode.

Standard Hydrogen Electrode:
$$2\,H^+ + 2\,e^- \rightleftarrows H_2 \quad E° = 0.000...\ V \qquad (8)$$

A SHE must have both hydrogen ions and hydrogen gas at an activity of 1.000. This is easy to achieve for the hydrogen ions, but work with hydrogen gas is more difficult and requires that hydrogen gas at a pressure of 1 bar be present around a platinum electrode. In addition, the platinum electrode is coated with a very porous form of platinum called "platinum black" that can absorb materials besides H_2 or H^+. These other materials can lead to "poisoning" of the platinum electrode and alter its properties, creating a system that no longer gives a reproducible potential.

Two more convenient and useful reference electrodes for potentiometry are those based on the **silver/silver chloride electrode** and the **calomel electrode** (or the mercury/mercury chloride electrode, in which "calomel" is another name for mercury(I) chloride). The half-reactions for these two electrodes are given below.

Silver/silver chloride electrode:

$$AgCl + e^- \rightleftarrows Ag + Cl^- \quad E° = 0.2222 \text{ V} \quad (9)$$

Calomel electrode:

$$Hg_2Cl_2 + 2\,e^- \rightleftarrows 2\,Hg + 2\,Cl^- \quad E° = 0.268 \text{ V} \quad (10)$$

The general designs of these electrodes are shown in Figure 3 and Figure 4. In each of these electrodes, an insoluble chloride salt coats the free element (Ag or Hg) and both the salt and free element are immersed in a KCl solution of known concentration (often saturated KCl). A calomel electrode that contains a saturated solution of KCl is also known as a *saturated calomel electrode (SCE)*, which has a potential of 0.242 V at 25°C.[7–10]

Indicator Electrodes. There are many indicator electrodes that can be used in potentiometry. These indicator electrodes can be divided into several categories based on how their signal is related to the activity of an analyte.[7,10] Table 3 lists four classes of indicator electrodes that make use of a metal. One possibility is the use of an inert metal as an electrode to oxidize or reduce another substance. This type of indicator electrode is known as a *metallic indicator electrode* and is made from a material such as platinum, palladium, or gold. An example of this type of electrode would be if we used a platinum wire as a cathode to reduce Fe^{3+} to Fe^{2+}. The half-reaction and Nernst equation for this part of the half-reaction are shown below.

Reduction Half-Reaction: $\quad Fe^{3+} + e^- \rightleftarrows Fe^{2+} \quad (11)$

Nernst Equation at 25°C:

$$E_{Fe^{3+}/Fe^{2+}} = E°_{Fe^{3+}/Fe^{2+}} - \frac{0.05916 \text{ V}}{1} \log \left[\frac{a_{Fe^{2+}}}{a_{Fe^{3+}}} \right] \quad (12)$$

Notice in the preceding equations that only Fe^{3+} and Fe^{2+} are shown as taking part in the half-reaction and measured response of this electrode. The reason for this is that the platinum electrode is merely acting as a source of electrons for this half-reaction but is not changed itself as part of this redox process.

A *class one electrode* ("electrode of the first kind") consists of a metal that is in contact with a solution that contains metal ions of that element. This type of electrode is used to produce a potential that is related to the activity of the metal ions in the solution-phase sample. An example of this type of electrode would be a silver wire that is immersed in a solution of silver nitrate. The potential of this electrode will depend on the activity and concentration of the Ag^+ ions in solution, as indicated by the Nernst equation for this electrode. (*Note:* An activity of 1.0 is used for Ag(s) in the Nernst equation because this represents a standard state for silver.)

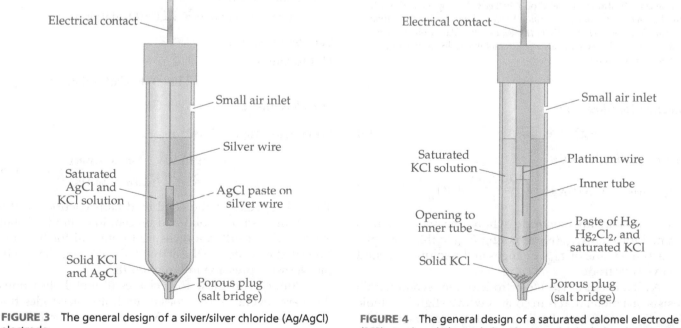

FIGURE 3 The general design of a silver/silver chloride (Ag/AgCl) electrode.

FIGURE 4 The general design of a saturated calomel electrode (SCE). A calomel electrode has the same basic design, but does not have solid KCl at the bottom. The calomel electrode has a lower, but fixed and known concentration of KCl instead of a saturated KCl solution.

TABLE 3   General Types of Indicator Electrodes Based on Metals

Type of Electrode[a]	Definition
Metallic redox indicator	An electrode made from an inert material such as platinum, palladium, or gold
Example:	A platinum electrode that serves as a site for electron exchange between Fe^{3+} and Fe^{2+}
Class one electrode	An electrode made of metal in contact with a solution that contains metal ions of the same element
Example:	A silver electrode in a solution that contains Ag^+
Class two electrode	An electrode made of metal in contact with a slightly soluble salt of that metal and in a solution containing the anion of the salt
Example:	A silver wire in contact with $AgCl(s)$ and in a solution that contains chloride ions
Class three electrode	An electrode made of metal in contact with a salt of the metal ion (or a complex of this metal ion) and a second, coupled reaction involving a similar salt (or complex) with a different metal ion
Example:	A lead wire in contact with insoluble lead oxalate, which is in contact with a solution that contains Ca^{2+} and in contact with insoluble calcium oxalate

[a]These classifications are based on J. Inczedy, T. Lengyel, and A. M. Ure, *International Union of Pure and Applied Chemistry—Compendium of Analytical Nomenclature: Definitive Rules 1997*, Blackwell Science, Malden, MA. This scheme also calls a metallic redox indicator a "class zero electrode."

Reduction Half-Reaction:

$$Ag^+ + e^- \rightleftharpoons Ag(s) \qquad (13)$$

Nernst Equation at 25°C:

$$E_{Ag^+/Ag(s)} = E°_{Ag^+/Ag(s)} - \frac{0.05916 \text{ V}}{1} \log \left[\frac{1}{a_{Ag^+}}\right] \qquad (14)$$

This results in an electrode where the value that is obtained for $E_{Ag^+/Ag(s)}$ (representing E_{Ind} in this example) varies as the value of a_{Ag^+} changes in the solution around the silver electrode.

A *class two electrode* ("electrode of the second kind") consists of a metal that is in contact with a slightly soluble salt of that metal and that is in a solution containing the anion of this salt. An example of a class 2 electrode would be a silver wire that is in contact with $AgCl(s)$ and that is immersed in a solution that contains chloride ions (the

anion that reacts with Ag^+ to form solid AgCl). The combined half-reaction and modified Nernst equation that we get for this overall process is shown below.

Reduction Half-Reaction: $Ag^+ + e^- \rightleftharpoons Ag(s)$

Solubility Reaction: $AgCl(s) \rightleftharpoons Ag^+ + Cl^-$

Combined Half-Reaction:

$$AgCl(s) + e^- \rightleftharpoons Ag(s) + Cl^- \qquad (15)$$

Overall Nernst Equation at 25°C:

$$E_{AgCl(s)/Ag(s)} = E°_{Ag^+/Ag(s)} - \frac{0.05916 \text{ V}}{1} \log \left[\frac{a_{Cl^-}}{K_{sp,AgCl}}\right] \qquad (16)$$

The result of this system is an electrode that now gives a response that is related to the activity of the anion (Cl^-) that is present in the surrounding solution.

A *class three electrode* ("electrode of the third kind") uses a metal electrode that is in contact with a salt of its metal ion (or a complex of this metal ion) and a second, coupled reaction involving a similar salt (or complex) with a different metal ion. This type of electrode is illustrated by the use of a lead wire that is in contact with insoluble lead oxalate, which in turn is in contact with a solution that contains Ca^{2+} and is in contact with insoluble calcium oxalate.

Reduction Half-Reaction:

$$Pb^{2+} + 2 e^- \rightleftharpoons Pb(s)$$

Solubility Reaction:

$$Pb(Oxalate)(s) \rightleftharpoons Pb^{2+} + Oxalate^{2-}$$

Precipitation Reaction:

$$Ca^{2+} + Oxalate^{2-} \rightleftharpoons Ca(Oxalate)(s)$$

Combined Half-Reaction:

$$Pb(Oxalate)(s) + Ca^{2+} + 2 e^- \rightleftharpoons Pb(s) + Ca(Oxalate)(s) \qquad (17)$$

Overall Nernst Equation at 25°C:

$$E_{Pb(Oxalate)(s)/Pb(s)} = E°_{Pb^{2+}/Pb(s)}$$
$$- \frac{0.05916 \text{ V}}{2} \left[\frac{K_{sp,Ca(Oxalate)}}{K_{sp,Pb(Oxalate)} \, a_{Ca^{2+}}}\right] \qquad (18)$$

The only species in the combined half-reaction for this system that is not a solid and present in a standard state is Ca^{2+}. The result is a measured potential for the electrode that is related to the activity of Ca^{2+}, as indicated by the Nernst expression in Equation 18.

Along with these four classes of metal electrodes, there are several other types of indicator electrodes that can be used in potentiometry. Most of these other indicator electrodes use a thin film or membrane as a recognition element to detect a particular analyte. We will come back to this other group of indicator electrodes in Section 3 when we discuss the pH electrode and other ion-selective electrodes.

Salt Bridges and Junction Potentials. If two electrodes are placed into separate solutions and connected to a potentiometer, no reading can be made. This occurs because some contact must be present between the two solutions. This contact is needed to allow the flow of ions to complete the electrical circuit. However, we do not want the solution by the reference electrode to be contaminated by the sample that is in contact with the indicator electrode. This problem can be solved by using a salt bridge to connect the two half-cells of this system and yet keep the contents of each half-cell separate.

A salt bridge can take many shapes but is often in the form of a U-shaped glass tube (see Figure 2). This tube is filled with agar that contains an aqueous solution of potassium chloride. Agar is a gel that will prevent mixing of solutions on either side of the salt bridge, while the solution within the agar will allow ions to travel between these solutions. When a solution in a half-cell on one side of this salt bridge begins to be depleted of negative charge, chloride ions from the salt bridge will migrate to this electrode to reestablish charge neutrality. At the same time, potassium ions in the salt bridge will move in the other direction to counter the excess of negative charge that has begun to appear at the other electrode. Potassium chloride is often used as a component of a salt bridge because K^+ and Cl^- ions have similar ionic mobilities in an aqueous environment. This feature means these ions will each be able to carry about the same amount of current in an aqueous solution and in the salt bridge. There are some situations in which salts other than KCl are used in the salt bridge. For instance, a salt other than KCl is needed when work is being carried out with a solution that contains Ag^+, which will precipitate in the presence of Cl^-.

Although salt bridges are necessary in most electrochemical cells, they do create an additional problem when this cell is being used for potentiometry. This problem arises from the creation of a **junction potential** at each interface between the salt bridge and one of the solutions. A junction potential is present whenever two solutions or regions exist in an electrochemical cell that have different chemical compositions.[9,10] Figure 5 shows an example of a *liquid junction potential*, which forms between two solutions of different composition, such as when an electrode is in an aqueous solution of 0.10 M HCl and this solution is in contact with an aqueous solution of 0.10 M NaCl that is in contact with a second electrode. At the boundary between these solutions there will be movement of ions across the interface to equalize the concentrations on each side. The rate of this movement due to a difference in concentration (known as "diffusion") will depend on the types of ions that are present on either side of the interface and their concentrations on each side.

In the example shown in Figure 5, chloride ions are already present at the same concentration in both solutions, so these ions will have no net movement across the boundary between these solutions. However, the concentrations of H^+ and Na^+ do differ from one side to the next, so some of these ions will tend to migrate to the other solution. Even though H^+ and Na^+ originally have equal concentrations in their respective solutions in Figure 5, H^+ has a much faster rate of travel in water than Na^+. This fact means H^+ will tend to travel across the solution boundary and into the NaCl solution faster than Na^+ can enter the HCl solution. The result of this initial process is that the charge at the boundary on the HCl side becomes slightly more negative than the side of the

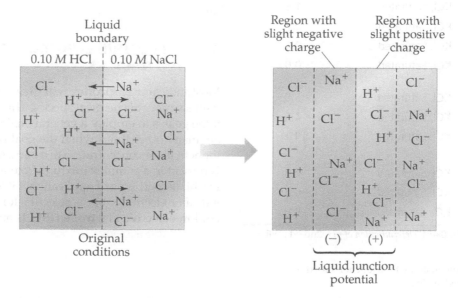

FIGURE 5 An example of the creation of a liquid junction potential.

An Introduction to Electrochemical Analysis

boundary that faces the NaCl solution. This difference in charge represents a small change in electrical potential that creates a junction potential.

Table 4 provides some examples of values for liquid junction potentials. These values are typically in the range of 5 to 30 mV. A liquid junction potential can be present even between two solutions that contain the same chemical but at different concentrations, as shown in Table 4 for various solutions of KCl that form a boundary with a saturated KCl solution. It is important to consider liquid junction potentials in potential measurements because this factor will contribute to the overall difference in a potential that is observed for an electrochemical cell. This effect is given by the following equation,

$$E_{Cell,Observed} = E_{Cell} + E_{Liq\ junction} \qquad (19)$$

in which $E_{Cell,Observed}$ is the experimentally measured cell potential, E_{Cell} is the true potential difference between the cathode and anode, and $E_{Liq\ junction}$ is the contribution due to a liquid junction potential. The exact size of the liquid junction potential is often an unknown quantity in an electrochemical cell. However, the size of this potential can be minimized by using in a salt bridge a salt like KCl that has a cation and anion with similar ionic mobilities. There are also cases in which a junction potential is intentionally created and used for chemical analysis. An example of this occurs in the use of a pH electrode, as is discussed in the next section.

TABLE 4 Examples of Liquid Junction Potentials*

Composition of Solutions at Boundary

Solution A	Solution B	Liquid Junction Potential (mV)[a]
KCl, 0.1 M	KCl, Saturated	1.8
KCl, 1.0 M	KCl, Saturated	0.7
KCl, 4.0 M	KCl, Saturated	0.1
KCl, Saturated	KCl, Saturated	0.0
HCl, 0.01 M	KCl, Saturated	3.0
HCl, 0.1 M	KCl, Saturated	4.6
HCl, 4.0 M	KCl, Saturated	14.1
NaOH, 0.01 M	KCl, Saturated	2.3
NaOH, 0.1 M	KCl, Saturated	−0.4
NaOH, 1.0 M	KCl, Saturated	−8.6

*These data are from R.G. Bates, *Determination of pH*, 2nd ed., Wiley, New York, 1973.

[a]These liquid junction potentials are for a junction based on Solution A | KCl, Saturated at 25°C.

2C Applications of Potentiometry

There are a number of applications for potentiometry in chemical analysis. One of the most common and powerful of these applications is the use of the potential measurements to give direct information on the activity or concentration of an analyte in a sample. The most successful use of potentiometry for this type of application is in pH measurements. This success is partly a result of the availability of inexpensive and reliable equipment for making such measurements (see Box 1 and Figure 6 regarding the invention of the pH meter).[11,12] Another reason for the success of potentiometry in this area is the selectivity with which pH measurements can be made by this approach. In the next section we consider how a pH electrode works and learn the reason why it has such a high selectivity for hydrogen ions.

Direct analyte measurements are not the only application for potentiometry. A closely related application is the use of potential measurements to follow the course of a titration, as occurs in a potentiometric titration. This approach is carried out by using an appropriate reference electrode and indicator electrode to follow the progress of a titration.

Potentiometry can also be combined with other methods for analyte detection. Two examples are the use of potential measurements to monitor electroactive analytes in samples that are being processed by flow-injection analysis or liquid chromatography. In both these techniques, potentiometry can be used to measure the concentration of certain analytes as they exit from a tube or column. In flow-injection analysis, the same analyte is measured in a sequence of samples that are being injected onto a flow-based system. In liquid chromatography, there are often several possible analytes in the same sample that are separated before detection is carried out by potentiometry. In either case, a graph of potential versus time can be prepared to show the amount of electroactive analytes that emerge from the system at a given point in time.[13,14]

3 ION-SELECTIVE ELECTRODES AND RELATED DEVICES

Most indicator electrodes will give a response or interact with a variety of chemical species. This can be an advantage if the goal is to employ a general method of analysis. There are many other times when the goal is to instead measure the activity or concentration of a particular analyte, even if it is present in a complex mixture. Potentiometry can be used for this second type of application if it is used along with an indicator electrode that is selective for the desired analyte. An **ion-selective electrode (ISE)** is an indicator electrode

BOX 1
Creation of the pH Meter

Early in the twentieth century most chemical analyses involved either gravimetry or titrimetry. This began to change in the 1930s with the introduction of instrumental techniques for chemical analysis. One of the key events to take place at this time was the development of the pH meter by Arnold Beckman in 1935 (Figure 6).

Beckman built his first pH meter to help a chemist in the California citrus industry who needed to measure the acidity of lemon juice. Beckman did this by constructing a potentiometer based on vacuum-tube amplification that would measure a potential with only a very small current. Many people had spent many years in examining the behavior of acids in solution

and the concept of pH had been developed many years earlier. Beckman's contribution was to design and build an instrument that could be easily used with an ion-selective electrode to make this important measurement.

With his device, the pH of a sample could now be measured in just a few seconds and with a device that did not affect the sample in any way. This was accomplished by having the instrument make a simple measurement of electrical potential involving an ion-selective electrode for hydrogen ions and converting this measured potential into a reading of pH. The result was a new and valuable method for chemical analysis that we still use to this day.

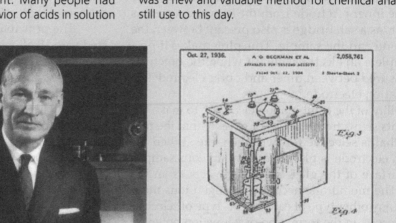

Arnold Beckman

FIGURE 6 Arnold Beckman (1900–2004) and a drawing from his 1936 patent for the original Beckman pH meter. (The photo on the right is reproduced with permission from the Chemical Heritage Foundation; the photo on the left is reproduced with permission from the Beckman Foundation.)

that can respond to individual types of anions or cations, and is one tool that can be utilized for such a task.[3,10]

3A Glass Membrane Electrodes

pH Electrode. The most common type of ISE is the **pH electrode**, an indicator electrode that is selective for the detection of hydrogen ions. The most common type of pH electrode is a **glass-membrane electrode**, which is a type of indicator electrode that uses a thin glass membrane for selectively detecting the desired ion (in this case, H^+). The glass used in a typical pH electrode is based on a special

mixture of lithium, barium, lanthanum, and silicon oxides (see Table 5). The glass membrane pH electrode was first used as part of an instrumental system for chemical analysis in the late 1930s.[12]

The design of a typical modern pH electrode is given in Figure 7. This design actually contains two electrodes in one, giving a device known as a *combination electrode*. Both the inner and outer electrodes in this device are Ag/AgCl electrodes. The outer part of this device contains a Ag/AgCl electrode that is surrounded by an enclosed solution saturated with AgCl and KCl. The inner part of this device has a second

TABLE 5   Composition of Ion-Selective Electrodes Based on Glass Membranes*

Type of Electrode	Composition of Glass	Usable Range (M)	Selectivity
pH Electrode	Li, Ba, La, and Si Oxides	$1-10^{-14}$	$H^+ \gg Li^+, Na^+ > K^+$
Sodium Electrode	Na, Al, and Si Oxides	$1-10^{-6}$	$Ag^+ > H^+ > Na^+ \gg Li^+, K^+, NH_4^+$
Electrode for Univalent Cations	Na, Al, and Si Oxides	$1-10^{-5}$	$K^+ > NH_4^+ > Na^+, H^+, Li^+$

*These data were obtained from T.S. Light, "Potentiometry: pH and Ion-Selective Electrodes." In *Analytical Instrumentation Handbook,* 2nd ed., G.W. Ewing, Ed., Marcel Dekker, New York, 1997, Chapter 18.

Ag/AgCl electrode and a saturated AgCl solution with a fixed concentration of HCl. A thin glass membrane separates the inner electrode from the sample. A porous plug that acts as a salt bridge is also present between the outer electrode and the sample. This plug makes it possible to complete an electrical circuit when the potential is to be measured between inner and outer electrodes in this combination electrode.[3,7]

The ability of the combination electrode to make pH measurements stems from the use of glass within the thin membrane that is selective for hydrogen ions. When the combination electrode is placed into an aqueous sample, the other surface of the glass membrane acts as an ion exchanger. The membrane accepts hydrogen ions more readily than any other type of cation. This type of selective interaction results in the formation of a junction potential between the glass membrane and the surrounding sample (see Section 2B). A similar junction potential is formed on the inside of the glass membrane where a fixed concentration of HCl is present. If the activity of hydrogen ions is different in the sample versus this interior solution, a difference will also be present in the two junction potentials that are formed. The difference in these junction potentials is then measured and used to provide a signal that is related to the hydrogen ion activity in the sample.

The relationship between the measured potential and hydrogen ion activity for a pH electrode can be described by the following equation.

$$E = K + 0.05916 \,(\text{pH})$$
$$\text{or } E = K - 0.05916 \log(a_{H^+}) \qquad (20)$$

This equation describes the difference in junction potentials between the inside and outside of the glass membrane in the case when the potentials of the inner and outer electrodes are otherwise equal, as they are for the device shown in Figure 7. The term K in this equation is a system constant that varies from one pH electrode to the next. However, it is still possible to use Equation 20 and the pH electrode for pH measurements by first calibrating this system with buffers that have known pH values. This calibration should be done for each type of pH meter that is being used. This process should also ideally

involve the use of at least two reference buffers with pH values that match the range of pHs that are expected in the samples.[3,7]

The principal interferences for this type of pH electrode are alkali metal ions, such as Na^+, Li^+, and K^+ (see Table 5). These ions also can interact with the external surface of the glass membrane and create a junction potential that is no longer related to just the hydrogen ion activity within the sample. Although Li^+ has the largest effect on these junction potentials, this type of interference is usually called a "sodium error" because sodium salts are much more commonly present in samples than lithium salts. This error only happens when the activity of hydrogen ions is low (representing a high pH). For instance, this error can occur if NaOH is used to adjust the pH of a solution to a high value. A simple way to reduce this effect is to use KOH instead of NaOH to adjust the pH of an aqueous solution when an accurate pH reading is

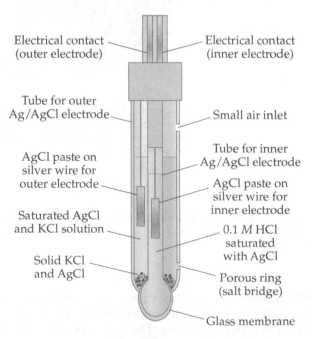

FIGURE 7 The design of a modern pH electrode. This is an example of a combination electrode, because both the indicator electrode and reference electrode are included with the same device.

needed. Another possible approach is to use a pH electrode that contains a glass membrane that has less interference in the presence of sodium ions.[3]

Sodium Ion-Selective Electrode. Various compositions of glass can be prepared to create ion-selective electrodes for cations besides H^+. One formulation based on a mixture of sodium, aluminum, and silicon oxides is used to make a *sodium ion–selective electrode*. This type of electrode creates a signal in the same general manner as a pH electrode. This signal is again based on a difference in the junction potentials that formed on both sides of the glass membrane in the presence of the sample on the outside of the electrode and a reference solution on the inside that contains a fixed concentration of the ion of interest.

The glass that is used in a sodium electrode still has a response that is almost 100 times greater for H^+ than for Na^+ when these ions are present at equal levels. This makes it necessary to use this type of electrode in an alkaline solution (i.e., one that has low hydrogen ion activity). A buffered solution is often added to samples and standards to control the pH (and ionic strength) for use with these electrodes and to help provide a response that is related to sodium ion concentration. The response of the sodium ion–selective electrode under these conditions will be proportional to the value of pNa, where $pNa = -\log(a_{Na^+}) \approx -\log([Na^+])$. This type of electrode will also have a strong response to silver ions. Yet another mixture of sodium, aluminum, and silicon oxides can be prepared to give an ion-selective electrode for a variety of univalent cations. This type of electrode gives a strong response for K^+, followed by a lower response for NH_4^+ and other cations.[3]

3B Solid-State Ion-Selective Electrodes

Other materials besides glass can be used to make ion-selective electrodes. An example is a **solid-state ion-selective electrode,** or "solid membrane electrode." This type of electrode contains a sensing element that is a crystalline material or a homogeneous pressed pellet. It is necessary in this type of electrode for the sensing element to have selective adsorption or interactions with the ion of interest. This element must also be able to conduct a small amount of current when it is used to provide a potential measurement. These are the same general requirements that are needed when using glass membranes in the pH electrode and other ion-selective electrodes.

The general design for this type of electrode is shown in Figure 8. This design consists of an internal reference electrode that is in contact with a reference solution containing a fixed concentration of the ion of interest. This reference solution is then in contact with the crystalline or pressed-pellet sensing element. The sensing element is also in contact with the sample solution on its outer surface. A separate reference electrode is also in contact with the sample and is used to complete the circuit for the potential measurement. The sensing element will preferentially interact with the desired ions in the solutions on both its interior and exterior surfaces. If these two solutions contain different activities of this ion, there will be different junction potentials created at these surfaces. The result is a difference in potential that is related to the activity of this ion in the sample.

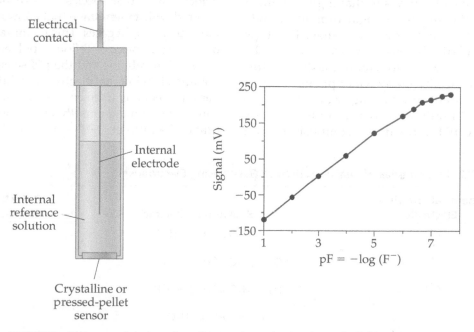

FIGURE 8 The general design of a solid-state ion-selective electrode (left), and an example of the response for a fluoride ion-selective electrode that is based on this design (right).

There are many types of solid-state ion-selective electrodes that have been developed. One common example is the *fluoride ion–selective electrode* that is used to measure fluoride in drinking water. In this case, the sensing element in the electrode is a pellet of lanthanum fluoride (LaF_3) that contains a trace amount of europium fluoride (EuF_2). LaF_3 is highly insoluble in water, with a K_{sp} value of only 7×10^{-17}. The surface of a crystal of LaF_3 will act as an ion exchanger for fluoride ions, as well as lanthanum ions. This feature makes such an electrode a useful tool in measuring the activity of fluoride in water samples. When LaF_3 is placed in water that contains no fluoride ions, some of this solid will dissolve according to the following solubility reaction and K_{sp} expression.

$$LaF_3(s) \rightleftarrows La^{3+} + 3\ F^-$$

$$K_{sp} = [La^{3+}][F^-]^3 = 7 \times 10^{-17} \qquad (21)$$

According to this K_{sp} expression, the maximum solubility of LaF_3 in water during this process will be given by $K_{sp} = [F^-]^4/3 = 7 \times 10^{-17}$, or $[F^-] = (2.1 \times 10^{-16})^{1/4} = 1.2 \times 10^{-4}\ M$. Whenever the fluoride concentration of a sample is much less than the solubility limit for LaF_3 of $1.2 \times 10^{-4}\ M$, the measured potential will begin to reflect the fluoride that has dissolved out of the electrode. At this point, the electrode becomes unresponsive to the actual fluoride content in the sample. This dissolution occurs slowly when the LaF_3 is in a compact pellet.

Figure 8 shows the response of a fluoride electrode when plotted as a function of pF, where $pF = -\log(a_{F^-}) \approx -\log([F^-])$. This response is typical of many ion-selective electrodes in that it gives a linear response versus the negative logarithm of analyte activity or concentration over a wide range. This type of electrode is relatively easy to use and can be employed as part of a system for continuously monitoring a sample, as is used by many water plants to monitor the fluoride content of drinking water. There are also some practical limitations to a fluoride electrode that are related to pH and sample composition. If a solution containing fluoride has a pH that is too low, the fluoride will mainly exist in solution as HF. Because the fluoride electrode responds to F^- and not HF, the pH that is used with this type of electrode should be at least two units above the pK_a of HF ($3.17 + 2 = 5.17$). At a pH greater than 10, another problem that can occur is that hydroxide ion (which has the same charge and a similar size to F^-) can also form an insoluble lanthanum salt, adsorb onto the surface of the LaF_3 crystal, and give a false high reading. If the sample contains metal ions such as Fe^{3+} or Al^{3+}, some of these metal ions can form soluble complex ions with fluoride and prevent this ion from interacting with the LaF_3 sensing element. To deal with these problems, a solution can first be added to each sample and standard to adjust the pH, control the ionic strength, and complex metal ions (e.g., Fe^{3+} and Al^{3+}) with ethylenediamine tetraacetic acid (EDTA).[3]

3C Compound Electrodes

Gas-Sensing Electrodes. Devices like the pH electrode are not limited to the detection of solution-phase chemicals, but can also be modified for used in other types of measurements. The modification of a pH electrode or other type of ion-selective electrode for the measurement of other analytes gives a device known as a *compound electrode*. One group of compound electrodes are those that have been modified for the analysis of certain gases. The result is known as a **gas-sensing electrode**. Some examples of gas-sensing electrodes are given in Table 6.

An ammonia gas-sensing electrode (illustrated in Figure 9) is both an electrode that can sense a gas and detect a molecular species. This device is a pH electrode covered with a membrane that allows passage of only low molecular-weight gases. This membrane is typically made of a very thin piece of Teflon or polyethylene. Between the covering membrane and the pH-sensitive glass is a small volume of an internal electrolyte solution (0.1 M KCl) that has an essentially fixed concentration of NH_4^+. When dissolved ammonia enters this solution through the membrane, the ratio of $[NH_4^+]$ to $[NH_3]$ is changed and the

TABLE 6   Examples of Reactions Used in Gas-Sensing Electrodes*

Chemical Entering Electrode	Reaction at Electrode	Detected Chemical
CO_2	$CO_2 + H_2O \rightleftarrows H^+ + HCO_3^-$	H^+
SO_2	$SO_2 + H_2O \rightleftarrows H^+ + HSO_3^-$	H^+
NH_3	$NH_3 + H_2O \rightleftarrows NH_4^+ + OH^-$	H^+
	$H^+ + OH^- \rightleftarrows H_2O$	
NO_2	$2\ NO_2 + H_2O \rightleftarrows NO_3^- + NO_2^- + 2\ H^+$	H^+ or NO_3^-

*Additional examples can be found in T.S. Light, "Potentiometry: pH and Ion-Selective Electrodes." In *Analytical Instrumentation Handbook*, 2nd ed., G.W. Ewing, Ed., Marcel Dekker, New York, 1997, Chapter 18.

pH is increased, as shown by the reactions in Table 6. This change creates a response by the pH electrode that is related to the activity of ammonia that was in the sample. Similar electrodes can be made to respond to other basic or acidic gases such as CO_2, SO_2, and NO_2.

Enzyme Electrodes. Even more elaborate electrodes can be created by using enzymes to convert analytes into products that can be measured by potentiometry. This type of compound electrode is called an **enzyme electrode** or "enzyme substrate electrode." An example is an enzyme electrode that has been created for the measurement of urea. This electrode is constructed by immobilizing the enzyme urease onto a semipermeable membrane. Urease catalyzes the hydrolysis of urea into ammonia and carbon dioxide.

$$H_2NC(O)NH_2 + H_2O \rightleftarrows 2\,NH_3 + CO_2 \qquad (22)$$

Because ammonia is so much more soluble than carbon dioxide in water, the CO_2 mainly bubbles out of solution and does not lower the pH. The ammonia, however, dissolves and goes through the membrane to raise the pH of an electrolyte solution that surrounds a pH electrode. The increase in pH is caused by a change in hydroxide ion activity and concentration, which is proportional to the amount of ammonia that has been produced by the enzyme and the original amount of urea that was in the sample. An ion-selective electrode for NH_4^+ can also

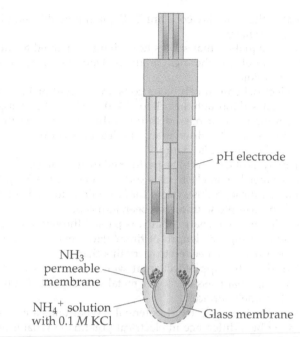

pH electrode

NH_3 permeable membrane

NH_4^+ solution with 0.1 M KCl

Glass membrane

FIGURE 9 Design of a gas-sensing electrode for ammonia, based on the use of a glass-membrane pH electrode for detection.

be used with such a system for the final measurement.[3] The use of other enzymes allows additional analytes to be detected by such an approach. Examples of other chemicals that can be detected through the use of enzyme electrodes include glucose, amino acids, alcohols, penicillin, and cholesterol.[3]

Key Words

Amperometry	Enzyme electrode	Junction potential	Silver/silver chloride
Calomel electrode	Gas sensing electrode	Ohm's law	electrode
Charge	Glass-membrane	pH electrode	Solid-state ion-selective
Coulometry	electrode	Potentiometry	electrode
Current	Indicator electrode	Resistance	Voltammetry
Electrochemical analysis	Ion-selective electrode		

Other Terms

Alternating current	Compound electrode	Fluoride ion–selective	Potentiometric titration
Class one electrode	Conductance	electrode	Saturated calomel
Class three electrode	Direct current	Liquid junction	electrode
Class two electrode	Electromotive force	potential	Sodium ion–selective
Combination electrode		Metallic indicator	electrode
		electrode	

Questions

UNITS OF ELECTRICAL MEASUREMENTS AND METHODS FOR ELECTROCHEMICAL ANALYSIS

1. What is meant by the term "electrochemical analysis"? Give one specific example for this type of analysis.

2. Define each of the following terms and state what units are employed with each of these parameters in the SI system.
   (a) Current
   (b) Charge
   (c) Electric potential
   (d) Resistance

3. What is the "Faraday constant"? Explain how this term is related to charge.

4. Give an equation that shows how charge is related to current in an electrochemical analysis. Define each term in this equation.

5. An electrochemical cell has a constant current of 125 μA that is passed through the cell for 500.0 s. What is the charge (in coulombs) that passed through this system over this length of time? How many moles of electrons were required to carry this charge?

6. An analysis of Cu^{2+} is to be performed by reducing Cu^{2+} to copper metal at an electrode's surface. A current of 560 μA is passed through this system for 2.50 min before all of the Cu^{2+} in a sample solution has been reduced.

   (a) What was the charge that was passed through the system during this length of time? How many moles of electrons were needed to carry this charge?

   (b) If all of the applied current went to reduce Cu^{2+} to Cu(s), what mass of copper metal was deposited at the electrode's surface?

7. Define the term "electrical potential." What units are used to describe a difference in electrical potential? What is an "electromotive force"?

8. What is meant by "resistance" in an electrochemical system? What units are used to describe resistance?

9. What is "conductance"? How is conductance related to resistance? What units are used to describe conductance?

10. What is "Ohm's law"? Explain how Ohm's law can be used to examine an electrochemical system.

11. What current must be present in an electrochemical cell if the potential is 140 mV and the resistance is 4×10^{12} ohms?

12. What must the resistance be across a certain part of an electrical circuit if the current through this component is 8.5 μA when the applied potential is 59.1 mV?

13. The glass membrane in a pH electrode has a resistance of 200,000,000 ohms. What current will be passed through this membrane if the measured potential is 400 mV?

14. Explain the difference between a "direct current" and an "alternating current". Give an example of an application for each of these two types of current.

15. Draw a graph of current versus time for a 5.0 A signal that is based on a direct current and a 5.0 A signal that is based on a 60 Hz alternating current.

TYPES OF METHODS FOR ELECTROCHEMICAL ANALYSIS

16. What is meant by the term "potentiometry"? Explain why the use of a fluoride ion–selective electrode is an example of potentiometry.

17. Define the terms "amperometry" and "voltammetry." How are these methods similar? How are these methods different?

18. What is "coulometry"? Explain why the Faraday constant is often used in coulometry.

CELL POTENTIALS AND THE NERNST EQUATION

19. Describe the general parts of an electrochemical cell that are used in potentiometry. Compare the general components of this cell to those for the study of oxidation–reduction reactions.

20. Why is it necessary in potentiometry to have "essentially zero flow of current"? What would happen if the current was not close to zero?

21. Discuss how the Nernst equation can be used in potentiometry.

22. What is meant by an "indicator electrode"? What is the role of this electrode in potentiometry?

23. What does it mean when a "negative" cell potential is measured in potentiometry? Explain how this type of situation can occur.

CELL COMPONENTS IN POTENTIOMETRY

24. Why is it uncommon for a standard hydrogen electrode to be used as a reference electrode in potentiometry?

25. Describe a silver/silver chloride electrode. What are the key components of this electrode and how does it work?

26. What is a "calomel electrode"? Describe how this type of electrode works.

27. What is a "saturated calomel electrode"?

28. List four types of metal indicator electrodes. Give an example of each type.

29. Determine whether each of the following electrodes is a metallic indicator electrode or a class one, two, or three electrode.

   (a) A copper wire in a solution of copper sulfate

   (b) A gold wire in a solution containing V(II) and V(III)

   (c) Mercury coated with Hg_2Cl_2 in a solution containing NaCl

30. A solution has a total concentration of iron ions of 0.0763 M in 1 M HCl. A platinum electrode that is placed in this solution gives a measured potential of 0.465 V versus SCE.

   (a) If there are no other species than Fe^{2+} and Fe^{3+} that are being detected, what is the ratio of $[Fe^{2+}]/[Fe^{3+}]$ in this solution?

   (b) What are the individual concentrations of Fe^{2+} and Fe^{3+} in this solution?

31. What is a "salt bridge"? What role does a salt bridge play in an electrochemical cell?

32. Define the term "junction potential." How does a junction potential affected the measured difference in potential for an electrochemical cell?

33. Explain how a junction potential can be formed by the presence of a salt bridge in an electrochemical cell.

34. What is a "liquid junction potential"? Give an example.

35. Sometimes both electrodes can be placed in the same solution, but this is unusual because then the redox reaction can occur in the beaker without influencing the electrodes. An example of a successful "junctionless cell" is one in which the first electrode is Ag/AgCl in a HCl solution and the other is a hydrogen electrode in the same HCl solution. What is a possible benefit of using this type of junctionless cell?

APPLICATIONS OF POTENTIOMETRY

36. What are some possible advantages of using potentiometry for chemical analysis? (*Hint*: Use the measurement of pH as an example.)

37. Calcium ion in a water sample was measured using a calcium-selective electrode. A 50 mL portion of the water showed a potential of −0.0650 V versus SCE. When a 1.0 mL portion of 0.0850 M Ca(NO$_3$)$_2$ solution was added, the potential changed to −0.0477 V. What was the original calcium concentration?

38. Explain how potentiometry can be used as part of a titration. Give a specific example of such an approach.

39. Discuss how potentiometry can be used with methods such as flow injection analysis or liquid chromatography. What do you think are some possible advantages for using these combinations of methods?

GLASS MEMBRANE ELECTRODES

40. Define the terms "ion-selective electrode" and "glass-membrane electrode." Illustrate both of these ideas using a typical pH electrode.

41. Describe how a modern pH electrode is constructed. Explain why this type of electrode is also known as a "combination electrode."

42. Explain how pH is measured by a pH electrode. What role does the glass membrane play in this process?

43. State why it is necessary to calibrate a pH electrode.

44. What is "sodium error"? Why is this type of error important to consider when using a pH electrode? What steps can be taken to minimize sodium error?

45. A pH meter reads pH = 2.50 when it is present in a dilute solution of HCl. Predict what would happen when solid NaCl is added to this solution.

46. Explain how a sodium ion–selective electrode works. How is this similar to a typical pH electrode? How are these two types of electrodes different?

47. The activity of a sodium ion as measured by a sodium-selective electrode is 0.0674 M. If the solution ionic strength is 0.0500, what is the concentration of the sodium ion in the solution?

48. A sodium-selective electrode has a response ratio of 2.00 for sodium compared to hydrogen ion. What is the lowest concentration of sodium ion that will have less than a 10% error if the measurement is made at pH 7.00?

SOLID-STATE ION-SELECTIVE ELECTRODES

49. What is a "solid-state ion-selective electrode"? How is this similar to a glass-membrane ion-selective electrode? How is it different?

50. Describe the general design of a solid-state ion-selective electrode.

51. Explain how a fluoride ion-selective electrode produces a signal that is related to fluoride activity or concentration.

52. State why it is often necessary to control the pH and ionic strength and to add EDTA to samples and standards when using a fluoride ion–selective electrode.

53. The following data represent potentials of a fluoride ion-selective electrode vs. SCE for several solutions. All solutions are made up in a way to control their pH and ionic strength, and contain added EDTA. Prepare a plot of the measured potential vs. pF based on this information and determine the concentration of fluoride in each unknown solution.

54. If a solution of silver ion and copper ion is precipitated by addition of sulfide ion, a mixture of Ag_2S and CuS is formed. This material when used in jewelry is called "niello." When this is collected by filtration, dried, and pressed into a thin pellet it can be made into a membrane suitable to make an electrode responsive to silver ion or copper ion. Because copper, especially, can be in equilibrium with ligands such as EDTA to give extremely low concentrations of Cu^{2+}, such an electrode can be used to detect the endpoint of a titration of copper by EDTA.

$$Cu^{2+} + H_2EDTA^{2-} \rightleftarrows CuEDTA^{2-} + 2\,H^+ \qquad (23)$$

The conditional formation constant for copper with EDTA is known to be greater than 10^{10} at a pH above 4.0. That means that if total copper concentration is 0.05 M and total EDTA concentration is 0.10 M, then the actual $[Cu^{2+}] < 10^{-10}$ M. The electrode can respond to such low concentrations. What is the value of pCu if the effective formation constant is 1.0×10^{14}, the total copper ion concentration is 0.050 M, and total EDTA concentration is 0.10 M.

COMPOUND ELECTRODES

55. What is meant by the term "compound electrode"? Give two general examples.

56. What is a "gas-sensing electrode"? Describe one specific example of a gas-sensing electrode.

57. Describe how a pH electrode can be modified for the detection of ammonia.

58. Using Table 6 as a guide, describe how the electrode in Figure 9 could be modified for the detection of CO_2 instead of ammonia.

59. The amount of protein in a wheat flour sample is to be measured. A 0.3476 gram portion is dissolved in concentrated sulfuric acid and heated to boiling in the presence of copper ion, which serves as a catalyst to destroy the biomolecules in the sample and convert the protein nitrogen into ammonium ion. After cooling, raising the pH with NaOH, and diluting the solution to 100 mL, an ammonia-selective electrode is used to measure the ammonium concentration to be 0.32 M. Protein is typically 16% nitrogen. Calculate the percent protein in this sample. Explain how an unscrupulous grain dealer could make the grain look more rich in protein by adding melamine ($C_3H_6N_6$).

60. A gas-sensing electrode is used to measure the concentration of carbonate in a solution that also contains other basic substances. Explain what will happen when the solution is made acidic with sulfuric acid while being monitored with a gas-sensing electrode.

61. What is an "enzyme electrode"? How is this similar to a gas-sensing electrode? How is it different?

62. Describe how a pH electrode can be made for the detection of urea through the use of enzymes.

Solution (M)	Potential (mV)
5.0×10^{-2}	-22.4
5.0×10^{-3}	36.8
5.0×10^{-4}	96.0
5.0×10^{-5}	155.2
Unknown 1	74.3
Unknown 2	190.6
Unknown 3	-54.3

An Introduction to Electrochemical Analysis

CHALLENGE PROBLEMS

63. Suppose that both a pH and a pF electrode are used during a titration of a solution of 0.10 M HF with 0.10 M NaOH. Sketch the response of both electrodes vs. volume of NaOH.

64. Obtain more information from sources such as Reference 3 on the calomel and saturated calomel electrodes. Use this information to explain why a 0.10 M KCl calomel electrode is superior to an SCE if the electrode is to be used at different temperatures.

65. Explain why the seemingly complicated electrode of the third type described in the chapter is used to measure pCa instead of a class one electrode utilizing elemental calcium.

66. Use the solubility product K_{sp} of AgBr to calculate the expected potential for a reference electrode that is similar in design to the Ag/AgCl electrode shown in Figure 4, but that uses AgBr in place of AgCl.

67. Barium sulfate is about as insoluble as is AgCl. Suggest why a $BaSO_4$ reference electrode has never been seriously considered.

68. What will be the error in measured pH if the true pH is 4.56, but the measured potential of a pH electrode is 1.0 mV too high?

69. A fluoride ion–selective electrode has about a 1000-fold higher response for F^- vs. Cl^- at the same concentration. Do you think an electrode would give reliable results for measurements of fluoride in seawater? Justify your answer.

TOPICS FOR DISCUSSION AND REPORTS

70. Contact a water-treatment plant in your area that practices water fluoridation. Ask workers at this facility about the approaches they use to follow the levels of fluoride that are added to the water. Discuss your findings.

71. Gas-sensing electrodes are often used in blood-gas measurements. Talk to a worker in a hospital laboratory or a surgical room to obtain more information on the use of blood-gas measurements.

72. Liquid-membrane electrodes are another class of devices that can be used in potentiometry for the selective detection of ions. Obtain more information on this topic and write a report on a specific example of this type of electrode.

73. Ion-selective field-effect transistors (ISFET) are yet another group of sensors that can be used in potentiometry. Locate a review article or book on this topic. Describe how this type of sensor works and list some of its applications.

References

1. L. W. Ripa, "A Half-Century of Community Water Fluoridation in the United States: Review and Commentary," *Journal of Public Health Dentistry*, 53 (1993) 17–44.
2. CDC, "Ten Great Public Heath Achievements—United States, 1900–1999," *Journal of the American Medical Association*, 281 (1999) 1481.
3. T. S. Light, "Potentiometry: pH and Ion-Selective Electrodes." In *Analytical Instrumentation Handbook*, 2nd ed., G. W. Ewing, Ed., Marcel Dekker, New York, 1997.
4. B. N. Taylor, Ed., *The International System of Units (SI)*, NIST Special Publication 330, National Institute of Standards and Technology, Gaithersburg, MD, 1991.
5. *Correct SI Metric Usage*, United States Metric Association.
6. *IUPAC Compendium of Chemical Terminology*, Electronic version, http://goldbook.iupac.org
7. J. Inczedy, T. Lengyel, and A. M. Ure, *International Union of Pure and Applied Chemistry—Compendium of Analytical Nomenclature: Definitive Rules 1997*, Blackwell Science, Malden, MA, 1998.
8. G. Maludzinska Ed., *Dictionary of Analytical Chemistry*, Elsevier, Amsterdam, the Netherlands, 1990.
9. A. J. Bard and L. R. Faulkner, *Electrochemical Methods: Fundamentals and Applications*, 2nd ed., Wiley, Hoboken, NJ, 2001.
10. D. A. Skoog, F. J. Holler, and T. A. Nieman, *Principles of Instrumental Analysis*, 5th ed., Saunders, Philadelphia, PA, 1998.
11. E. Wilson, "Arnold Beckman at 100," *Chemical and Engineering News*, 78(2000) 17–20.
12. J. Poudrier and J. Moynihan, "Instrumentation Hall of Fame." In *Made to Measure: A History of Analytical Instrumentation*, J. F. Ryan, Ed., American Chemical Society, Washington, DC, 1999, pp. 10–38.
13. J. Ruzicka and E. H. Hansen, *Flow Injection Methods*, 2nd ed., Wiley, New York, 1988.
14. C. F. Poole and S. K. Poole, *Chromatography Today*, Elsevier, New York, 1991.

Selected Answers

6

a. Charge = 0.0840 C, which corresponds to 5.24×10^{17} electrons

b. Mass of copper = 2.77×10^{-5} g

11 $I = 3.5 \times 10^{-14}$ A

29

a. Class one electrode

b. Metallic indicator electrode

c. Class two electrode

30

a. $[Fe^{2+}]/[Fe^{3+}] = 2.45$

b. $[Fe^{2+}] = 0.0542$ M, $[Fe^{3+}] = 0.0221$ M

47 $[Na^+] = 0.0625$ M

48 $[Na^+]$ must be greater than 5×10^{-7} M

53 [Unknown 1] = 1.16×10^{-3} M, [Unknown 2] = 1.26×10^{-5} M, [Unknown 3] = 1.73×10^{-1} M

Coulometry, Voltammetry, and Related Methods

From Chapter 16 of *Analytical Chemistry and Quantitative Analysis,* First Edition. David S. Hage, James D. Carr. Copyright © 2011 by Pearson Education, Inc. Published by Pearson Prentice Hall.

Coulometry, Voltammetry, and Related Methods

Chapter Outline

1 INTRODUCTION: THE DEAD ZONE

The concentration of dissolved oxygen in the ocean, rivers, and lakes is important to the survival of fish and other life in these waters. Oxygen is not very soluble in water, with only $2.9 \times 10^{-4} M$ being present in water that is saturated with air at 20°C. This solubility decreases at higher temperatures and if oxidizable solutes such as pollutants are present. Fish utilize dissolved oxygen much as we use oxygen in air as a necessary part of our metabolism. Green plants in the water give off oxygen while living, but remove oxygen when they die and decay. The corresponding lack of sufficient oxygen in water can lead to the creation of a region in the ocean or other bodies of water that is known as a "dead zone." The concentration of dissolved oxygen in natural waters is therefore an important quantity to measure to be able to avoid the creation of such a zone by pollution and to ensure that a proper oxygen content is present for fish and wildlife to live and thrive.[1,2]

It is difficult to take water samples from rivers or the ocean and return them to a laboratory for dissolved-oxygen measurements. This difficulty arises because contact with air or a change in temperature can affect the oxygen content of the sample. As a result, it is instead necessary to make a measurement of the dissolved oxygen levels in the field while the sample of water is still in its original setting. This task is often carried out by using a dissolved-oxygen electrode that measures the reduction of O_2 in water through a method known as *voltammetry* (see Figure 1).

In the last two chapters we have focused on an electrochemical method known as potentiometry, in which the measurement of a potential difference is used for chemical analysis. These measurements are all made in the presence of essentially zero current. Such conditions are used in potentiometry to ensure that no appreciable amounts of any oxidation–reduction reactions are taking place in the sample during the measurement, even though a difference in potential might exist that favors such a reaction. In this chapter, we will deal with other methods of electrochemical analysis in which a measurable current does flow between two electrodes, such as in the dissolved-oxygen electrode. Important examples of these methods include electrogravimetry, coulometry, voltammetry, and amperomentry.[3–5]

2 ELECTROGRAVIMETRY

Electrogravimetry, or "electrodeposition," is a type of gravimetric analysis where a dissolved analyte is converted into a solid by either oxidation or reduction in such a way that the product is tightly attached to an inert electrode. The increase in mass of the electrode after the analyte has been deposited on it can then be used as a direct measure of the amount of analyte that was originally in the sample.[6,7] Copper and silver are elements that can easily be measured by electrogravimetry through the following reduction half-reactions.

$$Cu^{2+} + 2\,e^- \rightleftharpoons Cu(s) \qquad (1)$$

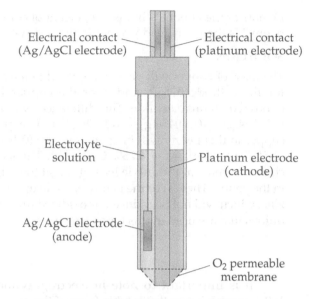

Anode: $Ag + Cl^- \rightleftharpoons AgCl(s) + e^-$

Cathode: $O_2 + 4H^+ + 4e^- \rightleftharpoons 2H_2O$

FIGURE 1 The general design of an electrode for measuring dissolved oxygen. This type of electrode is also known as a "Clark electrode" and is named after American chemist Leland Clark, who first developed such an electrode in the 1950s. The particular design shown here is an example of a combination electrode (a topic discussed in Chapter 14), in which both the anode and cathode are part of a single sensing device. The Ag/AgCl electrode in this device acts as the anode and reference electrode. The platinum electrode is the cathode and indicator electrode for oxygen that is able to cross the gas-permeable membrane and enter the electrolyte solution that surrounds this electrode.

$$Ag^+ + e^- \rightleftharpoons Ag(s) \qquad (2)$$

A necessary feature in this type of analysis is that essentially all of the analyte must be reduced and must attach to the electrode. This means the mass of any solute that is not reduced must be less than the smallest amount that can be detected by the balance, which is usually 0.0001 g.

The electrode employed in electrogravimetry is typically a piece of platinum gauze that has an area of several square centimeters, as illustrated by the system in Figure 2. Because reduction is occurring at this electrode, it represents the cathode in this electrochemical cell. In this situation, the cathode is electrically negative so that metal cations will be attracted to it and gain electrons as they convert from soluble ions into an insoluble metal. The other electrode, where oxidation occurs, represents the anode and is also made of platinum. The oxidation product that is created at this anode may involve the formation of oxygen gas from water, as shown in Equation 3, or the oxidation of some other component in the sample.

$$2H_2O \rightleftharpoons O_2 + 4H^+ + 4e^- \qquad (3)$$

Although reduction is often used in electrogravimetry for the analysis of metal ions, there are cases in which an oxidation reaction can also be employed. An example of a metal ion that can be converted to a solid form by means of oxidation is Pb^{2+}. The oxidation product of Pb^{2+} in an aqueous solution is PbO_2, which will adhere

to the anode as lead is oxidized from the +2 state in Pb^{2+} to the +4 state in PbO_2. The half-reaction for this oxidation step is as follows.

$$Pb^{2+} + 2H_2O \rightleftharpoons PbO_2 + 4H^+ + 2e^- \qquad (4)$$

When just one type of metal ion is present in a solution, it is relatively easy to select a potential that can be used for electrogravimetry. However, this situation becomes more complicated when more than one type of metal ion is present. This concept can be illustrated by using a mixture of Ag^+ and Cu^{2+} as an example. The standard reduction potential for silver is +0.80 V versus a standard hydrogen electrode (SHE), and for Cu^{2+} it is +0.34 V versus SHE. These values indicate that if Ag^+ and Cu^{2+} are in the same solution, the silver ions will be more easily reduced. Thus, it is possible to have selective electrode position for Ag^+ by using a potential that is high enough to reduce silver ions, but not high enough to reduce copper ions. This approach is called **controlled potential electrolysis**, and the device used to supply the desired potential is known as a **potentiostat**.

During electrodeposition, it is desirable to have the analyte deposited on an electrode in such a way that this deposited material can easily be weighed. This is not a problem for a metal such as copper, which forms a smooth adherent layer on a platinum electrode. However, the deposition of silver from an aqueous solution can result in large crystals that adhere poorly to a platinum electrode and often fall off. A smoother, more adherent silver deposit can be obtained by instead reducing Ag^+ from a

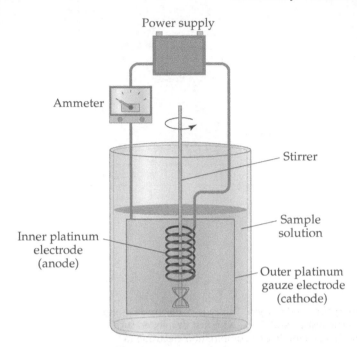

FIGURE 2 A system for the electrogravimetric analysis of metals. This device contains two concentric platinum electrodes. The outside platinum-gauze electrode acts as the cathode and is where a metal ion is reduced and deposited as solid metal. The interior platinum electrode acts as the anode. Mechanical stirring is used to promote the movement of the metal ions from the bulk of the sample solution to the surface of the cathode for reduction.

solution that contains a complexing agent such as cyanide. The net reduction reaction that then occurs is shown in Figure 5.

$$Ag(CN)_2^- + e^- \rightleftharpoons Ag(s) + 2\,CN^- \qquad (5)$$

There are also cases in which analytes can be deposited at both the cathode and anode when using electrogravimetry. This situation occurs during the measurement of copper ions and lead ions in a dissolved sample of brass. In this case, copper ions are reduced and deposited as copper metal at the cathode, according to the reduction half-reaction in Equation 1, and lead ions are oxidized and deposited at the anode as PbO_2, according to the oxidation half-reaction in Equation 4. After rinsing and drying each electrode, the mass of both metals in the original sample can be determined.

EXERCISE 1 **Using Electrogravimetry**

A new penny having a mass of 2.5133 g is dissolved in nitric acid and the resulting copper ions are plated out onto a platinum cathode that has a mass of 12.0476 g. After all the copper ions have been reduced, the measured mass at the cathode is 12.1454 g. There is no increase

---

in mass at the anode. What is the percent of copper in the penny? Is there any lead present in the penny?

SOLUTION

The mass of copper will be equal to the difference in mass for the cathode before and after the copper has been deposited on this electrode. This difference gives a mass of (12.1554 g) − (12.0476 g) = 0.1078 g Cu. The percent of copper in this penny will be given by 100 · (0.1078 g Cu)/(2.5133 g total mass) = **4.25% Cu (w/w)**. The lack of any change in mass at the anode indicates that there is no lead in the penny. The rest of the penny is made up of nearly all zinc, which will not be reduced or oxidized under the conditions that are used in this type of analysis.

It is important to note in electrogravimetry that 100% conversion of the soluble form of the analyte to the solid form is necessary, but 100% use of the applied current for this process is not necessarily required. If some water or other species are also oxidized or reduced, there will be no problem as long as these side reactions do not deposit any solid products on the electrodes. This is not the case in the next method we will consider, a technique known as "coulometry."

3 COULOMETRY

Coulometry is a technique that uses a measure of charge for chemical analysis.[6,8] In this method, the amount of an electroactive analyte can be determined based on a measurement of the total coulombs of electricity that are needed to quantitatively oxidize or reduce this analyte. For instance, the half-reaction for the reduction of Ag^+ to silver metal in Equation 1 indicates that one mole of electrons is needed for every mole of Ag^+ that is reduced to form $Ag(s)$. If we know the current and amount of time over which this current was applied to carry out this reduction, we can determine how much charge was required and use the Faraday constant (F, where F = a charge of 96,485 C per mole of electrons) to determine the moles of electrons that were needed to attain this current. Thus, we can use information on charge (as obtained from current and time) to measure the amount of Ag^+ that has undergone reduction. An example of this process is given in the following exercise.

EXERCISE 2 **Analyzing Silver Using Coulometry**

A constant current of 5.00 mA is allowed to flow through an electrochemical cell for 528 s as Ag^+ is reduced to silver metal from a 100.0 mL aqueous sample. If all the Ag^+ was reduced and all of the applied current was used for this reduction process, what was the original concentration of Ag^+ in the sample?

SOLUTION

We can first determine how many moles of electrons (n_e) were passed through this system by using Equations 14.1 and 14.2 see below, in which I is the current, t is the time, and Q is the corresponding charge.

Equation 14.2: $Q = I \cdot t$

$$= (5.00 \times 10^{-3}\,A)(528\,s) = 2.640\,C$$

Equation 14.1: $Q = n_e F$

$$2.640\,C = n_e(96{,}485\,C/mol)$$

$$n_e = (2.64\,C)/(96{,}485\,C/mol)$$

$$= 2.736 \times 10^{-5}\,mol$$

The reaction in Equation 1 indicates each mole of electrons that is consumed will result in the reduction of one mole of silver ions if the electrons are not taking part in any other oxidation–reduction reactions. Thus, the moles of Ag^+ that were reduced will also be 2.736×10^{-5} mol. This information can then be used to find the concentration of Ag^+ in the original sample.

$$\text{Conc. } Ag^+ = (2.736 \times 10^{-5}\,mol\,Ag^+)/(0.1000\,L)$$

$$= 2.74 \times 10^{-4}\,M$$

3A Direct Coulometry

The example in the preceding exercise involved the use of both constant current coulometry and direct coulometry. The term **constant current coulometry** refers to the fact that the current is maintained at a constant level during the analysis, while the phrase **direct coulometry** means that the analyte itself is what is being oxidized or reduced during the coulometric analysis. In order for this type of analysis to be accurate, two requirements must be met. First, there must be *100% current efficiency*.[6–8] This term means all the electrons that are passed through the electrochemical cell must be used to oxidize or reduce the analyte. In the previous exercise it was assumed this requirement was met by stating that all the applied current was being utilized to reduce silver ions and nothing else, such as water or hydrogen ions.

A second requirement is that essentially all of the analyte must be oxidized or reduced during the coulometric analysis. It can be challenging to meet both this requirement and the need for 100% current efficiency. In the last exercise, these conditions would require that Ag^+ be the most easily reduced species in the sample, even when its concentration becomes quite low after most of the silver has been reduced. If this is not the case, any other species that can undergo a similar reduction (or oxidation) must first be removed or masked so that they do not interfere in the analysis. Of course, it is theoretically impossible to reduce *all* of the silver ions in the last example, because

chemical equilibrium requires that some be left behind. This small amount will not create a problem as long as it is insignificant compared to the total amount of analyte and still provides the desired level of accuracy for the final measurement.

The progress of the coulometric reduction of Ag^+ can be monitored by potentiometry through the use of a silver electrode. In this case, the difference in potential between the silver electrode and a reference electrode will change as the silver ion concentration decreases (see Figure 3). The rapid change in potential as the reduction nears completion can be used to signal when this process should be stopped. The electrochemical system that is used to perform and follow this reduction will actually consist of four electrodes. Two of these electrodes will be used to carry out the reduction of Ag^+ by coulometry, with one electrode acting as the anode and the other as the cathode. There will also be two electrodes that will be used as the indicator electrode and reference electrode for the measurement of any remaining Ag^+ by potentiometry.

3B Coulometric Titrations

A **coulometric titration** is a special type of titration in which the titrant is generated by means of coulometry and in the presence of the analyte.[6,8] This method is in contrast to direct coulometry, in which electrons are used to directly reduce or oxidize the analyte. A good example of a coulometric titration is the determination of ascorbic acid, or vitamin C. Vitamin C ($C_6H_8O_6$, see structure given below) is found in many fruits and vegetables and is one of the more popular additives in food products. It is a moderately strong organic acid and a good reducing agent.

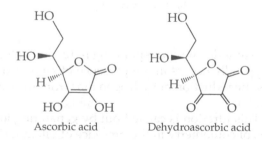

Ascorbic acid   Dehydroascorbic acid

It is difficult to measure vitamin C by direct coulometry, but this analyte can be measured by using a coulometric titration that uses iodine as an oxidizing agent. Equation 6 shows the reaction of vitamin C with iodine, in which the reduced product of vitamin C is dehydroascorbic acid ($C_6H_6O_6$).

$$C_6H_8O_6 + I_3^- \rightarrow C_6H_6O_6 + 2\,H^+ + 3\,I^- \qquad (6)$$

The volatility of I_2 makes it difficult to prepare and use in standard solutions for titrations, so an excess of I^- is also

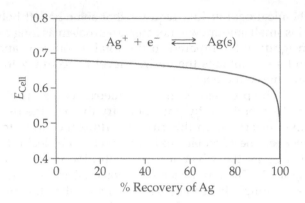

FIGURE 3 Expected change in the applied potential during the conversion of Ag^+ to $Ag(s)$ for analysis by electrogravimetry. This curve was calculated for an experiment conducted at 25°C and assumes that all of the current passing through the system goes toward the reduction of Ag^+ in a solution that initially contains this metal ion at a concentration of 0.010 M. The cell potential shown was calculated by utilizing the Nernst equation for this system and a standard hydrogen electrode as the reference electrode.

added to combine with I_2 and form the triiodide ion (I_3^-), which acts in Equation 6 as the actual titrant. A successful way of titrating something with iodine is to generate the I_2 (and I_3^-) through the oxidation of I^-. This production is carried out quantitatively between two platinum electrodes by controlling the current and time during which the oxidation of I^- is allowed to occur. The reactions that lead to the eventual formation of I_3^- during this process are given in Equations 7 and 8.

$$2\,I^- \rightleftharpoons I_2 + 2\,e^- \tag{7}$$

$$I_2 + I^- \rightleftharpoons I_3^- \tag{8}$$

At the cathode, the corresponding reduction half-reaction that typically occurs in the presence of an aqueous solution is the reduction of hydrogen ions from the surrounding water.

This titration is carried out by generating iodine by means of coulometry in the presence of vitamin C and by using starch as a visual indicator. When ascorbic acid is still present, the titrant reacts with it as quickly as iodine, and thus, I_3^- is formed. When no more vitamin C is present, the excess triiodide will react with starch to give the characteristic blue color that marks the end point. The time over which the current has been applied to reach the end point is then noted and used to determine how much analyte was present. An example of this type of analysis is provided in the color figures in the middle of this text. The calculations used in this approach are illustrated in the next exercise.

EXERCISE 3 · Coulometric Titrations

The vitamin C content in a 25.00 mL sample of a fruit drink is analyzed by a coulometric titration using I_3^- as the titrant and starch as the indicator. A current of 25.00 mA requires 6 min and 17 s to reach an end point during this titration. What is the concentration of vitamin C in the fruit drink (in units of g/L)?

SOLUTION

The moles of vitamin C can be found by using the fact that each mole of I_2 that is generated up to the end point will give one mole of I_3^-, which reacts with one mole of vitamin C. We can determine how many moles of I_2 were generated up to the end point by using the current and the exact amount of time this current was applied. The mass and concentration of vitamin C in the sample can then be found from this information, as shown below.

Mass of vitamin C = $(25.00 \times 10^{-3}\text{ C/s}) \cdot$
$(377\text{ s}) \cdot (1\text{ mol e}^-/96{,}485\text{ C}) \cdot$
$(1\text{ mol vitamin C/mol I}_2) \cdot$
$(1\text{ mol I}_2/2\text{ mol e}^-) \cdot$
$(176\text{ g vitamin C/mol})$
= 0.008596 g vitamin C

Conc. vitamin C = $(0.008596\text{ g})/(0.02500\text{ L})$ = **0.3438 g/L**

Another highly accurate coulometric titration is the titration of either strong or weak acids through the coulometric generation of hydroxide ions. These hydroxide ions are produced through the reduction of water, as given by the following reduction half-reaction.

$$2\,H_2O + 2\,e^- \rightleftharpoons H_2 + 2\,OH^- \tag{9}$$

When carried out carefully, six significant figures can be achieved in the final answer when using this method. The end point of this acid–base titration can be detected either through the use of an acid–base indicator or by using a pH electrode. As this and the previous example demonstrate, a great advantage of coulometric titrations compared to a volumetric titration is that there is no need to prepare or keep standard solutions of a titrant. Instead, the titrant is now generated in a known amount, as needed during the analysis.

Silver coulometry was an early method used for determining the value of the Faraday constant. A weighed mass of silver was dissolved and then reduced back to silver metal by using constant current coulometry. The product of the current and time was used to

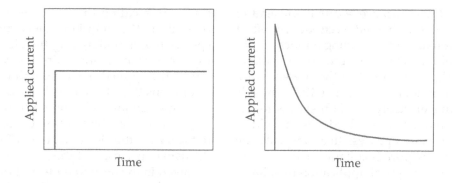

FIGURE 4 Typical plots of applied current versus time in constant current coulometry (left) and constant potential coulometry (right).

determine the number of coulombs that were needed to react with a known amount of silver. Because the atomic mass of silver was also known quite accurately from chemical methods, the Faraday constant could then be found by dividing the number of coulombs that were used by the moles of silver that had been reduced. This approach led to a value for the Faraday constant of 96,485 C/mol that is still used to this day, although more advanced and modern measurements have supplied additional significant figures for this value.

3C Constant Potential Coulometry

The potential needed for efficient oxidation or reduction in coulometry will change as the concentration of the analyte decreases. This can be illustrated through the Nernst equation.

Nernst Equation at 25°C:

$$E = E° - \frac{0.05916 \text{ V}}{n} \log\left(\frac{a_{Red}}{a_{Ox}}\right) \qquad (10)$$

In the case where an analyte is undergoing reduction, the ratio of $(a_{Red})/(a_{Ox})$ will increase as the analyte is reduced by coulometry. The decrease in this ratio means that a larger term is now being subtracted from $E°$, or that the electrode potential is becoming more negative. If another component of the sample can also be reduced at this lower potential, species other than the analyte will now begin to utilize some of the applied current.

A solution to this problem is to maintain the potential at a fixed value as the coulometry is carried out. This approach is known as **constant potential coulometry**. One complicating feature of this approach is that the current will now decrease as the coulometry is allowed to proceed and works with only a single species that will be decreasing in concentration over time. Under these conditions, the

charge that has been passed through the system will no longer be the simple product of current and time, but rather the integrated area of a current versus time plot (see Figure 4). This should not be surprising, because charge is defined as the integral of electrical current over time.[6,7]

4 VOLTAMMETRY AND AMPEROMETRY

Another important set of methods for electrochemical analysis are those in which current is measured as the potential is controlled. Techniques in this group include voltammetry and amperometry. **Voltammetry** is a method in which a current is measured as the potential is changed as a function of time. **Amperometry** is a method in which current is measured at a constant potential.[1] Many types of voltammetry are based on the reduction of analyte, but in some cases an oxidation process can also be employed. One example is the use of a dissolved oxygen electrode to measure O_2 in water, as we discussed at the beginning of this chapter.

4A Direct Current Voltammetry

The simplest kind of voltammetry is one in which the potential is gradually increased (or "ramped") from zero to a more negative value. This method is called "direct current voltammetry" or **DC voltammetry**. In order for a particular redox reaction to be studied by this method, or by any other type of voltammetry, the electroactive species of interest must be at the surface of the electrode when a potential is applied that is suitable for the desired redox reaction to occur. Of course, most species are out in solution far from the electrode surface. There are three means by which a solute ion can arrive at the electrode: convection, migration, and diffusion.[3,5]

Convection implies that the solvent is moving, which usually means the solution is being stirred. Thus, convection can be eliminated by simply using a quiet, unstirred solution. Migration occurs if the electrode and the analyte are oppositely charged. For instance, a cation will tend to migrate toward a negatively charged electrode. The effect of migration can be minimized by having a much higher concentration of nonelectroactive ions present in solution. Voltammetry is usually carried out in the presence of a high concentration of an inert salt such as KCl, which is used as a "supporting electrolyte." Diffusion is represented by the random motion of dissolved ions and solutes through the solvent. It is this process that is usually the desired mechanism of transport in voltammetry.[3,5]

An example of an analytical application of voltammetry is the use of this method to examine the concentration of cadmium ions in wastewater. The reduction half-reaction for this process is as follows.

$$Cd^{2+} + 2\,e^- \rightleftharpoons Cd(s) \tag{11}$$

Cadmium ions in a homogeneous sample of the wastewater will diffuse in all directions at a variety of speeds. A small fraction will hit the electrode, where they will have a chance of being reduced. If the electrode is not sufficiently negative, the cadmium ions will simply diffuse away again and not be reduced. However, as the applied potential at the electrode is made more negative, there is a good chance that the cadmium ions will be reduced as they reach the electrode's surface. This reduction will cause current to flow through the electrode and electrochemical cell.

A typical plot of current versus applied potential that is obtained for voltammetry (giving a graph known as a **voltammogram**) is shown in Figure 5. The current at the plateau of such a voltammogram is called the *limiting diffusion current* (I_d) and implies that 100% of the analyte hitting the surface is undergoing an oxidation–reduction reaction. In our example, all of the cadmium ions hitting the electrode at this point are being reduced to cadmium metal, which then adheres to the electrode. The potential half-way up the wave in

this plot is called the *half-wave potential* ($E_{1/2}$) and is related to the standard electrode potential for the species that is undergoing the electrochemical reaction. In our example, this point represents a situation in which the applied potential will reduce half of the cadmium ions that strike the electrode, while the other half diffuse away into solution without being reduced.[3,5]

The size of the limiting diffusion current is related to the size of the electrode, the diffusion coefficient of the diffusing species, and the number of electrons that are involved in the desired half-reaction. The size of this current is also directly proportional to the concentration of the analyte that is being examined in the solution. Thus, both qualitative information on the identity of this species (through the half-wave potential) and quantitative information on concentration (through the limiting diffusion current) can be obtained through this analysis. The general relationship between the limiting diffusion current and analyte concentration (C) is given by Equation 12.

$$I_d = k \cdot C \tag{12}$$

In this equation, the proportionality constant k is related to the analyte diffusion coefficient, electrode properties, number of electrons being transferred, and so on.[3,5] The exact value of this constant does not have to be known as long as it is constant during the analysis of the samples and standards. It is also necessary when using Equation 12 to subtract the background and charging current from the overall measured current at the plateau of the voltammogram in order to obtain the correct value for I_d.

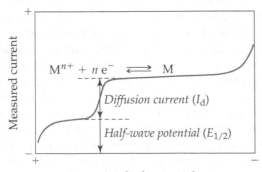

FIGURE 5   Examples of a general voltammogram for DC voltammetry. The size of the diffusion current (I_d) is related to the concentration of the analyte that is being reduced. The location of the half-wave potential ($E_{1/2}$) is related to the standard reduction potential for this analyte.

EXERCISE 4	Using Voltammetry

A standard solution that contains 3.50×10^{-3} M $CdCl_2$ is examined by voltammetry and gives a limited diffusion current at the plateau of 65.3 mA. An unknown water sample that is also thought to contain cadmium ions is analyzed under identical conditions and gives a limiting diffusion current of 45.3 mA. What is the concentration of Cd^{2+} in the sample?

SOLUTION

One way of solving for the concentration of Cd^{2+} in the unknown is to use the results for the standard to find the value of k in Equation 12. Rearranging Equation 12 to solve for this constant gives $k = I_d/C =$ (65.3 mA)/(3.50×10^{-3} M Cd^{2+}) = 1.866×10^4 mA/M. We can then use this value with Equation 12 and the measured current for the unknown to find the concentration of Cd^{2+} in the sample.

$$I_d = k \cdot C \Rightarrow 45.3\ \text{mA} = (1.866 \times 10^4\ \text{mA}/M)\,C$$

$$\therefore C = \mathbf{2.43 \times 10^{-3}}\ \boldsymbol{M}$$

The same answer is obtained by using Equation 12 to set up a simple ratio between the measured currents for the standard and unknown sample, where $C = (3.50 \times 10^{-3} M)(45.3 \text{ mA}/65.3 \text{ mA}) = 2.43 \times 10^{-3} M$. Both approaches assume that the reduction of Cd^{2+} is the only source of the limiting diffusion current during this measurement and that all other sources of current have been accounted for during the measurement of I_d.

There are two types of current that can be present during this measurement. The current that is created by the oxidation or reduction of the analyte or some other electroactive species is known as the *Faradaic current*. This is the current we wish to measure and relate to the concentration of an analyte that is undergoing oxidation or reduction in our sample. However, there is also a current that is produced when we first change the applied potential of an electrode. This "non-Faradaic" current is created by a charging of the electric double layer at the electrode solution interface when we change the potential and is known as the *charging current* or "double-layer current." This charging current is produced because the electrode and solution immediately in contact with this electrode act as a capacitor as the potential is changed and as an electric double layer of ions builds up at this interface. For instance, an electrode that is placed at a more negative potential will attract positively charged ions from the supporting electrolyte. This positive charge attracts negative ions in another diffusion layer until we eventually obtain the same composition of ions that we have in the bulk solution far away from the electrode. This accumulation of ions represents only a movement of charge and is not associated with an oxidation–reduction reaction. Thus, the Faradaic current we wish to measure must be greater than the charging current for us to make a useful measurement of an analyte by voltammetry (see Box 1 and Figure 6).[3,5,9]

Instead of using just two electrodes, voltammetry is usually performed using a system with three electrodes. First, there is a **working electrode** at which the reduction (or oxidation) of the analyte is carried out. This electrode is made from a material that is inert and that will not be oxidized or reduced itself as the analyte undergoes a redox reaction. For many years the working electrode was often liquid mercury, but now most modern voltammetry is done using a solid electrode that is made from a material like platinum, gold, or carbon. Second, there is a reference electrode that is used to control and set the potential of the working electrode. Enough current flows during an experiment in voltammetry that if that same current also goes through the reference electrode it would cause a chemical change within this electrode and change its potential over time. To overcome this problem, a third electrode is used that is called the **auxiliary electrode** or "counter electrode." It is this third electrode that is used

TABLE 1 Half-Wave Potentials for Cd^{2+} and Zn^{2+} versus a Saturated Calomel Electrode at 25°C*

Solution Conditions	$E_{1/2}$ for Cd^{2+} (V)	$E_{1/2}$ for Zn^{2+} (V)
1 *M* NaOH	−0.78	−1.53
2 *M* acetic acid/ammonium acetate	−0.65	−1.1
1 *M* KCl	−0.64	−1.00
1 *M* Na citrate + 0.1 *M* NaOH	−1.46	−1.43
1 *M* NH₃ + 1 *M* NH₄Cl	−0.81	−1.35

*Based on data from L. Meites, *Polarographic Techinques*, Interscience Publishers, New York, 1955.

to pass current and to provide the complementary half-reaction to that taking place at the working electrode (for instance, oxidation would occur here if reduction is happening at the working electrode). It is possible in this way to provide a complete electrical circuit without running the risk of changing the properties of the reference electrode over time.[3,5]

It is important to note that the solution composition and pH can cause the half-wave potential to be different for even seemingly simple situations. Table 1 shows the different half-wave potentials for a few solutes. If more than one reducible species is present in solution and if their half-wave potentials differ sufficiently, separate waves for these species can be seen. For instance, Cd^{2+} and Zn^{2+} in an acetate buffer will show two well-separated waves in DC voltammetry that can be used to measure both these species.

4B Amperometry

In the method of voltammetry, current is measured as the applied potential is changed over time. The measurement of current when the working electrode is held at a suitable, constant potential is called *amperometry*.[6] For example, an amperometric titration is carried out by measuring the current that is associated with the reduction (or oxidation) of an electroactive solute or titrant during the course of a titration. An example of this approach is the precipitation titration of lead by using chromate as the titrant.

$$Pb^{2+} + CrO_4^{2-} \rightleftharpoons PbCrO_4(s) \qquad (13)$$

If we measure the current that is associated with the reduction of Pb^{2+} as chromate is added, we will get a curve that approaches zero current as the lead ion concentration approaches zero. A useful feature for this titration is that one does not need data specifically at the end point. Instead, extrapolation of the response before and after the equivalence point can be used to determine the end point.

BOX 1
Cyclic Voltammetry

There are many ways in which the potential can be varied during an experiment that uses voltammetry. One popular approach that many electrochemists use for preliminary studies is the method of *cyclic voltammetry*. This is a type of voltammetry in which the potential is scanned back and forth in a linear fashion over time. The current that is produced by a sample is then measured during this scan at an electrode under conditions in which no convection is present in the solution. The result of this type of experiment is shown as a plot of the measured current versus applied potential and is called a *cyclic voltammogram*.

A typical cyclic voltammetry experiment is shown in Figure 6. In this particular case, only the oxidized form of the analyte is initially present at any significant concentration in solution. The experiment begins at a starting potential that is above the expected standard reduction potential ($E°$) for the analyte. This potential is ramped in a linear manner toward a more negative value (the "forward scan") while the resulting current at the working electrode is measured. As the potential approaches $E°$ for the analyte, this chemical will be reduced and a positive "cathodic" current will be measured. This reduction continues as the potential is made even more negative, but the

amount of analyte that can reach the electrode's surface soon becomes limited by diffusion and causes the current to decrease. A switch is then made and the potential is ramped back in a positive direction as part of a "reverse scan." This scan causes the analyte that has been reduced at the electrode to be reoxidized as the applied potential again approaches $E°$ for the analyte, producing a negative "anodic" current. This current eventually approaches zero as the potential is further increased and the amount of reduced analyte at the electrode is depleted.

Cyclic voltammetry can provide a variety of information on an oxidation–reduction reaction. For example, the number of waves that are observed can indicate how many oxidation–reduction events are occurring for an analyte. The location of these peaks will give the potentials at which these events occur. The difference in potential between the cathodic and anodic peaks is related to how many electrons are involved in an oxidation–reduction reaction. A comparison of the size of the peak cathodic current and peak anodic current will indicate whether the reaction is fully reversible or if the reduced and oxidized forms of the analyte have any side reactions. Changing the rate of the forward and reverse scans can also provide information on the rates of these side reactions.[5,8,9]

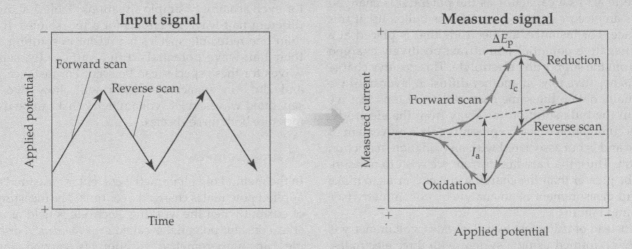

FIGURE 6 A general signal input and plotted response for cyclic voltammetry. The results shown in this case are for a reversible oxidation–reduction reaction with no side reactions. The peak currents that are measured for the cathodic current (I_c) and anodic current (I_a) are related to the amount of analyte that was reduced and oxidized again during the forward and reverse scans, respectively. The difference in the peak potentials (ΔE_p) is related to the number of electrons that are involved in this oxidation–reduction process.

EXERCISE 5	Using Amperometry

The half-wave potential for the reduction of Pb^{2+} to $Pb(s)$ occurs at about –0.5 V versus SHE. An amperometric titration is carried out at –0.7 V versus SHE on a 50.00 mL sample containing Pb^{2+} and using chromate as the titrant. The following results were obtained when this sample was titrated with 0.0654 M Na_2CrO_4. What was the original concentration of Pb^{2+} in the sample?

Titrant Volume (mL)	Measured Current (mA)
0.00	43.7
5.00	32.6
10.00	21.5
15.00	10.4
20.00	0.0
25.00	0.0

SOLUTION

When we prepare a plot of current versus titrant volume, the current reaches a value of 0.0 mA at 19.68 mL of added titrant. At this point, we have added $(0.01968\ L)(0.0654\ M\ CrO_4^{2-}) = 0.001287$ mol CrO_4^{2-}. The reaction in Equation 13 shows that Pb^{2+} will react with CrO_4^{2-} in a 1:1 ratio, so 0.001287 mol of Pb^{2+} must also have been present in the original sample. The concentration of Pb^{2+} would then be $[Pb^{2+}] = (0.001287\ mol)/(0.05000\ L) = \mathbf{2.57 \times 10^{-2}\ M}$.

A well-known analytical method that uses an amperometric detection scheme is the "Karl Fischer method" for measuring water in a sample. The key reaction in the Karl Fischer method is carried out in a methanol solution containing pyridine. Water from the sample is the limiting reagent that is titrated with a reagent that consists of a standard solution of SO_2 dissolved in methanol with pyridine and iodine. The overall titration reaction is shown in a simplified form below.

$$H_2O + SO_2 + I_2 \rightarrow 2\,HI + SO_3 \tag{14}$$

This titration is conducted in the presence of two electrodes, each of which has a controlled potential such that current will only flow when both iodine and iodide are present in solution. The Karl Fisher reagent is added until all the water has reacted. At that point, the next drop of titrant results in the presence of excess iodine, so that now both I_2 and I^- are present in the solution. Under these conditions a significant current will now be present, signaling that the end point of the titration has been reached. Because the potential of both electrodes is controlled in this approach, this method of detection is called *biamperometry*.[6,8]

Probably the most common type of analysis that is carried out by amperometry is the measurement of dissolved oxygen (see Figure 1). Oxygen is an excellent oxidizing agent and can easily be reduced at an electrode. At an applied potential that is more negative than about –1.5 V versus SHE, oxygen will be reduced to water in a four-electron process, as shown in Equation 15. This reduction gives a diffusion current that is proportional to the dissolved oxygen concentration.

$$O_2 + 4\,H^+ + 4\,e^- \rightleftharpoons 2\,H_2O \tag{15}$$

Special instruments designed to measure dissolved oxygen use a gold electrode that is covered with a thin plastic membrane. The membrane allows dissolved gasses to pass through, but prevents ions or large molecules from reaching the working electrode. Dissolved oxygen electrodes are often supplied with a long connecting cable and usually include a temperature sensor. Such features allow these electrodes to be used for the direct measurement of

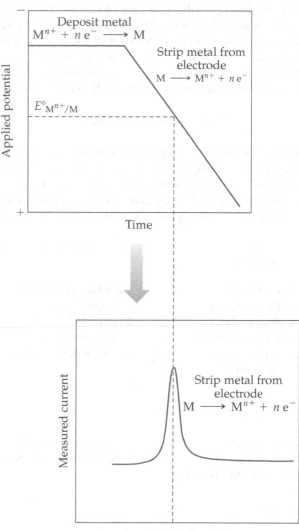

FIGURE 7 An illustration of the use of anodic stripping voltammetry for the reduction and later oxidation of a metal ion from a sample solution. The top graph shows how the applied potential is changed over time during this analysis. The bottom graph gives an example of the peak in current that is produced as the deposited metal is oxidized back into the form of metal ions. The size of this peak can be used with the analysis of similar standards for measuring the amount of the given metal ions in the original sample. This method can also allow several metal ions to be examined in one run if the corresponding metals have sufficient differences in their standard reduction potentials.

dissolved oxygen and temperature deep in the ocean, lakes, rivers, or wells.[6,9]

4C Anodic Stripping Voltammetry

Anodic stripping voltammetry is a combination of coulometry and voltammetry that is employed when measuring trace metal ions.[4,9] In this method, the working electrode is first set at a potential that is suitable for reduction of the analyte (see Figure 7). Reduction is allowed to occur at this potential for several minutes in a stirred solution. During this time, the reduction product is accumulating on the working electrode. The reduction is not exhaustive, as would be the case for direct coulometry or electrogravimetry, so most of the analyte remains dissolved in the sample. In the use of anodic stripping voltammetry to measure Pb^{2+}, the first step of this analysis would be represented by the following half-reaction.

$$Pb^{2+} + 2\,e^- \rightleftharpoons Pb(s) \qquad (18)$$

During the second step of this method, the applied potential is changed to a positive value and the previously reduced analyte is now reoxidized as the potential is scanned in a positive direction. In the example of the Pb^{2+} analysis, all of the lead that has been

accumulated at the electrode during the reduction step is now oxidized at a higher potential. The current and time required for reoxidation are then determined and used to determined how many moles of lead had been placed onto the electrode during the first step. This process is carried out for both the sample and a set of standards under the same set of analysis conditions. A comparison of these results then makes it possible to determine the concentration of the analyte in the sample. Simple mixtures of two or three low concentration and electroactive analytes in the range of 10^{-8} to 10^{-10} M can be examined by this method if these species can be reduced together, but have sufficiently different oxidation potentials.

Key Words

Amperometry
Anodic stripping
 voltammetry
Auxiliary electrode
Constant current
 coulometry

Constant potential
 coulometry
Controlled potential
 electrolysis
Coulometric titration

Coulometry
DC voltammetry
Direct coulometry
Electrogravimetry
Potentiostat

Voltammetry
Voltammogram
Working electrode

Other Terms

Biamperometry
Charging current
100% Current efficiency

Cyclic voltammetry
Cyclic voltammogram

Limiting diffusion
 current

Faradaic current
Half-wave potential

Questions

ELECTROGRAVIMETRY

1. What is "electrogravimetry"? How does this approach differ for a traditional gravimetric analysis?
2. Describe how electrogravimetry could be used for the analysis of metal ions such as Cu^{2+} or Ag^+.
3. How many moles of Cu^{2+} will be reduced during electrogravimetry if a current is 5.0 mA flowing for 7 min and 36 s?
4. What mass of copper will be reduced when electrogravimetry is performed at an appropriate potential on 150 mL of a 0.0764 M solution of $CuSO_4$?
5. A 250.0 mL portion of a solution containing copper ions and lead ions is subjected to electrogravimetric analysis. The cathode original mass is 23.9854 g and the anode mass is 10.6489 g. When the analysis is complete, the two electrodes have masses of 24.5673 g and 10.9858 g, respectively. What was the concentration of copper ions and lead ions in the original solution?
6. A 4.5631 g brass sample containing only copper and zinc is analyzed by electrogravimetry. The mass of the cathode increases by 3.7618 g and the mass of the anode does not change. What is the composition of the sample?
7. A 1.2764 g portion of copper ore was dissolved in acid, filtered to give a blue colored solution, and diluted to 250 mL. The solution was then subjected to electrogravimetry. The original mass of the platinum electrode was 15.7649 g and

after deposition was complete, it had a mass of 16.0467 g. What is the percent copper in the ore?
8. What is the expected precision of the silver ion concentration in a sample if a 25.00 mL pipet is used to deliver the sample for electrogravimetry if the mass of the cathode increases from 27.8645 to 28.7654 g?
9. What is meant by the phrase "controlled potential electrolysis"? Explain how this term is related to the method of electrogravimetry.
10. What is a "potentiostat"? What is the function of a potentiostat?

DIRECT COULOMETRY

11. What is "coulometry"? What is measured in this method and how is this information used for chemical analysis?
12. What is meant by the phrase "100% current efficiency"? Why is it important to have 100% current efficiency in coulometry but not in electrogravimetry?
13. Define what is meant by the terms "direct coulometry" and "constant current coulometry." Give an example of an analysis that makes use of these approaches.
14. A 25.00 mL portion of a nickel ion solution and a 25.00 mL portion of a silver ion solution each require the same amount of time to be fully reduced at the same constant current. Is it therefore correct to state that the concentrations of the two solutions are the same? Explain.

15. How many coulombs are necessary to give essentially 100% reduction of the Ag^+ that is present in a 100.0 mL solution of 0.100 M $AgNO_3$?

COULOMETRIC TITRATIONS

16. Describe how a typical coulometric titration is performed. How does this differ from a more traditional volumetric titration?

17. Analysis of a solid sample (250 mg) containing vitamin C gives an end point with starch as the indicator after 6 min and 24 s when analyzed by a constant current coulometric titration with iodine at a current of 30.00 mA. What is the percent vitamin C in the sample?

18. A forensic chemist wishes to measure the concentration of EDTA in a solution by coulometric generation of copper ions from copper metal. What is the EDTA concentration in a 100.0 mL portion of the sample if 198.5 s is needed to reach an end point when the current is 0.01000 A?

CONSTANT POTENTIAL COULOMETRY

19. Using the Nernst equation, explain why the potential changes when you are performing constant current coulometry.

20. What is "constant potential coulometry"? What are the advantages and disadvantages of this method compared to constant current coulometry?

21. The area beneath a current versus time graph of constant potential ($E = -0.320$ V) coulometric determination of nickel ions ($E° = -0.236$ V) in the presence of cadmium ions ($E° = -0.403$ V) is 458 A·s. The total solution volume is 250 mL. What can be said about the concentrations of these two ions in the solution?

DIRECT CURRENT VOLTAMMETRY

22. What is "voltammetry"? What parameter is measured in this method? What parameter is varied or controlled in this method?

23. What are three ways that a solute can arrive at the surface of an electrode during voltammetry?

24. What is DC voltammetry? How is this method performed and how can it be used in a chemical analysis?

25. Define or describe each of the following terms and explain how they are used in voltammetry.
    (a) Voltammogram
    (b) Limiting diffusion current
    (c) Half-wave potential

26. What is the difference between a Faradaic current and a charging current? How are each of these currents created? Which of these currents can be related to the concentration of an electroactive analyte?

27. Voltammetry can distinguish different oxidation states of the same element. For instance, CrO_4^{2-} is reduced to Cr^{3+} at a potential of 1.33 V, and Cr^{3+} is reduced to Cr^{2+} at −0.41 V, and Cr^{2+} is further reduced to $Cr(s)$ at −0.91 V. A voltammogram shows a limiting diffusion current of 34.5 mA at a potential where CrO_4^{2-} is reduced, 46.0 mA at a potential where Cr^{3+} is also reduced, and finally 69.0 mA at a potential where Cr^{2+} is reduced as well. What was these composition of the original sample in terms of these three soluble oxidation states? (*Note*: For the purpose of this problem, you can assume that the reaction of CrO_4^{2-} with Cr^{2+}

to give Cr^{3+} can be ignored; however, in practice this reaction will occur fairly rapidly and make it difficult to see all three waves for the given species in a voltammogram.)

28. Calculate the concentration of hydrogen peroxide (H_2O_2) in an aerated water sample at 20°C if a voltammogram shows a first wave having a diffusion current of 43.5 mA and a second wave of 104.6 mA total diffusion current.

29. A solution containing both copper ions and silver ions was subjected to voltammetry. Two cathodic waves were seen, the first having a diffusion current of 12.4 mA and the second having a total diffusion current of 34.2 mA. Which wave corresponds to which metal? What are the relative concentrations of the two metal ions? You may assume that the two ions have equal diffusion coefficients.

30. The charging current in a voltammetric measurement is 0.065 mA and a 2.5×10^{-2} M solution of $CdCl_2$ gives a diffusion current of 56.8 mA during this measurement. What is the limit of detection for this analysis if this detection limit is equal to the concentration of $CdCl_2$, which gives a Faradaic current that is three times the charging current?

31. Explain why a three-electrode system is used during voltammetry. What is the function for each of the electrodes within such a system?

32. Why is it important to control the pH and solution composition during a measurement that is based on voltammetry?

AMPEROMETRY

33. What is "amperometry?" Explain how this can be used as a tool to perform an amperometric titration.

34. Describe the Karl Fischer method. Give the titration reaction for this process and explain how the end point is detected.

35. Explain how amperometry is used to determine the concentration of dissolved oxygen in water.

36. A dissolved-oxygen probe is lowered into a deep lake from a canoe. This probe reads 8.0 ppm at the surface and for the first 15 ft of depth, but then suddenly changes to 2.3 ppm at 20 ft and the value continues to be decrease from 2.3 to 1.3 ppm when the probe reaches the lake bottom at 70 ft. Explain these observations.

ANODIC STRIPPING VOLTAMMETRY

37. Describe the method "anodic stripping voltammetry" and state how it is used for chemical analysis.

38. In an anodic stripping measurement of cadmium, 100 mL of sample solution is subjected to electrolysis for 500 s to reduce Cd^{2+} to elemental cadmium. The cadmium that is stripped is found to require 4.0×10^{-6} coulombs of charge to be reoxidized to Cd^{2+}.
    (a) What mass of cadmium was reduced in the electrolysis step?
    (b) How many coulombs of charge would be required if the electrolysis instead went on for 1000?
    (c) If the original solution had instead contained 4.5×10^{-8} M Cd^{2+}, what fraction of this original cadmium would have been reduced and later reoxidized?

39. The amount of lead ions in water is to be measured by using anodic stripping voltammetry. A 100 mL portion of sample solution is preelectrolyzed for exactly 10.0 min. Upon anodic stripping, the area of the peak corresponding to lead is 17.5×10^{-7} A·s. A standard lead solution (5.0×10^{-8} M) run in the same manner gave a peak area of

27.8×10^{-7} A·s. What is the concentration of lead ions in the sample? What fraction of the original lead was reduced in the preelectrolysis step?

CHALLENGE PROBLEMS

40. Why do you think it is important in electrogravimetry to use electrodes with large surface areas, although this is not important in coulometry or voltammetry?

41. Will an error be introduced in a coulometry experiment if distilled water is occasionally squirted in to rinse everything into the solution? Answer the same question if the measurement is done by voltammetry. Explain.

42. The dissolved oxygen concentration in a major river is measured at several positions upstream and downstream of a power plant that uses river water to remove excess heat. The following results are measured, all at a depth of 1.0 meter in the center of the river. Explain the difference in these measurements.

Position	Concentraction of Dissolved O_2 (ppm)
500 m upstream	7.3
25 m downstream	3.0
500 m downstream	3.2
2000 m downstream	7.0

TOPICS FOR DISCUSSION AND REPORTS

43. Obtain more information from the literature or the Internet on an oxygen-sensing probe that is used in the measurement of biological oxygen demand (BOD). Explain how this probe works.

44. Find out what the dissolved oxygen and temperature requirements are for fish and other aquatic organisms in your state. Are bodies of water in your state meeting these requirements?

45. The earliest successful voltammetry was carried out using a dropping-mercury electrode (DME). This electrode had a bulb of mercury attached to a small-diameter capillary from which drops of liquid mercury fell into the sample solution every few seconds. This technique is called *polarography*. Suggest some advantages and some disadvantages of such an electrode and a few reasons that this was so widely used for many years but is seldom used today.

46. The person who originally developed the method of polarography was Jaroslav Heyrovsky. Obtain more information about the life and scientific career of Heyrovsky and write a report on what you find.

47. Read about the history of the measurement of the Faraday constant and the role that electroanalytical methods have played in these measurements. Write a report on what you find.

48. Locate an article in a scientific journal in which the method of cyclic voltammetry is used for part of the study. Describe how this approach was used in that study and state what types of information this method was used to provide.

49. There are many types of voltammetry besides those that were discussed in this chapter. Below are a few examples. Obtain more information on any one of these methods. Write a short report that describes the way in which this method is performed and types of information it can provide on an electroactive analyte.

  (a) Differential pulse polarography
  (b) Square-wave voltammetry
  (c) Hydrodynamic voltammetry

50. There has been a great deal of recent interest in the use of microelectrodes and ultramicroelectrodes in voltammetry. Get some information on this topic and discuss the advantages that these small electrodes offer in electrochemical measurements.

References

1. R. J. Diaz and R. Rosenberg, "Spreading Dead Zones and Consequences for Marine Ecosystems," *Science* 321 (2008) 926–929.

2. D. T. Sawyer, A. Sobkowiak, and J. L. Roberts, Jr., *Electrochemistry for Chemists,* 2nd ed., Wiley, New York, 1995.

3. B. H. Vassos, "Voltammetry." In *Analytical Instrumentation Handbook,* 2nd ed., G. W. Ewing, Ed., Marcel Dekker, New York, 1997, Chapter 19.

4. J. Wang, "Instrumentation for Stripping Analysis." In *Analytical Instrumentation Handbook*, 2nd ed., G. W. Ewing Ed., Marcel Dekker, New York, 1997, Chapter 20.

5. A. J. Bard and L. R. Faulkner, *Electrochemical Methods: Fundamentals and Applications*, 2nd ed., Wiley, Hoboken, NJ, 2001.

6. J. Inczedy, T. Lengyel, and A. M. Ure, *International Union of Pure and Applied Chemistry—Compendium of Analytical Nomenclature: Definitive Rules 1997*, Blackwell Science, Malden, MA, 1998.

7. G. Maludzinska, Ed., *Dictionary of Analytical Chemistry*, Elsevier, Amsterdam, the Netherlands, 1990.

8. D. A. Skoog, F. J. Holler, and T. A. Nieman, *Principles of Instrumental Analysis*, 5th ed., Saunders, Philadelphia, PA, 1998.

9. W. R. Heineman and P. T. Kissinger, "Cyclic Voltammetry," *Journal of Chemical Education*, 60 (1983) 702–706.

Selected Answers

5 $[Pb^{2+}] = 4.88 \times 10^{-3}\ M$, $[Cu^{2+}] = 3.66 \times 10^{-2}\ M$

7 Copper content = 22.08% (w/w)

14 No, Ag^+ requires one electron per ion to be reduced to silver metal, while Ni^{2+} requires two electrons per ion to be reduced to nickel metal. Therefore, the original concentration of Ag^+ must have been double the original concentration of Ni^{2+} for this situation to occur.

17 Vitamin C content = 4.20% (w/w)

27 Only the relative levels of the three soluble oxidation states can be determined in this case (because no data for standards is provided), but these results do indicate that CrO_4^{2-}, Cr^{3+} and Cr^{2+} were all initially present at identical concentrations.

30 $[Ag^+]/[Cu^{2+}] = 1.14$

30 LOD for $[Cd^{2+}] = 8.6 \times 10^{-5}\ M$

36 The top 15 feet of the lake are in equilibrium with atmospheric oxygen. This no longer occurs below the "thermocline" mark at 15 feet. Water below that level is more highly reduced and has less oxygen. This effect becomes more pronounced as the depth increases from 15 to 75 feet below the surface.

38

  a. Mass of cadmium = 2.3×10^{-9} g

  b. Charge = 8.0×10^{-6} C

  c. Fraction of original cadmium that was reduced and later reoxidized = 0.0046

Index